The Family Of Hay

The Family of Hay

A

HISTORY OF THE PROGENITORS

AND

SOME SOUTH CAROLINA DESCENDANTS

OF

Col. Ann Hawkes Hay

WITH COLLATERAL GENEALOGIES

A. D. 500 — 1908

BY CHARLES J. COLCOCK, C. E.

Privately Printed for the author by
The Genealogical Association, New York, 1908

A FIREBIRD PRESS BOOK

PELICAN PUBLISHING COMPANY
Gretna 1998

THIS History of their Ancestors and Descendants is dedicated to the memories of Susan C. Hay and Eliza Hay Colcock as a token of his affection by the Author.

Manufactured in the United States of America
Published by Pelican Publishing Company, Inc.
1000 Burmaster Street, Gretna, Louisiana 70053

ILLUSTRATIONS

Ann Hawkes Hay		Frontispiece
The Hay Tartan	Opposite Pg.	18
The Emperor Charlemagne	" "	26
The Empress Hildegarde	" "	26
Alfred the Great	" "	27
Robert the Bruce at the Field of Bannockburn	" "	42
Coat of Arms of the Family of Hay of Erroll	" "	43
Slains Castle — Distant View	" "	58
Slains Castle	" "	59
Inshock Castle	" "	74
Delgaty Castle, Turriff, Scotland	" "	75
Judge Martin Wilkins	" "	90
Chancellor William Smith, Supreme Court of New York	" "	91
Mrs. William Smith, wife of the Chancellor	" "	106
Lewis Scott Hay	" "	107
Harriet Yonge Johnson Hay	" "	107
Col. Frederick J. Hay	" "	122
Susan Cynthia Brown, wife of Col. Hay	" "	123
Dr. Joel Wyman	" "	138

ILLUSTRATIONS — Continued

Dr. William D. Ellis and his wife, Susan Emily Hay	Opposite	Pg.	139
Judge William D. Ellis	"	"	170
Phoebe Caroline Prioleau Ellis	"	"	170
Eugene Gordon Hay	"	"	171
Julia Caroline Oakman Hay	"	"	171
Rev. Samuel Hutson Hay	"	"	186
Mary Peck, wife of Rev. Samuel Hutson Hay	"	"	187
Map of Haverstraw, New York at the time of the Revolution		Pg.	196
Susan Cynthia Hay	Opposite	"	200
Martha Hutson Hay	"	"	201
Frances Snowden Hay	"	"	216
Badge worn by the Hay Clan in battle	"	"	217
Dr. Walter Scott Hay	"	"	232
Mary Susan Hay	"	"	232
Mac Garadh Mhor—The Countess of Erroll	"	"	233
Townsend Hay, Chief of American Branch of Clan Hay	"	"	248
Ben Hay Hammet of the American Clan Hay dressed in the Hay plaid	"	"	248
March of the Clan to Delgaty Castle	"	"	248
The Hay house at Beaufort, South Carolina	"	"	249
"Belmont," Joshua Hett Smith's house at Haverstraw, N. Y.	"	"	249

EDITOR'S NOTE TO SECOND EDITION

In 1908 the late Charles J. Colcock, after years of research, published "The Family of Hay," the genealogy of Colonel Ann Hawkes Hay, which gave a history of his progenitors and much information about his direct as well as collateral descendants. The scarcity of this valuable work has induced me to reprint it so that later generations might have copies. Col. Hay's descendants are now living from New York to Florida and in other states and many of them will be interested.

This second edition of "The Family of Hay" is an exact copy of the first edition — as far as it is humanly possible to set it in type again without mistakes.

New material has been added and many lines brought down to the present time. Quite a number of pictures, reproductions of paintings in possession of the editor, and the Hay tartan in color are included. There are nearly one third more pages in the new edition.

    —Erroldine Hay (Mrs. T. D. Bateman)
    Editor and compiler of the
    second edition of "The Family
    of Hay."

Preface

SEVEN years ago, the writer of this little volume secured the services of a capable agent, Mrs. Laura Nichols Graham (her present address, "The Cumberland," Washington, D. C.), who embarking at Boston, Massachusetts, set sail for Kingston, Island of Jamaica, duly commissioned with the task of examining all records on file relating to Michael and his only son, Colonel Ann Hawkes Hay.

It was known that the former, emigrating from Scotland in the early part of the eighteenth century, had settled at Kingston; whilst the latter, with a half uncle, later the Rev. Isaac Wilkins, D. D., had been sent to New York to be educated, and married there when eighteen years of age Martha, a daughter of the Hon. William Smith, Judge of the Supreme Court of New York and a native of England.

Of twelve children surviving from this union, left orphans at a tender age by the early death of their father, the eldest son had remained in the State of New York, where he married and left descendants; a daughter, Janet, marrying Mr. Campbell, had removed to the State of Louisiana; whilst the remainder and a widowed mother had settled finally in the State of South Carolina.

Scarce more than infants when their father died, his valuable papers having been destroyed at his home in Haverstraw on the Hudson during the war of the American Revolution, the lineage of Colonel Hay was unknown to his children beyond the tradition that he was directly descended from an ancient house, Hay of Erroll, confirmed by the following coat armor handed down to them: "A field argent charged with three shields gules within a bordure nebule of the last; for crest, a hand proper holding an ox-yoke; motto, 'Laboranti Palma.'"

PREFACE

Faithfully did Mrs. Graham execute the laborious duty assigned to her. Guided by "Archer's Monumental Inscriptions," after a diligent search under a tropical sun in July, she found herself sweeping the accumulated dust of one and a half centuries from the foot-worn marble slab fitted over a vault in the centre aisle of the Kingston parish church, and transcribing therefrom the half obliterated superscription relating to what had been animate of the remains of Michael Hay, his daughter Isabella Richmond, and his wife's cousin german, Mrs. Alexander Grant. In one grave, just outside the church, had been interred the bodies of three infant children of Colonel Hay and his wife Martha Smith, their burial records being preserved at Spanish Town, to which the Jamaica archives had been removed for safe keeping.

The documents copied by Mrs. Graham at Spanish Town show that Michael Hay had been a wealthy planter possessed of several estates and many slaves in Jamaica, and had married soon after his arrival in that island Esther, daughter of the eminent Judge Martin Wilkins, one of the Associate Justices of Jamaica Island, whose family had emigrated from Glamorganshire, Wales.

To the above marriage one son had been born, Ann Hawkes Hay, whose peculiar name was bestowed in compliment to a maternal great aunt, Ann Wilkins Mister, who made him her heir after the death, with no surviving issue, of her daughter Martha, wife of Dr. Alexander Grant of Jamaica, whose family may be distinguished by his coat of arms charged with three crowns to be seen on his tombstone.

From a paragraph in the testament of Michael Hay mentioning "The children of my sister Jane, spouse of Dr. George Bethune of Cupar, Fifeshire, Scotland," the services of Mr. Henry Paton, 120 Polwarth Terrace, Recorder in Edinburgh, were secured, and he was empowered to delve amongst the musty volumes in the Scottish offices of registry for mention of Michael Hay and Jean Hay Bethune in the hope that this would reveal their parentage.

It may be seen by examining the documents presented later in this work that this expectation was realized by evidence showing that the parents of Michael were Thomas Hay, writer in Edinburgh, and writer to the Signet, who died in 1728, and his wife Isabel Balfour, who died in 1745, naming in her testament her husband Thomas

PREFACE

Hay, writer in Edinburgh, and three children, Michael, Andrew, and Jean, spouse of Dr. George Bethune of Cupar, Fifeshire.

Mr. Paton also extracted a paper executed by Michael Hay, in which he describes himself "Eldest lawful son and apparent heir to Thomas Hay, writer in Edinburgh," dated 1745, Kingston, Jamaica; and another drawn by Jean Hay, dated Cupar, 1746, describing herself "Spouse of Dr. George Bethune of Cupar, Fifeshire, and lawful daughter to Thomas Hay, writer in Edinburgh." Both of these were executed just after their mother's death in 1745.

Thus was found, what in genealogical tracing is the most difficult link in a chain of descent, the connection between the first American ancestor and his progenitors in Great Britain.

The parentage of Thomas Hay, writer in Edinburgh, was next established by "A Letter of Factory," dated Rome, Italy, 1721, written by Andrew Hay, describing himself "lawful son of James Hay of Carriber," and appointing as his legal representative in Scotland "Thomas Hay, writer in Edinburgh, my brother german, in whom I have every confidence"; and also by a document dated 17—, "by Andrew Hay of Bridgehouse, son of Thomas Hay of Carriber, writer in Edinburgh and writer to the Signet," together with a deed executed by "Thomas Hay, writer in Edinburgh," referring to his estate of Bridgehouse formerly belonging to Sir David Balfour of Forrett (his wife's father), witnessed by Michael Balfour (his brother-in-law for whom his son Michael had been named). The will of James Hay of Carriber, drawn up many years before his decease, mentions his wife Magdalen Robertson, his brother Mr. John Hay of Woodcockdale, and three sons, John, George, and Andrew; and provides for children not yet born.

That James subsequently had a son Thomas is shown by the letter of factory written by his son Andrew, extracted from above; and that he had two daughters, Christian and Grizel (Grace), is shown in the will of their brother John, which mentions them and their husbands, Andrew Marjoribank, and Thomas Boyes.

In a "History of Writers to the Signet," published in Edinburgh, occurs a sketch of James Hay of Carriber, which mentions his death in 1702, and states that he married Magdalen Robertson, and was the son of Mr. David Hay of Woodcockdale, Clerk of Sessions; while a legal document dated 1646, extracted from the Edinburgh records by Mr. Paton, refers to Mr. David Hay of Woodcockdale and his spouse Jean Winrame (or Winrihame).

Thus, by documents secured through the invaluable assistance of Mrs. Graham in Jamaica and Mr. Paton in Edinburgh, the lineage of Colonel Ann Hawkes Hay was successfully traced back through four generations in Scotland, and it became known with what families of Great Britain he was related.

The aid of some of these kinsmen was now invoked by correspondence, and much valuable information afforded by letters to the writer received from the Duke of Sutherland, Sir Lewis John Erroll Hay, 9th Baronet of Park, Sir Archibald Dunbar of Elgin, Sir James Balfour Paul, Lord Lyon of Scotland, and the Rev. James Bonallo of Auldearn, and a very complete chart from Mr. William Hay of Edinburgh, which connects Thomas Hay, writer in Edinburgh, 1725, with his progenitor William de la Hay, who died 1170, and was the cup-bearer to Malcolm IV. and William the Lion.

In one of his letters, Sir Lewis Erroll Hay enclosed a little pamphlet, "The Culbin Sands," in which the author, Mr. George Bain of Nairn, Scotland, made a beautiful reference to the Hays of Lochloy, ancestors to Hay of Woodcockdale.

This led to a correspondence with Mr. Bain replete with most valuable information germain to this work. In this place, the writer begs to express his most sincere gratitude to Mr. Bain for his great kindness in contributing to this little work, freely and without price, from his extensive store of knowledge relating to "The Hays of Lochloy." But for such assistance this family history would have been very incomplete, and every descendant of "the knightly family of Hay of Lochloy" or of "Rose, Barons of Kilravock," or of any prominent family of Nairnshire, is urged to secure a copy of this "History of Nairnshire," which may be had by enclosing three dollars and sixty cents to Mr. George Bain, Editor of the Nairnshire Telegraph, Nairn, Scotland.

The following authorities are among those consulted in preparation of this work:

The books of Baronetage and Peerage by Burke, by Douglas, by Sharp, and by Debrett; Burke's "History of the Commoners," the "Encyclopædia Britannica," Chambers' Encyclopœdia, and "The National Biography"; the histories of Scotland by Scott, by Robertson, and by Lang; Browne's "History of the Scotch Highlanders"; "The American Archives"; "Smith's History of New York"; "New York in The Revolution"; "A Genealogical Deduction of the Family of Rose, barons of Kilravock"; "A History of Nairnshire," by Mr. George Bain; "Great Historic Families of Scotland," by Dr. Taylor, and "The Bruces and Cumyns," by Mrs. Cumyns Bruce.

Acknowledgment is likewise made to Miss Mary Erskine Hay for her valuable assistance in verifying records, and to any others who have aided by supplying information for this modest little work which though full of faults, it is hoped may yet be free from errors.

Should any feel inclined to criticise the introduction of collateral ancestors, so styled, into this family history, let them realize it is the design of the author to set forth the lineage of Colonel Hay, that it is a convention of man which transmits the name to the male posterity, inheriting the blood and characteristics of the mother equally with those of the father, and frequently to a more pronounced degree—a law of nature recognized by the ancient Gael in the custom of "Tanistry" regulating the succession of his kings. Who, attempting to describe a mighty stream flowing into the broad ocean, would neglect to take into account its tributary sources, which, intermingling with the central current, blend to form the perfect whole rolling on in majesty, having acquired dignity from its length and grandeur from its breadth?

If any Hay progenitors, as those of many another American family, are of noble and royal lineage, even in a democratic country, this circumstance should not preclude their introduction into a work designed as a monument to its past, in which are to be engraven the names of ancestors who have borne important parts in shaping the world's history, bequeathing to posterity records of greatness for inspiration, and examples of usefulness for imitation.

In preparing this volume, the writer hopes he may incite others of South Carolina to follow his example, each perpetuating the memory of his fathers in form more durable than marble or brass; and while drawing much of his material from the history of the past, he yet adds material that is new, moulding it into such coherency that it may serve some useful purpose to the historian of the future.

Such is the ambition of this delver in the ashes of the past—the ashes of those who have experienced the soft emotions of love and been stirred by the turbid passions of ambition, which, breaking down the artificial divisions of time, prove universal humanity akin, and thus will his labor serve an end more extensive than is generally implied in a family genealogy, of a dignity, however, sufficient in itself to justify its compilation.

Errollton Cottage,   C. J. C.
Lyndhurst, South Carolina,
25 July 1907.

PART I

Early History

WHICH presents to the reader a review of a section of the early history of Scotland, and introduces Colonel Hay's Gaelic ancestors, whose names in this sketch are distinguished from other names by being marked with a star. The authorities from whose works these facts are extracted have been mentioned in the preface to this work.

The Scoto-Irish, a branch of the great Celtic family, are supposed to have crossed to Ireland from North Britain and settled in Ulster. The most powerful of its two tribes was the Cruithne.

About the year 250, Carmac, King of Ireland, sent his cousin, General *Cairbre-Riada, to quell disturbances among these kindred Gaelic clans, who conquered a territory of about thirty miles extent in northeast Ireland, which was granted to him by the king, and over its inhabitants his posterity ruled for several ages, giving to its natives the name of Dal-Riads.

A colony of the Dalriadic Celts, who were Christians, crossed over to Scotland, then inhabited by the Picts.

In the year 503, a second colony of the Dalriads (the first having been driven back to Ireland), under three brothers—Lorn, Fergus, and Angus—son of *Erc, a descendant of Cairbre-Riada, settled in what is now Cantyre. From these brothers spring the Scoto-Irish, or Gaelic, kings of Scotland.

During the reign of Conal, fifth in line, his kinsman, St. Columba, with twelve disciples, crossed from Ireland and founded in the island of "I" the monastery of Iona, and thence made pilgrimages among the Picts, whom he Christianized, building monasteries as centres of religion.

THE FAMILY OF HAY

The period between 503 and 836 was spent in struggles between the Scots, the Picts, and the Saxons of Northumberland, resulting finally in a conquest of the Picts (oppressed on the coast by the Nord Vikings), under their last king, Wred, by the Scots under *Kenneth, son of *Alpin, son of *Eocha IV. by his wife *Urgusia, daughter of a King of the Picts. *Kenneth Macalpin united the rival kingdoms of Picts and Scots, and transmitted the Celtic blood to his descendant *Malcolm Cawnmohr, who, by his marriage to the Saxon princess *Margaret, daughter of *Aedward the Aetheling, added the blood of *Aelfred the Great to the stem of sovereigns of Scotland and of England and of their posterity.

The following chronological table of the Scoto-Irish kings connects the three sons of Erc with Malcolm III. In this line, and in the "Saga of Harald Haarfager," the ancestors of Colonel Ann Hawkes Hay are distinguished from other names by being marked by an asterisk:

1. Lorn, *Fergus, and Angus reigned 503-506.
2. *Domangart, son of Fergus, 506-511.
3. Comgal, son of Domangart, 511-535.
4. *Gauran, son of Domangart, 535-557.
5. Conal, son of Comgal, 557-571.
6. *Aidan, son of Gauran, 571-605,
7. *Eocha-Bui, son of Aidan, 605-621.
8. Kenneth I., son of Eocha-Bui, 621-621.
9. Ferchar, son of Eogan, 1st of race of Lorn, 621-637.
10. *Donald-Breac, son of Eochar-Bui, 637-642.
11. Conal II., grandson of Conal I.
12. Dongal, who reigned several years with Conal, 642-652.
13. Donal-Buin, son of Conal, 652-55.
14. Maol-Duin, son of Conal, 655-81.
15. Fercha-Fada, grandson of Fercha I., 681-702.
16. *Eochar II., son of Domangart, grandson of Donal-Breac, 702-705.
17. Ainbhcealach, son of Fercha-Fada, 705-706.
18. Silvach, son of Fercha-Fada, reigned over Lorn 706-729.
19. Duncha-Beg, reigned over Cantyre and Argail until 720, and over Lorn 729-733.
20. *Eocha III., son of Eocha II., reigned over Lorn 720-729.
21. Muredach, son of Ainbhcealach, 733-736.
22. Eogan, son of Muredach, reigned over Lorn, 736-739.
23. *Aodh-Fin, son of Eocha III., reigned over Lorn 739-769.
24. Fergus, son of Aodh-Fin, reigned 769-772.
25. Selvach II., son of Eogan, 772-796.

THE FAMILY OF HAY

26. *Eocha IV. (sometimes called Achaius), son of Aodh-Fin, married *Urgusia of Furgusia, daughter of Fergus, King of the Picts, reigned from 796 to 826, 30 years.
27. Dungal, son of Selvach II., reigned from 826 to 833.
28. *Alpin, son of Eocha IV. (or Achaius) by his Pictish wife, the Princess Urgusia, succeeded to the throne of the Scots, and claimed the kingdom of the Picts A.D. 833. He had two sons:—Kenneth and Donald.
29. *Kenneth II., son of Alpin, known as Kenneth MacAlpin, reigned from 836 to 843. The warlike Picts offered no great resistance, perhaps submitted without resistance, to his claim to the throne by virtue of descent from their Princess Urgusia. Thus was united the races which formed the elements of the picturesque Scotch Highlander, and thus was the blood of the Picts and Scots transmitted to the dynasty of Kenneth Macalpine, which continues as follows:—
    He had two sons:—Constantine and Eth.
30. Donald, brother of Kenneth II., reigned from 859 to 863.
31. *Constantine II., son of Kenneth Macalpin, was taken captive by the Danes and beheaded in 878.
32. Eth, or Aodh, or Hugh, brother of Constantine II., reigned one year and was slain by Grig in fight near Strathallan.
    He left sons:—Constantine (from whom descended the royal family of Scotland, the Bruces, and the Baliols) and Doir, the Thane of Lochaber.
    The Thanes of Lochaber, and the Great Stewards of Scotland also claim descent from Eth through Fleance, son of Banquo.
33. Grig, Gregory, or Cyric, now usurped the throne, and associated with him Eocha, grandson of Kenneth M'Alpine by his daughter who had married Cu, British prince of Strath-Clyde.
    In 803 Eocha died, and Donald, son of Constantine II, took Eocha's place.
34. *Donald II., son of Constantine II., outlived Grig four years and was killed at Fores in a struggle to subdue the province of Moray. He transferred the seat of government from Fort-Teviot to Scone.
35. Constantine III., son of Eth, succeeded, and after a long reign retired to a monastary A.D. 943, and d. at St. Andrews 952.
36. *Malcolm I., son of Donald II., succeeded, and was slain by the Moray men two miles from Fores.
    He left three sons:—Duff, Kenneth, and Mogall, the father of Grim.
37. Indulph, son of Constantine, succeeded, and was the first King of Scotland to take Edwinsburgh. He was slain by the Norsemen at Invercullen, A.D. 962, and left two sons:—Culin (Colin) and Eocha.
38. Duff, eldest son of Malcolm I., succeeded, but was opposed by Culin, and was murdered at Fores by Donald, the Governor of Fores Castle, a partisan of Culin. Duffus Castle was the northern residence of Duff.

39. Culin succeeded and reigned four years, when he fell with his brother Eocha, in a battle with the Britons of Strath-Clyde.
40. *Kenneth III., brother of Duff and son of Malcolm I., succeeded. He married a daughter of William Long-Epee, Duke of Normandy, by whom he had children:—Malcolm, and Duncleda, who married Kenneth, Thane of Lochaber, and was the mother of Banquo.

    He was assassinated by the Lady Fenella, daughter of Cruichne, Earl of Angus, who was the agent of disaffected claimants to the succession under the law of tanistry, which Kenneth abolished.
41. Constantine IV., son of Culin, usurped the throne, but was slain in battle on the Almond River, in battle with Malcolm, son of Kenneth.
42. Grim, son of Mogall, nephew of Duff, usurped the throne north of Forth. He is sometimes called Kenneth M'Duff.
43. *Malcolm II., son of Kenneth III., succeeded on the death of Grim. His reign was disturbed by Uchtred, son of Waltheof, Earl of Northumberland. He was attacked when 80 years of age, near Glamis, by a ruffian band, and died three days after from loss of blood. He settled his dominions upon his grandson Duncan.

    He had three daughters:—

    i. *Bethoc, or Beatrix, m. Crynan (or Grimus), Chief of Athol, lay-abbot of Dunkeld, and Abthane of the Western Isles, by whom a son Duncan.

    ii. *Alice or Olith, m. Sigurd Lodvison, Earl of Orkney, and was great-grandmother of Hace, Earl of Orkney, whose daughter and heiress Margaret, Countess of Orkney, m. Madoch, Earl of Atholl, from whom descend the Scandinavian earls of Orkney, the St. Clairs, and Colonel Ann Hawkes Hay, who also descends from Bethoc.

    iii. *Dovada, wife of Earl Finlath, and mother of M'Beth, is also said to have been a daughter of King Malcolm.

44. *Duncan, son of Bethoc by Crinan, grandson of Malcolm, succeeded to the throne. He had three sons:

    i. *Malcolm, afterward King Malcolm Cawnmohr.
    ii. *Donald Bane (vide Comyn, sec. vi., part ii.).
    iii. *Melmare, Earl of Atholl, whose son Madoch, Earl of Atholl, m. his cousin Margaret, Countess of Orkney.

    All of these children were ancestors of Colonel Hay. Duncan was slain by Macbeth, under the influence of his wife the Lady Gruach, the Lady Macbeth of Shapespeare, granddaughter of Kenneth IV., who by her first husband Gilcomgain had a son Lulach who d. 1058, leaving a line of claimants to the throne.

    It is said, but not credited, that King Malcolm II. put to death M'Boede (son of Boede, son of Kenneth III.),

THE FAMILY OF HAY 5

brother of the Lady Gruach, and this caused the murder of King Duncan.

45. Macbeth, who slew King Duncan circa 1040, usurped the throne in the name of his step-son's rights, and reigned with great ability until 1058, when he was slain in battle by MacDuff, Thane of Fife, whose descendants were granted the privilege of crowning the subsequent kings of Scotland.

46. *Malcolm III., surnamed Cawnmohr, son of Duncan I., now ascended the throne, and was one of Scotland's greatest sovereigns. He married Margaret (called for her sanctity St. Margaret), sister of Aedgar the Aetheling, daughter of Aedward the Aetheling, lineal descendant of King Aelfred the Great, and by her Malcolm had sons: Alexander; Edgar; and David (successively kings); and a daughter Matilda m. King Henry I., of England.

The history of Scotland will now be resumed where it was interrupted by this genealogical digression.

Malcolm III., surnamed Cawnmohr, reigned from 1058 to 1093. He m. 1st Ingebiorge dau. of the Northman, Earl Thorfinn, and had by her a son Duncan. The King married 2d Margaret, the beautiful and saintly sister of the Aetheling, at Dunfermline, "where the King in the ballad sits drinking his blood-red wine."

*Gospatrick, kinsman of Malcolm, and descended from Crinan's line, was Earl of Northumberland, but, engaging in an insurrection against William the Conquerer, took refuge in Scotland, A. D. 1068, and was granted by the king, the lands of Dunbar, and founded the house of Dunbar and March, so famous in later years for both good and evil.

*Waltheof, son of Earl Eiward, by Elfleda, daughter of Earl Aldred, was made Earl of Northumberland by King William, and married Judith, the Conqueror's niece, by whom he was later betrayed to her uncle, and William's ill fortune has been dated from the cruel execution of Earl Waltheof, who, having been invited to engage in a rebellion against the Normans, refused, but, in loyalty to his friends, failed to expose the conspiracy.

On November 13, 1093, King Malcolm was slain near Alnwick while leading an army against Rufus, his son Edward falling with him. St. Margaret died broken-hearted at Edinburgh Castle and was laid to rest at Dunfermline.

His son Duncan had been carried as a hostage to England by William after a meeting with Malcolm at Abernethey on the

Tay, and by Queen Margaret he left surviving children, Eadmund, Aethelred lay Abbot of Dunkeld, Aedagar, Alexander, and David later the First.

He left brothers Donald Bane (from whom in the female line descended the Red Comyn) and Melmare.

Donald Bane was made king by the Celtic element, was driven from the throne by his nephew Duncan, who was slain six months later by the men of Moearn and their Mormaor, Malpeter Macloen, and Donald Bane restored who ruled north of Forth while his nephew Aedmund ruled in Lothian, until with the aid of his maternal uncle, Aedgar the Aetheling, the younger brother Aedgar was placed upon the throne, who put out the eyes of his paternal uncle Donald while his brother Aedmund died in an English cloister. With Donald Bane was ended the reign of the pure Celtic line in Scotland.

Aedgar reigned from 1097 to 1107. His sister Eadgyth, or Matilda, married *Henry I. of England, bequeathing the blood of *Aelfred the Great to its successive sovereigns. Eadgar died 1107 and Alexander I., his brother, became King of the Scots, while *David became Earl of Lothian and Cumbria, residing for a lengthy period at his sister's court in London.

Alexander I. was styled "The Fierce" for his retaliation on the Celts of Moray and Mearns, who attacked him at Invergowrie, hard by Dundee, and nearly took his life. After his victory against them at Spey, he founded the monastery of Scone, and its charters were attested by Heth of Moray, who married the daughter of Lulach, son of Gruach — The Lady Macbeth of Shakespeare — granddaughter of Kenneth IV.; the descendants and pretended posterity of this marriage became a disturbing element to later reigns. Other witnesses to this charter were Madach of Athol, *Malise Earl of Strathearn, Dufagan of Fife, Gratnach and Rory (of Angus, Buchan or Mar).

He was the first to introduce charters north of Forth, and the last Scottish king who relied mainly upon the old Celtic and Anglo-Norse element; his successor being educated at the English court, encouraged the Anglo-Normans to settle in North Scotland, deporting many of the Highland Scots into the lowlands to make room for the Southrons, no doubt causing them much suffering and distress.

Alexander was a resolute and astute Prince; he married Sibylla, a daughter of Henry I., but died at Stirling 25 Apl. 1124, and was succeeded by his brother David.

With *David I. (1124-1153) Anglo-Norman and English influence was established in Scotland, for he had lived many years at his sister's court in London, and was partial to the Norman and his customs. It has been shown that David was the youngest son of *Malcolm Cawnmohr by his wife the Saxon *Princess Margaret, daughter of Aedward the Aetheling, who while a refugee in Europe had married a Hungarian lady of rank. *David had married Matilda (or Maud), widow of Simon of St. Liz, heiress of Watheof by his wife *Judith, niece of William the Conqueror, and thus brought Scotland the unfortunate claim upon Northumberland. On August 22, 1138, at Cowton Moor, near Northallerton, David and his chivalrous son *Prince Henry led the Scots in the Battle of The Standard, in which was present *Malise Earl of Strathearn. A graphic account of this battle has been given by Ailred, Abbot of Riveaux, who shows that in England Prince Henry was held in admiration.

While at Stephen's court, Henry married Ada, youngest daughter of the *Earl of Warrene. He died 12 June 1152, before coming to the throne, and even the English chroniclers bewail him "as though he had been the Chevalier Bayard or Sir Philip Sidney of his age." Henry left sons Malcolm b. 1142, William the Lion, and *David Earl of Huntington, whose births followed at intervals of about a year.

*King David I. died at Carlisle 24 May 1153, leaving a reputation for virtue, bravery, and benevolence; he founded the lowland abbeys of Holyrood, Melrose, Jedburgh, Kelso, Dryburgh, and others, centres of letters and civilizaton, "and brought Scotland within the circle of European chivalry, manners, trade, and education."

Malcolm IV., son of Prince Henry, was crowned at Scone at the age of eleven years. Henry II. of England took advantage of his youth by wresting from him Northumberland, a part of his grandmother's dowry to her husband.

The quarrel was, however, temporarily made up, and Malcolm, called "The Maiden" on account of his great beauty, later accompanied Henry to Toulouse and was knighted at Tours, winning distinction by his bravery.

He was soon called upon to quell a rebellion of the Celts led by Somerled, Earl of Argyl, and Lord of the Isles, and, later, others led by the descendants of Lulach, step-son of MacBeath and son of his wife Gruach, granddaughter of Kenneth III., who left issue to contest the claims of the descendants of *Duncan, grandson of Malcolm II.

A daughter of Lulach had married Heth, Earl of the turbulent province of Moray, and bore him sons Angus and Malcolm. These had led an insurrection against David I., when absent in England, but, at North Esk, were defeated by the Constable of Scotland and Angus slain. Malcolm had carried on a guerilla warfare with increasing forces and successes, and David had been forced to call to his aid his Norman friends under Walter Espec. Later Malcolm was betrayed to David and imprisoned at Roxburgh. It was a son of this Malcolm MacHeth by a sister of Somerled who was now disturbing the reign of Prince Henry's son, Malcolm IV.

Galloway subdued and the Celts of The Isles defeated, Malcolm IV. died 1165, and was succeeded by his brother William.

William the Lion reigned from 1165 to 1214—forty-eight years. He was a brave and in his early years a warlike Prince, but was captured while making an exhibition of rash valor at Alnwich, kept captive for many years by Henry II., who only released him after exacting his signature to "The Treaty of Falaise," which placed Scotland in feudal subjection to England, the exactions of which treaty were generously annulled by Richard Cœur de Lion.

The Firebrand of William's reign was Donald Bane, "pretendant" son of William, son of Duncan, son of *Malcolm Cawnmohr by his Norse wife Ingebiorg, daughter of *Earl Thorfinn. Donald fell in battle near Inverness in 1187, and his son was hanged in 1212.

Such Normans as William settled in Northern Scotland were succeeded by Celticized descendants.

William the Lion died 4 December 1214, after a long reign

of great vicissitude, begun by a youthful show of rash valor at Aln, and terminated by practice of the cool diplomacy of age.

Alexander II., son of William the Lion, succeeded and reigned from 1214 to 1249. He joined the English barons in their struggle with King John, who came north and burned Berwick. The accession of Henry III. to the English throne ended this war, Alexander doing homage for his English fiefs. In 1221, Alexander married the English princess, Joanna. He soon reduced the Celtic province of Argyll to a sheriffdom, which had been in the hands of the Campbells of Loch Awe, of the house of MacArthur. He left, however, the race of Somerled as chief lords, who were to be later won over, as Clan Ranald, to the cause of Bruce, and who held the Isles and included Clan Donald, while the mainland of Ayr was under Clan Dougal.

During this reign the claimants having been beheaded, the claims of the MacWilliams and the MacHeths to the Scotch crown were ended. Joanna having died in 1238 without leaving him an heir to the throne, Alexander wedded Marie de Courci, to whom a son was born in 1241. The king died in 1249, at Kerrera, during an effort to subdue Argyll and make himself Lord of the Isles.

He had, in his reign, destroyed the blood of the "pretendants" to give place to strife among the great nobles destined to trouble his successors. He was succeeded by his son.

Alexander III. reigned from 1249 to 1286—about thirty-seven years. He was knighted at York, on Christmas Day, 1251, by Henry III., and the day following married his daughter, the Princess Margaret of England. Then followed a coalition between Alan Durward and Walter Comyn, Earl of Menteith, for custody of the royal children, and the government of Scotland, in which Henry took part and a regency was established. His minority ended in 1263, Alexander contended with Hakon, King of Norway, and Magnus, King of Man, for possession of The Isles, which were ceded in 1266 by Hakon, excepting Shetland and the Orkneys; but the title of Lord of The Isles remained with the descendants of Somerled till the close of the fifteenth century.

Alexander did much to break the power of the Vikings in Scotch waters as allies to the Celts. Edward I. having ascended the English throne in 1272, Alexander did him homage for fiefs held in English territory, but refused to do homage for his own kingdom, which, he said, he held of God.

In 1281, his daughter Margaret married Eric, King of Norway, and his eldest son married Margaret of Flanders. Margaret of Norway died 1283, giving birth to a daughter, and her brother expired without issue. The succession to the throne now rested with this infant—The Maid of Norway—to whom it was secured by an assembly of the nobles and the estates of Scotland.

Alexander married again Yolet, daughter of the Count of Dru, but met his death one stormy night in 1286, his horse falling over a cliff on the Fifeshire coast; he had refused to take shelter from the storm, he must reach wife and home that night.

The storm which caused the death of the King portended for Scotland a prolonged period of gloom. On her political horizon are gathering lurid clouds, destined to rain blood over her lands now fair and smiling with peace, and soon the rising flood shall sweep to destruction brave lives and strong castles, leaving desolation in its wake; while southern blasts will hurl army after army of the Anglo-Norman over the border to harry a country weakened by internecine strife, yet uniting to resist the claims of English sovereigns whose ambition had persuaded them to regard free and independent Scotland as a fief. At the close of this now impending struggle, the dispensation of an over-ruling Providence will give the stronger kingdom to be governed by a king of the weaker northern nation, foreordaining that James VI. of Scotland and James I. of England shall be one and the same.

On the death of Alexander III., Scotland's sovereign was a girl, but three years old, in distant Norway.

Six custodians of the realm were appointed in 1286 to govern the kingdom, viz.: Fraser, Bishop of St. Andrews; the Earl of Fife; Alexander Comyn, Earl of Buchan; John Comyn, Lord of Badenoch; Wishart, Bishop of Glasgow; and James the Steward.

Six months later, at "Turnberry Castle," in Carrick, the following nobles "banded" to support each other "save against their fealty to the King of England, and the person who shall obtain the Scottish throne being of the blood of Alexander III. and according to the ancient custom of Scotland":

Patrick, Earl of Dunbar and his sons; Walter Stewart, Earl

of Menteith; *Bruce, Earl of Annandale and his son *Robert, Earl of Carrick; James the Steward of Scotland, son-in-law of the Earl of Dunbar; Angus Mohr Macdonald of the Isles, and Alexander his son; Richard de Burgh, Earl of Ulster; and Thomas de Clare, brother of the Earl of Gloucester, and nephew to the wife of Bruce; this pointed to the later claims of Bruce.

In 1289 Scotland was on the eve of civil war, which was the opportunity of Edward I., who arranged with the Pope and Eric of Norway for a marriage between the Prince Edward and The Maid of Norway. A treaty of marriage was accepted by Scotland, and the young queen sailed in a Norwegian vessel for the Orkneys, where she died in September, 1290.

John Baliol and his partisans were soon in arms asserting his claim to the throne, resisted by the counter claim of *Robert Bruce, Earl of Annandale.

These claims and those of others are contained in the following table:

*Prince Henry of Scotland, who died before his father King David I., by his wife the Lady Adeline, daughter of William, Earl of Warren and Surrey, left three sons:—

   i.   Malcolm, who succeeded his father to the throne.
   ii.   William the Lion, who succeeded his brother to the throne.
   iii. *David, Earl of Huntingdon in England, who m. Maud, the youngest daughter of Ranulph, Earl of Chester, and had by her a son and four daughters:—
      i.   John, surnamed "Le Scot," Earl of Chester d. s. p.
      ii.   Margaret m. Alan, Lord of Galloway, and had two daughters.
          i.   Divorgal m. John of Baliol, and had children.
             i.   John, the present claimant to the throne.
             ii.   Ada m. Sir William de Lindsay, and had a daughter, Christiana, wife of Ingelram, Sire de Courcy.
          ii.   Marjory m. John Comyn, Lord of Badenoch, descended from King Donald Bane; and had a son.
             i.   John, styled "The Red Comyn."
      iii. *Isabel m. Robert de Brus, and had a son.
          i.   *Robert, Earl of Annandale, competitor with Baliol.
      iv. Maud, d. s.
      v.   Ada m. Henry of Hastings, and had a son.
          i.   Henry of Hastings, whose son or grandson John, 2d. Bar Hastings was a competitor for the crown.

Now is made the celebrated protest of the seven earls against

the conduct of Fraser, Bishop of St. Andrews, and John Comyn, who have espoused the cause of Baliol.

The friends of Bruce, the elder, place themselves under the protection of King Edward I., asserting Bruce's claim to the throne as grandson of David (Baliol was a great-grandson), and also as the choice of Alexander II. when childless in 1233, a choice ratified by a council of nobles.

The well-known events now follow where Edward as Lord Paramount declares in favor of John Baliol (which would seem a fair decision), to become a mere puppet to the English king, who probably before rendering a decision had weighed the characters of the rivals.

At length Edward's humiliating demands upon John Baliol drove him to the assertion of Scotland's independence.

Edward led an army against Scotland, and besieged Berwick. defended—but in vain—by *William Douglas, a name which becoming prominent for the first time in Scottish history, is destined to play an important part, and wield powerful influence, for many generations to come.

In a brief period, Edward having crossed the border, is master of all the strong castles, and receives the submission of the nobles. King John is forced to resign his crown and is imprisoned in the Tower of London, but eventually is permitted to retire to France to his Norman estates. *Bruce has joined the crowd of Anglo-Norman nobles to give in their submission to Edward. Proud Scotland lies prostrate at the feet of the greatest of the Plantagenets, who, having penetrated as far north as Elgin, in 1296 retired south from Berwick, leaving Cressingham as Treasurer, Warren Earl of Surrey, Guardian; and Ormsby, Justiciar of Scotland.

Who now dare stand forth and strike a blow in the cause of Scottish rights and liberties!!

"The Wallaces had come north with the Fitz Alans, and the younger son of Sir Malcolm Wallace of Elderslie in Renfrewshire was not a man to endure insult, and it is said at Lanark his wife had been killed in a brutal manner by the English."

A lion was then aroused, and Wallace slew the English sheriff Hazelrig, responding to the call of Wishart and the Steward to

THE FAMILY OF HAY

lead the Celts in an effort to drive out the hated English. It was a revolt of "the people." Edward was on the continent and the Scots' rising spread. On 11 Sept. 1297, Wallace, at the head of 40,000 men, fought a battle at Stirling Bridge, in which the English were defeated with great slaughter, Cressingham slain, and Warren driven to Berwick.

For the ensuing seven years followed a struggle between Scotland and Edward, in which was much changing of sides by the nobles, but throughout it all Sir William Wallace was inflexible. In this interval was fought the Battle of Falkirk, 22 July 1298. Stirling Castle, bravely defended by Sir William Oliphant, fell in 1304, and Wallace, a fugitive, was finally taken near Glasgow, it is said, through the treachery of the second son of Walter Stewart, Sir John Menteith.

Wallace was beheaded, drawn, and quartered, 23 August, 1305, and his limbs exposed at Berwick, New Castle, Stirling, and Perth, but his name had been written imperishable in Scotland's history, in romance, and in tradition, to shine with undimmed lustre through all time to come, as that of an uncompromising martyr to love of country and victim to English tyranny.

*Robert Bruce the Younger held many English estates in possession, for which he owed fealty to the English sovereign.

He was, likewise, Lord of Annandale and Earl of Carrick, estates that lay in Southwest Scotland. The following tables show that flowing in his veins was the blood of a long line of Norman ancestors, mingled with that of the Gael, the Saxon, and the Dane, by virtue of descent from Kenneth Macalpin, Aelfred the Great, Earl Siwald, and William the Conqueror by Matilda of Flanders, whose lineage later will be traced to Henry the Great Prince of Saxony, and the Emperor Charlemagne.

1. *Sir Robert de Brus, a noble Norman, accompanied William the Conquerer to England and acquired ninety-four lordships in the county of York alone. He married as his second wife Agnes Anand, a great Scotch heiress, by whom he obtained the Lordship of Annandale.
2. *Robert de Brus, their son, married and left issue:—
3. *William de Brus, who married and left a son:—
4. *Robert de Brus, who married the Lady Isabel, dau. of Prince David, Earl of Huntingdon by his wife Maud, dau. of Hugh, Earl of Chester. David, Earl of Huntingdon, was grandson of King

Malcolm Cawnmohr and the Saxon Princess Margaret, dau. of Aedward the Aetheling, in direct line of descent from Aelfred the Great; David was descended from Kenneth Macalpin and the Scoto-Celtic kings. They had a son:—

5. *Robert de Brus, Lord of Annandale, Contestant for the Crown, m. 1st. Isabel, dau. of Gilbert de Clare, Earl of Gloucester; and m. 2d. a daughter of the Earl of Carrick, by whom among other children a son:—
6. *Robert de Brus, Earl of Carrick, b. 1245, m. Marjorie, dau. Niel, Earl of Carrick, A. D. 1271, by whom among other children:—
7. *Robert the Bruce, Earl of Carrick, who became King Robert I.

Lineage of Maud, who married David of Huntingdon

1. *Maud, sister of Hugh Lupus, m. Ralph de Meschines, and had a son.
2. *Ranulph de Meschines, Viscount of Bayeux in Normandy, had conferred upon him by King Henry I., on the death of his cousin Richard de Abrinan, the earldom of Chester—he was also Earl of Cumberland and Carlisle—and married Lucia, widow of Roger de Romara, Earl of Lincoln, and daughter of Algar, Earl of Mercia.
3. *Ranulph de Meschines, their son, was born in Gernon Castle, Normandy, and was Earl of Chester, marrying Maud, daughter of Robert, Earl of Gloucester, son of King Henry I. of England, by whom,
4. *Hugh, Earl of Chester, their son, married Bertrad, daughter of Simon, Earl of Evereux in Normandy.
5. *Maud, their daughter, married David, Earl of Huntingdon; these were the great-grandparents of King Robert the Bruce. (It will be later shown the lawful ancestor of Colonel Hay.)

*Robert Bruce, owing fealty to the English sovereigns, had rendered important service to Edward I., who had decided adversely to his father's claims.

The Scottish clergy were ever hostile to the subordination of ecclesiastical Scotland to ecclesiastical England, and during the siege of Stirling, a "band" was made between Bruce and Lamberton, Bishop of St. Andrews, looking to Bruce's elevation to the throne.

In the meantime Edward had organized his Scottish kingdom, appointing his nephew John of Brittany as Viceroy, and summoning the Scotch nobles to his parliament.

A combination was formed in 1306 to place Bruce on the throne of Scotland. In its way stood John Comyn, son of the contestant, who was unwilling to join the revolt, and—it is said—kept

Edward informed in the details of the intrigue. During an interview with Bruce in the Church of the Minorite Friars at Dumfries, Bruce slew "The Red Comyn," and by this murderous deed was transformed from the vacillating follower of Edward to the, thenceforth, patient and dauntless defender of Scottish liberties and his own claims to the crown; never again to abandon the cause he now espoused, but carry it to a triumphant conclusion, after enduring trials and in the face of difficulties that might well appall the most determined resolution.

When Edward heard of the murder of Comyn, and that Bruce had been crowned at Scone by aid of the Countess of Buchan of the traditional house of Macduff (but not seated on the "Stone of Destiny," which had been transported to England), he swore vengeance against indomitable Scotland and prepared to return once again, and bring to the block the heads of all who had dared befriend the cause of liberty.

Having knighted three hundred young gentlemen at Westminster desirous of winning their spurs, he marched north with an army to pour out the vials of his wrath upon the devoted heads of the irrepressible Scots.

Robert Bruce now revealed that noble manhood of his nature hitherto dormant and unsuspected. His faithful friends, in this period of darkness, were James, brother of *Sir William Douglas, who, taken captive at Berwick, had died in an English dungeon; Gilbert Hay, Lord of Erroll; Thomas Randolph, Lennox, Athol (to die on a gibbet), Somerville of Carnwarth, and a brother of *Simon Fraser.

Aymer de Valence, as forerunner of Edward, had led his forces to Perth. Bruce challenged him to come forth to combat. "On the morrow," he replied, "I will fight, but not today."

Accepting this assurance in good faith, the Scots went into bivouac, scattering for the day. Aymer sallied forth unexpectedly, and, suddenly falling upon them, despite the heroic efforts of Bruce and Seton (later taken and hanged), Randolph, and many other nobles were captured, and the Battle of Methven was lost to Bruce. Many cruel executions of the Scotch nobles followed, and the patriot Simon Fraser's head was placed beside that of Wallace.

Then shone resplendent the grand qualities of *Robert Bruce. A refugee, his cause desperate, his wife given up to the English by the Earl of Ross, his daughter and sister in Edward's power, he wanders with a few faithful friends in the wilds of Western Scotland, cheering them by reading aloud adventurous tales of the knights of the olden time, encouraging them by his personal prowess and lion heart, to endure immortal on the Douglas shield.

With "The Gentle James" and Gilbert Hay for companions, he crosses Loch Lomond, and befriended by Angus Og of Isla, finally escapes to Rathlin, an island on the Irish coast, where he is reanimated to renewed effort by "the spider and his web."

"From Rathlin Douglas makes a foray on Arran, and Bruce soon follows, Douglas and Boyd responding to three blasts of his horn. Hence he looks longingly across to his own lands of Carrick, in Percy's hands, sending Cuthbert over to light a beacon if all be well. By some strange chance, the beacon is lighted by another hand, and Bruce crosses to confront new dangers, from which he escapes by his wonderful genius, undaunted courage, and great strength and energy. His brothers Thomas and Alexander are taken by Dougal Macdowal of Galloway, carried to Enward at Carlisle and hanged. Nigel had been already beheaded, and the future looked dark and hopeless.

In Galloway Bruce was soon surrounded on all sides by human sleuth-hounds, vying with his own bloodhounds to run him down. It was now that Douglas, stealing to his own lands, "wrought the massacre of 'the Douglas Larder,'" making the reputation of "Castle Dangerous," where fair ladies were wont to test the courage of their suitors.

A gleam of light shone through the darkness on the 10 May 1307, when—reversing their attitudes at Methven—Bruce won the victory of Loudon Hill, where Aymer, having challenged Bruce to an open fight, was defeated. Edward, enraged, advanced, but died at Burgh-on-Sands, with Scotland full in sight, with his last breath bequeathing to his son, as a legacy, the conquest of Bruce and Scotland.

Through bitter trials patiently borne, by dauntless courage exhibited in every extremity of peril, excommunicated by the Pope,

THE FAMILY OF HAY

and an object of jealousy to the other Scottish nobles, beleaguered on all sides by treacherous friends and open foes, having lost three brothers at the block, Bruce is winning the admiration and confidence of a large part of Scotland. His success at Loudon, the cruelty of the English executions, and the opportune death of Edward I. encouraged them openly to proclaim allegiance to this descendant of David of Huntingdon, of the race of Macalpin.

The tide had turned, and Bruce has expiated that hasty deed of sudden passion at Gray Friars. Like David of old, he had sinned; like David had repented; and who dare say that, unlike David, he was not forgiven by a God, who first ordained, as an expiation, so much of hardship and suffering.

In this sketch, the events in the life of Bruce in his days of prosperity must of necessity be touched upon but lightly. Gradually the strong places are won back from the English, and their defences destroyed to prevent reoccupation by the enemy. Through the prowess of Randolph and Douglas, bravery of Edward and commanding genius of Robert Bruce, the English are at length driven from their Scotch strongholds, and Stirling Castle agrees to surrender at the end of a year unless rescue is given in that period.

These terms appealing to the chivalrous pride of England to send assistance, and to Scotland to prevent it from reaching Stirling, led to Bruce's great victory of Bannockburn, in which Edward II. and 100,000 of England's best warriors were rolled back in bloody defeat.

On the issue of this battle—nay, on the swing of Bruce's battle axe on the eve of the great battle—hung the fate of Scotland. The result welded the disaffected, seating Bruce firmly on the throne, and the Queen and her husband were no longer as "little children playing at being king and queen."

Bruce's confiscations of those refusing to come into his peace, while it enriched his friends, among whom were *Randolph, Douglas, *Sir Christopher Seton, Sir Andrew Murray (son of Wallace's comrade and later Regent), the Hays, the *Steward, *Sinclairs, *Gordons, *Flemings, and others, yet it created a party of disaffected nobles, who in the later reigns of David Bruce, banded together and espoused the cause of Edward Baliol. Perhaps it had been wiser had measures less harsh than confiscation been adopted —but such was the policy of the age.

A treaty with Edward III. was concluded at Northampton, 4 May 1328, in which was arranged the marriage of David Bruce, then five years old, to Joanna, a maid of seven years, the sister of King Edward; of this union there were no surviving children.

The great *King Robert died in his fifty-fifth year, 7 June 1329, and his body was buried at Dunfermline under a marble tomb brought from Paris. His heart was carried to the Holy Land by his friend James Douglas to expiate the death of Comyn, and later deposited at Melrose Abbey; on the passage there or back, Douglas was slain by the Saracens in Spain in a chivalrous attempt to aid in expelling them from that country.

Bruce had married first the Lady Isabella, daughter of Donald, 10th Earl of Marr, and was succeeded by their son David.

The reign of David II. was begun 1329 and ended Feb. 1370-1, when he died in Edinburgh Castle.

Unlike King Robert I., Robert II., and Robert III., he was not an ancestor of Colonel Hay, and we shall hasten over the events of his degenerate reign, presenting only what is required to give coherency to this historical recapitulation.

While yet a child, for safety, he was sent to France, and a regency established, administered by Andrew Murray, by Randolph, and the Steward. Then followed an unhappy struggle between the national party of Scottish nobles, resisting the party of disinherited nobles banded with Edward Baliol and aided by King Edward III.

At length, Baliol's adherents quarreling among themselves, David, at the age of eighteen years, landed in Scotland to strike a blow for possession of his kingdom. He was not wanting in personal bravery.

The Battle of Durham, or Neville's Cross, was fought 17 Oct. 1346, where the best blood of Scotland was sacrificed. Among those who fell thick around their king were Moray, the last male heir of Randolph; Hay, the High Constable of Scotland; Keith, the Marichal; Charteris, and thirty others; March and the Steward escaped unhurt, while King David, William Douglas the Knight of Liddesdale, Fife, and Menteith were taken and the last cruelly executed.

Tartan of the Hay Family

The capture of David was the culmination of Scotland's misfortunes; for his ransom, fixed at 100,000 merks, was to prove a grevious burden upon his country. While at the English Court a prisoner, he practically resigned his kingdom to Edward III., agreeing to recognize him as feudal lord, and promising to fix the Scottish succession upon Prince Lionel, should he have no issue.

While David was in captivity the Steward (later Robert II.) was regent, and William Douglas (son of Archibald), returning from France, drove the English out of Douglasdale and Ettrick, and Copeland, the captor of David, out of Teviotdale; and a little later he slew the Knight of Liddesdale in Ettrick Forest—a deed probably justified if the ballad commemorating the event be true.

During this reign *Sir Alexander Ramsay of Dalhousie, one of Scotland's bravest patriots, had gone to the rescue of "Blach Agnes," daughter of Thomas Randolph and wife of Patrick Dunbar, Earl of March, who, in the absence of her husband, was successfully conducting the defence of Dunbar Castle against the English under Salisbury.

"Agnes' love-shafts go straight to the heart," remarked Salisbury as an English knight fell beside him pierced by an arrow sent from the castle, while the "chatellaine," in plain view, walked the parapet, and with her handkerchief contemptuously "flecked" the dust from the spots where fell the English missiles.

Sir Alexander also stormed Roxburgh Castle, and received in reward the Sheriffdom of Teviotdale, formerly held by William Douglas, Knight of Liddesdale. The Knight of Liddesdale in revenge seized his former friend while holding court, threw him across a horse and bore him to "The Castle Hermitage," cast him into a dungeon, and starved him to death. It is related that the noble prisoner existed seventeen days on grain that sifted through cracks in the ceiling overhead — the floor of a room used as a granary.

Perhaps Lord Douglas had this in mind—as well as his private quarrel—when he took the life of his kinsman of the same name, styled "The Flower of Chivalry."—(Lord William of Douglasdale slaying Sir William of Liddesdale.)

David was finally permitted to return to Scotland by Edward and dispossess Edward Baliol of the crown. The remainder of this reign was one of strife among the nobles, border wars and efforts to discharge the ransom of the king. In 1370-1 David died in Edinburgh Castle, leaving upon Scotland the burden of about 45,000 merks indebtedness to England of unpaid ransom. The taste of individual power enjoyed by the nobles during David's long captivity was destined to linger and give trouble to his successors, down to the period of James IV.

David left no children and was succeeded by his nephew, *John Stewart, son of *Marjorie Bruce, by her husband, *Walter the Steward. John changed his name to Robert, as Baliol had brought the name of John into disrepute. In 1332 Edward Baliol, supported by the nobles disinherited by Robert Bruce, taking advantage of David's youth and absence from Scotland, had preferred his claim to the throne. He began his career with the promise of brilliant success, winning against odds the Battle of Duplin, in which the Regent *Donald, 12th Earl of Mar, was slain.

Later, King, he was driven from the throne by David and his adherents, and passing into England, ended his days fishing for pike, probably deriving more enjoyment from this innocent sport than when bearing the weight of a crown and surrounded by turbulent subjects, all of whom he could not please, and many regarding him as an interloper. Yet, by descent, the claims of this royal fisherman to the Scottish crown were superior to those of the Bruce and his descendants.

The succession to the throne of Scotland had been secured by act of Parliament to Robert, son of Marjory Bruce and Walter the Steward, whose first and third wives were Alice, daughter of Sir John Erskine of Erskine, and Isabella Graham.

By his marriage with Alice, Walter Stewart had three sons and one daughter; the eldest son, Sir John Stewart of Railston, left two sons and three daughters—Marjory, Egidia and Margaret. Margaret married, 1388, Sir John Hay of Boyne and Enzie in Banff and of Tullibdy in Clackmannan, receiving a dowry of 100 marks from her uncle, King Robert II. Their daughter, Egidia, became the wife of Alexander, Earl of Huntly, the founder of the Seton family. (The foregoing information is furnished by Mr. George Bain and by The Lord Lyon of Scotland) [Lord Lyon is father to the present Queen Mother of England.]

*Robert II. had many children by *Elizabeth Mure, whom he married in 1349, and after her decease married, second, Eupheme Ross. The Earl of Atholl, living in the reign of James I., was descended from the last marriage, while Robert III. and almost all the crown heads of Europe spring from the first wife.

Robert gave his daughter Isabel in marriage to James, 2d Earl of Douglas, the hero of Otterburne, brother to *George, 1st Earl of Angus, to whom Robert III. gave his daughter Mary for wife. (Ancestors of Colonel Hay.)

Ascending the throne at middle age, Robert was a lover of peace, yet his warlike nobles waged continual border warfare on the Marches of the two kingdoms; at one time Richard II., invading Scotland in retaliation, advanced into Aberdeenshire.

On the 14th of August, 1388, was fought by moonlight, near Alnwick, the Battle of Otterburne, celebrated in Scotch ballads. The Scots were led by James, 2d Earl of Douglas, the King's son-in-law, Warden of the eastern Marches, who fell in the fight and was found dying by James Lindsay, *John Sinclair, and his brother Walter.

"How fares it with you, cousin?" asked John Sinclair. "Ill," replied the dying Earl. "Few of my fathers died in their beds; raise my banner and cry, 'Douglas!' and tell not where I am to friend or foe."

The Scots rallied to the cry, and although far outnumbered by the English, the Percies were taken, and "a dead Douglas won the field."

These border forays were generally in the nature of tournays of chivalry, conducted without bitterness, and the prisoners admitted to light ransom. If death came, it was the warrior's fortune to go to his last sleep on the battle field, and not in his bed, as an old woman.

The politician of this reign was Robert's second son, the Duke of Albany and Earl of Fife, fated to cast the shadow of his influence over the succeeding reign.

Worn by years of responsibility and toil before he came to the throne, as Regent of Scotland during the captivity of his uncle in England, *Robert II. died in 1390, having reigned twenty years as king, and was succeeded by his eldest son, Robert.

The good King Robert III. began his reign 14 August 1390, and died 4 April 1406—reigning about sixteen years.

The hereditary tragedies of the Stewart kings were inaugurated during this reign in the sad death of Prince David, Duke of Rothesay, the King's eldest born. He was wild and wilful, but brave and generous. Mutual jealousy existed between his uncle Albany and himself—and strife. The King, having received an injury from a horse in early life, was incapacitated for a life of activity, and found it necessary to delegate a portion of his royal duties. By act of Parliament Rothesay was made "Lieutenant of Scotland" for three years, and at the end of that period, for some prank, his father was persuaded by Albany to place him in temporary restraint. He was arrested on the St. Andrews Links, warded in the Bishop's Castle, hurried to Falkland in a storm, and there mysteriously met his death, as related in "The Fair Maid of Perth."

Albany stands accused by historians for the murder of his nephew, but while circumstantial evidence points strongly to his guilt, yet direct proof is wanting.

Not long after this the King's second son, James, was sent to France—perhaps his father was afraid of ambitious Albany—but on the way was taken prisoner by England, Scott says in time of truce between the nations.

The double blow broke King Robert's heart, who, on the 4th of April, 1406, was removed by death from evils which he was not strong enough to control, and amid which he was too good to dwell in happiness.

During this reign, in 1396, occurred the celebrated clan fight of thirty against thirty, an account of which is given later in this work. Also Elgin Cathedral was burned by Alexander Stewart, "The Wolf of Badenoch"—the King's mad half-brother. He was the father of Alexander Stewart, Earl of Mar, who, in 1408, commanded the lowland nobles at the Battle of Harlaw, where the hordes of Highlanders, under Donald of The Isles, were halted in an attempt to sack Aberdeen and overrun the lowlands; this may be accepted as atonement by the son for the father's act in 1398.

In the border wars of Robert's reign, the Earl of Northumberland and Hotspur won the battle at Nisbet Moor in the Merse, followed a few days later by Homildon Hill, where Douglas and

THE FAMILY OF HAY

Murdoch, Albany's son, were defeated with great slaughter while leading an army of 10,000 men, who were victims of England's crossbows.

In this border battle the chivalrous *Sir Adam Gordon seeing Sir John Swinton, with whom he was at deadly feud, about to lead a hopeless charge with a handful of cavalry, in admiration for his valor begged to be reconciled and to receive from his hand the accolade of Knighthood, and rode with him to death.

The Percies, wardens of the Marches, were victors, but incensed because forbidden by Henry IV. to ransom their prisoners, after the custom of border warfare, they rebelled. Not long after, at the Battle of Shrewsbury, in which Prince Henry, Percy and Douglas had displayed heroic valor, Hotspur was slain and Douglas taken captive.

Having traced the history of Scotland from Colonel Hay's first royal ancestor to his last—from *Fergus the Dalriad, who came over to Cantyre in 503, to *Robert III., who died in 1406, covering a period of nine hundred years—this historical review is brought to a close.

It will now be shown how the names marked in the First Part with an asterisk are the names of progenitors of Colonel Ann Hawkes Hay, and his descent will be brought down from William de Haya, who accompanied Duke William of Normandy to England in 1066.

PART II

First Generation

WILLIAM DE LA HAY is mentioned in local history as having been cup-bearer to Malcolm IV. and William the Lion, whose reigns extended over the period 1153 to 1214—sixty-one years.

He married Julianne de Soulis, daughter of Ranulph (Randolph) de Soulis, Lord of Liddesdale and Castle Hermitage. It is probable that Ranulph was descended from Count de Soulis, maternal uncle of Richard the Fearless, Duke of Normandy, great-grandfather of William the Conqueror.

The origin of the ennobling of the family of Hay is thus told by Boethius and other early historians of Scotland.

The tradition is taken from "A Genealogical Deduction of the Family of Kilravock or Rose—written by Mr. Hew Rose, Minister of Nairne 1683, and completed by the Rev. Lachlan Shaw, Minister of Elgin in 1753, with Illustrative Documents from the Family Charter Room," printed under the auspices of "The Spalding Club of Aberdeen" in 1848, at a time when its president was the Earl of Aberdeen, K. T.; and vice-presidents, the Duke of Richmond, K. G.; Duke of Sutherland, K. G.; Earl of Airlie; Earl of Seafield; Lord Saltoun, etc.

"I doubt not that the originall and antiquitie of this familie is as clearly demonstrable from undoubted historie as anie in the nation; for all of our histiographers write of the Battell of Loncartie, and never write of that without giving the originall of the familie.

Anno 984, or therabout, and in the reigne of Kenneth III, the Danes invade Scotland; the Scots fight them at Loncartie (not far from Perth) and are put to flight. But a countrie man named HAY with his two sons being at their labour in the field, did with the yoaks of their oxen stop the flying Scots at a narrow passage, forcing them not only to return upon the Danes, but also entering with their homilie weapons amongst the thickest of the enemies. By their valour and encouraging example the Danes were put to flight and Scotland preserved from slaverie.

In reward of such signallie good service, the King giving him several options, he accepted of what lands a falcon letten flie, should fly over before she alighted, which were the lands of Erroll and others very considerable, which were enjoyed by his descendants, till sold off in the minoritie of Gilbert, late Earl of Erroll, having continued in the familie near seven hundred years." The account continues:—"The first HAY may match any of the heroes. After his glorious achievement, when King and subjects heaped praises upon him deservedly, he was not elated but carried moderately and soberlie, refusing to be gorgeously attired, but marching with his sons bearing their yoaks befoure the King to St. Johnstoune. His courage, his modest composednes after so much glorie, show that he was probably noblie descended. I am sure they prouve he was of noble spirit, as fitt stem for such a brave descent who have frequentlie been pillars of their prince and native countrie. Of this noble familie was that Sir Gilbert Hay who when King Robert Bruce was at the lowest, and the whole nation, yet never deserted the person of his king in all his fortunes, attending him in his lurking places when not owned by anie, still waiting for opportunie to act for his oppressed prince and countrie then appearing to breathe their last.

So that if Alexander the Great could say of his friends that Clytus loved the King, and Hephistion Alexander, it may be trulie said that this noble gentleman was to King Robert Bruce both Hephistion and Clytus.

This Sir Gilbert Hay (as he well deserved) was created, by Robert Bruce, Lord High Constable of Scotland, which office was not only honourable but of eminent authoritie and advantage whilst our kings resided in Scotland, and is yet a very great jurisdiction while Parliament is sitting; besydes that therebye the Earls of Erroll are still counsellors as it were by birthright, without particular commissions. To this Sir Gilbert, King Robert gave the half of the whole estate belonging to the Earl of Buchan, of the surname of Cuming, which was great, and makes now a considerable part of the patromonie of the familie of Erroll.

William, Lord Hay, Constable of Scotland, with his whole kindred and the Southern nobilitie (through the contrivance of Andrew Murray of Tullibardin) were cut off at Duplin 1332, and at that time the whole name of Hay had been extinct, if the said William and other kinsmen's wives had not given posthumous birth to boys who restored the race."

The following account of the origin of the name is attributed by James Taylor, M. A., D. D., F. S. A., author of "The Great Historic Families of Scotland," to Mr. Hay Allan, who rests it upon the authority of a manuscript "History of the Hays":—

"MacGaradh is the ancient name of the Hays. It is of genuine Gaelic origin, and was given first to the family in allusion to the celebrated action by which the first Hay raised himself from obscurity. It is very expressive of the circumstances. Its literal signification is a dyke, or barrier, and was given to the ancestor of the

Hays for his conduct at the Battle of Loncarty, where he stood between the fleeing Scots and the victorious Danes like a wall of defence.

"Surnames did not come into use in England until the time of the Conqueror, and into Scotland a little subsequently. That of Garadh was given to the ancestor of the Hays about one hundred and fifty years before this, and had not been retained by his descendants as an individual designation, but as the name of the whole race, as Clann na Garadh, and particularly as the patronymic of the chief who was designated Mac Mhic Garadh Mor an Sgithan Deang, the son of the son of Garadh of the red shields. * * * * * * In the reign of Mac Beath there were two brothers of the direct descendants of Garadh, and during the trouble of that tyrant's usurpation, the younger, 'being right bauld and stalwart of heart,' went into Normandy, where he married the daughter and heiress of one of the barons of the dukedom. * * * * * He assumed the name of De la Haye, which is a sufficiently literal translation of Garadh, the first signifying hedge or fence, the latter dyke or barrier.

"In the reign of Malcolm Bean Mor, the son of the first De la Haye, was one of the warriors who accompanied William of Normandy into England. Some time after the Conquest, he made a journey into Scotland to visit his uncle, the chief of the Clan na Garadh, then grown to an advanced age and without children. During his visit the old chief died, and there being no other heir, De La Haye was declared his successor, residing in Scotland. The name became hereditary to the descendants of Garadh and the old appelation dropped into oblivion."

Sir Lewis John Erroll Hay, Bart., sent the writer the following verses, commenting as follows:—

"Copied out of an odd leaf pasted in an old MS. history of the Hays. It is composed in imitation of a Highland Pibroch. The two long stanzas of 'The Gathering' are said to be of considerable antiquity. Of the first there is a version in Gaelic. The second is not older than 1646, for Hay of Yester did not receive the title of Tweeddale until that period. The rest of 'The Gathering' is said to have been written by Captain James Hay in 1715." The slogan of the Hays was "Hollen MacGaradh."

The Gathering Of The Hays

"MacGaradh, MacGaradh, red race of the Tay,
Ho gather! Ho gather! like hawks to the prey;
MacGaradh, MacGaradh, MacGaradh comes fast,
The flame's on the beacon, the horn's on the blast,
The standard of Erroll unfurls its white breast
And the Falcon of Luncartie stirs in her nest;
Come away, come away, come to the tryst!
Come in, MacGaradh, from east and from west.
MacGaradh, MacGaradh, MacGaradh, come forth,

THE EMPEROR CHARLEMAGNE

The Hays have four lines of descent from the Emperor Charlemagne and his Empress Hildegarde; the great king of the Franks and Emperor over all the Roman Empire.

THE EMPRESS HILDEGARDE

Charlemagne's wife — known as "Hildegarde the Fair."

King Alfred the Great. This statue was unveiled at Winchester on the Thousandth Anniversary of his death. The great progenitor of the family of Hay.

THE FAMILY OF HAY

Come from your bowers from south and from north,
Come in all Gowrie, Kinnoul, and Tweeddale,
Drumelyier and Naughton, come locked in your mail;
Come Stuart! Come Stuart! set up your white rose,
Killour and Buccleugh, bring your bills and your bows;
Come in, MacGaradh, come armed for the fray,
For wide is the war-cry, and dark is the day.

Quick March.

"The Hay, the Hay, the Hay, the Hay!
MacGaradh is coming, give way, give way.
"The Hay, the Hay, the Hay, the Hay!
MacGaradh is coming, hurra!
MacGaradh is coming like beam of war,
The blood-red shields are glinting far,
The Stuart is up, his banner white,
Is flung to the breeze like flash of light;
Dark as the mountain's heather wave
The 'Rose' and the 'Misle' are coming brave,
Bright as the sun which gilds its thread
King James's tartan is flashing red,—
Upon them, MacGaradh! bill and bow!
Cry, Hollen MacGaradh, Hollen, Hollen!

Charge.

"MacGaradh is coming like stream from the hill,
MacGaradh is coming lance, claymore, and bill;
Like thunder's wild rattle is mingled the battle
With cry of the falling, and shout of the charge—
The lances are flashing, the claymores are clashing,
And ringing the arrows on buckler and targe.

Battle.

"MacGaradh is coming, the banners are shaking,
The war tide is turning, the phalanx is breaking,
The Southrons are flying, 'St. George!' vainly crying,
And Brunswick's white horse on the field is borne down,
The red Cross is shattered, the red roses scattered,
And bloody and torn, the white plume in its crown.

Pursuit.

"Far shows the dark field like the streams of Cairn Gorm,
Wild, broken, and red in the skirt of the storm—
Give the spur to the steed, give the war-cry, it's 'Hollen,'
Cast loose to wild speed, shake the bridle and follen,
The rout's in the battle like blast in the cloud,
The flight's mingled rattle peals thickly and loud,
Then 'Hollen, MacGaradh!' 'Hollen, MacGaradh!'
'Hollen-Hollen-Hollen, MacGaradh!'"

THE FAMILY OF HAY

Hay and his two sons who arrested the fleeing Scots at Loncarty have been immortalized by Shakespeare in the drama of "Cymbeline," where they are introduced as Bellisarius, a banished lord in disguise, and Guiderius and Arviragus, supposed to be sons of Bellisarius, but really the sons of King Cymbeline.

The battle is lost, the Britons (Scots) are fleeing, when enter Bellisarius and his sons:—

Bellisarius— "Stand, stand! We have the advantage
Of the ground;
The lane is guarded; nothing routs us
But the villainy of our fears.
Guiderius—
Arviragus— Stand, stand! And fight!

Posthumus relates as follows what then took place:—

Posthumus— "The army broken
And but the backs of Scots seen, all flying
Through a straight lane; the enemy full hearted
Lolling the tongue with slaughtering, having work
More plentiful than tools to do't, struck down
Some mortally, some slightly touch'd, some falling
Merely through fear; that the straight pass was damm'd
With dead men hurt behind, and cowards living
To die with lengthen'd shame—
Lord— Where was this lane?
Post.— Close by the battle, ditch'd, and wall'd with turf;
Which gave advantage to an ancient soldier—
An honest one I warrant; who deserv'd
So long a breeding as his white beard came to,
In doing this for's country. Athwart the lane
He, with two striplings—lads more like to run
The country base than to commit such slaughter;
With faces fit for masks, or rather fairer
Than those for preservation cas'd, or shame—
Made good the passage; cried to those that fled;
'Our (Scotland's) harts die flying, not our men:
To darkness! fleet souls that flie backwards.
Stand! or we are (Danes), and will give you that
Like beasts that you shun beastly, and may save
But to look back in frown—Stand! Stand!"
These three, three thousand confident, in act as many—
For three performers are the file when all the rest do
Nothing,—with this word 'Stand, stand,'

THE FAMILY OF HAY

               Accommodated by the place, more charming
               With their own nobleness, which could have turn'd
               A distaff to a lance, gilded pale looks,
               Part shame, part spirit renew'd; that some turn'd **coward**
               But by example,—O, a sin in war, damm'd in the **first**
               Beginners!—'gan to look the way they did,
               And grin like lions upon the pikes of hunters. Then began
               A stop i' the chaser, a retire; anon
               A rout, confusion thick: forthwith they fly
               Chichens, the way which they stoop'd eagles; slaves
               The strides they victors made: and now our cowards
               Like fragments in hard voyages, became
               The life o' the need; having found the back door open
               Of the unguarded hearts, heavens! how they wound!
               Some slain before, some dying, some their friends
               O'er-borne i' the former wave: ten chas'd by one
               Are now each one the slaughter man of twenty:
               Those that would die or ere resist are grown
               The mortal bugs of the field.
Lord—   This was strange chance:
               A narrow lane, an old man, and two boys?
Post.—   Nay, do not wonder at it: you have made
               Rather to wonder at the things you hear
               Than to work any; will you rhyme upon't
               And vent it for a mockery? here is one:
               "Two boys, an old man twice a boy, a lane
               Preserv'd the (Scots) and was the (Danish) bane."

(Note:—In the above extract, "Scot" and "Dane" have been substituted for "Briton" and "Roman" — restitution for Shakespeare's robbery.)

The name in Scotland now emerges from the mists of tradition and enters a period illuminated by the light of historical research. Mr. Taylor in his book, "The Great Historic Families of Scotland," says:—

"The Hays are a branch of the Norman family of de Haya. * * * * * * * * Their armorial bearings are the same as those borne by the families of the name in Italy, France, and England. A Sieur de la Haya, accompanied William the Conqueror to England in 1066. A William de la Haya who married the daughter of Ranulph de Soulis, Lord of Liddesdale, was cup-bearer to Malcolm IV., about the middle of the twelfth century, and to his brother William the Lion, who bestowed on him the lands of Erroll."

This William de la Haya was, no doubt, the son or grandson

of the Sieur de la Haya, who came to England with Duke William, who had found his way to Scotland, the land of his ancestors, as told by Mr. Hay Allan. He died in the year 1170, and left by his wife Julianne de Soulis the following three sons:—

    i.   SIR WILLIAM DE LA HAY, LORD OF ERROLL, whose history follows.

    ii.   Robert de Hay, from whom descend the seven Lords of Yester, created 1488, the title then changing 1646 to Earl of Tweeddale, and in 1694 changed to that of Marquis of Tweeddale.

    iii.   Peter de la Hay, living in 1196.

Second Generation

SIR WILLIAM DE LA HAY, LORD OF ERROLL was the eldest son of William de la Hay, the Cupbearer. He was living in 1160.

He was a courtier of William the Lion, and became one of the hostages for payment of his ranson. He went on a special mission to King John of England, and returned with King William to the north.

Mr. Bain writes in his "History of Nairnshire":—

"Amongst the great nobles at the court when King William was in Moray was William de Hay. He is a signatory to some five different charters granted by the King and recorded in the Chartulary of Moray. The King had in his gift the lands of Auldearn, and it is extremely probable that the Sir William de la Hay so frequently mentioned in the charters of the period received the grant of the lands of Lochloy at this time, in addition to his possessions elsewhere."

He died in 1199, and left issue by his spouse Eva de Petenalin, a wealthy heiress, the following six children:—

i. Sir David de la Hay, of whom later.
ii. William de la Hay.
iii. John de la Hay, from whom descend the Hays of Naughton.
iv. Thomas de la Hay.
v. Robert de la Hay.
vi. Nicholas de la Hay.

Third Generation

SIR DAVID DE LA HAY, LORD OF ERROLL, was the eldest son of Sir William de la Hay by his wife Eva de Petenalin. In 1188-99, he had charters to hold the Lands of Erroll "as freely as his father had held them." He married Helen, daughter of Gilbert, 3d Earl of Strathearn, by his wife, the Countess Matilda, daughter of William D'Aubigny, Earl of Albemarle.

Earldom of Strathearn

1. Malisius, Earl of Strathearn, testibus in the foundation charter of the monastary of Scone by King Alexander I., anno 1115; was at the battle of the Standard, anno 1138.
2. Ferquhard, second earl, was at Perth with Malcolmn IV. (Fordun, vol. i, p. 1153, 450). He left two sons: Gilbert; and Malise, who is designed in the foundation charter of Inchaffray "Frater Gilberti, Comites de Strathearn," anno 1198.
3. Gilbert, third earl, married Maude or Matilda, daughter of William D'Aubigny, Earl of Albermarle, and had five sons and two daughters:—i. Gilbert d.s.p.; ii. William d.s.p.; iii. Ferquhard d.s.p.; iv. Robert, who became the heir; v. Fergus, "frater Domini Roberti, Comites de Strathearn"; vi. Christian, married Sir Walter Oliphant; vii. Helen, married David de la Hay, Lord of Erroll.
4. Robert, 4th earl, witness to the charter of the whole earldom of Fife, granted by Alexander II. to Malcolm, son of Earl Duncan. He d. ante 1244, leaving a son Malise, and three daughters: Annabella, m. to Sir David Graham; Matilda, m. Malcolm, Earl of Fife; Lucia, m. Sir William Sinclair of Roslin.
5. Malise, 5th earl, one of the guarantees of the truce in 1224 with England, m. Mary, daughter of Eugene of Ergada, relict of the King of Man. "Malisius Comes of Strathearn, viduam regis Manniæ, filium Eugenii de Ergadia uxorem duxit," etc.—Fordun v. ii., p. 109.
   He died anno 1271, and was buried at Dunblane, and was succeeded by Malise, his son.
6. Malise, 6th earl, agreed to the marriage of the Princess Margaret, daugter of Alexander III., with Eric of Norway A.D. 1281. And to the marriage of her daughter, the Maiden Queen, with Prince Edward

of England in 1290. He was one of the Bruce's chosen arbiters in 1292. He m. Egidia, dau. of Alexander Cumyn, 2d Earl of Buchan, and left by her Malise his heir, and Mary m. to Sir John Murray of Drumsargard, whose son afterward became Earl of Strathearn.

7. Malise, 7th earl, was an adherent of Robert Bruce. He signed the letter to the Pope in 1320, asserting the independence of Scotland. He appears to have been three times married, but left no male heir. His first wife, mother of the Countess Johanna, was the daughter of Sir John Menteith.

His second wife, Marjorie, was daughter of "Robert de Muschamp."

His third wife, according to Sir James Balfour, was Matilda, daughter and heiress of Magnus, Earl of Orkney and Caithness, by whom he had four daughters—of whom the first m. William, Earl of Ross, who had A.D. 1344, from Malise, a gift of the earldom of Caithness; but this was not confirmed by David II. until 1362. Isabel, the second sister, m. Sir William Sinclair of Roslin. The third, "Matilda de Strathearn," m. Hugh of Arthe, and was mother of Alexander of Arthe. The fourth m. Reginald Cheyne, and was mother of Mariot Cheyne. These four daughters of Malise, Earl of Strathearn, inherited the earldom of Orkney and Caithness, in right of their mother, daughter and heiress of Earl Magnus, untouched by their father's forfeiture.

Sir Robert Gordon says:—"Malisius, Earl of Caithness, Orkney and Strathearn, gave the earldom of Caithness to William, Earl of Ross, in marriage with his daughter Isabel, which was not confirmed by Robert II. until 1362; Malise himself being attainted in 1343 by King David for giving the title of "Earl of Strathearn" to David's enemy, the Earl of Warrenne, who m. Johanna, Malise's daughter. It must have been Johanna's mother, and not herself, who was implicated in the plot against King Robert and condemned to perpetual imprisonment, anno 1320.—Fordun vol. ii., p. 274.

Mariot Cheyne had a fourth part of the earldom of Caithness, on her own resignation, and a charter of half the barony of Strabrock, as wife of the deceased John Douglas.

Alexander of Arth, representative of the Earls of Strathearn, inherited and resigned the earldom of Caithness to Robert II.

The Earldom of Strathearn, on the forfeiture of Malise, 7th earl, was conferred on his nephew Sir Maurice Moray, eldest son of Mary, his sister, m. to Sir John Moray of Drumsargard, Lord of Clydesdale, who had joined the Steward at the seige of Perth in 1339, and had many charters from David II., and the ward of Walter Cumyn of Rowallan.

8. Mauritius, Comes de Strathearn by charter from David II., accompanied King David into England, and was killed at the Battle of Durham in 1346, and having no issue, the earldom, which was left to him and

heirs male, returned to the Crown, he being succeeded in his other estates by his younger brother, Sir Alexander Moray of Abercairney. It remained in the Crown until it was erected into a County Palatine by King Robert II. in favor of his eldest son David Rothesay, by his marriage to Eufame, dau. of Hugh, Earl of Ross.

9. Prince David thus became Earl of Strathearn. He left an only child, the Lady Euphemia, designed "Comitessa Palitina de Strathearn," who m. Sir Patrick Graham, Lord of Kincardine and Dunduff.

Sir James Dalrymple says:—"In the Chartulary of Inchaffray, Insula Missasarum, are many particulars concerning the Earls of Strathearn which have escaped genealogists."—Mrs. Cumming Bruce, pp. 551-554.

It has been seen that the monastary of Inchaffray was founded by Gilbert, 3d Earl of Strathearn, and his Countess Matilda, whose parentage is shown by the following extract from the charter:—"Ego Gilbertus, filius Ferquhardi, Comites de Strathearn, et Ego, Matilda, filia Willelmus D'Aubigny," etc.

Sir David de la Hay by his wife Helen, dau. of Gilbert, 3d Earl of Strathearn, and his Countess Matilda D'Aubigny, had sons:—

 i.   Gilbert de la Hay, Lord of Erroll (vide immediately below).
 ii.   Sir William de la Hay of Leys; his history follows presently in Section IV.

Fourth Generation

SIR WILLIAM DE LA HAY OF LEYS was the second son of David de la Hay, Lord of Erroll, by his wife Helen, youngest daughter of Gilbert, 3d Earl of Strathearn, by his countess Matilda, daughter of Willam D'Aubigny, Earl of Albemarle.
(Vide Burke and also "The Bruces and the Cumyns" p. 552, and Hist. Nairn.)

"When the crisis arises in regard to the succession to the Scottish throne, William de la Hay exhibits his seal to the 'Letter of the Community of Scotland,' 1289. During the time the Guardians of Scotland administered the affairs of the nation, his son Sir John figures in the history of the period. When the claims of Bruce and Baliol were submitted to Edward, Bruce nominated William de la Hay as one of his Commissioners, and Dr. Taylor in his 'History of Edward I., in the North Scotland,' states that this William de la Hay was the representative of the family of Hay of Lochloy in the County of Nairne.

"In support of Robert Bruce the Elder, he joined the Scottish nobles at Dunbar, and was taken prisoner and sent to the Castle of Berkhampstead. He was soon liberated, however, and swore fealty to Edward, 28 August 1296, and came north with him. He was then appointed Sheriff of Inverness, and in that capacity he received the oaths of fealty of the principal officers in the North, amongst others that of William de Monte Alto, Sheriff of Dingwall.

"Sir William de la Hay was also appointed Warden of Ross, and was practically Governor of the North. So valiant a knight was too valuable an officer to be left in civil employment, and Edward summoned him to accompany him on an expedition to Flanders. He responded, and the payments made him for services in Flanders are recorded in the Exchequer Rolls. His son joined the patriotic party and adhered to Bruce and in 1304 one Oliver Avenal petitioned Edward to give him the lands of John de la Hay in the County of Inverness, promised him in the late war. After the War of Independence, the Hays were reinstated in their lands in Inverness and Nairn."—Mr. Bain in Hist. Nairn, pp. 206-07. He had two sons mentioned in contemporary history:—

i. A son from whom descend Hay of Leys, ancestors to the Earls of Kinnoul created 1633, the two James Earls of Carlisle created Lord Sauley 1615, who m. Lucy Percy, dau. of the Earl of Northumberland, and many other Hays distinguished in the history of Scotland and England.

ii. Sir John de la Hay, Lord of Tholybothil, whose history is given in Section V.

Fifth Generation

SIR JOHN DE LA HAY was the son of Sir William de la Hay of Leys. He adhered to the cause of Robert Bruce and mention is made in "The History of Nairnshire" that Edward I. was petitioned by Oliver Avenal to bestow upon him the promised lands of Sir John Hay. These lands were afterward restored by King Robert the Bruce to the family. He is a witness to a charter of Alexander of Moravia. He married the daughter and heiress of Sir Andrew Fraser of Touch and Tullibody, who in 1296 was Sheriff of Stirling.

Fraser

The Frasers, like most of the other great Scottish houses, were of Norman descent. Their original designation was Frissell, which occurs in the roll of Battle Abbey, and is still given to them in various parts of the country.

It is said their ancestor came to Scotland in the reign of Charlemagne along with the French ambassadors that monarch is reputed to have sent over to form a league with King Achaius.

In reality the first of the name settled in Scotland in the reign of Malcolm Cawnmohr, and appears to have obtained from that monarch a grant of the lands of East Lothian. In the reign of David I., Sir Simon Fraser possessed half of the lands of Keith, called from him Keith Simon. Hervey, the ancestor of the Keiths, Earls Mareschal, who married Simon's granddaughter, was proprietor of the other half, named from him Keith Hervey.

1. Another member of the family, Sir Gilbert Fraser, obtained the lands of North Hailes, and also a large estate in Tweeddale. Oliver Castle, a celebrated stronghold of the Frasers, was built by his oldest son Oliver Fraser.
2. Sir Andrew Fraser, 2d son of Sir Gilbert Fraser, and uncle of Sir Simon, became, on the death of the patriot, the male representative of the Fraser family.
    He possessed the lands of Touch in Stirlingshire, and of Stuthers in Fife, afterward the property of the Lindsays, Earls of Crawford. "He was," says Anderson, "the historian of the family, the first of the name of Fraser who established an interest for himself and descendants

in the northern parts of Scotland, and more especially in Inverness-shire, where they have ever since figured with such renown and distinction."

3. A daughter of the foregoing Sir Andrew, who was her father's heiress, m. Sir John de la Hay, and it will be seen later that the property of "Touch" acquired by this marriage is transmitted to Sir Alexander Seton of Touch, one of the descendants of this pair.

Sir John de la Hay, by his spouse Miss Fraser, the heiress of Touch and Tullibody, had a son:— (The Bruces and the Cumyns.)

    i. John de la Hay, Lord of Tholybothil, whose history follows.

Sixth Generation

SIR JOHN DE LA HAY, LORD OF THOLYBO-THIL in 1369, and in his mother's right, possessed of the lands of Touch and Tullibody, was the son of Sir John de la Hay by his wife Miss Fraser, daughter of Sir Andrew Fraser of Inverness-shire.

"In 1350 he granted lands in Nairn and Sutherland, and Strathpeffer in Ross, to his brother-in-law, Thomas Sinclair, with his sister Euphemia; and in 1374 mortifies an annuity out of the lands of Lochloy and Raits to the chapel of St. Mary at Kinraize, with consent of John, his son and heir."—The Bruces and Cumyns.

The following extract from the "History of Nairnshire," by Mr. George Bain, evidently refers to this grant:—

"In 1364, John de la Hay, Lord of Tullibothil, was Sheriff of Inverness and with consent of his son John granted out of his lands of Lochloy and Wester Raite an endowment for the chapel of Kincraggie. He also possessed the lands of Awn (the Enzie) and others.

Mention is made of David II., having given in 1362, a grant of all the lands lying between the Spey and the rivulet called the Tynot in the Forest of Awne to John de la Hay of Lochloy and Tullibothil, for the purpose of being cultivated. Out of these lands in 1374 he gave a donation of four pounds for the support of a chaplain in the chapel of Geth."

Sir John Hay of Tholybothil married in 1364, Christian Keith, daughter of Sir William de Keith, Great Mareschal of Scotland, by his spouse Marjorie Comyn, 3d daughter of William Comyn, 1st Earl of Buchan, Great Justiciar of Scotland 1209. (Mrs. Cumming Bruce and Mr. Bain.)

Keith

The family of Keith descend traditionally from Robert, leader of the Catti, who emigrated from Germany in the reign of Malcolm II. and gained a signal victory over the Danes in 1010, in which he slew their leader "Canus."

King Malcolm dipped his finger in the blood of the dead general, and drew

THE FAMILY OF HAY

three strokes on the upper part of Robert's shield, which his descendants bear on their arms in pale, and created him "Hereditable Great Mareschal of Scotland." (This is probably mythical.)

1. Warin de Keith, descended from Robert, was Great Mareschal of Scotland.
2. Hervius de Keith, son and heir, was living in time David I.
3. Hervius de Keith, son and heir, died in 1196.
4. Malcolm de Keith, son and heir, Great Mareschal, living 1183.
5. Philip de Keith, son and heir, married Eda, daughter of Hugh Laurens by his wife, Eda, daughter and heiress of Simon Fraser, and died about 1220.
6. Hervius de Keith, Great Mareschal, son and heir, died 1242-50.
7. Sir John de Keith, Great Mareschal, son and heir, married Marjorie, youngest daughter of William Cumyn, b. 1163, Great Justiciar of Scotland in 1209, First Earl of Buchan in right of his 2d wife Marjorie, Countess of Buchan—William Cumyn's first wife was Matilda Urquhart, daughter of Banquo, from which marriage sprang the House of Badenoch, one of whom was John the Red Comyn.

    By his second marriage William Cumyn, Earl of Buchan, had Marjorie, who, we have seen, married Sir John de Keith.
8. Sir William de Keith, Great Mareschal, son and heir, married Barbara, daughter of Sechar or Sirlo de Seton, and d. anent 1290.
9. Christian de Keith, daughter of Sir William de Keith by his wife Barbara, married 1364, Sir John de la Hay, Lord of Tholybothil.

Line of Comyn

(De Comin, Comyn, Cumine, Cominge, Cumming)

1. John, Count de Comyn and Baron de Tonsberg, Normandy, was the son of Baldwin, founder of the House of Blois, the son of Baldwin, son of Godfrey, a distinguished soldier of the cross, grandson of Charles, Duc d'Ingeheim, fifth son of the Emperor Charlemagne.

    (Vide Burke's Extinct Peerage on Moreton or De Burge, Earl of Cornwall A.D. 1068; also vide "The Bruces and the Cummings," pp. 391-401, from which most of the following is taken.)

    John had two sons:—Eustace of whom presently; and Harlowen de Burg, founder of the Abbey of Grestein in Normandy, died vit. pat. having married Arlotta, mother of William the Conqueror, by whom he left two sons present with their half-brother, Duke William, at the Battle of Hastings 1066, viz.:

    i. Robert, Count of Moreton or Mortein, Normandy, created Earl of Cornwall, with grants for 793 Manors, slain in Northumbria A.D. 1087; and left a son William, who rebelled against Henry I., demanding the earldom of Kent, which his Uncle Odo had held. William left a son Adelm from whom derive the House of Clanricarde.

THE FAMILY OF HAY

    ii. Odo, Bishop of Bayeux, created Earl of Kent in 1067, died 1096-98—vide Selsden's Titles of Nobility, p. 527.

2. Eustace, Count of Comyn and Baron of Tonsberg, had son:—

3. Robertus de Comyn, Earl and Governor of Northumberland, progenitor of all of the name in Scotland. King William sent him 700 veteran Normans to enforce his authority in Northumberland, and these soldiers having committed outrages at Durham, the natives rebelled, and Earl Robert and his 700 men were all killed save one. (1068-9.)

    Upon the death of Comyn, Cospatrick, son of Maldred by Algitha, daughter of Uchtred (who had been Earl of Northumberland in the reign of Canute) bought the earldom from King William, but it being discovered he had countenanced the murder of Robert Cumyn, he was forced to fly from the wrath of William, and took refuge with Malcolm III., who made him Earl of Dunbar and Defender of the Marches.

    Cospatrick's race still exists in the Dunbars and Dundasses, although there is no longer a "Counte des Marches d'Ecosses"—though, oddly enough, he who held that title by lineal descent from Cospatrick in 1400 claimed cousinship with Henry IV. of England through the "blude of the Cummyn," Henry claiming a like descent.

    Robert had two sons:—John, and William, who was bred a cleric by Gaufred or Geoffrey; he became Chancellor to David I. of Scotland, and was nominated Bishop of Durham by Queen Matilda; d. ante 1144.

4. John Comyn, son of Robert, was killed in the wars between King Stephen and Matilda, the Empress Queen, circa 1135. He must have married one of the heirs of Andrew Gifford of Fonthill, and left a son:

5. William Comyn, son and heir, held in 1120 one-third of the lands Fonthill, in Wiltshire. He died before 1140, when his widow Maud, daughter of Thurston Banaster of Basset, married 2d William de Hastings.

    He had large possessions in Tynedale, and left two sons:—William, the eldest d.s.p., was killed in the contest for the Bishopric in 1144. His death caused his uncle to give up the struggle, and Northallerton and other lands were settled on the younger brother:—

6. Richard Comyn, second son of William, had a grant of the lands and honours of Northallerton in 1144.

    He married Hextilda, daughter of the Countess of Etheltela, daughter of the Count de St. Pol by his wife Bethoc (Beatrix), daughter of King Donald Bane, second son of King Duncan, murdered by Macbeth.

    (It is remarkable, and it will show how the noble families of Scotland have intermarried, when it is observed that King Duncan had three sons, Malcolm Cawnmohr, Donald Bane, and Melmare, Earl of Athol, and each of these brothers was an ancestor of Colonel Ann Hawkes Hay.)

Richard Comyn obtained from Prince Henry lands in Peebleshire, viz., the lands of Lynton-Ruderic now West Linton.

"We find in 'Origines Parochials Scotiæ' that between the years 1152 and 1159, Richard Comyn (the second of a race which rose within a century to a height of power which no other family in the land ever reached or attained in after times) gave to the monks of St. Mary of Kelso the Church of Lynton Ruderic," etc.

By his wife Hextilda, Countess of Etheletela, whom he m. 1152, he had children:—

  i.   John, died in lifetime of his father, bu. at Gelso.
  ii. William, his heir, vide below.
  iii. Odo, a Priest.
  iv. David, m. Isabel de Valoines, progenitors of the Cumyns of Kilbride, who in turn were progenitors of the Hamiltons.

7. William Comyn, son and heir of Richard, b. 1163; was great Justiciar of Scotland in 1209; and d. in 1233, aetat. 70.

He married 1st Matilda Urquhart, dau. of Coetisa, dau. of Banquo, by whom he left i. Margaret, m. Bartime Seton; ii. Agnes, m. Philip de Melgdrum; iii. Richard, Lord of Kirkentilt, whose only son John m. Matilda, Countess of Angus, and d. in France, 1242, leaving an infant son Bertraldt; the Countess m. 2d. Gilbert de Umphraville. iv. Walter Cumyn, m. 1231, the eldest daughter of Maurice, Earl of Menteith, and became Earl of Menteith in her right; he was Guardian and Regent of Scotland in 1249, and had a gift of Badenoch from Alexander II., and died without issue, 1258; v. John, the Red Comyn (No. 1), who m. Marian, as some say, daughter of the Lord of Galloway and sister of Devorgoile, according to others daughter of the Lord of the Isles. He d. 1273, and John Comyn, murdered by Bruce, was his grandson.

William, son of Richard, married 2d Marjorie, daughter of Fergus, the last of the old line of earls, and in her right became 1st Earl of Buchan of the house of Comyn.

By her he had of the house of Buchan:—

  i.   Alexander, 2d Earl of Buchan, succeeded his mother 1237; he m. Elizabeth, 2d dau. of Roger de Quincy, Earl of Winchester, by Alena, eldest dau. of Alan, Lord of Galloway by his first wife. Alexander was Great Justiciar in 1251, High Chancellor in 1270, till his death in 1289.
  ii. Fergus.
  iii. Elizabeth, m. William, 9th Earl of Mar.

(Which gives Colonel Hay a second line of decent from the House of Comyn.)

Robert the Bruce arrives at the Field of Bannockburn. The Hays have five lines of descent from this Scottish hero and king. (Courtesy of Chivas Brothers, Ltd. of Aberdeen)

Coat of Arms of the Family of Hay of Erroll. A field of argent charged with three gules within a bordure nebule of the Past; for crest, a hand proper holding an ox yoke; motto—"Laboranti Palma".

THE FAMILY OF HAY

    iv.   Jean, m. Sir Gilbert de la Hay, Regent with his brother-in-law 1255-58.
    v.   Marjorie, m. Sir William de Keith, Great Mareschal.
    vi.   Isabel, m. Francis, Lord Cheyne of Inverugie and Cassilmont.

8. Marjorie, daughter of William Comyn, 1st Earl of Buchan, by her husband Sir William de Keith, 6th Great Mareschal, had a daughter.
9. Christian, who married 1364, Sir John de la Hay, Lord of Tholybothil, who are in the direct line of Colonel Hay's ancestors, conveying to him a second strain of Comyn blood. (Vide Elizabeth suprs.)

    Of Sir John de la Hay, Lord of Tholybothil, Douglas says, he was so great a lord that he was given on his shield as an extra mark of distinction—A Bend Dexter.

(It may be of interest to our readers to trace the descent of King Henry IV. of England from William Comyn, 1st Earl of Buchan; this was as follows:—William, 1st Earl of Buchan and his wife Marjorie, had a son: Alexander, who had a son:—Alexander, who had a daughter:—Alice, m. Henry de Beaumont, and had a daughter:—Isabel, m. Henry Plantagenet, Duke of Lancaster, and had a daughter:—The Lady Blanche Plantagenet, m. John of Gaunt, third son of Edward III., and a son:—Henry IV., King of England, who was proud of his Comyn blood, and claimed to be half a Scot.)—The Lineage of Comyn is taken from the book of Mrs. Cumming-Bruce, "The Bruces and Cumyns."

    Sir John de la Hay, Lord of Tholybothil, by his wife, Christian, daughter of Sir William de Keith (vide "Keith" 8 and 9) by his wife Marjorie Comyn, daughter of William, 1st Earl of Buchan (vide "Comyn" 6 and 7) had a son:—

    i.   Sir John de la Hay, 2d Lord of Tholybothil; history follows.

Seventh Generation

SIR JOHN DE LA HAY, 2d Lord of Tholybothil, was the son of Sir John de la Hay by his spouse, Christian Keith, daughter of Sir William de Keith, Great Mareschal of Scotland, and was living A. D. 1380. He also possessed the lands of Park and Lochloy in Nairnshire; Boyne and Enzie in Banffshire; Touch and Tullibody in Clackmannanshire; and is frequently styled: "John Hay of Boyne and Enzie."

He married A.D. 1388, Margaret Stewart, the youngest daughter of Sir John Stewart of Railston, the eldest son of Walter the Steward by his 1st wife Alice Erskine, a daughter of Sir John Erskine of Erskine, great-grandson of Henry de Erskine, who, during the reign of Alexander II., possessed the barony of Erskine in Renfrewshire, south of the Clyde.

As King Robert II. was the only child of Walter the Steward by his 2d wife Marjorie Bruce, daughter of King Robert I., he was a half-brother of Sir John Stewart of Railston, and a half-uncle to Margaret Stewart, the latter's daughter; thus it follows, that upon the occasion of Margaret's marriage to Sir John Hay, King Robert II., in a gift of dowry, refers to her as his niece.

(For mention of this marriage vide: "The Bruces and Cumyns," p. 618, and "The History of Nairnshire," p. 108. Sir James Balfour Paul, Lord Lyon of Scotland, in a letter to the writer says: "Sir John Hay of Boyne and Enzie" married Margaret, a half-niece of King Robert II.)

Colonel Hay was descended from Walter the Steward by the latter's marriages to Alice Erskine and to Marjorie Bruce, therefore we introduce the pedigree of Margaret Stewart.

Line of Stewart

2. Alan obtained soon after the Conquest a grant of the Castle of Oswestry, in which grant he is spoken of as the son of Fiaald. He married the daughter and heiress of Warine, Sheriff of Shropshire, in the time of William the Conqueror, and had three sons:—i. William,

THE FAMILY OF HAY

from whom descend the Earls of Arundel, and Duke of Norfolk; ii. Walter Fitzalan, vide below; iii. Simon, who accompanied his brother Walter to Scotland and founded the family of Boyd, from which, we have seen, descend the Earls of Erroll.

Walter Fitzalan, 2d son of Alan, was made by King David I. High Steward of Scotland. He married Eschina, daughter of Thomas de Londoniis, heiress of Molla and Huntlaw, in Roxburghshire, and died A.D. 1177, leaving an only son.

Alan, his son, who was 2d High Steward.

Walter, his son, who was 3d High Steward.

Alexander, his son, who was 4th High Steward, who had two sons:—
James, vide below; and John, who married Margaret, the daughter and heiress of Sir John Bonkyl of Bonkyl, and from them descended some of the most considerable branches of the name, among whom was Lord Darnley Stewart, Earl of Lennox, who married his cousin, Mary Queen of Scots, from whom were James I., of England, and almost all the sovereigns of Europe.

Sir John Stewart in right of Margaret his wife is known as Sir John Stewart Bonkyl, and by her he had a son, Sir Alexander Stewart of Bonkyl, who succeeded to his maternal grandfather's estate and had a daughter, Isabella Stewart, who married Donald, 12th Earl of Mar, by whom she had a daughter Mary, married Kenneth, 4th Earl of Sutherland.

These were progenitors of Colonel Hay as will be seen later in the lineage of Janet Sutherland.

James, eldest son of Alexander, was the 5th High Steward.

Walter, son of James, was 6th High Steward of Scotland. He espoused the cause of Robert the Bruce, and was present at the Battle of Bannockburn.

He married 1st Alice Erskine, daughter of Sir John Erskine, and had three sons and one daughter—the eldest son was Sir John Stewart of Railston, whose daughter Margaret married Sir John Hay, Lord of Tholybothil, Boyne, and Enzie. (For their posterity vide below.)

Walter the Steward married 2d Marjorie Bruce, the only daughter of King Robert I., and had a son King Robert II., who had a son King Robert III., whose daughter Mary married George Douglas, 1st. Earl of Angus, who were ancestors of Colonel Hay: (vide "The Line of Douglas" given later in this work.)

Walter the Steward married 3d Isobel Graham.

Sir John Stewart of Railston, son of Walter the Steward by his 1st. wife Alice Erskine, had among other children:—

Margaret Stewart, half-niece of King Robert II., who makes to her on her marriage a gift of dowry, she married, as has been shown, Sir John Hay, Lord of Tholybothil, Lochloy, Boyce, and Enzie, had issue:— ("The Bruces and Cumyns," p. 618.)

THE FAMILY OF HAY

i. Sir James Hay of Enzie, Boyne, Touch, and Tullibody, who left sons:

Sir John Hay, who married a daughter of the Earl of Ross, and died ante 1425, leaving a daughter and heiress—Egidia Hay, who married Alexander, 1st Earl of Huntly (created 1449), by whom she had a son—Sir Alexander of Touch, 1st. Lord Seton,—from whom the Setons of Touch.

Sir Gilbert Hay, 2d. son of Sir James, married Margaret Gordon of Strathbolgie and left two sons:—David d.s.p.; and Andrew Hay, who had a son Alexander d.s.p. and a daughter —Helen Hay, who married an Abercrombie, whence the lords Abercrombie of Tullibody.

ii. William Hay of Lochloy, whose history is given in Section VIII. and is in direct line of Colonel Hay's pedigree.

iii. John Hay, who left a daughter, Euphemia Hay, who married Sir John Sinclair of Deskford (who raised the fallen banner of the dying Douglas at Otterburn) and his daughter Margaret Sinclair married Sir Walter Ogilvie, from whom descend the Earls of Findlater (and also Colonel Hay, who derives also from Sir Alexander Seton, 1st Earl of Huntly, by his 3d marriage to Margaret Crichton).

Eighth Generation

WILLIAM HAY OF LOCHLOY was the second son of Sir John Hay of Boyne, Enzie, Tholybothil, Touch, Tullibody, and Lochloy, by his spouse Margaret Stewart, half-niece of King Robert II., and daughter of Sir John Stewart of Railston. (Vide "Stewart," Sec. VII.)

"His monument is still to be seen at Elgin Cathedral—the oldest tomb but one of a layman within the sacred precincts. The monument is in the transept. It consists of a stone sarcophagus with the colossal figure of a knight in complete armour with dirk and spurs still visible. The feet rest upon a lion couchant and the stone bears an inscription." The following is the inscription sent the writer by Sir Archibald Dunbar, Bart., of Elgin:—Hic Jacet Wills. de la Hay, quonda aens. de Lochloy, qui obiit viii die mensis Decembris anno Dom. MCCCCXXI. — (We now resume our extract from "The History of Nairn," by George Bain):

"Mention is made of this old Knight at a great gathering of northern gentry at the kirkyard of Chanonry of Rosemarkie, 16th August 1420. Amongst those present were John, Bishop of Ross; Dame Mary of the Isles and of Ross; Hugh Fraser Lord Lovat; John M'Leod Lord of Glenelg; Angus Gothrason of the Isles; Sir William Fraser Dean of Ross; Walter Douglas Sheriff of Elgin; Walter Innes Lord of that ilk; Urquhart of Cromarty; Donald of Kaledor; Thane of that ilk; Sinclair of Deskford; John the Rose Lord of Kilravock; John of Nairn Lord of Ardmuthack; with many others.

"The object of the meeting was to witness the resignation of the lands of Kerdale, Inverness-shire, by William the Graeme into the hands of 'a noble lord and a michty, Thomas Earl of Murray,' over-lord of the barony of Kerdale, and the earl conveys back the said lands to Graham and his heirs male, failing which to William Hay, his 'good-father,' Lord of Lochloy, and his male heirs."

Mr. Bain continues:

"The proceedings at Rosemarkie meant more than appears on the face of the deed, which was simply a regulation of succession. There was matchmaking in the business. The Earl of Moray had at this time a particular interest in the Hays of Lochloy, for John, William de la Hay's son, was engaged to marry the earl's daughter. But John proved fickle. He fell in love with a daughter of the Thane of Cawdor, and wished to be off with the old love.

"He received a communication from the Earl of Moray, and never did a disappointed father-in-law write a more tender, dignified and generous letter in such delicate circumstances." (This letter will be given in the next section, which is devoted to John de la Hay.)

The "History of Nairnshire" continues:—

"The Hays of Lochloy in the course of a generation or two became extensive land owners. Besides Lochloy, they had: Inshock, Park, Kinnudie, Meikle Urchany, Wester Raite, Foynesfield, Dallas, and other possessions in the north and south. They were at the height of their prosperity about the close of the sixteenth century. David Hay of Lochloy married Marie Rose of Kilavock in 1605. She lived to see her eighty-eighth year, and when she died it is stated there were descended of her no less than one hundred and ten persons then in life."—Mr. George Bain in the "History of Nairnshire"; from his writings we also quote the following beautiful descriptions of Inshoch Castle, three miles to the east of Auldearn, and of Lochloy as he saw it a few years since on the coast of Moray, not far to the east of the town of Nairn:—

"The ancient and knightly family of Hay of Lochloy, near neighbors of the Brodies, acquired at a very early period lands in Nairnshire. It was one of the oldest branches of the Hays of Erroll.

The first mention of Lochloy was in connection with the landing of Harold, Earl of Caithness, at the port of Lochloy to make submission to King William the Lion, at the Castle of Nairn. * * * * * * We now come to one of the prettiest and most interesting bits of scenery of its kind in this part of the country.

It is entitled to be called the Lake District, and no description can convey an idea of its beauty, but here are its elements:—

There is the dense wood of Lochloy forming a dark background to the deep-blue water of the lake lying at its foot.

The Loch, which wears a somewhat cold and wintry look on the hottest days, loses itself westward in a morass of rushes and aquatic plants. Along its northern edge, the sward, cut up into plots and patches, is the greenest of the green.

You look eastward and see the Loch rounded by another patch of green turf; and it is succeeded by another sheet of water known as the Cran Loch, and the water—being for the most part shallow—the light plays upon the surface in brightest colors, giving us 'Green Isles set in amber.'

The carse beyond has been planted, but has wonderful open spaces; so that you have beautiful glades, far-stretching avenues, up which you momentarily expect to see some gay cavalcade or fairy procession advancing.

THE FAMILY OF HAY 49

To the eye the scene is really charming and then it teems with life, with bird life especially. In the far plantations you hear the familiar songsters of the grove piping their lays unceasingly, and you are startled by the plaintive note of the cuckoo—'telling its name to all the wood.' A flock of wild geese are feeding among the sedgy reeds of Lochloy, and it may be, as it often happens, a pair of wild swans are floating majestically in the centre of the great loch. As you move eastward the air becomes thick with water fowl.

The coot, with a hoarse cry, rises from its nest, and plunges awkwardly into the loch, ploughing it as it goes. The pee-wits, which have long ere this become unwelcome attendants, now thoroughly alarmed at your intrusion, make threatening swoops at your head; while flocks of little ducklings, most comical looking in their newly fledged state, go racing and swimming about as for dear life. And for nests,—at the end of April or early May is the nesting season, every second or third tuft of grass on the island contains one. But what need to describe a scene made classical to all lovers of natural history by the graphic pen of the late Mr. St. John! In his books you will read of his shooting swans at Lochloy; watching flocks of geese on the shore; hunting roe and foxes in the Black Wood close by; and having perilous encounters with seals on the Old Bar. Mr. St. John was an English gentleman, who tired of fashionable life, and betook himself to this part of the country. He was a keen sportsman, and at the same time a most observant naturalist, and his book, 'Wild Sport and Natural History of The Highlands,' is full of incident and adventure. To his pleasant pages I refer you for further information respecting the wild denizens of the marshes of Lochloy. His early volume, 'Sport in Moray,' gives the fullest particulars about Lochloy.

But a word of two before we leave the spot about the family history of Lochloy. At a very early date we read of John de la Hay of Lochloy. He was one of the supporters of Baliol as against Bruce. The family was a branch of the Hays of Erroll. Doubtless they had a house at Lochloy, but in later centuries the old Castle of Inshoch was the family residence. The property at one time included Knockoudie and Park. One of the recumbent stone figures in Elgin Cathedral, representing in life size a warrior taking his rest, is a memorial of William Hay of Lochloy, and in Auldearn church-yard we have the last resting place of Hay of Lochloy, with a large tablet giving an account of the glories of the Hays. who were ranked among the nobles of the land in the olden time. * * * * * Immediately to the east of Lochloy is the town of Mavistown."

Does not this poetical description rest our readers in their plodding through these pages? Let us now go a few miles south of Lochloy to a spot a few miles east of Auldearn, on a line with Park and Cawdor Castle to the west of that historical town, and pausing a moment on the moor, search for traces of the witches who foretold to Macbeth his fortune—they should be there if such beings leave an impression of themselves behind. What we do find is the picturesque ruin of an old castle once belonging to the Hays of

Lochloy—Inshoch Castle thus described by our friend, Mr. Bain:—

"The Hays originally had a residence at Lochloy on the site now occupied by the house of the Baillies of Lochloy—a position on the coast commanding a wide view of the Moray Firth. At a very early period, however, a second castle was built more inland, namely, at Inshoch, and remains of it still exist. It was protected on one side by an impassable peat moss, and as the name would indicate, 'Insh-ach,' the island field, was surrounded with ditches formed by the overflow of the bog. The Castle had its entrance on the ground floor. On the landing of the stair adjoining the hall, a stone basin in a pretty little gothic arch was provided for washing the hands, with a drain for carrying off the water. The Hall itself was a handsome, well-lighted apartment, thirty feet by seventeen feet, with plastered walls, a large fireplace with moulded gambs, above which is a shield displaying the armorial bearings of the Hays of Lochloy—the insignia that had floated on many a field of battle.

The oldest part of the building shows a simple keep with round towers placed diagonally, so as to command the four sides of the main building, and turrets in the angles.

The original building appears to have been altered and additions made to it, doubtless to meet the requirements of a more advanced civilization. The ground floor was vaulted throughout and contained a kitchen with very large fireplace, and numerous cellars. Except the kitchen window, which may have been enlarged, the basement was lighted with narrow loops. A stone sink is fitted into the kitchen window, connected by a drain to the outside.

In the larger turret to the southwest, there is a very pretty little private room, commanding a charming view and provided with stone seats—doubtless my lady's boudoir.

The ruins are in a dilapiated state, and a considerable portion fell in the great storm of 1879, the night of the Tay Bridge disaster * * * * * * The family declined in the middle of the seventeenth century and the lands are now possessed by Brodie of Brodie."

In another publication, "Guide to Nairn and Its Neighborhood," Mr. Bain writes:—

"Leaving Auldearn and pursuing your way eastward, the Castle of Inshoch comes full into view. * * * * * * * It is built in the usual castellated style common to the period and is a most picturesque ruin. * * * * * * The curious construction of the old staircase leading up to the 'Lookout' is well seen through the broken masonry and with the assistance of a ladder adventurous youths still climb to the top. In years long gone this ancient castle was the stronghold of the Hays of Lochloy, a family that long flourished as one of the most powerful of northern 'septs' and figures largely in local tradition. * * * * * * But we are not far from the classic ground of the Hard-muir, "The Blasted Heath of Macbeth." On a hillock near the old Toll-house, a little off the road, marked by a few old pines, danced the witches, whose singular greeting of Macbeth

THE FAMILY OF HAY

by the titles of Thane of Glamis, Thane of Cawdor, and 'King Hereafter,' first fired his ambition and led him to murder his king. As the witches danced they sang—

> 'The weird sisters, hand in hand,
> Posters of the sea and land,
> Thrice do go about, about;
> Thrice to thine and thrice to mine,
> And thrice again to make up nine.'

After the overthrow of the conspiracy by Macdonald of the Isles and the Thane of Cawdor with the King of Norway, and the subjugation of the Western Isles, Macbeth and Banquo return from the west coast.

The news of the great victory they had achieved had reached Forres, where King Duncan was, first by the wounded Sergeant and then by the Thane of Ross. Crossing the moor after fatiguing journey, 'So foul and fair a day,' exclaimed Banquo, 'I have not seen', he impatiently asks—

'How far is't called to Forres?'

Before answer can be made he is startled by the appearance of three withered hags, whom he boldly addresses—

> '—What are these,
> So withered and so wild in their attire,
> That look not like the inhabitants of the earth,
> And yet are on it. Live you? or are you aught
> That man may question? You seem to understand me.
> By each at once her chappy fingers laying
> Upon her skinny lips! You should be women
> And yet your beards forbid me to interpret
> That you are so.

Macbeth—	Speak if you can, what are you?
First Witch—	All hail, Macbeth! Hail to thee, Thane of Glamis!
Second Witch—	All hail, Macbeth! Hail to thee, Thane of Cawdor!
Third Witch—	All hail, Macbeth! Thou shalt be king hereafter!'

Macbeth afterward eagerly demanded an explanation of their mystic word.

> '—Stay, you imperfect speakers, tell me more,
> By Sinel's death, I know I am Thane of Glamis.
> But how of Cawdor? The Thane of Cawdor lives
> A prosperous gentleman; and to be king
> Stands not within the prospect of belief,
> No more than to be Cawdor. Say from whence
> You owe this strange intelligence? or why
> Upon this blasted heath you stop our way
> With such prophetic greeting? Speak, I charge you!'

The heath is now under cultivation and has lost its bleak aspect, but who, so near the spot of such a remarkable scene in this tragedy of the immortal bard, would not indulge his fancy in viewing it, although historically regarded as fictitious."

Each square inch of Scotland's soil is historic ground, and here we are surrounded by the amphitheatre of scenes which have stirred the pulses of the world—but two of these we may glance at in passing. A few miles west of Inshoch Castle was fought in early May-1645, the Battle of Auldearn, where the noble Marquis of Montrose, a descendant of a Hay, defeated General Hurry with twice the number of the Highland forces. In this battle fought Hay of Kinnudie and Hay of Lochloy; the former was slain. A century later the celebrated Battle of Culloden was lost to the brave and romantic Charles Edward Stewart, about a half-day's ride from Auldearn toward the west. The day preceding the fatal fight, the Prince and his secretary, Mr. Hay, formed a party at dinner with their hosts, Rose, Baron of Kilravock; and his Lady, at Kilravock Castle, and the next night at this same castle was entertained His Highness, the Duke of Cumberland, whose exhibition of cruelty in putting to death the Highlanders lying wounded and helpless on the battlefield, will for all time brand him with the stigma we would fain see unmerited. "Fraser of Inverallochy, severely wounded, leaned wearily on the turf dyke, when Hawley riding by demanded, "To whom do you belong?" "To the Prince, sire," was the Chieftain's unhesitating reply. "Shoot that dog!" said Hawley to his aide-de-camp. "No sire! I am a soldier, not an executioner. My commission is at your disposal, but I can not and will not shoot him," replied the young officer. It was Wolfe, the hero of Quebec, who thus refused to act the butcher. It is a Highland tradition that thirteen years later, when General Wolfe on the Heights of Abraham fell back mortally wounded, it was the arms of Fraser of Lovat which received him, and, along with Simon Fraser, the younger brother of Inverallochy, bore him tenderly off the field." In the "Story of Culloden Moor," by Mr. Bain, the account of this battle —and the campaign leading to it—is set forth in a most delightful, simple, chaste, and masterly style.

Mr. Robert Leslie Moir of Aberdeenshire, Scotland, a descendant of the Hays, sent the writer the following touching account of a visit he paid to Culloden:—

THE FAMILY OF HAY 53

"The battlefield at the present time is under the plough, all except where the thickest of the fight took place. This has been preserved practically as it was on the day of the battle and surrounded by a belt of wood, by the good taste, I believe, of Duncan of Forbes. The principal object on the moor is the cairn, erected to the memory of the clansmen who fell that day. You are supposed to add a stone to it. On each side of the road leading through the actual place of conflict (this road did not exist in 1746) are the graves of the Highlanders who fought so well that fatal day, each clan by themselves. After the battle, they were identified by their tartans and buried in heaps—Macintoshes, Frasers, Macdonalds, Macgillivrays, Camerons, Stuarts of Appin, and many more.

There are also two trenches of 'Mixed Clans,' to my mind the saddest thought of all. They were, indeed, 'mixed' at Culloden. The 'Well of the Dead,' where the young chief of the 'Macgillivrays' fell, is still to be seen; but no one drinks from it now, as his blood still reddens the water. Macgillivray was wounded, but managed to get his back against a wall or stone fence hard by, and fought there until literally cut to pieces. I have been told that fourteen dead Englishmen were found near his body next day. Near by is 'The Field of the English Dead,' where the Englishry lie buried. This, when I was there, was being sown with corn. (Without doubt there were sad hearts in England, too, after the carnage of Drumossie Moor.) A little farther on is the stone from which Cumberland directed the battle; and although there is nothing to mark the spot, an old man pointed out the place where Prince Charles Edward stood and watched the conflict. If this was the place, why no stone to mark it? One to 'The Butcher, but not one to our own 'King of the Hielan Hearts'? Oh, shame!

The deep stillness of the place broken only by the distant call of some wild creature of the moors, the great hills looking down on the battlefield just as they looked on the day of action, the mounds of the mighty dead, the romance and glamor of the whole scene, powerfully excite the imagination; and in fancy I almost saw the wave of the tartans, and heard the slogan of the clansmen, as, impatient of inaction (like true Highlanders) and maddened by the havoc wrought in their ranks by the artillery of the enemy, they burst, like one of their own mountain torrents, on the Hanoverian lines, to the scream of their native pipes, and the boom of the English cannon. In vain, brave hearts, in vain! All that valor, all that desperation could do was done, but the star of the Stuarts was set, and the mighty heart of Scotland broken.

The shadows of evening were beginning to gather, warning me it was time to be moving; so, with bared head and reverent heart, I stooped me down and plucked a bit of heather from each hallowed mound, beneath which lay, in the silent sleep of death, so many of the brave, the noble, and the true.

To many lands have these mountain flowers been sent, to clansmen in Canada, in India, and in Africa, to help to keep the memory green of those gallant hearts, who, famished, exhausted, and broken, yet faced the Hanoverian host in the blinding sleet and hail of that fatal April day so long ago, and died the death of heroes for Scotland and Prince Charlie."

The following lines were inspired by some heather sent by the writer of the above description to a South Carolina daughter of the Hays of Erroll and Lochloy, and will show that though separated from Scotland by many generations and many thousand miles, she is still leal to "her ain countrie."

The Heather-bell

"Only a spray of heather from those Scotch hills far away.
From moors of waving purple, where my spirit loves to stray,
Yet it brings a fragrant message from the land I love so well,
And tenderly I'll cherish the bonnie heather-bell.
"I feel as I gaze on its beauty, and hold it so close in my hand.
Some day I must cross the broad ocean, and among the sweet heather-bells stand,
And there, as they wave in the breezes, full many a tale will they tell
Of noble deeds when my fathers dwelt in the land of the heather-bell.
"My pulse throbs warm as I listen to tales of her warriors brave,
Who with hearts that were leal, and arms that were strong, stood ready their country to save;
And tho' in the battle full many, by swift flying darts, were laid low,
With last labor'd breath, their cry was 'Advance!' they died with their face to the foe.
"There in the dusk of a terrible day, their forms lie silent and cold,
The moon, when it rose, shed a pitying ray, on the faces of young and of old,
And one grasps his sword in a firm, rigid hand, the other is press'd to his side
To stay the sharp pain of a deep, cruel wound, and stifle a groan ere he died.
"Here rests the form of a brave, noble lad, who fell on a heather-clad mound,
All stain'd with his life-blood, while clasp'd in his hand a bunch of the blossoms is found,
Press'd close to his heart, while the look on his face a story of love seems to tell.
Of one who is waiting to crown him at home with a garland of sweet heather-bell.
"And the sad winds wail and whisper of that time now dead and gone,
When the heather-bells were tolling a requiem forlorn,
In dreams I love to wander o'er those shadowy banks and braes,
To hear the echo'd message from their vanish'd, hallow'd days.
"So I bless this spray of heather, which brings to me these dreams
Of mossy banks and bonnie braes and gentle flowing streams,
And when the shadows lengthen, and I lay me down to rest,
May a kind hand place the heather upon my pulseless breast."

—Patti Lee Hay Colcock.

We must, however, resist the spell tempting us to linger by the wayside of Scottish romance and poetry, and proceed with tracing the footprints left behind by a family of Scotland.

William de la Hay, Lord of Lochloy, married Janet Macintosh, eldest daughter of William Macintosh, by his 2d marriage late

THE FAMILY OF HAY

in life to Margaret, daughter of Rurorie (Rorie) Mor M'Leod of Lewis, who was the seventh Chief of the Macintosh Clan.

(In a letter to the writer of this work, Mr. George Bain, Historian of Nairnshire, writes:— "According to the Kinrara Manuscript, William Macintosh, reckoned 7th Chief of the Macintosh Clan, by his 2d marriage late in life with Margaret, daughter of Rurorie Mor M'Leod of Lewes, had one son Malcolm Beg (who became 10th Chief) and five daughters, the eldest of whom, Janet, he gave in marriage to the Lord of Lochloy, surnamed Hay."

Mr. Bain continues in his letter:— "Mr. A. M. Macintosh, the historian of the family, informs me that this marriage may be placed early in the 15th century; Janet's brother, Malcolm 10th Chief, was alive in 1457, but must at that time have been very old."

The above marriage of William Hay of Lochloy is likewise given by Mrs. Cumming-Bruce in her work, "The Bruces and the Cummings."

Clan of Mackintosh

(From "The Family of Kilravock," printed by The Spalding Club):—

" 'Tis allowed that Macintosh is descended of Mac Duff, Thane of Fyfe. So the name signifies, viz.: 'Mac,' that is 'son,' and 'Tosche' (in the British Twisoc from Tus, i. e. 'Chief') 'Thane.'

Schaw, son of Duncan M'Duff, Thane and Earl of Fyfe who died in the year 1154, is said to have come into the north with King Malcolm IV., in his expedition against the Moravienses about 1160, and to have been made by him Governor of the Castle of Inverness, with a gift of lands in Petty and in Strathearn; and, rearing a family, separate from his father, assumed the surname of Macintosh (son of the chief) in memory of his descent. * * * * * The sixth from this Schaw inclusive was Angus Macintosh, who about the year 1291 married Eve Catach, the daughter and heir of Donal or Dougal, Chief of the Clanchatan, and with her he got the lands of Strathlochy, Glenly, and Locharkeg, which remained in the family of Macintosh until sold to the Earl of Argyle (of whom Lociel holds them) in 1665, for 70,000 merks Scots. * * * * * Eve Catach, who married Macintosh, was the heir female (Clunie's ancestor being the heir male) and had Macintosh assumed her surname, he would (say the MacPhersons) have been the Chief of the Clanchatan according to the custom of Scotland. * * * * * *

Be this as it will, Macintosh's predecessors were, for above three hundred years, designed "Captains' of Clanchatan in royal charters and commissions, in bonds, contracts, history, heraldic, etc.; the occasion of which title was that several tribes or clans (every clan retaining its own surname) united in the general designation of 'Clanchatan'; and of this incorporated body Macintosh was the head, leader, or captain.

These united tribes were: MacIntosh, MacPherson, Davidson, Shaw, MacBean, MacGilivray, MacQueen, Smith, MacIntrye, Mac Phail, etc.

In those times of barbarity and violence, small and weak tribes found it necessary to unite with more numerous and powerful tribes. As long as the tribes of Clanchatan remained united (which was until the family of Gordon breaking with the family of Macintosh, broke their coalition) they were able to defend themselves against any other clan."

In this connection the following incident will be recalled by our readers:

"Sept. 28, 1396, the Clanchatan under Schaw Macintosh fight against the Clancaie for precedence, thrittie against thrittie, at Saint Johnstone, North Inch of Perth, west bank of Tay, the place.

Schaw is third in succession, is acknowledged chief, and drops his first name as indicating descent from the Thayne of Fyfe. (It follows from this that both MacDuff of Fife, and MacIintosh of Clanchatan are ancestors of Colonel Hay).

An account of this fight is thus recorded in Scottish History:

"There being a great debate for precedence between Clanchatan and Clancaie —the first commanded by Statte Beg, the last by Gillichrist M'Kean—which occasioned much bloodshed among themselves, and robberies in the country about them, the quarrel being irreconcilable, by advice of the Earl of Crawford and Thomas Dunbar, Earl of Murray, they resolve to fight for it, thirty against thirty, with swords only, before the King.

The day is appointed, St. Johnstone and North Inch, there the place. One of the Clanchatan is wanting, and so the appointment is near deserted, till Henry Wynd, a saddler, for a small piece of money, and assurance of maintenance if maimed, undertakes to supply the place of the absent.

A desperate and bloody combat follows in presence of King and nobilitie till the whole clan were killed except one who leaped into Tay, and escaped by swimming.

Of the other clan, ten and the saddler survived, but were wounded. The saddler fought notably, 'for his own hand,' he said.

This made Macintosh predecessor Captain of the whole clanchatan, though there had been two or three before. This was the year 1396."

William Hay of Lochloy, by his wife Janet Macintosh, daughter of William Macintosh, seventh chief of the clan Macintosh, had one son:— ("The Bruces and Cummings," p. 618)

i. John de la Hay, Lord of Lochloy. (Vide Section IX.)
ii. A daughter who married William Graeme, Baron of Kerdale in Inverness-shire; (vide a letter from Thomas Dunbar, Earl of Moray to John de la Hay, releasing him from an engagement to his daughter, in which William Graeme is referred to as "your brother").

Ninth Generation

JOHN DE LA HAY, LORD OF LOCHLOY, was the only son of William of Lochloy, by his spouse Janet MacIntosh, eldest daughter of William MacIntosh, 7th Chief of the clan MacIntosh. He died A. D. 1431.

"He espouses a daughter of his beloved cousin, Donald, Thane of Cawdor, at Elgin, the xvth daie of Fev. 1422."— (Mr. Bain and Mrs. Cumming-Bruce).

It had been arranged at Rosemarkie (vide section VIII.) between William de la Hay and the Earl of Moray that the son of the former was to marry the daughter of the latter, but John losing his heart to a daughter of Donald, Thane of Cawdor, the latter requested the Earl of Moray to release John de la Hay from this engagement.

The following will show how generously this request was granted in a letter which bears the legend "Thomas Dunbar, Comitis Morauie":— ("The Kilravock Family" and "The His. Nairn").

"Thomas Erle of Murreff til our richt well belovit Jone the Haye, Lord of Lochloy, greeting:

"It is in fresh memorie with you, as we understand, that throu certain tailye made betwix us and your fadir, ye are oblisit to spouse a douchter of ours, for the quhilk thing to be done, we confermit to your fadir a tailye betwix him and the lord of Dolas apon the lordship of Dolas, and forgiff till him fourtez poundez, the quhilk suld haf bene paiit tilus for the relife of that land; and awls for that ilke marriage, we confermit til your fadir a tailye betwix him and your brither Wilyame the Grahame, apon the landez of half the barony of Kerdale, and resavit you to the like landez upon the said tailye; and now of new, we haf herd be certain relacion of our luffit cusine, Donaldo, thayne of Caldor, that you wald be releschit from your oblising til us of the saide mariage, and haf our licence, freedome, and gude will, to spouse a douchter of the saide Donaldo, thayne of Caldor, with sic commands, freedomes, and rewards as are forspokyn, and we grantit unto you of beforetyme.

"Quharfore, he the tenor of thir our letteris, of your oblising made to us of beforetyme, baith be your fadir and be yourselff, for the mariage of our douchter, we relsche you, dischargis you, and quitclemis you for ever, gifing and granting to you our council, our licence, and gude will to spouse and til haf to your wif, the douchter of the said Donaldo, thayne of Caldor, with sic freedoms, profitis, and rewardis, as war forspokyn in our first commands, togidder wid our help, suppout, and maintenance, in al your lachful and liveful errandis in al tyme to cum; thereatour we haf grantit and gifin, and be thir our lettris grantis and gifis to the said Donaldo, thayne of Caldor, fourte markez of the relese of your landez of the half of the barony of Kerdale, the quihilk Wilyame the Haye, your fadir, was oblisit to pay til us, of the quihilk we quitcleme you for ever be the teneur of thir lettre, to the quihilk our sele we haf girt beput, at Elgin, the xv dia of the moneth of Feueryere, the yere of our Lord a thousand four hunder twenti and twa yere."

(We think our readers will agree with us in the opinion that the English and spelling of the nineteenth century is an improvement upon that of the fifteenth, and we shall not ourselves attempt a translation of the above, leaving them to do so.)

(The following is based upon "The History of Nairnshire" and "Guide to Nairn," by Mr. George Bain.)

The Early Thanes of Cawdor

The original patrimony of the Thanes of Cawdor appear to have been limited to the fertile valley between Brackla and Barivan. The first addition to their early heritage were the lands of Highland Boath and Banchor—at one time held by the illustrious family of Durward by charter of Alexander II.

The Thanes of Cawdor, says Shaw, the historian of Moray, as Constables of the King's house resided in the Castle of Nairn, and had a country seat at what is now called "Old Cawdor," a half-mile north from the present seat (about 10 miles south of the town of Nairn, and a few miles west of Auldearn but to the east of the river Nairn). Here they had a house on a small moat with ditch and drawbridge, the vestiges of which were still to be seen in 1720.

But another building was erected and the appearance of the Castle is most imposing. It is protected by a fosse and its entrance secured by a quaint old drawbridge, and stands among the hills a half-mile south of their original country seat.

The tradition is that the Thane of Cawdor, anxious to build another house, but hesitating as to its site, was directed in a dream to bind the coffer containing the treasures collected for the architectural purpose to an ass, and set the animal free, and build wherever it might stop. The ass came to a first hawthorn tree, looked at it but passed on; it came to a second tree, rubbed against it but still passed on; when it came to the third hawthorn tree, on the bank of the burn, it lay down beside it with its treasure burden. Around this tree the Thane built his castle, and in the lowest vault of the tower, the trunk of a hawthorn, firm and sound,

Distant view of Slains Castle. Seat of the Hays of Erroll in Aberdeenshire, Scotland. It is right on the North Sea.

Slains Castle. From a group of photographs made especially for Erroldine Hay (Bateman) and given to her by the late Earl of Erroll.

THE FAMILY OF HAY 59

growing out of a rock and reaching to the top of the vault, is still to be seen. Strangers are brought to stand around it, each to take a chip of it, and then to drink to the hawthorn tree, and prosperity to the house of Caldor or Cawdor.

The Cawdor genealogical tree gives the following succession of Thanes:—

(1) Donald, Thane of Cawdor, 1295; (2) William, Thane of Cawdor, who obtained a charter of the thanage from Robert I. in 1310; (3) William, Thane of Cawdor about 1350; (4) Andrew, Thane of Cawdor, who was enfeft in the Sheriffship and Constabulary of Nairn and half of Dunmaglass, and died about 1405—said to have been murdered by Sir Alexander Raite of Raite; (5) Donal, Thane of Cawdor, served heir to his father in 1405, and acquired the other half of Dunmaglass, of Moy, near Forres, and Little Urchany; it is mentioned in the family genealogy that a daughter of Thane Donald married John de la Hay (vide the letter given above from Thomas Dunbar, Earl of Murray, to John de la Hay).

According to tradition, Schaw MacIntosh, (vide the preceding Section VIII.) married Helen, dau. of the second Thane of Cawdor, and thus was obtained the first half of Dunmaglass. Urchanybeg was purchased from the Bishop of Moray in 1421.

The office of Sheriff of the shire, and Constable of the Castle, carried with it considerable emoluments as well as local inffuence, and the family at an early date possessed the lands of Balmakeith, Millbank, the Gallowslands, and the Skateraw, and had a charter to the lands formerly belonging to Fergus the Dempster.

William succeeded his father Donald and was the 6th Thane of Cawdor. Looking out for a good match for William, his son, he found that living at the old Castle of Dunbeath on the Caithness coast, on the Moray Firth, was an untitled, but very wealthy Chief, Alexander Sutherland, whose wife was a daughter of Donald, Lord of the Isles.

The hand of his youngest daughter, Mariot, was sought, and she married the young Thane, William.

Marjory of Cawdor, one daughter of this marriage, married Philorth Fraser; Marion, another daughter, married three years later, Hugh Allanson MacIntosh; a third daughter married William Dallas, heir of Budgate and, we believe, General Meade of the Battle of Gettysburg, was a descendant of this pair.

Mariot or Marion Sutherland, wife of William, Thane of Cawdor, died leaving him sons, but the eldest, William, was weak in body, and became Vicar of Barrivan, preferring the church to secular life with its struggles. William, the Thane, then fixed the succession of the title upon John, a natural son afterward legitimated, who had married Isabella Rose, daughter of the Baron of Kilravock.

Of this marriage of John to Isabella Rose were born Janet and Muriel, and the latter while a child was carried off under romantic circumstances and the ward of her marriage was granted to Argyle, and on the completion of her twelfth year she was married to Sir John Campbell, son of the Earl of Argyle; they were married 1510.

Thus the Thanage of Cawdor passed from the old Thanes to the family of Campbell.

It is interesting to note here in passing the origin of the poem "Glenara," by the Scotch poet, Campbell:—

M'Lean of Duart, an inhuman wretch, had married Lady Elizabeth Campbell, a sister of the above mentioned Sir John Campbell, the new Thane of Cawdor. Through some mad freak of temper, M'Lean took the lady out to sea, and left her on a barren rock in the ocean, covered at high tide, and expected her to perish there. At the point of death, she was rescued by a passing boat. Sir John's indignation led him to avenge the insult by following M'Lean to Edinburgh, and slaying him in his bed. Remission for the slaughter under such exceptional provocation was granted by King James V., and Sir John and Lady Muriel took up their residence at Cawdor, making it their home, visiting only occasionally their possessions in Argyle.

Sir John was succeeded by his son Sir Archibald Campbell, who married a daughter of James Grant of Freuchy, and died 1551 leaving a son John, who married Mary Keith, daughter of the Earl Mareschal, and sister of the Countess of Argyle. In consequence of this marriage he removed to shores of Argyle, where later he met with a tragic end.

John de la Hay died A.D. 1431, and, by his wife, a daughter of Donald, 5th Thane of Cawdor, left a son:—

    i.   William de la Hay, whose history follows:

Tenth Generation

WILLIAM DE LA HAY OF LOCHLOY, PARK, AND DOLAS, was a son of John de la Hay, Lord of Lochloy, by his spouse, a daughter of Donald, Fifth Thane of Cawdor, "his luffit cousin." (History of Nairnshire and Mrs. Cumming-Bruce in "The Bruces and the Cummings.")

He held charters bearing date 1431. Thomas Cumyn of Altyre redeemed the lands of Dolas from him in 1460, and an Indenture of Friendship between them bears date 22 July 1476.

He probably married a daughter of the house of Cumyn, by whom he had Dolas, and died 1480, leaving two sons:—

   i. John de Hay, history follows in Section XI.
   ii. Alexander Hay of Mayne, living 1484, had a son:—William Hay of Mayne, living 1541, who had two sons:—John Hay of Mayne, living 1544; and William Hay of Mayne, who d. 1558, leaving a younger son, William, d. 1598, and an elder son:—James Hay of Mayne, d. 1561, leaving a son:—William Hay of Mayne, living 1590-1618, who left issue:—
      i. James, living 1618; ii. Francis, living 1618; iii. Alexander.

Eleventh Generation

JOHN THE HAY OF LOCHLOY AND PARK was the eldest son of William the Hay, and succeeded his father to the lands of Park and Lochloy in 1480. (These lands of Park were in Nairnshire west of Auldearn.) It does not appear when he married, but by his spouse he left sons:—

- i. William Hay of Park and Lochloy, history follows in Sec. XII.
- ii. Alexander Hay, living in 1511.
- iii. Andrew Hay, living in 1511.

The Hays of Park and Lochloy must not be confounded with the later Hay of Park.

The latter Baronets of Park were created 1663, and descended from Alexander Hay of Dalgetty, descending from the Hays of Erroll, and these last lands of Park are in Wigtonshire, and were of the abbey lands of Glenluce. In this line is Sir Lewis John Erroll Hay, 9th Bart., who has most kindly supplied the writer with much valuable information, copied from his father's family chart which, he states, was once borrowed by the Countess of Erroll to settle a point in dispute with the Marchioness of Tweeddale, and was photographed in London at that time. For this courtesy of his kinsman, the writer makes grateful acknowledgment.

Twelfth Generation

WILLIAM THE HAY OF PARK AND LOCHLOY, was the eldest son of John the Hay of Park and Lochloy, and held charters dated 1509-1511. His name occurs in the following solemn settlement, by arbiter, of the church lands of Croy:—

"At Nairne the thretene day of August the yer of God ane thousand four hundredth nynte and twa yeres, we, Alexander Dunbar of Vestfield, James Dunbar of Cromnoch, Knychtis, Adam Gordon chantar, Wilyame Winchester treasurer of the cathedral Kirk of Murray," etc.

Also from an Indenture made at Elgin 10 May 1492 between William, Thane of Calder and John his son with Hugh Rose, Baron of Kilravock, the following names are taken:— "Alexander Innes, Alexander Stewart, Chancellor of Murra, Master Thomas Grant official of Murra, William Hay of Lochloy."

A royal writ of this period begins as follows:— "James, by the grace of God, King of the Scots, till our Sheriffs of Elgin and Fore, and thri deputies, and to our lovitt John Chene, William Hay of the Park, John Paterson, Andra Ferquharson, and Alexander Urquhart, ouer Sheriffs in that part * * * * * given under our signet in Edinburgh xvi. dai of May and of ouer reigne the first yere.—Ex deliberatione dominorum concilii."

The following is accounted an important document in North Country History, and relates to an Inquest of 11 Feb. 1431, undertaken at the instance of Alexander Stewart, son of the Wolf of Badenoch, for ascertaining former tenure of lands.

It is given for the mention it makes of John, the father of William the Hay, and for that of other names:—

"Ad quam declarationem electi fuerunt et Jurati isti subscripti: Walterus de Innes de eodem, Donaldus de Calder, Hugo Rose de Balnagown, Alexander M'Cullagh, Johannes Hay de

Lochquhloy, Walterus Andree, Wilelmus Calder, Johannes Willelm de Fothnes, Nicholaus Man, Laurencius Curran, Gaufridus Schrres, Angusius Horaldi, Andreas Grame, Dauid Lommysden, Thomas de Chisholm, Willelmus Mykill, et Hugo Ade."—Copied from "The Family of Kilravock," published by the "Spalding Club."

William Hay of Lochloy and Park married Katherine Urquhart of Cromartie. This marriage is given in "The Bruces and the Cummings," by Mrs. Cumming-Bruce, of whom they were ancestors; it is also given by Mr. George Bain, Historian of Nairnshire, in correspondence with the writer.

The following is an extract from Mr. George Bain's letter, and will serve as an introduction to the distinguished pedigree of Katherine Urquhart Hay, given presently:—

Nairn, North Britain, 17th April 1907.

"Dear Professor Colcock,

"I am in receipt of your favor with remittance to cover cost of 'The History of Nairnshire' and hope it has arrived safely, as it was posted at the same time as 'Lord Brodie.' * * * * * * I shall be glad to assist you in connection with the Hays of Lochloy. Some of the information you ask for will require some searching, but I purpose sending you notes just as I get them ready, without waiting till I have the whole finished. It may interest you to have a view of Inshoch Castle, the last residence of the Hays of Lochloy, which I enclose.

"I am glad Mrs. Colcock is pleased with 'Lord Brodie.' The old gentleman, I think, has never got justice done him—he is bitterly attacked for his moderation from opposite sides, but after all he was sound in the faith, and right in the main.

"I enclose a few notes which may be of use to you. You may depend upon their accuracy.

"Yours Faithfully,

(Signed) "GEORGE BAIN."

Mr. Bain's notes on Katherine Urquhart:—

"Katherine Urquhart of Cromartie was wife of William Hay of Lochloy (1509).

The Urquharts of Cromartie have been traced up to Adam and Eve by Sir Thomas Urquhart, without a single break in the genealogy! Sir Thomas was a famous scholar, a friend of the 'Admirable Crichton,' but a most eccentric character.

The first Urquhart of Cromartie known to history, however, is Adam—Sir Thomas is right in this. The following is the state of the case according to the documents:— In the 13th century, the family of Mowat (then de Monte Alto) were in possession of Cromartie, but early in the following century the estate had accrued to King Robert the Bruce, who granted Cromarty to Sir Hugh Ross,

THE FAMILY OF HAY

eldest son of William, Earl of Ross, in 1315, and by him it was afterward, in the reign of David Bruce (1329-77), given to Adam de Urquhart.

"There are two places which bear the name of Urquhart—a church foundation in Moray and a large estate in Inverness. These (Glen Urquhart) with a famous old Castle on Loch Ness.

"The accepted account is that one Conacher, a mighty warrior, received the territories of Urquhart and its castle from the King as a reward for services in the war of 1160. He is said to be an Irishman of the royal house of Ulster, and the families of Forbes, Mackay, and Urquhart, look back to him as their common ancestor.

"Adam of Cromartie was descended from Conacher the Great's third son; his son John; his son William; his son William; and his son Alexander of Cromartie, Sheriff of Cromarty in 1501, father of Katherine, who married William Hay of Lochloy; his other daughter, Agnes, married Rose of Kilravock (from whom the family of Rose in Charleston, S. C.).

"The Urquharts had large estates in Aberdeenshire, and are said to have had seven mansion houses. They were, many of them, leading personages in Church and State in Scotland."

We shall now give on the authority of Burke's Peerage.

Lineage of Katherine Urquhart

1. William Urquhart of Cromarty, Hereditary Sheriff of that county, married 1st Lilias, daughter of Hugh, Earl of Ross, by his wife, the Princess Maud, daughter of King Robert the Bruce by his second wife Elizabeth, daughter of Aylmer de Burgh, Earl of Ulster. (1314)
2. Adam Urquhart of Cromarty, their son, held charters from William, Earl of Ross, for lands of Inch, and Rory, in Rosshire, in 1338, and a charter in 1357, from David Bruce, for the Sheriffdom of Cromarty, and married Brigidia, daughter of Sir Patrick Fleming of Biggar, ancestor of the Earls of Wigton, by his wife, the youngest daughter of Sir Simon Fraser of Oliver Castle, the patriot, whose other daughter married Sir Gilbert Hay from whom descend the Earls of Tweeddale.
3. John Urquhart of Cromarty, his son and heir, living in 1368, married Agnes, daughter of Sir Alexander Ramsay, ancestor of the Earls of Dalhousie—vide the 1st part of this book, reign of David II., for an account of Sir Alexander, who was starved to death in the dungeon of William Douglas of Liddesdale.
4. Sir William Urquhart of Cromarty, eldest son and heir, was Knighted by Robert III., married a daughter of Sir Alexander, 1st Lord Forbes, by his wife the Lady Elizabeth Douglas (who married 2nd David Hay of Yester), daughter of George Douglas, 1st Earl of Angus, by his spouse the Princess Mary, daughter of King Robert III. (Vide the Line of Forbes which follows presently. (1448)

5. Alexander Urquhart of Cromarty, second son, made Hereditary Sheriff of Cromarty, had a charter under the Great Seal from James IV. "Terrarum de Felthar," etc., dated 25 Aug. 1503, married Katherine, daughter of Sir James Ogilvie of Deskford. (Vide the Line of Oglivie which is given presently).
6. Katherine Urquhart, daughter, married William the Hay, mentioned at the head of this section; and they were ancestors of Colonel Ann Hawkes Hay.

Sir William Urquhart of paragraph 4 above, married a daughter of Sir Alexander, First Lord Forbes; we now give his pedigree:—

Line of Forbes

1. The name is derived from the Lands of Forbes, Douside, Aberdeenshire.
   John of Forbes was living in the reign of William the Lion.
2. Furgus of Forbes, his son, held charters in 1236, from Alexander, Earl of Buchan.
3. Alexander of Forbes, son and heir, held charters to the same lands from Alexander III., A.D., 1271.
4. John of Forbes, son and heir, besides the lands of Forbes, which he held from the Crown, held charters for Edinbanchirg and Craiglogy from the Earl of Mar, and was Sheriff of Aberdeen.
   He married Margaret.
5. Sir John Forbes, son and heir, was knighted circa 1390, and died -1406; he married Elizabeth, daughter of Kennedy of Denure, ancestor of the noble house of Cassilis.
6. Alexander, First Lord Forbes, eldest son and heir, was made a Lord of Parliament in 1442, and died A.D. 1448.
   He married 1423, Elizabeth, daughter of George Douglas, 1st Earl of Angus (vide the Line of Douglas, given presently).
7. A daughter married Sir William Urquhart of Cromarty, and from them descends Colonel Hay. (Vide paragraph 4 in the line of Katherine Urquhart, given above.)

Sir Alexander Urquhart of Cromarty, father of Katherine Urquhart, who married William the Hay (vide paragraph 5 of her lineage) married Katherine, daughter of Sir James Ogilvie of Deskford.

We shall now give:—

Line of Ogilvie

(Consult Burke, Edition for 1853, under "Seafield.")

1. Sir Walter Ogilvie, Knight of Auchleven, 2d son of the High Treasurer of Scotland, by Isabel Durward, heiress of Lintraithin, obtained permission from the crown in 1455 to fortify his Castle of Findlater; he died 1473.
   He married Margaret Sinclair, only daughter of Sir John Sin-

THE FAMILY OF HAY

clair of Deskford and Findlater, who raised the banner of the dying Douglas, at the Battle of Otterburn in 1338, the brother of George, 1st Earl of Angus.

2. Sir James Ogilvie, Knight of Deskford and Findlater, son of Sir Walter, married Margaret, eldest daughter of Sir Robert Innes of Innes, and died in 1510.
3. Sir James Ogilvie, son, died 1505, in his father's lifetime. He married Agnes, daughter of George, 2d Earl of Huntly.
4. Katherine Ogilvie, daughter of Sir James, granddaughter of George, 2d Earl of Huntly, married Alexander Urquhart, Hereditary Sheriff of Cromarty, who held a royal charter dated 1503.

(Vide paragraph 5 in the "Line of Katherine Urquhart." These were ancestors of Colonel Hay.)

Under "The Line of Forbes," paragraph 6, it will be noted that Alexander, First Lord Forbes, married Elizabeth Douglas, daughter of George Douglas, First Earl of Angus.

We shall now give her pedigree to be found in the following:—

Line of Douglas

"'In the story of Scotland,' says Mr. Froude, 'weakness is nowhere; power, energy, and will are everywhere'; and this national vigour, determined will, and indomitable resolution seem to have culminated in the 'Doughty Douglases,'

"Their stalwart, and tough physical frames, and the strong, resolute, unbending character of such men as 'William the Hardy,' 'Archibald the Grim,' and 'Archibald, Bell the Cat,' types of their race, eminently fitted them to be 'premier peers.'—leaders of men. From the War of Independence down to the era of the Reformation, no other family played such a conspicuous part in the affairs of Scotland as the Douglases.

"They intermarried no less than eleven times with the royal family of Scotland, and once with that of England. They enjoyed the privilege of leading the van of the Scottish army in battle, of carrying the crown at the coronation of the sovereign, and of giving the first vote in Parliament. A Douglas received the last words of Robert the Bruce, a Douglas spoke the epitaph of John Knox. The Douglases were celebrated in the prose of Froissart and the verse of Shakespeare. They have been sung by antique Barbour and by Walter Scott, by the minstrels of Otterburn and by Robert Burns. * * * * * They contributed greatly to the crowning victory of Bannockburn. They sent two hundred gentlemen of their name, with the heir of their earldom, to die at Flodden. There was a time when they could raise thirty thousand men, and they were for centuries the bulwark of the Scottish border against 'our auld enemies of England.' * * * * * They have gathered their laurels on many a bloody battlefield of France, where they held the rank of Princes, and in Spain, and in the Netherlands, as well as in England and Scotland.

"They have produced men not only of doughty character, but of the gentle and chivalric type, also, like the 'Good Sir James,' and the William Douglas, who married the Princess Egidia, justifying the exclamation of the author of the 'Buke of the Howlat'—

'O Douglas, Douglas,
Tender and true!'

"The cradle of the race was in Douglasdale, but their origin is hid in obscurity. 'We do not know them,' says Godscroft, 'in the fountain but in the stream; not in the root but in the stem; for we know not who was the first mean man that raised himself above the vulgar.' * * * * * * It is alleged by Chalmers that the founder of the family came from Flanders about the year 1147, and was named Theolbald the Fleming, and received from Arnold, Abbot of Kelso, a grant of lands on Douglas Water (DhuGlas, the 'Dark Stream') from which the family derived its name. Wyntoun is of the opinion that the Douglases had the same origin as the Murrays, either by lineal descent or by collateral branch, as they have the same arms, the same stars set in the same manner. Through the innate energy of their character they seem to have sprung at a single bound to the first rank of Scottish nobles."—Dr. Taylor in "The Great Historic Families of Scotland."

We now give Colonel Hay's Douglas ancestors as given in "The House of Douglas," by Mrs. Cumming-Bruce in her book, "The Bruces and the Cummings," page 529:

1. Archibald, 4th Lord of Douglas, testibus to charters, died 1240. Married Margaret, daughter and co-heiress of Sir John Crauford, by whom two sons:—Sir William, his heir; and Andrew, by some said to be the ancestor of the Earls of Morton.

2. William, 5th Lord of Douglas, son and heir, on Palm Sunday, at Edinburgh, 1240, signs an Indenture for the marriage of his son Hugh with the daughter of the Lord of Abernethy, settling on them all his lands, and furthermore, those "quae sunt in calumnia inter me et heredes Johannis Crauforde." He died 1276.

He married Martha, daughter of Duncan, and sister of Niel, Earl of Carrick (1240-50), and aunt of Marjorie, Countess of Carrick, who married Robert de Brus, and was mother of King Robert.

They left two sons: Hugh, 6th Lord of Douglas, who married Marjorie, daughter of Alexander and sister of Hugh, Lords of Abernethy d.s.p. and William. (This makes a fourth line of descent of Colonel Hay from the family of Bruce.)

3. William the Hardy, 7th Lord of Douglas, 2d son, succeeded his brother Hugh, who d.s.p.; in 1288, he imprisoned William of Abernethy in Douglas Castle for the murder of Duncan, Earl of Fife; he died in York after seven years of captivity, having been betrayed by his English wife.

He married 1st Lord Keith's sister, by whom he had two sons: i. Sir James, 8th Lord of Douglas, surnamed "The Good," the friend of Bruce, killed in Spain on his way to the Holy Land with

THE FAMILY OF HAY 69

the heart of Bruce (A.D. 1330-31); ii. Hugh, 9th Lord, survived his brother James for nine or ten years, resigned in favor of his nephew William, son of his half-brother Archibald, in 1341-42; iii. Archibald.

4. Archibald Douglas, Lord of Galloway, Regent of Scotland from March to July, 1333, when he was killed at Halidon Hill. He defeated the Balliols at Annan in 1332.

He married Dornagilla, daughter of John Cumyn of Badenoch by Mary of Galloway, by whom two sons and a daughter, viz.: t. William, 1st Earl of Douglas; ii. Archibald, Lord of Galloway; iii. Alianore, married Alexander, 8th Earl of Carrick, son of Edward Bruce. Alexander was killed with his father-in-law, Archibald Douglas, at Halidon Hill.

John Comyn of Badenoch was styled "John the Black Comyn," and was a Competitor for the Crown in 1292, when he gave in his pedigree; he married Marjorie, a sister to John Balliol; he was the son of John the Red Comyn (No. 1) by his wife Marian, believed by some the daughter of the Lord of Galloway and sister of Devorgoile, by others the daughter of The Lord of the Isles.

John the 1st Red Comyn was the 3d son of William Comyn, Great Justiciar of Scotland in 1209, and 1st Earl of Buchan, by his 1st wife Matilda Urquhart, daughter of Coetisa, daughter of Banquo. (This is a 2d line of descent for Colonel Hay from William 1st Earl of Buchan, and also one from Banquo, and four from the Emperor Chalemagne. Vide "The Line of Comyn," Section VI.)

Archibald Douglas, the 2d son of Archibald the Regent, was made Lord of Galloway after the death of Thomas de Brus A.D. 1380, by King David II.; he left no legitimate heir, but William the Black Douglas was his natural son, and for his great worth and bravery was given with the lordship of Nithsdale by King Robert II. his beautiful daughter Egidia, by whom he left an only daughter Egidia, who married Henry, Earl of Orkney. His male line extinct. In France William the Black Douglas was Prince of Ranskin and Duke of Spruce.

Alianore or Eleanor m. 1st Alexander of Brus, 8th Earl of Carrick, and had an only dau. Alianore who m. Sir William Cunningham, and had a grant in 1361, of the earldom of Carrick.

Alianore m. 2d Sir James of Sandilands, who was given by her brother William Douglas the barony of West Calder; her son and heir, Sir James Sandilands, m. Joanna, dau. of King Robert II., the lords Torphichen being their lineal descendants.

Alianore m. 3d William of Touris; m. 4th Duncan Walys of Sundrum and m. 5th and last by dispensation (1376) Sir Patrick Hepburn of Hailes.

5. A. D. 1342.—William, 1st Earl of Douglas, and 5th Lord of Douglas,

was sent as a hostage to England for the King, at which time he is first styled Earl of Douglas.

By some authorities he is said to have married three times, by others only once. He, however, styled Margaret Stewart "My Wife," and it is extremely probable they were married.

He m. 1st ante 1343, Margaret of Mar, who, on the death of her brother Thomas, 13th Earl of Mar (A. D. 1377), became Countess of Mar and Lady Garioch, by whom he had James Douglas, the hero of Otterburn, where he fell A. D. 1388, and Isabel, afterward Countess of Mar.

It is said that Earl William divorced this lady, who m. 2d Sir John Swinton of Swinton, and that the Earl m. 2d Margaret, daughter of the Earl of Dunbar and March, by whom he had Archibald the Grim, who succeeded his brother James as Earl of Douglas in 1388. The Earl of Douglas m. 3d (and with doubtful legality) Margaret Stewart, daughter of the Earl of Angus (who died of the plague 1357-58) and widow of the Earl of Mar who d. 1377, by whom he had a son:—

6. George Douglas, 1st Earl of Angus, youngest son of William, 1st Earl of Douglas, by his 3d wife.

    On the 24 May 1397, he married the Princess Mary, granddaughter of King Robert II., daughter of the king's son later Robert III., by his wife Annabella Drummond, daughter of Sir John Drummond of Stobhall. (The Drummonds were celebrated for their good looks.) Mary was the full sister of David, the unfortunate Duke of Rothsay, whose sad fate is portrayed in "The Fair Maid of Perth," and of James, later King James I., of Scotland, the ablest of the Stewart sovereigns, who was murdered.

7. The Lady Elizabeth Douglas, daughter of George, 1st Earl of Angus, by his wife the Princess Mary, daughter of King Robert III. and his Queen, Annabella Drummond, married in 1423, Alexander, the First Lord Forbes. (Vide Line of Forbes.)

8. The Lady Forbes, daughter, married Sir William Urquhart of Cromarty, Sheriff of Cromarty. (Vide Line of Urquhart.)

9. Katherine Urquhart, daughter, married William the Hay. (Mr. George Bain, Historian of Nairnshire, and "The Bruces and Cumyns," p. 619.)

William the Hay by his wife Katherine Urquhart of Cromartie had a son:— "The Bruces and Cumyns," p. 619).

i. John Hay of Lochloy and Park, history follows, in Sect. XIII.

Stewart-Earls of Angus

George Douglas, 1st Earl of Angus, married 3d Margaret, widow of Thomas, 3th Earl of Mar, and daughter of Thomas Stewart, 2d Earl of Angus in the Stewart line. We shall give this line:—

THE FAMILY OF HAY

"Sir John Stewart, who fell at Falkirk with Sir John the Graham in July, 1298, was the uncle of Walter, who married Marjorie Bruce. Sir John married Margaret, only daughter and heir of Sir Alexander Bonkyl of Bonkyl, by whom he had seven sons, and an only daughter who married Thomas Randolph, Earl of Moray and Regent of Scotland.

By some it is said that his eldest son, Sir Alexander Stewart, was created Earl of Angus by Robert the Bruce, but in England the Umphravilles were still so entitled, but

1. John Stewart, son of Sir Alexander, is the first Stewart whose name appears as a witness when Randolph was 'custos regni Scotiae' as Earl of Angus, Lord of Bonkyl and Abernethy, having married in 1329, by special dispensation, Margaret, eldest daughter of Sir Alexander de Abernethy. John had a sister Isabel married 1st to Donald, Earl of Mar, by whom she had Thomas, 13th Earl of Mar, and Margaret, who succeeded her brother and married William, 1st Earl of Douglas.
2. Thomas Stewart, 2d Earl of Angus, only son, married Margaret, only daughter of Sir William Sinclair of Roslin. He assisted in the taking of Berwick in 1352; but suspected of conspiracy by David II. was imprisoned in Dumbarton Castle, where he d. of the plague, 1321.
3. Lady Margaret, daughter, married 1st her cousin Thomas 13th Earl of Mar, who d.s.p. in 1377; she married 2d William, 1st Earl of Douglas, by whom:
4. George Douglas, 1st Earl of Angus, on the resignation of his mother when he was seven years old.
   He married, at the age of sixteen, Mary, daughter of Robert III., as has been already set forth.
5. The Lady Elizabeth Douglas, daughter, married Alexander, 1st Lord Forbes, in 1423.
6. Lady Forbes, daughter, married Sir William Urquhart of Cromarty.
7. Katherine Urquhart, daughter, married William the Hay, Lord of Lochloy and Park, by whom:—
   i. John Hay of Lochloy and Park, history follows in Section XIII.

Under the preceding table—The Stewart-Earls of Angus—it is shown in paragraph 3, that Thomas Stewart married Margaret, daughter of Sir William Sinclair (St. Clair) of Roslin. This marriage may also be seen in the 1853 edition of Burke, p. 152, where is given the lineage of Sir William St. Clair, and it is there stated that he married Isabel, daughter of Malise Earl of Strathearn (he was 7th Earl) by his 3d wife Matilda, daughter of Magnus, Earl of Orkney and Caithness. (Vide "Earldom of Strathearn" of this book, Section II., paragraph 7.)

Matilda's Norse origin from "Earl Rognvald, The Wise and Mighty" is full of interest and we give it in the next table. Earl Rognvald was also an ancestor of Colonel Hay through William the Conqueror descended from Rollo his son, and also an ancestor of Colonel Hay through the line of King Robert Bruce—therefore this early Scandinavian Count Rognvald should possess peculiar interest to our readers—who are trebly his descendants. The lines of Bruce and William the Conqueror will be given later—we shall now present the Norse origin of Matilda, wife of Sir William St. Clair of Roslin circa 1318, which is to be found in the following:—

Earldom of Orkney and Caithness

(Taken principally from "The Bruces and Cumyns.")

"It is to Scandivania and its sages we must look for the history of our Pagan ancestors and their conversion to Christianity.

"The Scalds who wrote the sagas were mostly Icelanders; but from the day of Harald Haarfager, families had become so dispersed that hereditary interests and the rights to property in Iceland and Orkney were involved in what was transpiring in Northumberland and Norway, as well as at Dromtheim.

"The Odhal or Udal Holding was the only tenure of lands recognized in Scandinavian kingdoms. It was transmitted by Odin's followers to their offspring as the dearest of their free institutions.

"It was a tacit entail upon the primal occupant and his heirs, inalienable while one udal-bron descendant should live to claim it—or to reclaim it from the stranger, if alienated in his absence or childhood. The sagas, therefore, were far from being fairy tales, as some appear to suppose, but were registers of public and private events, by means of which each man might claim his rights on his return from distant lands. Let us then refer to the Saga of Harald Haarfager:—

"King Harald Haarfager, or the Fair-haired, succeeded when he was ten years of age, to the dominions of his father, Halfdan the Black. His mother, Queen Ragnhilda, daughter of Sigurt Hiort, a king in Ringerige, had a brother, 'Guttorm,' who was Harald's guardian. Harald sent to ask Gyda, daughter of King Eric of Hordaland, in marriage, but she refused unless he made himself king of all Norway. * * * * * * Upon this Harald vowed to become sole king, and, with Guttorm's help, he became so.

"Harald fought and conquered in many battles and over each district he set an earl, in place of the king he had subdued.

"At last, after the battle of Haversfiord, A. D. 885, he became sole king of Norway, and made Drontheim his capital. Many of the discontents fled and it was then Iceland and the Faroe Isles were discovered and peopled. There was also a great resort to Shetland, and many took to viking in the West Sea. In winter they were in the Orkneys and the Hebrides, and in summer they marauded in Norway, and did great damage. Therefore one summer King Harald sailed with his fleet right out into the West Sea. First he came to Shetland and slew all the vikings who could not save themselves by flight; then southward, to the Orkneys, and cleared them of all vikings, then to the Hebrides, and slew many vikings who had men at arms under them. He then plundered, far and wide, in Scotland itself, and had a battle there. Afterward he went to the Isle of Man, but the people had all fled.

"In this war fell 'Ivar,' eldest son of *Earl Rognvald. Earl Rognvald was the son of *Eistein Glumre, and was Harald's greatest friend. When the kings were conquered, Rognvald was made Earl of North and South More or Moeri, and afterward of Raumdal also; and it was at a feast at Rognvald's house in Moeri that Harald received the name of 'Haarfager,' Fair-haired, having taken a bath and had his hair cut and combed, after ten years, for he had taken a vow not to do so till he had conquered all Norway; so Earl Rognvald called him 'The Fair-haired,' and all men thought it just.

"Now when Ivar fell, King Harald gave Earl Rognvald the Orkney and Shetland Islands as a compensation for the loss of his son; but Rognvald immediately gave both to his brother 'Sigurt,' who remained there; and Harald, before sailing eastward, gave him the earldom. * * * * *

"Earl Rognvald was the son of Eistein Glumre, who was the son of *Thebotan, Duke of Sleswick and Stermace A. D. 721, who fled into Norway by reason of the Danish tyranny, and married *Jocunda,' daughter of Hunheafter, King of North and South Moeri.

"Thebotan married second *Ascrida, daughter of Rognvald, son of Olaus, King of Norway, whose sons were: 1, *Rognvald; 2, Sigurt.

"Sigurt, therefore, became the first Jarl of Orkney and Shetland, and soon made himself very powerful, conquering Caithness, Ross, Moray, and the Sudrlands. Elgin is said to have been founded by him and called after his favorite general, 'Helgy.' * * * * * * We are not told how long Sigurt held it, nor the date of his death. He died at Burghead—the Phoroton Strapeton of the Romans, the 'Broch' of the Danes and Norwegians—after a great battle in which he slew his opponent, the Scottish earl, 'Melbrigd' (probably the grandfather of Macbeth); but the dead man's projecting tooth did what his armed hand could not do, inflicted a wound on Sigurt's leg as he carried off the head slung to his saddlebow, and caused his death.

"Earl Sigurt married Jocunda, daughter of Olaus the White, King of the Danes in Dublin. With her brother, 'Thornstein the Red,' he entered into a partnership, and they overran Scotland, and took possession of all north of the Oichel River.

"Gulthorm, Sigurt's only son, succeeded, but dying within a year without heirs, the Earldom returned to Earl Rognvald, who was still alive.

"And here we may remark that although Harald had appointed sixteen earls in Norway—one over each district—when he suppressed the small kings, they appear to have been merely collectors of his 'scatts' or land tax, with the exception of 'Rognvald, the Wise and Mighty,' whose family were the only hereditary nobles under the Norwegian crown exercising a kind of feudal power. The Earls of Orkney of this line became almost independent, only paying military service and a nominal quit-rent when obliged to do so.

"Hallad, or Halloden, was next sent by his father, Earl Rognvald, to be Jarl of Orkney, but finding the vikings troublesome, soon returned to Norway and took up his udal rights again. When Earl Rognvald heard this he was ill pleased, and said his sons were very unlike their forefathers. Then said his son 'Eynor,' 'I have enjoyed little affection or honor amongst you, and if you will give me force enough, I will go west; and I promise you, at any rate, what will please you, that you shall never see me again.' So Earl Rognvald gave Eynor his son a ship fully equipped, and he sailed for the West Sea in harvest.

"When he came to the Orkney Isles, two vikings, 'Thorar Treaskeg' and 'Kalf Sturfa,' were in his way with two vessels, and he attacked and slew them both, and slew the vikings. He was therefore Earl, and a mighty man o'er those seas. * * * * * * He was called 'Turf Eynor' because he taught the people to cut turf for fuel, there being no wood in Orkney.

"Besides Ivar, who was killed, Earl Rognvald had five sons:— Thorer, who became his successor in Moeri; Hallad or Halloden; *Eynor; Hrollong; Rollo or Rolf Ganger, the famous conqueror of Normandy, whose mother was *Hilda, daughter of *Rolf Naefia. Earl Rognvald's daughter Hilda married Sigurt Rice, King Harald's son. Meanwhile Harald m. Gyda; and it is recorded that when he took to wife 'Ragnhilda the Mighty,' daughter of King Eric of Jutland, he put away nine wives.

"Ragnhilda was the mother of 'Eric Bloodyaxe,' the most beloved son of the king, who intended him to be head king over all the others, but the people preferred Halfdan the Black.

"By Asa he had four sons. Gulturm, the eldest, was fostered by Duke Gulturm, uncle to the king—who poured water over him, calling him by his own name—and Harald gave him the government of Viken when he died in his bed at Tonsberg before 893.

"Halfdan the Black and Halfdan the White were twins, also sons of Asa, and Sigfrod also.

"By Gyda, daughter of Eric king of Hordeland, he had Alaf, his daughter Hraerick, Sigfrig, Frode, and Thorgill—the two last were kings in Ireland.

"By Swanhilda, daughter of Earl Eistein, he had Olaf Geistadalf, Biorn, and Ragnor Ryskill.

'By Ashilda, daughter of King Dagson, he had Dag, Skirra, and Ingegred.

"By Snaefrig, a beautiful Laplander, he had Sigurt Rice, Halfdan Haaleg, Gudrod Liome, and Rognvald Rettilbeen.

"After a time, as the sons of Harald Haarfager grew up (when he was about forty years of age, circa 889), they became jealous of the power of Earl Rognvald. Two of them, Gudred Liome and Halfdan Haaleg, assembled forces, surrounded Earl Rognvald's house, and burnt him and sixty men in it. Then Gudrod took possession of the earldoms of Moeri and Raumdal, but Halfdan took three long ships and sailed for Orkney. King Harald assembled a large force and drove his son Gudrod out of Moeri and banished him, and installed Thorer

INSHOCK CASTLE

Illustration from the original edition of "The Family of Hay." Once the seat of the Hays of Lochloy — a branch of the Hays of Erroll — now only a ruin. Nearby is the classic ground where the witches danced, made famous by the "immortal bard" in Macbeth.

Delgaty Castle, Turriff, Scotland. Headquarters of the Clan Hay.

the Silent, eldest son of Rognvald by Hilda, daughter of Rolf Naefia, in his father's dominions, giving him his daughter Alaf Arbot in marriage.

"When Halfdan Haaleg arrived in Orkney, *Eynor, who was earl there, fled at first to the mainland, but soon came back and had a battle with Haaleg, who was defeated and took to flight.

"Eynor and his men lay all night upon the ground and in the morning sought the whole island for Haaleg. Then Eynor said, 'What is that I see upon the Island of Ronaldsha? Is it a man or bird? Sometimes it raises itself up, and sometimes lies down again.' They went and found it was Halfdan, and they took him prisoner and killed him by cutting a spread eagle on his back, to avenge the burning of Earl Rognvald. Then Eynor sang:—

> " 'Where is the spear of Hrollong? Where
> Is stout Rolf Ganger's bloody spear?
> I see them not—yet never fear!
> For Eynor will not vengeance spare
> Against his father's murderers though
> Hrollong and Rolf are rather slow,
> And silent "Thorer" sits and dreams
> At home beside the mead-bowls' streams.'
>
> —Laing's Sea Kings of Norway.

"When the tidings of Haaleg's death reached Norway, his brothers took it much to heart, and thought his fate demanded vengeance. So King Harald ordered a levy and proceeded to Orkney in great force, and Eynor fled to Katenes; but men and messages passed betwixt them, and at last a conference was held, when the Earl submitted to the King's decision that he and his people should pay him sixty marks of gold. But Eynor took upon himself to pay the whole fine on condition that his people resigned to him their udal rights, which thus became vested in the earl, and so continued until the days of Sigurd Lodvison (ante 1014).

"When King Harald was seventy years of age, he had another son by 'Thora,' who came to be king and was called 'Hakon the Good,' or 'Hakon Adalstein's fostre'—Athelstane's foster-son—for his father sent him to England to be fostered by King Athelstane, who had him baptised and brought him up a Christian.

"Hakon was much beloved by all good men and especially by Athelstane, who gave him a sword of which the hilt and handle were of gold, and the blade so fine that it cut through a millstone to the centre eye; and the sword was called 'Quernbiter.' He was the youngest of all King Harald's sons, and the only one who escaped being murdered by 'Eric Bloodyaxe.'

*Rollo or Rolf, sometimes called the 'Ganger,' Earl Rognvald's son, became a great Viking. He maruded in England, and in summer landed on the coast of Norway and made a cattle foray; and King Harald hearing of it assembled a Thing, and made Rollo an outlaw all over Norway. When Rolf Ganger's mother, Hilda, heard this, she hastened to the King to entreat his pardon, but the King was so angry that he would not listen. Then she sang:—

> " 'Think'st thou, King Harald, in thine anger
> To drive away my brave Rolf Ganger
> Like a mad wolf from out the land?
> Why banish Naefia's gallant name-son,
> The brother of the brave udal-men?
> Why is thy cruelty so fell?
> Bethink thee, monarch, it is ill
> With such a wolf at wolf to play,
> Who, driven to the wild woods away,
> May make the King's best deer his prey?'
> Laing's Sea Kings of Norway.

"Rollo went over the seas, west to the Hebrides, or Sudreyar, our Sodor, and Man, and from thence to Valland, where he subdued a great earldom, which he peopled with Northmen, and from them it was called Normandy."

It is not possible within the limits set for this little volume to reproduce the sagas of the remaining early kings of Scandinavia. If our readers are interested in these interesting details relating to their Scandinavian origin, they should read Mrs. Bruce Cumming's most valuable work, "The Family Records of the Cummings and the Bruces"—a standard work, and magazine of genealogical and historical lore.

The author was the wife of the Hon. Charles Lennox Cumming, M. P., representing Inverness, who assumed the name and arms of Bruce by right of his wife. She was a granddaughter of James Bruce, the celebrated Abysinnian traveler and author of African Explorations. James Bruce was really James Hay, a great-grandson of David Hay of Woodcockdale, and a son of David Hay who, marrying Helen Bruce of Kinnaird, assumed her name under the requirements of her father's will regulating the succession of his property.

Thus Mrs. Cumming-Bruce was related to Colonel Hay, and as their origin was the same in many lines, we shall quote frequently from her work.

In the above saga all names starred are progenitors of Colonel Hay. In order that our readers—his descendants—may understand this, the following table is here introduced for their benefit:—

1. *Olaus or Olaf, King of Norway, had two sons, Rognvald and Sigurt.
2. *Rognvald, his son, having married had a daughter:—
3. *Ascrida, married Thebotan, Duke of Sleswich and Stermace, A.D. 721,

THE FAMILY OF HAY   77

who had fled from the tyranny of the Danes. They had a son:—
4. *Eistein Glumre, who married and had a son:—
5. *Rognvald the Mighty, Earl of Moeri, in Norway, and of Orkney, he died 890, and had a son:—
6. *Torf Eynor, Earl of Orkney 910, who had a son:—
7. *Thorfinn the Skull Splitter, Earl of Orkney 950, who had a son:—
8. *Hlodver, Earl of Orkney, 870, and had a son:—
9. *Sigurd the Stout, Earl of Orkney, slain at Contarf 1014; had son:—
10. *Thorfin, the famous Earl of the Orkneys and Caithness, grandson of King Malcolm II. of Scotland, had a son:—
11. *Paul, Earl of Orkney 1090, had a son:—
12. *Hakon, Earl of Orkney 1100, had a daughter:—
13. *Margaret, married Maddad, Earl of Athol circa 1140, had a son:—
14. *Harald Madadson, Earl of Orkney 1139 to 1206, married 2d a daughter of MacHeth, Earl of Ross and Moray, descended from Gruach, Lady Macbeth, and also sprung from Somerled, Lord of The Isles: By 2d wife he had sons:—Henry, who claimed his mother's rights over Ross and Moray; David; and John.

    Harald married first Affreca, a daughter of Duncan, Earl of Fife, by whom a son Thorfin, who died a hostage circa 1202.
15. *John, youngest son of Harald by his second wife, was the last Norse Earl of Orkney and Caithness, and died 1231.

    King Alexander II. came from Jedburgh to Caithness and after some negotiation, took from him Sutherland, which he gave to Hugh Freskyn, whose son William was created first Earl of Sutherland in 1232.
16. Daughter of John, last Norse Earl of Orkney and Caithness, married *Gilbride (Gilbert), Earl of Angus; they had a son:—
17. *Magnus II., acknowledged Jarl of Orkney by Hacon IV. of Norway, and Earl of Caithness by Alexander II. of Scotland. (1240)
18. *Gilbride, son of Magnus II., Earl of Caithness, had son:—(1250)
19. *Magnus III., Earl of Caithness, (1260)
20. *John, Earl of Caithness, son, married a daughter of Eric, King of Norway, (1300)
21. *Magnus IV., his son, married and had son:—
22. *Magnus V., last of the male line of Angus Earls of Orkney and Caithness. He married Sophia, daughter of Ferquhard, Earl of Ross, and left an heiress:—
23. *Matilda, married Malyse, Earl of Strathearn, who became in her right Earl of Orkney and Caithness. Besides a son Ferquhard, they had daughters:—i. Matilda, m. William, Earl of Ross, and had a gift of the earldom of Caithness confirmed by David II., 1362; their line ended in Euphemia, Countess of Ross, m. Sir Walter Leslie, and Lady Joanna, m. Sir Alexander Fraser of Philorth. ii. Isabel, m. William St. Clair of Roslyn, had Henry, whose homage was accepted by

Hacon VI. of Norway, 1379, Earl of Orkney. iii. Matlida, m. Hugh de Arth and had a son Alexander, who in 1375 was styled "Representative of the Earls of Strathearn, when he inherited and resigned the earldom of Caithness to Robert II., who thereupon granted two charters to David Stewart his eldest son by second marriage. iv. Mariot, who married Reginald le Cheyne.

24. *Isabel, daughter of Matilda and Malyse, married Sir William St. Clair of Roslyn (vide Burke A.D. 1353, p. 152.)
25. *Margaret St .Clair of Roslyn, daughter, married Thomas Stewart, 2d Earl of Angus.
26. *Lady Margaret Stewart, daughter, married 2d William, 1st Earl and 5th Lord of Douglas. (Was his 3d wife.)
27. *George Douglasson, 1st Earl of Angus in the Douglas line, married the Princess Mary, daughter of King Robert III. of Scotland.
28. *The Lady Elizabeth Douglas, daughter, married Alexander, 1st Lord Forbes.
29. *Lady Forbes, daughter, married Sir William Urquhart of Cromarty.
30. *Katherine Urquhart, daughter, married William de la Hay, Lord of Lochloy and Park; by whom:—
    i. *John Hay of Lochloy and Park, whose history follows in Section XIII.

Thirteenth Generation

JOHN HAY OF LOCHLOY AND PARK was the eldest son of William the Hay, Lord of Lochloy and Park, by his spouse Katherine Urquhart, daughter of Sir William Urquhart, Sheriff of that ilk. He died A. D. 1563. John married Isobel Dunbar, who died A. D. 1554, and was buried with her husband in the graveyard of the cathedral of Auldearn, where the inscription of their deaths on a monument in the chancel was recently sent us by the Rev. James Bonallo of Auldearn, who married a daughter of the "Dowager Lady Dunbar of Boath."

The following is an extract from one of the Rev. Mr. Bonallo's letters, with extracts also from a letter written him by Mr. Bain:—

"I duly received yours of the 28th of December and handed it to our local historian, Mr. Bain, and I enclose his reply. He knows more about these matters than any other of my acquaintance. It turns out strangely enough that your wife and my wife—who is daughter of Dowager Lady Boath in this parish—are Scotch cousins. I may explain that Sir Alexander Dunbar of Boath, to whom you wrote, died some years ago.

"Yours faithfully,
"JAMES BONALLO."

"I have looked over Prof. Colcock's genealogical record and find it quite correct in the older period, though I am satisfied the Hays had possession of Lochloy at a much earlier date than is assigned them. You will find my reason stated at page 206 of my History of Nairnshire, also see page 257 for further information.

1. Bennangefield, or Bennetsfield, is in Ross-shire and now forms part of the Rosehaugh estates. The Dunbars of Bennangefield were descended from Patrick, sixth son of Sir Archibald Dunbar of Westfield, the same ancestor as that of Mrs. Bonallo, so that your American correspondent and your wife are Scotch cousins.

2. John, who married Isobel Dunbar in 1554, died in 1563, leaving several sons:—John, who succeeded him; David and Alexander of Foynfield; and George, who dying in 1600, left a son Alexander, who married Catherine Skene, and became Sir Alexander Hay of Fosterseat.

The Hays of Kinfauns, of Monckton, of Woodcockdale, and of Carruber, all derive from the Hays of Lochloy about this period.

3. David Hay of Lochloy (No. 8 in list) married Marie Rose of Kilravock in 1605, and when she died it is said no less than 110 of her descendants were then in life."—From Mr. Bain to Mr. Bonallo.

We now introduce the inscriptions sent us by the Rev. James Bonallo, copied by him from the monument in the chancel of the Cathedral of Auldearn, relating to the foregoing John Hay of Lochloy, his son John, and the latter's son Master Alexander Hay of Kinnudie:—

"This is the sepulcre of Johe Hay of Lochloy, who departed in the yeir of God 1563, and of Isobel Dunbar his spous, who diet in the yeare of God 155-; as also of Johne Hay of Lochloy, Laird of Park, his son, who diet in the moneth of Januar, in the yeir of God 1598, and of Janet Sutherland his spous, who diet in the moneth of Januar, in the yeir of God 1587, parentis to Master Alexander Hay of Kinnoudie."

"Monumentum Sepulturae M. A. H. de Kinnoudie, qui obiit 1 April 1616 ejusque posterorum."

"In ecclesiaste ornamentum conditum mutatur mundus mundique illustria cuneta tempore flaccescunt more fluentis aquae en tres in triuno tumulo conduntur at una germani fratres filius atque patris est haeros genitor grandaemus nobilis Inschoche."

Translation of the last inscription:—The world is changed into an elevated church-memorial, and all the noble things of earth at this time are beginning to pass away after the manner of flowing water. Behold three full brothers find a resting place together in a single grave, while another son of his father, a grand and noble chief, lies at Inschoch.

The above inscription agrees exactly with the one given by Mrs. Cumming-Bruce, with the exception of the date of the death of Janet Sutherland, and she likewise gives an additional Latin inscription recounting some of the glories of the Hays of Lochloy.

The lineage of Isobel Dunbar will be found in the following:—

Earldoms of Dunbar, March and Moray

The Dunbars were descended from Gospatrick, Earl of Northumberland in 1068, who was implicated in the death of Robertus de Comyn, and fled from the wrath of King William I., to the court of his kinsman, Malcolm III., King of Scotland. King Malcolm granted him the earldom of Dunbar and made him Defender of the Marches.

Gospatrick was the son of Maldred by Algitha, daughter of Uchtred, who had been Earl of Northumberland in the reign of Canute, and was likewise a descendant of Malcolm II.

THE FAMILY OF HAY

In this line was Patrick, 9th Earl of Dunbar and March, to whom we shall return presently.

After the death of Edward Bruce, the king's brother, his nephew Thomas Randolph, was appointed Guardian of the Realm, and of the heir, in case of his being under age at the time of the death of Robert I. and failing him these offices to devolve to Lord James of Douglas.

1. Thomas Randolph, Earl of Moray, died, leaving by his countess Isabel, daughter of Sir John Stewart of Bonkyl, two sons, Thomas and John, and two daughters, Agnes and Egidia.
2. Thomas, second Earl, died without issue twenty-three days after his father.
3. John Randolph, 3d Earl of Moray, a prisoner in England from 1335 to 1341, married the Lady Euphemia de Ross, who married secondly by Papal dispensation King Robert II., in 1355.
   John was killed at Durham in October, 1346, leaving no heir.
4. On the death of both her brothers, the heroic Lady Agnes Randolph, who had married Patrick, 9th Earl of Dunbar and March, assumed the title of Countess of Moray, and thus in Patrick was united the three earldoms of Dunbar, March and Moray, which descended and was confirmed to their second son:—
5. John Dunbar, 2d son, on his marriage to Marjorie, daughter of King Robert II., by his 1st marriage for which a Papal dispensation had been obtained. (This gives another line of descent for Colonel Hay from the Bruces.)
   John was killed in a tournay in 1394, leaving two sons, Thomas and Alexander, and a daughter Mabella, married Robert, 6th Earl of Sutherland.
6. Thomas de Dunbar, Earl of Moray, was taken prisoner at Homildon, in 1402, afterward hostage for the King, died in England leaving a son Thomas de Dunbar, Earl of Moray in 1408, who signed the marriage contract of his sister Euffame with Sir Alexander Cumyn of Altyre. He likewise had a daughter, Janet, married to Hugh, Lord Lovat. contract dated at Findleteer Castle 9 August 1422 but his uncle's son became the earl. (It was this Thomas, Earl of Moray, who released John Hay from an engagement to marry his daughter, and we hope this daughter was Janet, for if so she was not long left disconsolate. Vide Sec. IX. of this work.)
7. Alexander de Dunbar, second son of John, the 4th Earl, married Maud Fraser of Lovat, and left:—
8. James Dunbar, son, who succeeded his cousin Thomas in the earldom. He married 1st his second cousin Isobel, daughter of Sir Walter Innes of Innes. She died before the Papal dispensation arrived, and the marriage was not recognized as legal on account of the relationship.
   James married 2nd Lady Janet Gordon, eldest daughter of Alex-

THE FAMILY OF HAY

ander, 1st Earl of Huntly, and dying in 1430 was succeeded by the husbands of his daughters—the eldest having married Sir William Creighton, got Frendraught in tocher; the second marrying Archibald Douglas, brother to the Earl of Douglas, possessed the earldom until 1425 when he was attained.

9. Sir Alexander Dunbar of Westfield, son of James Dunbar, 5th Earl of Moray by his first wife, Isobel Innes, was debarred the succession, and became the stem (says Mr. Hew Rose) of all the extant families of Dunbar.

He married Isobel Sutherland, daughter of Alexander Sutherland, Lord of Duffus, by his wife Morella (or Muriel) Chisholm, heiress of Quarrelwood, and by her had issue:—

    i. Sir James Dunbar of Cumnock, who died in 1504.
    ii. Sir John Dunbar of Mochrum, who was killed in 1505.
    iii. Alexander Dunbar of Kilbinack, killed in 1498.
    iv. Gavin Dunbar, Bishop of Moray, died in 1532.
    v. David Dunbar of Durres and Grangehill, who died in 1521, and was succeeded by his son:—Alexander in 1523, who was succeeded by his son:—Robert, who m. Christian Zearmouth, and was s. by his son:—David, obtained charter of erection of Durres into a barony in 1569, and was s. by his son:—Mark, served heir to his father in 1569, and sold the estate of Durres to Sir John Campbell of Cawdor, and purchased the lands of Grangehill in Moray, and was s. by his son:—Ninian Dunbar of Grangehill, who m. 1st a dau. of Lord Banff, m. 2d a daug. of Dunbar of Bennangefield, and was s. by his son:—Sir Robert Dunbar, who was knighted by Charles II., and married Grizzel, only dau. of Alexander Brodie of Brodie, styled Lord Brodie, who was s. by:—Alexander his brother, who was s. by:—Thomas, son, m. Janet Dunbar, heiress of Westfield in 1749, who sold the property of Grangehill, and ceased to be connected with Moray.
    vi. Patrick Dunbar, Chancellor of Aberdeen and Caithness. He died in 1595, ad was founder of the family of Bennangefield. The following is an inscription on a tombstone in Elgin Cathedral:—"Here lies Mr. John Dunbar of Bennethfield, who died 2nd Dec. 1590, and Margaret and Isobel Dunbar his spouses, who died 3d Nov. 1590, and 4th Dec. 1603," etc.
    vii. Janet Dunbar, who was Lady Innerugie.

It would appear from the above that Isobel Dunbar, who married her neighbor John Hay of Lochloy and Park, and named one of her sons Patrick (a name appearing for the first time in the family of Hay), was a daughter of either David Dunbar of Durres and Grangehill, or of Patrick Dunbar, Chancellor of Aberdeen and Caithness, or a granddaughter.

John Hay of Lochloy and Park, by his spouse Isobel Dunbar, had the following sons:

i. John Hay of Lochloy and Park. His history follows in Section XIV.
ii. David Hay of Foynfield. He was witness in 1571 to his nephew's marriage contract.
iii. Alexander Hay of Foynfield (sometimes Tynefield). He m. 1st a daughter of Innes of Innes, and m. 2d a Hepburn (1577).
iv. George Hay, died ante 1606, leaving a son Sir Alexander Hay of Fosterseat, who m. Catherine Skene, charters 1603-30; he had a son:—Alexander Hay of Warriston:—whose son left a daughter:—Janet Hay (1625).
v. Patrick Hay. (Vide "The Bruces and the Cumyns," p. 619.)
vi. John Hay the 2nd.

As Colonel Hay descends from Morella or Muriel Chisholm by at least two lines, and since living in Charleston, S. C., is another family—the family of Dr. Arthur Rose—which likewise descends from Morella Chisholm, we give the following note relating to their origin:—

"The name of Chisholm was right ancient in the south, where Chisholm of that ilk enjoyed a good fortune in Teviotdale. * * * * * * I have not learned upon what occasion they sold their lands in the south and made a purchase in the north, if it was not upon their being made Governors of the Castle of Urquhart. That castle with the barony of Urquhart was originally a portion of the estate of Cumyn, Lord Badenoch. But upon the forfeiture of that family in the reign of Robert Bruce, the castle became a royal fort whose governors were appointed by the crown to which it was annexed in 1455.

In 1334, Robert Louder was Governor of the Castle, and probably his grandson, Sir Robert Chisholm, succeeded him. I do not find Sir Robert Chisholm left any issue except the Lady Kilravock (Rose), and he was succeeded by his brother Sir John Chisholm, who, upon the demise of his grandfather Sir Robert Louder of Quarelwood, got the lands of Quarelwood, Brightmonie, Kinisterie, etc.

John Chisholm having a son Sir Robert Chisholm of Quarelwood, the latter had only a daughter Morella (Muriel), who married Alexander Sutherland of Duffus, which brought into that family a rich accession of lands formerly belonging to the Louders."—From "Fam. of Kil."

Extract from "History of Nairnshire," p. 227:—

"The old castle stood on a high ridge commanding a wide view both of the country inland and of the coast seaward. Dinner at that time was a mid-day meal, and the sun was hardly in the zenith when Queen Mary was once more in the saddle and riding down the brae of Moyness toward Auldearn. Her host at Moyness was John Dunbar, of the family of Westfield, hereditary sheriffs of Moray, and if the Dean of Moray was in his own parish at the time, the Queen would have made the acquaintance of another Dunbar, whose stately mansion, rising three stories in height, and surrounded by fine trees, must have attracted her attention.

The old Kirk of Auldearn standing on the high ground which the present edifice still occupies must have been a prominent object at the time. The village itself was a hamlet of detached houses and gardens on the slope, with the mill and brew-house on the low ground in front. Kinnudie would have been visible from the high road, and on the slope further to the south were the homesteads of Knockaudie, Park, and Ballacraggan, with numerous cottar houses belonging to the Hays and their subtenants. Anchnacloich was possessed at this time by a family of the Roses."

In this connection the following little clipping, full of pathos, will be of interest to our readers:—

"January 22—For twa hundred year an' mair, there's been a Baxter at Burnbrae, and a Hay at Kilspindie; ane was just a workin' farmer, and the other a belted earl, but gude freends and faithfu'; an', ma Lord, Burnbrae was as dear to our folk as the castle was tae yours.

"A' mind that day the Viscount cam o' age, an we gaithered to wis' him weel, that a' saw the pictures o' the auld Hays on yir walls, an' thocht hoo monie were the ties that bound ye tae yir hame.

"We haena pictures nor gowden treasures, but ther's an auld chair at oor fireside an' a' saw ma grandfather in it when a' wes a laddie at the schule, an' a' mind him tellin' me that his grandfather had sat in it lang afore.

"Its na worth muckle, an' it's been aften mended, but a'll na like tae see it carried oot frae Burnbrae."—The Days of Auld Lang Syne.

Fourteenth Generation

JOHN HAY, LAIRD OF PARK AND LOCHLOY, was the eldest son and heir of John Hay of Lochloy and Park, by his spouse Isobel Dunbar, and died in 1598 (vide tombstone inscription of previous section, also p. 619 of "The Bruces and the Cumyns," and "History Nairnshire").

The following extract is taken from page 258 of the publication "The Family of Kilravock," published by "The Spalding Club":—

"I Johne Hay of Lochtloy grantis me to have ressauit fra ane rycht honorable man Huchone Rose of Killraock the sum of four hundrycht marks usuall money of Scotland, in part of payment of ane muir sum promisit me by the said Hucheon Rose, in name of doit and tocher guid, be contrak of mariage solemnizet betuixt my sone and apparent heir Johne Hay and Margaret Rose dowthir of the said Hucheon. * * * * * * At Elgin the xxj day of October, the yeir of God 1m 5c threescor eleven yeirs, before the witness Alexander Hay of Fynesfield, William Hay burgess of Elgin, Daniel Hay, and William Douglas, Notary Publict."

John Hay of Lochloy and Park married Janet Sutherland, who died A. D. 1587, the daughter of William Sutherland of Duffus.

(This marriage is mentioned in "The Bruces and the Cumyns," pp. 619-20; by Mr. Bain, the author of "The History of Nairnshire," and by Burke in "The History of The Commoners," p. 594, with a statement that William Sutherland was descended from the earls of Sutherland and was the ancestor to the Lords Duffus.)

The following letter to the writer gives Sir Robert Gordon, A. D. 1630, as authority for the lineage of William Sutherland, of Duffus, the father of Janet:—

"Stafford House, London, S. W., Mar. 28, 1906.

Dear Sir,

The Duke of Sutherland desires me to acknowledge your letter of the 28th ult., and in reply to forward the enclosed copy of part of a genealogical table of the House of Sutherland, which gives the information you ask for.

THE FAMILY OF HAY

This table was of a series very carefully prepared by Sir Robert Gordon, Historian of Sutherland in 1630. * * * * * *

Yours faithfully,
ALEXANDER SIMPSON,
Private Secretary."

The following is the record:—

Sutherland-Duffus

1. Four traditional ancestors who were Thanes of Sutherland from whom Freskyn, Baron of Strathbrock, West Lothian; and of Duffus in Moray under King David I., 1124-53; who had sons:—Hugh Freskyn c. 1214; William, who had charter of Duffus from William the Lion; and Andrew.
2. William, son, 1st Earl of Sutherland, c. 1235, d. 1248.
3. William, 2d Earl of Sutherland, son, d. 1307; had sons:—William and Kenneth.
4. William, 3d Earl of Sutherland, d.s.p.
5. Kenneth, 4th Earl of Sutherland, son of William, 2d Earl, had sons:— William and Nicholas (by his wife, Mary, dau. Donald, 12th Earl of Mar).
6. William, 5th Earl, married the Princess Margaret Bruce, d. 1370. From him descended the later Earls of Sutherland.
7. Nicholas, Lord Duffus, 2d son of Kenneth the 4th Earl, married Mary, daughter of Reginald le Cheyne by Mary, Lady of Duffus and had two sons:—John d.s.p. and Henry.
8. Henry, Lord Duffus, who succeeded his brother.
9. Alexander, Lord of Duffus, son, married Muriel Chisholm (daughter of Sir Robert Chisholm of Quarelwood, vide Section XIII.), d. ante 1487 and had issue:—
    i. Alexander, who died before his father, and left a daughter Christian, m. William Oliphant, whose succession was contested and got shorn of lands in 1507.
    ii. William, see below.
    iii. Isabel, who married Sir Alexander Dunbar of Westfield (not given in the record of the Duke of Sutherland).
10. William of Berydale and Duffus, 2d son, died in 1507.
11. William Sutherland of Duffus, married Janet, daughter of Alexander Innes of Innes, by whom issue:—i. William; ii. Alexander, Dean of Caithness; iii. Elizabeth, m. John, 3d Earl of Caithness.
12. William Sutherland of Duffus, eldest son, died 1529, and left:—
13. William Sutherland of Duffus, son, died ante 1549.

(The table sent us continues the line down to George, 7th and last Lord Duffus, who d.s. 28 Aug. 1875.)

THE FAMILY OF HAY

Janet Sutherland, daughter of the above William Sutherland of Duffus, married John Hay of Lochloy and Park; he died 1598, she died 1587, and their remains were interred at Auldearn, with an inscription still to be seen on a monument in the chancel of the cathedral of that town. They left children:—(Mr. Bain, historian, and "The Bruces and Cumyns.")

    i.   John Hay, died in life of his father, having married in 1571, Margaret, daughter of Hugh Rose of Kilravock, and left three sons:—i. John Hay of Lochloy, who s. his grandfather in 1598, and d.s. in 1600; ii. David Hay, who s. his brother in 1600, was brought up by Sir Alexander Hay, Clerk Register, and his great-uncle Sir Alexander Hay of Fosterseat, married Marie Rose of Kilravock, by whom:—John Hay of Lochloy, died in 1640 (married 1629, Jean Cumyn, dau. of James Cumyn, Baron of Altyre, by Margaret Fraser, sister of Simon, Lord Lovat, and had a son Sir John Hay and Colonel William Hay of Lochloy and Park in 1704, etc.), William, 2d son, and Hugh Hay of Brightmonie, d. 20 Jan. 1664; iii. Robert Hay of Strowie and Park.

    ii.   George Hay, history follows in Section XV.

    iii.   Mr. Alexander Hay of Kinnudie, who married Elizabeth Monro, and left a son Walter Hay.

During the Battle of Auldearn, 1645, MacDonald, in command of the Gordon Highlanders, was forced to fall back, defending his body with a large target, he resisted single handed the assaults of the enemy. When he had just reached the garden gate, Hay of Kinnudie, tall and powerful, uncle to young Hay of Lochloy, pressed MacDonald hard who called out, "My men are coming up behind you!"

Hay turned round and MacDonald, with a single sweep of his broadsword, cut him down. Another minute and MacDonald's own sword was shivered to pieces. History of Nairnshire.

Fifteenth Generation

GEORGE HAY was the second son of John Hay of Lochloy and Park by his wife Janet, daughter of William Sutherland of Duffus, and died ante 1598, during the lifetime of his father.

His younger brother was Mr. Alexander Hay of Kinnudie, who had a son Walter, while the properties of Lochloy and Park passed down to David, the son of George's eldest brother John.

We extract the following from "The History of Nairnshire," pages 253 and 254, relating to this David:—

"The Laird of Brodie and Brodie of Lethen, as might be expected, signed the National Covenant. David Hay of Lochloy also adhibited his name. David had had rather an adventurous career. He was the second son and in the year 1600 succeeded his brother John. A letter of his has been preserved which gives a curious account of the upbringing of a Nairnshire lad in these early days.

"He says that in his minority, being under the government of (his uncle and cousin) Alexander Hay of Kinnudie and Walter, then his curators (his uncle George having died), he was transported from the county of Moray to Lothian for education in the schools there. He remained there until the year of the Plague. He was left desolate until Sir Alexander Hay, Clerk of the Register, at the earnest entreaty of Sir Alexander Hay of Fosterseat, removed him to Whittinghame, where he was lovingly entertained for a year.

"The origin of the Hays of Fosterseat may thus be traced—John of Lochloy, the hero of the breach of promise case (he who had requested release from an engagement to marry the daughter of Thomas Dunbar, Earl of Moray in order to marry the daughter of Donald, Thane of Cawdor) was succeeded by his son William of Lochloy, Dallas, and Park; he was succeeded by his son John in 1480; John's eldest son William succeeded him, marrying Katherine Urquhart of Cromarty, by whom he had John, who married Isobel Dunbar in 1554, and died in 1563, leaving several sons:—John, who succeeded him; David and Alexander of Foynesfield, and George Hay, who dying before 1600, left a son Alexander, who married Catherine Skene, and became Sir Alexander Hay of Fosterseat.

"The Hays of Kinfauns, of Wariston, of Easter Kennet, of Monckton, of Woodcockdale, and of Carriber, can all be traced to the Hays of Lochloy.

"It happened that when the young Laird of Lochloy, David, came on the

THE FAMILY OF HAY 89

visit to Sir Alexander Hay, at Kelso, and was invited to accompany him and—writes young Lochloy, 'transported me with horse and abutments effeiring to my rank to the City of London, to the effect that I might see and understand good manners and fashions.'

"His expenses in London for breakfast, dinner, supper, and bed, 'conform to the order of England,' were 36s Scots per day, his horse 6d, hay 6d, oats 2d, and bread 14s Scots.

"He remained in London from September till March, and thereafter till his marriage, and his kinsman, Sir Alexander, defrayed all his expenses, and when trouble arose with his uncles and cousins of Kinnudie and Foynesfield in regard to count and reckoning during his minority, Hay of Fosterseat helped him most lovingly to redeem his property and to recover his woods, which were, he says, 'the pleasure of my estate.' David married Marie Rose of Kilravock and left a numerous family."

By referring to the table of "Sutherland-Duffus" in the preceding section, it will be seen that Kenneth, the 4th Earl of Sutherland, married Mary of Mar. He was slain at the Battle of Homildon Hall A. D. 1333, along with many nobles. The lineage of Mary will be found in the following account of:—

The Earldom of Mar

1. Martacus, 1st Earl of Mar, witnessed a charter to the Culdees of Loch Leven by Malcolm Cawn Mohr, A. D. 1065.
2. Gratnach, 2d Earl of Mar, son, witnessed the foundation charter for the Monastery of Scone by King Alexander I., 1114.
3. Margundus, 3d Earl of Mar, son, witnessed charters of King David I., and of King Malcolm IV.
4. Gillocher, 4th Earl of Mar, son, witnessed charter of Malcolm IV.
5. Morgundus, 5th Earl, son, married Margaret, and was reinvested in the earldom by King William I., A. D. 1171.
6. Gilbert, 6th Earl of Mar, son, was living A. D. 1180.
7. Gilchrist, 7th Earl of Mar, brother, was living 1214.
8. Duncan, 8th Earl of Mar, son and heir, married Arabella, daughter of William, son of Nescius, Lord of Latherisk.
9. William, 9th, Earl of Mar, son and heir, was one of the Regents of Scotland in 1258, Great Chamberlain in 1265, married Elizabeth, daughter of William Cumyn, Earl of Buchan. She died 1267; the earl went on a special mission to King Henry III., and died soon after.
10. Donald, 10th Earl of Mar, son and heir, was a nominee on the part of Robert Bruce in his contest for the Crown, A. D. 1290. His daughter, the Lady Isabella, married King Robert I.; the earl d. 1294.

THE FAMILY OF HAY

11. Gratney, 11th Earl of Mar, son and heir, married Christian, daughter of Robert Bruce, Earl of Carrick, sister of King Robert I., (she married 2d Sir Christopher Seton and 3d Sir A. Murray of Bothwell) and had children: i. Donald; ii. Elyne, who married Sir John Menteith, Earl of Arran.
12. Donald, 12th Earl of Mar, son and heir, married Isabel Stewart, daughter of Sir Alexander Stewart of Bonkill.

    On defeat of his uncle, King Robert I., he was imprisoned but not chained in respect to his youth; after Bannockburn, he was exchanged with the Queen for the Earl of Hereford. As Regent of Scotland after the death of Randolph, Earl of Moray, he was defeated by Edward Balliol at Dupplin, A. D. 1332, and slain.

    He had daughters, Margaret, Countess of Mar, who married William, Earl of Douglas and 2d Sir John Swinton; and Mary, who married Kenneth, 4th Earl of Sutherland.
13. Nicholas Sutherland, Lord Duffus, 2d son, married Marie, daughter of Reginald le Cheyne by his wife Mariot, 4th daughter of Malyse, 7th Earl of Strathearn by his wife Matilda, daughter of Magnus V., the last Angus Earl of Orkney and Caithness (vide Earls of Strathearn in Section III).

Reference to the "Sutherland-Duffus" table of Section XIV. No. 7 shows the continuation of this line as follows:—

Nicholas Sutherland, Lord of Duffus, who had a son:—Henry Sutherland, Lord of Duffus, who had a son:—Alexander Sutherland, Lord of Duffus, who had a son:—William Sutherland of Berydale and Duffus, who had a son:—William Sutherland of Duffus, who had a son:—William Sutherland of Duffus, who had a son:—William Sutherland of Duffus, who died ante 1549, and had a daughter:—Janet Sutherland, who married John Hay of Lochloy and Park, and had sons: i. John Hay, heir to the lands of Lochloy and Park; ii. George Hay, ancestor of Colonel Ann Hawkes Hay; iii. Alexander Hay of Kinnudie.

George Hay, second son mentioned above, seems to have drifted to the South, and acquired property in Clackmannanshire, in the last probably by marriage, and by his wife left issue:—

(Vide "The Bruces and the Cumyns," p. 619).

i. David Hay.
ii. Alexander Hay of Easter Kennet; history follows in Section XVI.
iii. James Hay.

Judge Martin Wilkins of the Island of Jamaica.
Grandfather of Col. Ann Hawkes Hay.

Chancellor William Smith, Judge of the Supreme Court of New York while a province under Great Britain.

Sixteenth Generation

ALEXANDER HAY, LORD EASTER KENNET, was the 2d son of George Hay, and was possessed of the lands of Bridgemark in Kirkcudbright, and Easter Kennet in Clackmannanshire. He died A. D. 1594.

In 1564 he was nominated by Maitland of Lethington for the office of Clerk of the Privy Council, and was Director of the Chancery in 1577. He was appointed Clerk Register in 1579, and admitted Senator to the College of Justice with the title of Lord Easter Kennet.

In 1579 he was a member of the Commission for the Jurisdiction of the Kirk, and in 1581 was a member of the commission for the visitation and reformation of hospitals, and acted as arbitrator in the feud between the families of Gordon and Forbes. After the "Raid of Ruthven," in November, 1581, he carried to Lennox the King's commands that he must quit the kingdom and during the absence of Maitland was "Interim Secretary for the Scotch Language" in 1589. In 1592 he received grants of numerous charters for his good services, and died 15 September 1594.

Letters from and to him were published by his son Alexander Lord Newton, and in "Thorp's Cal. State Papers," Scot. Series between 1573-84; he is mentioned in "Brinton and Haig's Senators of the Royal College of Justice," Anderson's Scottish Nation; Acts of the Scottish Parliament iii., 138, 219, 231, 626; Books of Sederunt; Keith's App. 174; Melville Mem. p. 205; Spotiswood p. 379; Mayse pp. 71-72; Monteith's Theatre of Morality p. 54. (Vide "Dictionary of National Biography").

From the Nairnshire Telegraph, June 11, 1907, we extract the following:—

"The old ruined castle of Inshoch is the only visible object reminding us of the knightly family of Hay of Lochloy, save the memorials of the race in the

Churchyard of Auldearn and the effigy of the warrior in armour in the Cathedral of Elgin. * * * * * *

"The main line of the Hays of Lochloy died out about a generation ago but not a few of its branches from younger sons still flourish. One of these—strange to say—is in the Southern States of America—in South Carolina— * * * * * * and curiously enough the old religious fervor, so characteristic of the Hays of Lochloy in Reformation and Covenanting times, manifests itself under the warm sunshine of South Carolina, in respect that out of one family of Hays there are several of them ministers of the Presbyterian Church. Occasionally the Hays gave a Priestary to the Episcopal Church—it would have been unfair to have kept all their sons for one side. * * * * * * But we must pass over several generations of Johns and Williams of Lochloy until we come to John Hay who died in 1563. This Laird of Lochloy and Park left at least six sons. At this time the estate of Park and Lochloy had attached to it several small properties, such as Kinnudie, Brightmonie, part of Rait, and Foynesfield.

"The eldest son, John, of course, gets Lochloy; the second and third sons, David and Alexander, are settled at Foynesfield; and the fourth son, George, gets the small property of Foresterseat, near Elgin, an old possession of the Hays of Lochloy. The younger generation seek in the South a wider sphere for their energies; and George's son Alexander becomes a prominent man of affairs in Edinburgh. He becomes Clerk Register, is knighted, and takes a leading part in Scottish political affairs as Sir Alexander Hay of Foresterseat. His father died in 1606, when he succeeded to Foresterseat.

"His cousin George, son of the Laird of Lochloy, had several sons to be provided for, and the second son, Alexander, went south, and also rose rapidly in the legal profession, and acquired, along with other properties, Easter Kennet in Clackmannan. Alexander was knighted by King James, he became Clerk to the Privy Council, Director of the Chancery, Clerk Register, and a Lord of Session, and took the title of Lord Easter Kennet. He was a great favorite of King James, and when the King went to Denmark for a wife, he took Hay of Easter Kennet with him as Interim Secretary of the Scottish language.

"Young David Hay of Lochloy, who succeeded his brother, had been sent to school by his uncle of Kinnudie. The Plague appeared, and the school was broken up. The poor boy, so far from home, would have been left in a desolate condition had not Sir Alexander Hay of Easter Kennet come to his rescue. After a time Sir Alexander transferred David to the guardianship of Sir Alexander Hay of Foresterseat, who brought him up; and never was pupil more grateful to his guardian. In after years when David was comfortably seated at Inshoch, and had married Marie Rose, daughter of the 'gentle baron of Kilravock,' he draws up a formal deed, expressing his obligations to him, not only for his upbringing, but also for paying off the debts on his estate and settling several other troublesome questions.

"There was some dispute about Foynesfield which was referred to two arbiters, one of whom was Sir Alexander Hay of Easter Kennet, and although these last Hays in the south had become men of great wealth and high position

THE FAMILY OF HAY

in the land, they never forgot their old friends in Nairnshire and, in more cases than that of David of Lochloy, did they set the lairds on their feet again.

"Sir Alexander Hay of Easter Kennet died in 1594. His youngest son, Sir Alexander Hay of Newton and Whiteburgh, was also a Lord of Session in 1610 under the title of Lord Newton, and he was appointed Lord Clerk Register in 1612, and died in 1616, of whom are the Hays of Moncton. Hay of Easter Kennet's eldest son John married Mariot Drummond," etc.

(We reserve the remainder of this article on the Hays of Lochloy by Mr. Bain, the historian of Nairnshire, for the next section, where it properly belongs.)

Sir Alexander Hay of Easter Kennet m. Mariot Farquhar (vide charter of 1582) by whom three sons:— ("The Bruces and the Cumyns," p. 619.)

    i.   John Hay, whose history follows in Section XVII.
    ii.   Daniel Hay.
    iii. Sir Alexander Hay of Whiteburgh in 1600; died in 1616, and left a son:—Alexander Hay of Moncton 1646, who had a son:—Alexander Hay of Moncton living 1683.

Seventeenth Generation

MR. JOHN HAY OF EASTER KENNET was the eldest son and heir of Sir Alexander Hay, Lord Easter Kennet, by his spouse Mariot Farquhar, descended from an ancient family of Gilmerscroft, North Britain. He was living A. D. 1600, and married Mariot (or Marian) Drummond. In continuation of our extract introduced into the last section from Mr. Bain's sketch of "The Hays of Lochloy," we quote:—

"Sir Alexander Hay of Easter Kennet died in 1594. * * * * * * His eldest son, John, married Mariot Drummond and left two sons:—

"i. Alexander Hay, who left three daughters; ii. David Hay, of Woodcockdale, who acquired the estates of his father, now very extensive, and who sold Easter Kennet in 1638, and contiguous property, to the Bruces of Clackmannan and Wester Kennet, for the sum of 16,000 merks. The Hay family acquired the property of Woodcockdale in Linlithgow and Bridgemark in Kirkcudbright and other properties.

"By a singular piece of good fortune, the old Easter Kennet estates returned to them. Alexander Bruce of Kinnaird (grandson of Mr. Robert, the minister), married a daughter of Sir Robert Bruce of Clackmannan, and the lands were settled upon an elder daughter of the marriage, failing a male heir, on condition of her marrying a gentleman of the name of Bruce or one who should assume the name and arms of Bruce. Such a gentleman was found in David Hay, the younger son of Hay of Woodcockdale, the former owner of the property. David Hay married Helen Bruce, the Lady of Kinnaird, and assumed the name of Bruce. Of their four sons only the younger survived and he assumed the name of Bruce, while his sisters stuck by the name of Hay.

"David Bruce (sic lege Hay) by his first wife had two sons,

the youngest of whom, James Bruce, alone survived. This James Bruce (in reality Hay) was the famous Abyssinian traveler—really a Hay of Lochloy by male descent.

"The late Mrs. Cumming-Bruce of Dunphail was his great-granddaughter.

"It is from one of the sons of Hay of Easter Kennet that the family of Hays of South Carolina and a professor in one of the educational institutions of Charleston, S. C., descend."

The above refers to a member of one of the branches of the family of Colcock, which likewise descends from the Hays of Erroll and Lochloy.

Mr. John Hay of Easter Kennet by his spouse Mariot Drummond had two sons:— ("The Bruces and the Cumyns," and Mr. Bain.)

i. Mr. Alexander Hay, one of the Clerks of Session, who left daughters:—Margaret, Anna, and Ellen, provided for out of Easter Kennet, one of whom married Sir John Gibson.

ii. Mr. David Hay of Woodcockdale, Easter Kennet, Craigtown, and Kennet Paus, sold to Bruce of Clackmannan and of Wester Kennet, in 1638, for 16,000 merks. History follows in Section XVIII.

Eighteenth Generation

MR. DAVID HAY OF WOODCOCKDALE was the 2d son of Mr. John Hay of Easter Kennet by his spouse Mariot Drummond. He d. A. D. 1662. After the decease of his elder brother, Mr. Alexander Hay, who left no male heirs, David Hay acquired the properties of Craigtown, Kennet Paus, and Easter Kennet, and sold this last estate in 1638, to Bruce of Clackmannan and Wester Kennet for the sum of 16,000 merks.

He held the office in Edinburgh of a Clerk of Session, and married Jean Winrhame (or Jean Winrahame).

The following abstracts were sent up by Mr. Henry Paton, 120 Polwarth Terrace, Edinburgh, Scotland, and relate to the above:—

"Action by Mr. David Hay of Woodcockdale, against Captain Robert Drummond, brother, son, and lawfully charged to enter heir to the deceased Mr. John Drummond of Woodcockdale, his uncle, in which mention is made of Jean Winrahame (Winrhame), the pursuor's spouse, and of the alienation to him and her and their heirs, of the lands of Woodcockdale on the 8th and 22d of March, 1644." (Register of Acts and Decrees, Volume 533.)

"1652, August 18th.—Action at the instance of Mr. David Hay of Woodcockdale, for himself and as executor to the deceased Bethia Hay, spouse to the deceased John Durham of Duntervie, his sister, against Mr. Alexander Hay, writer in Edinburgh, and John Vaus in Barnbarrs, for his interest, mentioning that the deceased James Hay of Brigmark, as principal, and the pursuor as cautioner for him, granted a Bond on the 27th Nov. 1647, to the said deceased Bithia Hay, for 600 merks, and the said James Hay also by his bond, dated 17 May 1648, promised to pay 1,000 merks to the pursuor, and Mr. Alexander Hay now of Brigmark, as son and heir to the deceased James, having renonced to enter heir to his father, the pursuor seeks adjudication to be made of certain lands and teinds, etc., to which the said James Hay of Brigmark might have claim." (Ibid, Vol. 558.)

Mr. David Hay of Woodcockdale, by his spouse Jean Winrhame, had the following children:—("The Bruces and the Cumyns," also from an extract of his family chart sent us by Sir Lewis Erroll Hay, Bart., and "The Hay Tables.")

 i. Mr. John Hay of Woodcockdale, (vide below).

THE FAMILY OF HAY 97

ii. James Hay of Carriber (or Carruber), whose history will be presented in Section XIX.

iii. Andrew Hay. (Not given by the authorities cited above, but proved by the will of his father, James Hay of Carriber.)

James Bruce (sic lege James Hay), the celebrated Abyssinian explorer, was a second cousin of Michael, the father of Colonel Ann Hawks Hay. The latter was a great-grandson of James Hay of Carriber, while the former was a great-grandson of Mr. John Hay of Woodcockdale, and therefore we introduce an account of the descendants of John of Woodcockdale, which should be interesting to their cousins—the posterity of James of Carriber.

We abstract first from "The Bruces and the Cumyns," a very elaborate work by Mrs. Cumming-Bruce, great-granddaughter of the Abyssinian traveler:—

1. Mr. John Hay of Woodcockdale was the eldest son of Mr. David Hay of Woodcockdale, and had sons:—David Hay, Andrew Hay, and John Hay. (Mackenzie's Deeds, Vol. 79.)

2. David Hay, eldest son of John, married in 1687, Helen Bruce, dau. Alexander Bruce of Kinnaird, of the same stock as Robert I., and by the terms of the will of her grandfather, assumed the name of Bruce, and thus became David Bruce.

    His descendant, Mrs. Cumming-Bruce, now says:—

    "From an old family Bible, printed in 1561, the same which Mr. Robert Bruce called for on his deathbed, I copy the following entries by Helen Bruce, who married David Hay:—

    i. "Helen Hay, our first child, was born in January, 1689, and was baptised on the 12th day by Mr. Sutherland, Minister of Larbert. Witnesses—James Hay of Carriber, Mr. John Hay of Carriber, Mr. John Hay of Woodcockdale, and John Drummond of Newton."

    She married later Counsellor Hamilton of London, brother of Alexander Hamilton of Wishaw, and had among other children a son, William Gerard Hamilton, better known as "Single Speech Hamilton," who was by some supposed to be the author of "The Letters of Junius."

    ii. "Alexander (Hay) was b. in Jan., 1691, and bap. by Mr. Sutherland before the same witnesses."

    iii. "John (Hay) was b. in January, 1693, and bap. on the 10th of that month by Mr. Paterson, Minister of Borthwick, before the same witnesses."

    iv. "James (Hay) was b. in January, 1694, and was bap. the 8th of that month by Mr. Paterson. Witnesses—Carriber and

    Woodcockdale, James Galloway of Balgair, and Andrew Kerr.
 v. "Margaret (Hay) was b. 11th of August, 1695, and bap. by Mr. Sutherland the same day before the same witnesses. (She died later unmarried.)
 vi. "David (Hay) was b. the 25th of November, 1696, and bap. by Mr. Sutherland, before the same witnesses."
    On the death of her husband David Hay, Helen married 2d Robert Boyd, brother of Major Ninian Boyd of the Scotch Greys. She died in 1728, and of her four sons only David, the youngest, survived his mother, the Lady of Kinnaird.

3. David (sic lege Hay), the youngest child of David Hay by his spouse Helen Bruce of Kinnaird, assumed the name of his mother and became David Bruce.

  He married 1st Marion Graham, eldest daughter of James Graham, Advocate and Judge of the High Court of Admiralty, by his first wife Marion Hamilton, eldest sister of Alexander Hamilton of Pencaitland (Judge Graham married 2d Lady Mary Livingston from whom the present family of Grahams of Airth descends).

  On November 12th, 1715, David, with many other young gentlemen, one of whom was probably Michael Hay his cousin, had been taken prisoner at Preston, when Judge Graham went to Carlisle at his own expense, to plead for them A. D. 1717.

  David married 2d Agnes Glen, sister of Governor Glen of South Carolina, and sister of Andrew Glen of Longcroft, co. Linlithgow (whose only daughter Elizabeth Glen, married in 1767, George, 8th earl of Dalhousie, and was grandmother of the late earl, she died A. D. 1907).

  David by his 1st wife Marion Graham had a surviving son:
 i. James Bruce (Hay), the Abyssinian traveler.

  By his 2d wife Agnes, the sister of Governor Glen of South Carolina, David had issue:—
 ii. Alexander Bruce (Hay), bred an advocate to the Scotch bar. d.s.p.
 iii. Andrew Bruce (Hay), who settled the "Bruce Hermitage" in Dec. 1775, in the Island of St. Vincent. d.s.p.
 iv. David Bruce (Hay), an officer in the Duke of Richmond's regiment, and was mortally wounded in the breach of the fortress called "the Morro," at Havana, while fighting as a volunteer in the forlorn hope. d.s.p.
 v. Captain William Bruce (Hay), in the service of the East India Company, proposed and led the attack on the 3d August 1780, in which was captured from the Mahrattras, the fortress of Gualior until then deemed impregnable. d.s.p.

vi. Thomas Bruce (Hay), who was agent in St. Vincent. d.s.p.

vii. Robert Bruce (Hay), physician at Lucknow, died May, 1800, at Serampore, leaving a considerable fortune, and large claims for money lent to the Nabob of Oude which were never settled. His large collections of Natural History were purchased by the Duke of Marlborough. d.s.p.

4. James Bruce (Hay), the Abyssinian traveler, eldest son mentioned above, of David Bruce (Hay) by his wife Marion Graham, was born at the family residence of Kinnaird, co. Sterling, Scotland, on the 14th Dec., 1730.

"His father, David, was the eldest son of David Hay of Woodcockdale, in the shire of Linlithgow, by Helen, dau. of Alexander Bruce of Kinnaird, who dying without male issue, transferred to her and her descendants his name and estate.

"The family of Woodcockdale was sprung from the Hays of Park (and Lochloy), in the province of Moray, an old branch of the Hays of Erroll, whose bravery distinguished them at a remote period of our national history. * * * * * In Feb., 1728, David married Marion Graham, daughter of James Graham of Airth, Dean of the Faculty of Advocates, and Judge of the High Court of Admiralty in Scotland. * * * * * * His father married a few years after the death of his first wife, Miss Glen, daughter of James Glen in Longcroft, in shire of Linlithgow, and sister of James Glen, who was for a long time Governor of South Carolina. * * * * * *

On Saturday, the 26th Apl. 1794, having entertained company at Kinnaird, as he was going down stairs about eight o'clock in the evening to hand a lady into her carriage, his foot slipped and he fell headlong to the ground * * * * * and he expired early the next morning.

He was 6 feet 4 inches tall, large and well proportioned, of strength corresponding to his stature, his features and face elegantly formed, his air noble and commanding. He was attentive to his dress and particularly successful in wearing the dress of the nations through which he passed in his travels, in an easy and graceful manner, to which he was indebted in part for his good reception, especially in Abyssinia."—Extracts from Alexander Murray's "Accounts of the Life and Writings of James Bruce of Kinnaird," who was in reality James Hay and a second cousin of Michael Hay.

James Bruce (Hay) was well educated, master of many languages and accomplishments, and for many years in foreign countries led a life full of interesting and daring adventure. He made many collections of great value to the world, and wrote a history of his explorations in Africa.

He married 2d, 20 May 1776, Mary Dundas, daughter of Thomas Dundas of Fingask, by Lady Janet Maitland, daughter of the 6th Earl of Lauderdale, by whom among other children:—

5. James, who was b. 28 June 1780, and had a son:—
6. James Bruce (Hay), s. his father in 1794, but being still a minor was entrusted for his education to Dr. Knox, and subsequently to the poet, Hector M'Neil.

    He married Elizabeth, daughter of William Spicer of Wear, co. Devon by Elizabeth Parker, dau. of Francis Parker of Blagden, uncle of the 1st Lord Boringdon.

    He died in Edinburgh, June, 1810, and left an only daughter:—

7. Mary Elizabeth Bruce (Hay), succeeded her father in 1810. She married 21 June 1820, Charles Lennox Cumming, 2d son of Sir Alexander Cumming Gordon of Altyre and Gordonstown, Bart. She was the author of "The Bruces and the Cumyns," from which we have extracted largely in our work, and which is recognized as a compilation of great historical and genealogical value, based on original documents.
8. Elizabeth Mary, daughter, m. 1841, James Lord Bruce, who s. his father as 8th Earl of Elgin, and 12th Earl of Kincardine. They had a daughter:—Lady Elma Bruce, m. Hon. T. Hovell-Thurlow, by whom a son:—James Frederick.

Nineteenth Generation

JAMES HAY OF CARRIBER was the second son of Mr. David Hay of Woodcockdale, Craigtown, and Easter Kennet, by his spouse Jean Winrhame. He married Magdalen Robertson, descended of Strowan, was a Writer to the Signet, and died A. D. 1702.

The following abstracts sent us by Mr. Henry Paton of Edinburgh, are offered as supplying information relating to the foregoing James Hay, W. S., of Carruber:—

"Factory by George Hay, only lawful son to the deceased John Hay, uncle to the Earl of Erroll, who is going forth of this kingdom to London, and being confident of the kindness and care of James Hay of Carruber, appoints him his factor and commissioner to uplift certain sums due to him, especially a debt due by the deceased James, Earl of Tullibardine, since 1682, contained in a bond granted by him to his said deceased father, therein designed lawful son to George Hay, grand-uncle to the Earl of Erroll, dated at Edinburgh, 29th September, A. D. 1697."—(Durie Deeds, Vol. 98.)

"1703, December 15th.—Testament Testamenter of James Hay of Carriber, who died in 17—, given up by himself upon the 16th September 1690, and by Magdalen Robertson, his widow.

"This estate is valued to 1,333 pounds, 6 shillings 8 pence, and consists of some debts due to him by William Lockhart of Birkhill, and Jean Bruce, his mother, and the tenants and possessors of their lands.

"This testament is dated at Edinburgh 16th September 1690, and in it he appoints his spouse Magdalen Robertson, his only executrix. She is to have the life rent use of his estate, and after her death it is to devolve on John Hay, his eldest son, whom failing on George Hay his 2d son, whom failing on Andrew Hay his 3d son, whom failing on any other son he may yet have (he lived twelve years longer), and failing sons it is to go to his daughters successively according to age.

"He nominates his spouse only tutrix to his children, and failing her by death or marriage, he nominates Sir John Foulis of Ravelston, Sir Alexander Gibson of Pentland, George Drummond of Blair, Mr. John Hay of Woodcockdale, George Robertson, Clerk to the Register of Hormineys; Andrew Hay, 'my brother;' James Crawford, 'my nephew;' John Robertson and Dr. James Robertson, 'my brethren-in-law,' or any three of these to be tutors to his said children.

"Confirmed as above. John Hay of Carriber as cautioner. (Edinburgh Testaments Vol. 82)."

Note in the above abstract of the will of James Hay of Carriber:—that he gives in this will twelve years before his death and the testament may have been drawn up many years before he gives it in, that he makes conditional provision for any other son he may yet have and was outlived by his wife and must have had other children, that he names a brother Andrew and also a son Andrew, that he refers to Mr. Drummond of Blair, and names James and John Robertson as his brothers-in-law, and a nephew James Crawford.

"1743, Sept. 6th.—Testament Dative of John Hay of Carriber (eldest son of above James Hay), who died there on — October 1708, given up by Andrew Hay, late of Mugdrum, and Grizel Hay, widow of Thomas Boyes, W. S., brother and sister german to the defunct.

"Thomas Boyes (nephew), Writer in Edinburgh and lawful son to the said deceased Thomas Boyes, cautioner. (Edinburgh Testaments, Vol. 107.)"

"James Hay of Carriber, 2d son of David Hay of Woodcockdale, Linlithgow, died December, 1702, married Magdalen Robertson." (Extracted by Mrs. Graham from "The Society of Writers to the Signet 1594-1890," p. 96.)

"1671, Admission of James Hay, son of the deceased Mr. David Hay of Woodcockdale." (Ibid, p. 313.)

"10 Dec. 1702. Andrew Marjoribank of that Ilk. Apprentice (at law) to James Hay of Carriber. Eldest son to Thomas Marjoribank of that Ilk. Died 13 April 1742. Married A. D. 1700, Christian, daughter of James Hay of Carriber, Linlithgowshire. Commissary of Edinburgh. Entered as a member to the Society of Writers to the Signet. (Ibid, p. 139.)"

"Fiscal 1710-17. Thomas Boyes. Died about 1718. Married 19 April 1708, Grizel, daughter of James Hay of Carriber, Linlithgowshire. Entered as member of Writers to the Signet admitted 1704. (Ibid, p. 369.)"

"Under List of Members—p. 140.—Andrew Marjoribank of that Ilk. Eldest son of Andrew Marjoribank of that Ilk. W. S. (by wife Christian Hay). Died 20 Feb. 1766. Married 1st Mary Chalmers in 1744, and 2d Jean, daughter of Thomas Boyes, Deputy-Clerk of Session, in Feb. 1755."

"Under Abstract of Minutes, p. 364.

"16 Nov. 1702. Admission of Andrew Marjoribank from the office of James Hay of Carriber."

"Ibid.—1708, 10th Jan. Committee consisting of Thomas Boyes, Andrew Marjoribank and eight others, appointed to meet and enquire into the records of the signet, etc."

"Ibid.—Commission by the Earl of Mar (John Erskine) to Thomas Boyes and thirteen others to be Commissioners, dated at Edinburgh 7th Nov. 1713."

THE FAMILY OF HAY

"Ibid, p. 321.—1681, 13th July. Commission by Alexander, Earl of Moray, sole Secretary of State for Scotland, appointing James Hay and other Commissioners for regulating the calling of the Writers to the Signet."

"P. 322.—James Hay and others appointed to take account of the box, 5th Dec. 1681."

"P. 323.—James Hay and other, to remove abuses."

"P. 328.—Admission of Mr. Alexander Drummond, lately prentice and servitor to James Hay, 14th Nov. 1684."

'P. 344.—Admission of Andrew Kerr from the office of James Hay, 2d October 1696."

In Nisbet's Heraldry, Vol. 1, p. 324, mention is made of Mr. John Robertson and Mr. James Robertsohn "descended of Strowan," also to John Crawford, Dean of Guild in Linlithgow, descended of Haining, of Marjoribanks descended of the Johnstones—which evidently refers to the brothers-in-law of James Hay of Carriber, and the family of his nephew and son-in-law. It will be remembered that the great Scotch minister was a Robertson descended of Strowan.

From documents before us it is shown that James Hay of Carriber in addition to Carriber, partly in Linlithgowshire and partly in Stirlingshire, possessed the lands of Craigend and Easter and Wester Gaw, and that by his spouse Magdalen Robertson, who survived him (he died A. D. 1702), he left the following children:—

i. John Hay of Carriber, who d. in 1708, and left two sons:—John of Carriber and Andrew. The former had a son Andrew, who sold the lands of Carriber and died A. D. 1764.
ii. George Hay.
iii. Andrew Hay of Mugdrum.
iv. Thomas Hay of Bridgehouse, whose history follows in Section XX.
v. Christian Hay, who married A. D. 1700, Andrew Marjoribanks, writer to the Signet, Commissary of Edinburgh, and by him had a son Andrew Marjoribanks.
vi. Grizel (or Grace) Hay, who married Thomas Boyes, W. S., in the year 1708, 19th April, and had children: Thomas Boyes, and Jean Boyes, who married her cousin Marjoribanks.

For evidence showing that James Hay of Carriber had a fourth son Thomas Hay, born after his will was drawn up, see the Letter of Factory written by his brother Andrew Hay, and dated Rome, Italy, 4th April 1721, in which he appoints as his agent in Scotland during his absence, "My brother german, Thomas Hay, Writer in Edinburgh," and in the letter describes himself as being a "son of James Hay of Carriber."

It is hardly necessary to explain that "brother german" means a lawful brother where both parents are in common.

That this Thomas Hay was the father of Michael Hay is proved by the wills of Isabel Balfour and of letters of renunciation by Michael Hay and his sister Jean Hay, to be given in the next Section XX.

Twentieth Generation

THOMAS HAY OF BRIDGEHOUSE, WRITER IN EDINBURGH, was the 4th son of James Hay of Carriber, W. S., by his spouse Magdalen Robertson. He married Isabel Balfour, daughter of Sir David Balfour of Forret, and sister of Michael Balfour of Forret. He died 28 January 1733. We have before us many references to the above Thomas Hay, Writer in Edinburgh, extracted for us by Mr. Henry Paton, 120 Polwarth Terrace, Edinburgh, and he must be carefully distinguished from his kinsman, Thomas Hay, W. S., who married Anna Gibson, and was founder of the house of Alderston, in Haddintonshire, who belonged to an older generation.

It is not always an easy task in tracing a pedigree to find absolutely convincing proof connecting our first American ancestor with his continental parentage, and unless this link in the chain of evidence be incontestable, all is unsatisfactory, no matter how plausible. In this case we have been especially fortunate, and in order that our readers—Colonel Hay's descendants—may be perfectly assured of the certainty of their descent, at the risk of proving tiresome, we propose to be as explicit as the circumstances demand.

We first offer some extracts from a few letters from a gentleman in Edinburgh whose reputation for ability and integrity is well appreciated in his native city, and whose work often leads him to delve among the original charters and records of the past.

These extracts are as follows:—

"120 Polwark Terrace, Edinburgh, 17 Feb. 1905.

"Dear Sir:—

"I have to acknowledge your favor of the 22d ult. and also of the previous one of Dec. 18th to which I have been giving effect by instituting a special search for information, the results of which I am enclosing. I have found positive proof of Michael Hay having a sister Jean, who married Dr. George Bethune of

Cupar, Fife, and a brother Andrew, the mother of all being Isabel Balfour, so that the point is now the parentage of Thomas Hay, their father.

"He is mentioned as sometimes of Cupar and sometimes of Edinburgh, but I searched both registers and others, but could find no traces of the birth of his children. The Hays are a numerous family in some parts of Scotland, and I have examined a large number of wills, also other registers, but without, as yet, attaining certainty," etc.

"Yours faithfully,
"(Signed) Henry Paton."

In a letter from same to same dated 30th May 1905:—

"I was just deploring with myself that I must write you by this mail that after a long search through many volumes of records I had still no success when this day I came upon a deed which will satisfy you.

"I feel very thankful it has turned up before I wrote, for I know what disappointment it would cause you to have received my negative letter. The deed is a Letter of Factory by Andrew Hay, son of the deceased James Hay of Carriber, to Thomas Hay, Writer in Edinburgh, his brother german, in whose fidelity and fitness he has entire confidence, to uplift all moneys due to him and transact necessary business on his behalf. The Factory is dated at Rome 4th April 1721, and recorded on the 15th May following, in the Register of Deeds (Durie's Office) Vol. 160. It thus proved that Thomas Hay was son of James Hay of Carriber."

In a letter from same, bearing date 17 August 1906.

"I send you herewith enclosed the certified copy of the Factory. It is copied from the original deed itself, and this copy is as valid in any Court of Justice as the original. * * * * * I am frequently among old charters in private collections, and something further of interesting nature may turn up."

We now append an extra copy of this certified copy of the Letter of Factory as sent us by Mr. Paton:

"Public Records of Scotland"

"At Edinburgh the Fifteenth day of May One thousand seven hundred and twenty one years.

"In presence of the Lords of Council and Session Compeared Mr. Mathew McKell Advocate Edinburgh as Procurator for the Party after named and designed and gave in the Factory underwritten desiring the same might be registered in their Lordship's Books conform to Law which desire the said Lords found reasonable and ordained the same to be done accordingly whereof the tenor follows viz:—

"I Andrew Hay Lawfull son of the Deceaset James Hay of Carriber Having an entire confidence of the fidelity and fitness of Thomas Hay Writer in Edinburgh my Brother german for discharging the trust underwritten Do therefore by these presents make and constitute the said Thomas Hay my lawful factor and Commissioner and hereby give and grant to him my full power warrand and commission for me in my name and upon my behalf To uplift and receive all and sundry debts and sums of money due and adebted to me by whatsoever persons

Mrs. William Smith, wife of Chancellor Smith of New York, née Mary Hett of Huguenot parentage.

Lewis Scott Hay, sixth son of Col. Ann Hawkes Hay, was born at Fishkill on the Hudson River, New York State. He followed his older brother to South Carolina and settled in the coastal region there.

Harriet Yonge Johnson, wife of Lewis Scott Hay. She was a native of Wadmalow Island, S.C.

Recepits or discharges thereof to grant which shall be so sufficient as granted by myself and if need be to pursue thereof and such sum so to be raised to lay out upon new security and generally to do every other thing requisite there-anent and anent the managing and disposing of any other my effects and concerns in Britain in the same manner as if I were personally present Promising to hold the same Firm and Stable With this Provision always that the sd. Thomas Hay shall be accountable to me for his intermissions by verture hereof whereunto by the acceptation of these presents he binds and obliges Himself consenting to the registration hereof in the books of Council and Session or any other Judges books competent in Scotland therein to remain for preservation and thereunto I constitute the said Mr. Mathew McKell Advocate my Procurator.

"In Witness whereof I have written and subscribed these presents at Rome the fourth day of Aprile old stile in the year of God One thousand seven hundred and twenty one.

"(Signed) ANDREW HAY.

"Extracted on this and the two preceding pages by me, Deputy Keeper of the Records of Scotland.

"(Signed) GEORGE A. J. LEE.

"The principal Deed above extracted is impressed with a Duty of sixpence.
"Certified by me,
"GEORGE A. J. LEE."

Impressed with the official seal, "Ab Archivis Publicis Scotiae."

"1756. January 28th.—Testament Testamentary and Inventory of the goods, etc., of Isabel Balfour, widow of Thomas Hay, Writer in Edinburgh, thereafter in Cupar, in the parish of Cupar and sheriffdom of Fife, who died on —— given up by Mrs. Jean Hay, daughter of the said Isabel Balfour, and spouse of Dr. George Bethune, physician in Cupar of Fife, in terms of a Disposition by the Defunct to her which is engrossed, etc., bears that Isabel Balfour, widow of Thomas Hay, Writer in Edinburgh, for the love and affection which she bears to Jean Hay, only daughter now in life procreated between her and the said deceased Thomas Hay, assigns to her all her effects and other goods of which she may die possessed, appointing her sole executrix to her, but reserving the power to alter. —Dated at Edinburgh 2 Feb. 1734. Witnesses:—Andrew Marjoribanks of that Ilk and Thomas Boyes, Writer in Edinburgh.

"The Estate is valued to 1524:17:8 pounds and consists of debts due to her, made up as follows: Bill dated 19 July 1723, drawn by Helen Gordon, widow of James Pitcairn, Writer in Edinburgh, and accepted by the said Thomas Hay for 6:8:6 pounds sterling with interest; and it is said there is a decreet at the instance of the said Helen Gordon against Michael, Andrew, and Jean Hay and their tutors and curators, as representing the deceased Thomas Hay, their father, before the sheriff of Fife, dated 12th Feb. 1734, decreeing them to pay to her the said sum and interest due thereupon.

"To this sum the said Isabel Balfour has right by the latter's will and testament of the said Helen Gordon, in which she appoints the said Isabel Balfour, her only Executor, which testament is dated 5 April 1723, which sum was due to the said Isabel Balfour at the time of her death, with 500 pounds Scots as the expenses of the said Thomas Hay's funeral, and fourteen pounds sterling for mourning to the said Thomas Hay's children and 200 merks for the maintenance of these children from 28th January then last, being the day of the said Thomas Hay's death, to the term of Whitsunday then next, and which three sums last above mentioned are contained in a decree of cognition obtained before the Commissary of St. Andrews * * * * * * against the said Michael, Andrew, and Jean Hay, dated 28 November 1733.

"Confirmed 28 January 1756. John Pilmore, Writer in St. Andrews, cautioner. (Register of Edinburgh Testaments, Vol. 22)"

It will be noted that the witnesses to Isabel's will are Andrew Marjoribanks and Thomas Boyes, who, it will be seen by reference to the table in Section XIX, were nephews of the testator's husband, Thomas Hay, and sons of Christian and Grizel, daughters of James Hay of Carriber. The date of Thomas Hay's death is likewise given in the will as having been 28th Jan. 1733, while his wife Isabel Balfour died A. D. 1756.

We shall next give abstracts from documents which will show the lineage of Isabel Balfour, reserving for the next section of our work, two deeds of renunciation—one by Michael Hay, dated Kingston, Jamaica, 1757, the other by "Jean Hay, spouse of Dr. George Bethune," dated 1757, at Cupar, Fife, executed in the year following their mother's death. The abstract follows:—

"Disposition by Thomas Hay, Writer in Edinburgh, narrating that Andrew Hay of Mugdrum (his brother german) had paid to him 5,000 merks, and therefore he sells to him and his heirs and assignees, the lands of Bridgehouse in the parish of Logie, and shire of Fyfe, and assigns to him the dispositions of the lands and teinds granted by the deceased Sr. James Ramsay of Logie, with consent of Dame Lilias Seton his spouse and David, Robert, William, and Margaret Ramsay, his children, to the deceased Sir David Balfour of Forret, one of the Senators of the College of Justice, dated 23d August 1682 and 2d April 1684.

"This disposition is dated at Cupar 6th February, 1729, one witness being Michael Balfour of Forret. (Durie, Vol. 219.)"

"1691, November 27th.—Sasine, 2d October, of Mrs. Marie Hay, lawful daughter of Peter Hay, elder of Leyes, (by her Attorney, George Wilson, servitor to Michell Balfour of Forret) upon her contract of marriage with Mr. James Balfour of Randerstoun, dated 21st Nov. 1690, in an annual rent out of the lands of Randerstoun in liferent; among the witnesses to the contract being Michael Balfour of Forret, James Arnot of Woodmiln, Mr. Peter Hay, younger of Leyes, etc. (Fife Sassines Vol. 15.)

"1692, June 10th.—Sasine, 7th June, of Barbara Hay, second lawful daugh-

THE FAMILY OF HAY

ter of the deceased John Hay of Parish in terms of her contract of marriage with George Hay of Mortoun, in the half lands of Mortoun, in the parish of St. Fillans, Fife, in life rent."

"Testament Testamentary of Mrs. Ann Hay, 3d lawful daughter of the deceased Mr. Peter Hay of Leyes, in the parish of Errol and sheriffdom of Perth, who died in June, 1702, given up by Helen Hay her sister german, widow of the deceased John Pilmore (it is to be observed that John Pilmore was cautioner for the will of Isabel Balfour-Hay), sometime merchant in Dundee as her executrix. * * * * * * She appoints her said sister german her executrix and leaves the following legacies:—To Ann Hay, lawful daughter of Peter Hay of Leyes, her lawful brother, 1000 merks, or should she die before marriage or attaining the age of twenty one years, then to George Han, second lawful son to the said Peter; to Anna Balfour, lawful daughter of Mr. James Balfour of Randerstoun, 1000 merks, and failing her as above to Jean Balfour, her eldest sister, and failing both to the other children procreated between Mr. James (Balfour) and Marie Hay, his spouse, her sister * * * * * * This is dated—Leyes 15th January 1702, among the witnesses being Alexander Drummond, lawful son of Adam Drummond.

"Confirmed 18th May 1705, Robert Pilmuir, merchant in Dundee, cautioner. (Vol. 16.)"

"Sasine of Mr. James Balfour in the lands and barony of Randerstoun. He is 2d lawful son of Sir David Balfour of Forret, Knight, one of the Senators of Justice.

"The destination is to the said Mr. James Balfour and his heirs male and female; whom failing to Michael Balfour, eldest lawful son to Sir. Andrew Balfour, M.D., Knight (probably a brother of Sir David) and his heirs male lawfully procreated of his body; whom failing also, to Michael Balfour, now of Denmilne, Knight-Baronet (evidently a 2d brother of Sir David Balfour), and his heirs male, etc. (Fife Sassines, Vol. 15.)"

"1737, April 16th.—Factory by Andrew Blair (sic lege Hay) of Bridgehouse, Esq., lawful son to the deceased Thomas Hay of Carriber, Writer, (being to go out of Scotland) to Thomas Trotter, brother german to Henry Trotter of Morton Hall; dated at Edinburgh, 15 Apl. 1737. (Durie Deeds, Vol. 195.)"

"1740, March 20th.—Factory by Andrew Hay of Bridgehouse, narrating that as he resides outside of Scotland, he cannot transact his own business there, and appoints Thomas Trotter (as above) his factor.

"Dated at London, 13 March 1740. (Ibid, Vol. 201.)"

"Testament Dative of Andrew Hay, Esq., of Bridgehouse, residentur in Edinburgh, who died in October 1754, given up by Mrs. Margaret Nicholson, his widow, daughter of Sir. William Nicholson of Glenberry, in whose favor the defunct made a Disposition and Settlement on the 5th of April 1754.

"Mention is made in the deed of Andrew's father, Thomas Hay, Writer in Edinburgh. Alexander Innes was cautioner. (Edinburgh Testaments, Vol. 116.)"

It would appear from the evidence of the foregoing abstracts of wills, inventories, and factories, that Isabel Balfour was the granddaughter of Sir David Balfour of Forret, Knight and Senator of Justice. Sir David Balfour of Forret had two brothers (Sir Andrew, Knight, and Sir Micheal, Knight-Baronet, each of whom had a son Michael) and two sons—Michael Balfour and James Balfour of Randerstoun, who married Marie, daughter of Mr. Peter Hay of Leyes. (The Earls of Kinnoul were descended from Peter Hay of Leyes, as also the James Hays, Earls of Carlisle.)

Isabel Balfour was a daughter of either the eldest of the above sons of Sir David Balfour, Michael, or of the second son James Balfour of Randerstoun, it is not certain which one.

The lands of Bridgehouse (an estate three miles west of Bathgate, in Linlithgowshire, not far from the lands and castle of Carriber), and other property originally belonging to Sir James Ramsay of Logie, were alienated to Sir David Balfour of Forret, and descended to Thomas Hay of Carriber, Writer in Edinburgh, through his marriage to Isabel Balfour, granddaughter of Sir David.

Bridgehouse was then alienated by Thomas Hay to his brother Andrew Hay of Mugdrum, after the latter's return from Italy, for 5,000 merks, and Andrew Hay of Mugdrum leaves this property to his nephew (and probable namesake) Andrew, 2d son of his brother Thomas Hay, who, on his death, disposed and settled them on his wife Margaret, daughter of Sir William Nicholson of Glenberry; we do not know whether Andrew left any children. (This Andrew was the uncle of Colonel Ann Hawkes Hay.) Neither do we know what was the lineage of Sir. David Balfour of Forret, Knight and Senator of the College of Justice, but it should not be difficult to establish.

Thomas Hay of Bridgehouse (sometimes designated of Carriber), 4th son of James Hay of Carriber, had the following children by his spouse Isabel Balfour, granddaughter of Sir David Balfour of Forret, Knight and Senator of Justice:—

 i. Michael Hay, whose history follows in Section XXI.
 ii. Andrew Hay of Bridgehouse, who married Margaret, a daughter of Sir William Nicholson of Glenberry, and d. A. D. 1754.
 iii. Jean Hay, who married Dr. George Bethune of Cupar and Kingask, in Fifeshire, son of Dr. James Bethune by his wife Ann Hatray, whom he married A. D. 29th April 1704, daughter of the celebrated Dr. Sylvester Hatray by his spouse Helen Inglis.
   Dr. George Bethune was the first Grand Master of the St. Regulus

Masonic Lodge of St. Andrews, and was succeeded in that office by the Earl of Elgin. He was of a celebrated family of Bethunes (or Beatons), hereditary physicians to the Lords of the Isle, and is supposed to be of the family of Maximilian Bethune, Duke of Sully, the great Minister of France in the reign of Henry IV.

Janet Bethune (or Beaton) is prominent in Scot's "Lay of the Last Minstrel."

The property of Kingask in Fifeshire had been possessed by James Hay, Earl of Carlise, in 1598; and descended to Agnes Hay, Countess of Glencairn, his daughter. It was possessed in 1710 by Thomas Bethune, in 1720 by Dr. James Bethune, and descended to his son Dr. George Bethune, who sold it to Sir Philip Anstruther.

Dr. George Bethune, whose coat armor bore an otter's head erased and whose crest was a physician's cap, died in February, 1774, and was buried with masonic honors. His widow, Jean Hay, died A. D. 1778, and had three children:—i. Margaret Bethune, b. 1740; ii. James Bethune, b. 1743; and iii. a daughter, born 1746.

Twenty-first Generation

MICHAEL HAY, GENTLEMAN OF KINGSTON, JAMAICA, was the oldest son of Thomas Hay of Bridgehouse, Writer in Edinburgh, by his spouse, Isabel Balfour, granddaughter of Sir. David Balfour of Forret. He married 2d in Jamaica Esther, daughter of Judge Martin Wilkins.

It has been suggested to us in our Scotch correspondence by one of his name, that he was involved in the political differences of 1715, and after the Battle of Preston, leaving Scotland, took refuge in the West Indies. His kinsmen the Earls of Carlisle and Kinnoul had been Governors of Barbadoes.

It will be seen by referring to Section XVIII, No. 3, that Judge Graham went to Carlise at his own expense, to defend his grandson David Bruce (sic lege Hay) and other young gentlemen who had engaged in the rising of 1715, and been taken prisoners at Preston. The above mentioned David was a cousin of Michael, from the same neighborhood, and we believe it probable that Michael was out for the Stewart in the "rising." His name appears in the records of the West Indies for the first time about 1740. John Hay of Restalrig was active in the insurrection of 1745, and present at Culloden, where he held the position of Secretary and Treasurer for Prince Charles Edward; after that defeat, so disastrous to the cause of the Stewarts, John Hay was forced to flee the country.

A story is told relating an incident of the pretty little Scotch lass, Grizel (or Grace) Hay, who, escaping secretly from the house for several days with food hidden beneath her hood, kept her uncle John Hay from starvation, until the vigilance of Cumberland's butchers slept, and her charge made a safe escape from his refuge in a tomb.

At times she was followed by the soldiers, but a precocious feminine shrewdness, and high courage born of affection and loyalty, enabled her to elude the human sleuth-hounds following in her trail; boldly confronting them, she baffled their curiosity by her girlish wit. Or, perhaps — to the honor of manhood — his henchmen were not so eager for the blood of a passive victim as their master, and Cumberland must be satisfied by the assumption on the part of his followers of a vindictiveness that hid in them a generous mercy foreign to his unfeeling heart.

What we have learned of Michael Hay in the Island of Jamaica can be most explicitly set forth by extracting from the ample documents supplied us by our faithful and very intelligent agent Mrs. Laura Nichols Graham, whose address at present is "The Cumberland," Washington. She was not the first lady who journeyed to the West Indies on such a mission, but the result was more gratifying than that of Gertrude Atherton seeking the paternity of Alexander Hamilton, whose father was a kinsman of Michael Hay.

On the 28th of May, 1901, writing from the Hotel Essex, Boston, Massachusetts, Mrs. Graham announces her intention of sailing the following day on the "Admiral Farragut," of the United Fruit Company's Line, for Port Antonio, Jamaica, the remainder of the journey to be made by rail.

We extract from her report of about one month later:

"New York City, 2d July 1901.

"Dear Mr. Colcock,

"After a charming trip of five days, I arrived in Kingston early Tuesday morning, and almost immediately set out to the Parish Church. * * * * * Assisted by the Archdeacon, Mr. Downer, and his servant, I began my search for the tombstone, which lasted three burning afternoons before success was met. It must have been a pathetic sight to see me out in the churchyard in the broiling sun, sweeping the old tombstones which lay flat and half covered by soil and leaves. Just as I was giving up in despair, I paused in the centre aisle of the dimly lighted church for a moment, and glancing down at my feet saw the name "Grant" on an almost obliterated tombstone of white marble, forming a part of the floor. I was standing on it!

"All that is discernible of the coat-of-arms is the left side of the shield, surrounded by an oak wreath. * * * * * The names of Martha Grant, Michael Hay, and Isabella Richmond, having been perhaps more deeply chiseled than the rest of the inscription, were perfectly readable, but the rest is more or less worn by the feet of many generations of parishioners, being in the centre aisle of the church. The location of this vault proves that the persons who lie there were people of prominence in Kingston. * * * * * * This tombstone is now partially protected from further wear by benches fastened to the floor, placed there since the church was rebuilt. * * * * * *

"About nine feet to the right of this tombstone is that of William Hay of Westmoreland. Between them lies Waterhouse of Fernelly, Esq., who was born about the same year as William Hay, and his crest is a dog holding something in its mouth. To the left of Michael lies Dr. Samuel Knight, and Bassilia Hawkes is buried nearer the main entrance.

'The gentlemen upon whom I called for advice and assistance from time to time, and from whom I received the greatest courtesy, were:—Mr. Twells, Vice-Consul, acting for Mr. Watts; Mr. W. Anthony Baker of the Surveyor-General's Office; Mr. Frank Cundall, Secretary of the Jamaica Institute; O'Conner DeCordova, Registrar of the Supreme Court; Mr. S. P. Smeeton, Registrar-General of the Island Record Office, at Spanish Town; and Archbishop George W. Downer of the Parish Church.

"I found it necessary to go out to Spanish Town where the earliest records are kept. The Church of England registers of the different parishes, recopied, together with the wills and deeds, constitute the only vital records of the Island. Of many of the parishes, 1750 is the earliest record, that of Kingston being one of the earliest. Many of the parishes have been amalgamated, and this makes the work of searching more complex. There is now no St. Dorothy, but it is possible that Hay's Savannah, now in Clarendon, was formerly in that parish.

"There were Hawkes in Port Royal, and Michael Hay owned lands there. A land patent in Port Royal was granted to one, John Hay, 15th Sept. 1668.

"I am inclined to believe that Michael Hay had no living relatives in Jamaica except those mentioned in his will. * * * * * He mentions his sister Jean, who married Dr. George Bethune of Cupar in Fife, Scotland. The Bethunes are of noble lineage, and are now known as the Lindsay-Bethunes. It would seem that the Ballards, Ellises, and Beckfords, all eminent families in Jamaica, were connected with the Lindsay-Bethunes, as Sir David Lindsay of Evelick, subsequent to 1752, married Susanna Charlotte Long, widow of George Ellis, while Edward Long married Mary Ballard, daughter of Thomas Beckford. * * * * * *

'Michael Hay appears in Jamaica records about the time of his marriage to Esther, only daughter of Judge Martin Wilkins and wife Ann. She was the widow of John Sharpington. His marriage to Ann seems to have brought additional lands to his already large estate, and her property descends to Ann Hawkes Hay through the will of his grandfather Wilkins.

"Upon the death of his wife Ann, Martin Wilkins married Johanna Roberts, 'a gentlewoman of Vere,' who (probably) outlived him. She was the mother of Isaac Wilkins, and three other children; the latter died young.

"The sister of Judge Martin Wilkins, Mrs. Ann Mister, who was a widow for many years, left her property to Ann Hawkes Hay, and she is doubtless the great-aunt for whom he was named Ann.

"The name of Hawkes I cannot trace in the family. That there was an Ann

Hawkes in Jamaica is proved by the burial record of 'Edward Hawkes' the property of Ann in Port Royal, 2d Nov. 1737. * * * * * *

"You will see that I have copied the wills of Michael Hay and Martin Wilkins and abstracted the wills and deeds of the contemporary Hays in Jamaica. The records are ample, and I could have spent another fortnight to advantage. * * * * * * That the estates of Ann Hawkes Hay in Jamaica were valuable is proven by the fact that two suits in Chancery were sustained by them—proceedings at that time no less expensive and tedious than at the present day. * * * * * * Michael Hay, after wife Esther's death, married Elizabeth Webb, widow of Archibald Campbell, who was Assistant Governor of Jamaica. His signature, dated 1780 or 90, thereabouts, is preserved at the Jamaica Institute. Of this marriage there was no issue, but Mary Campbell of Scotland may have been her daughter by her first marriage.

"Michael Hay owned property in the parishes of Saint Dorothy, Saint Andrew, Saint David, Port Royal, and the parish and town of Kingston. He was administrator of the estate of Martin Wilkins (although his widow Johanna was appointed in the will) and was guardian of Isaac Wilkins. He was likewise administrator of the estate of his wife Elizabeth's grandmother, Elizabeth Villers; and was duly appointed guardian of his son Ann Hawkes Hay, for whom he held in trust the estates of Martin Wilkins and Ann Mister.

"Michael Hay's daughter Isabella (named undoubtedly for his mother Isabel Balfour) married Walter Richmond, and died soon after, probably without children, as no Richmond baptisms could be found during the period of their marriage.

"At her death, her interest in the Hay estate ceased; her husband remarried. I could not find his will. Nor could I find wills of Isabella Richmond, or Johanna Wilkins, as married females could not devise property at that time.

"The last record of Ann Hawkes Hay in Jamaica was A. D. 1771. * * * * * * Could not find will of Mary Patty Macey's deceased husband Thomas; he must have died elsewhere.

"Did not find marriage of Dr. George Bethune and Jean Hay, but will write to Cooper in Fife with a view of learning her father's name. Will also try through Demarara and New York records to learn the parentage of Dr. George Bethune and his brother Divie (David), mentioned in "Duffeld Family."

"Spring Garden Estate is one of the most prosperous in the Island. The old maps at the Surveyor-General's office show two tracts of land in the name of Hay, adjoining Spring Garden in St. Dorothy's, now held by the heirs of Charles Verley, who died while I was in Kingston. Hunt's Bay is quite near Kingston. * * * * * * The nearest railway station to Hay's Savannah is May Pen. * * * * * * There appears in the old maps an estate called 'Willikyns,' forming part of Bushy Park. Martin Wilkins was the proprietor of Nightingale Pen and Old Pen in the Savannah (later called Hay's Savannah). * * * * * *

"Although Ann Hawkes Hay made many transfers of his property, I fancy they were for the most part leases. The 99 years' lease made by his own grandmother, Ann, expired in 1817. (After his death.) I believe there is property in Jamaica which rightfully belongs to the heirs of Colonel Hay.

"I found it necessary to go back and forth to Spanish Town every day, as the local accommodations were poor. By taking the train leaving Kingston at 7:30 in the morning, I was able to spend six hours each day at the Record Office, returning at 5:30, and reaching the hotel in time for dinner. This was my life in Jamaica—working all the time, with an occasional afternoon at the Library Office of the Institute, or seeking information elsewhere. I have taken the liberty of including the cost of these trips among my items of expense which I submit to you for approval.

"At last I have found the motto 'Laboranti Palma' among the Hay crests. In Fairbairn's 'Crests of Great Britain and Ireland,' appears 'Hay. Scotland, An arm from elbow, in hand an ox yoke with bows gu. Motto: Laboranti Palma.' * * * * * *

"Yours very respectfully,
"Laura S. N. Graham."

Not far from the vault that holds the remains of Michael, the father of Colonel Ann Hawkes Hay, is the stone over the dust of Basilia Hawkes, and on this stone is written the following inscription:—

"Here lyes Basilia Hawkes
who died after her Brother Richard the 17th Feb. 1739.
"Go; fair example of untainted youth,
Of modest wisdom and pacific truth,
Compos'd in suffering and in joy sedate,
Good without Noise, without Pretention Great;
Just of thy word, in every thought sincere,
Who knew no wish but that the world might hear;
Of softest manners, unaffected mind;
Lover of Peace, and friend of Human kind,
Go, live! for Heaven's Eternall Year is thine.
Go, and Exalt thy Morall to Divine.
And thou blest Maid, attendant on his doom,
Pensive hast followed to the Silent Tomb,
Steer'd the same course to the same quiet Shore,
Not parted long, and now to part no more.
Go, then! where only Bliss Sincere is known,
Go, where to live and to enjoy are one!
Yett take these tears, Mortality's relief,
And till I share your joys, forgive my grief.
These little Rites; a stone, a verse receive,
They are all a Mother, all a Friend can give."

The Will and Codicil of Michael Hay

"In the name of God Amen. I, Michael Hay, of the Parish of St. Andrews, in the Island of Jamaica, Esquire, being in good health and of perfect mind and memory, do make this my last Will and Testament in manner following:

THE FAMILY OF HAY

"First, I desire that all my just debts and Funeral expenses be fully paid and satisfied. Item: I give and bequeath unto my friend James Alves of the Parish of Kingston, Gentleman, the house in which he lives, with the appurtenances, Situate in Princess Street in the Town of Kingston, To hold to him during his natural life and afterward to revert to my Heir at Law hereinafter named. Item: I give and bequeath unto Isabella Hay, the Daughter of Ann Main late of the Parish of Kingston the yearly sum or annuity of eighty pounds Current Money of Jamaica to be paid to her out of the Rents and Profits of my estate during her natural life by two equal half-yearly payments, the first payment to be made six months after my decease and so forth thereafter, and I do Hereby Charge and Subject my whole Estate real and personal to the payment of the said annuity to the said Isabella Hay. Item: I give, devise and bequeath all the rest and residue and remainder of my Estate both real and personal or of whatever kind or quality the same may be, unto my son Ann Hawkes Hay, and to the heirs of his body lawfully to be begotten forever.

"But in case my said son shall happen to die before he attains his age of Twenty one years, and without lawful issue, or in case after his attaining the age of Twenty one years, he shall happen to die without disposing of my said real estate bequeathed to him, then and in that case, I give and bequeath one full moiety or Equal Half Part of my said real and personal estate unto the several children of my sister Jane Bethune, the wife of Dr. George Bethune of Cooper in Fife, in that part of Great Britain called Scotland, begotten or to be begotten, to be equally divided among them, share and share alike, and to their heirs forever; and the other moiety or equal half of my said estate, I give and devise and bequeath unto the above named Isabella Hay to hold to her and the heirs of her body for ever, but in case the said Isabella Hay shall happen to die without lawful issue, then I give, devise and bequeath the moiety of my Estate so bequeathed to her, unto the said children of my said sister Jane, to be equally divided among them share and share alike in the same manner with the other moiety of my said Estate bequeathed to them as aforesaid. * * * * * *

"And I do hereby nominate and appoint Henry Livingston and John McLean both of the Parish of Kingston in the Island aforesaid, merchants, Executors of this my last Will and Testament, and Guardians of my said son Ann Hawkes Hay until he shall attain the age of twenty one years, and I hereby revoke all former wills by me heretofore made, and declare this to be my last Will and Testament.

"In witness whereof I, the said Michael Hay the Testator have hereunto set my hand and seal this Twenty Sixth Day of April in the year of our Lord one thousand seven hundred and fifty nine (1759).

MICH: HAY (Seal)"

"Witnesses: James Brown; Robert Gordon; John Stancliffe.
"Proved, 19th August 1762, by James Brown, before W. H. Lyttelton.
(Island Record Office, Spanish Town, Jamaica, West Indies: Wills: Liber 34, folios 12 and 13; Enr. 19th August 1762, Jamaica Island.)

Codicil

"I, Michael Hay, of the Parish of St. Andrew, in the Island of Jamaica aforesaid, Esquire, do make and publish this Codicil to my last Will and Testament in manner and form following:—

"Imprimis, I give unto Dr. John Kydd of the Parish of Kingston and Martha, his wife, and unto my daughter Isabella Hay, the sum of Forty Pistoles each, to buy them mourning. Item: I give also and bequeath unto the said Martha Kydd and the said Isabella Hay the rents issues and profits of the Penn commonly called or known by the name of Tittles Penn, now leased to me by Daniel Moore, to have receive take and enjoy the same during the remainder of the term therein yet to come, free and clear of and from the payment of the rent reserved to be paid for the same to the said Daniel Moore; and I hereby subject my other Estate with the payment of the said rent and every part thereof. I also give unto the said Martha Kydd and Isabella Hay all the furniture belonging to me at the said Penn, together with all the Sheep, Goats, and Small Stock thereon, to be to them their Executors administrators and assigns in equal proportions Share and Share alike. And I likewise give unto them, the said Martha Kydd and Isabella Hay, the use of the following negroes (my own property) during the remainder of the term of the said lease yet to come, videlicet, Monimia, Sarah, Celia, and Eve, with their increase, and from and after the termination of the said lease, I will that the said negroes do revert and become a part of my residuary Estate.

"Item: I give unto the said Martha Kydd one piece of plate belonging to me called the Jorum-Cup and Cover. I give unto the said Dr. John Kydd my New England Horse and Kittoreen and likewise one small Bay Horse now at Mount Pelior Estate in the Parish of St. David. And lastly it is my desire that this Codicil be annexed to and taken as part of my Last Will and Testament. In Witness whereof I have hereunto set my hand and affixed my seal this first day of February in the year of our Lord one thousand seven hundred and sixty two.

"MICHAEL HAY.

"Witnesses: William Forbes; David Thomas; Campbell Scrogie."

It will be observed in the will of Michael Hay that he refers to a daughter by Ann Main, whom he provides with an annuity of about $450, together with the profits, rents, live stock and negro slaves of Tyttles Penn, which last is to be divided with Martha, wife of Dr. John Kydd. It is probable that Martha Kydd was a sister of Ann Main, and aunt of Isabella Hay, who was entrusted to her care on her mother's death. The names of Kydd, Alves, Forbes, Gordon, Campbell, Livingstone, M'Lean, are found among the landed gentry around Edinburgh, Scotland, and it is not unlikely that some of them came to Jamaica at the same time and under the same circumstances as did Michael, and friendships existed between them in the mother country.

THE FAMILY OF HAY

In his will Michael devises one-half of his estate, under certain conditions, to the children of "my sister Jane Bethune, wife of Dr. George Bethune in Cooper, Fife, in that part of Great Britain called Scotland." Compare this with the will of Isabel Balfour, who speaks of her husband Thomas Hay, Writer in Edinburgh, and their children: Michael, Andrew, and Jean, spouse of Dr. George Bethune in Cupar, Fife, and with the two documents given below, and it will be seen that the parentage of Michael Hay is established beyond any question, while that of his father Thomas is proved by the Factory of Andrew his brother, son of James Hay of Carriber, to be seen in the preceding section of this work. It will be recalled that Isabel Balfour-Hay d. in 1756. We now introduce these two deeds, sent by Mr. Henry Paton:—

"1757, January 12th.—Registration in Register of Deeds (Durie, Vol. 216) of Renunciation by Michael Hay, eldest lawful son and apparent heir to the deceased Thomas Hay, Writer in Edinburgh, narrating that he has been charged at the instance of Rachel and Katherine Erskine, daughter of the deceased Mr. Thomas Erskine, Advocate, to enter heir to the said deceased Thomas Hay, his father, * * * * * but that he, seeing that by serving himself heir may incur great damage, rather renounces his right as heir to his said father's estate and property. Dated at Kingston in the Island of Jamaica 27th April 1756; witnesses, Robert Forester of the Parish of Kingston, merchant there, and William Forbes of the said parish, gentleman."

"1757, January 11th.—Renunciation by Mrs. Jane Hay, daughter to the deceased Thomas Hay, Writer in Edinburgh, spouse to Dr. George Bethune, physician in Cupar of Fife, narrating that they have been charged at the instance of James Blair of Ardblair and David Green, Writer in Edinburgh, to enter heir to the said deceased Thomas Hay, her father, which if she do she will incur great damage thereby. She therefore, with her said husband's consent, discharges herself to enter heir to her said father. This is dated at Cupar, Fife, 5th January 1757. (Edinburgh Deeds, Vol. 107)."

Rachel and Catherine Erskine, mentioned in the Renunciation of Michael Hay, were born the one in 1728, the other in 1729, and were the youngest of seven children of Thomas Erskine, advocate, and Rachel Liberton. It is interesting to observe that Thomas Erskine, their father, was a son of Henry Erskine, third Lord Cardross, of Kirkhill, County Linlithgow, and of Uphall, West Lothian, who established a colony at Beaufort, South Carolina, which was destroyed by the Spaniards. Broken in fortune, but not dispirited by misfortune, he returned to Europe, attaching himself to the friends of liberty in Holland. He died at Edinburgh 21 May 1693, in the 44th year of his age. He was a distant kinsman of Michael Hay.

The family of Grant in Jamaica was one of considerable distinction. Their arms were: Gule, a chevron eng. ermine between three antique crowns or. Crest, a mountain in flames, sometimes described as a burning hill.

John Grant was Chief Justice of Jamaica. Sir Alexander Grant, Bart., was the proprietor of Charlemont Pen (grass farm), near Iry Sugar Estate in St. Thomas; also one of the proprietors of Bryan Castle, Great House, Trelawny, originally settled by Bryan Edwards, Esq., Historian of the West Indies.

In Liber 29, Folio 67, of Jamaica Wills, is registered the testament of the mother of Mrs. Alexander Grant of Jamaica, Ann Mister, widow (nee Ann Wilkins), in which "all lands owned by her in any part of the world are left to Michael Hay, in trust for her great-nephew, Ann Hawkes Hay, until the latter shall become of age; and five hundred pounds in cash to Isaac, son of her brother Martin Wilkins, deceased. In case Isaac shall survive Ann Hawkes Hay, then Isaac shall receive," etc.

Wilkins

The family of Wilkins in Jamaica was descended of an eminent family of that name in Wales. They were related to Oliver Cromwell, Protector of England, and the branch of the family which settled in Jamaica removed from Glamorganshire, Wales.

Judge Martin Wilkins was one of the five Assistant Judges for the Island under the Act of 1744, and a wealthy planter possessed of large estates and many slaves.

He married 1st 10 Nov. 1718, Ann Pichell, the widow of John Sharpington, son of Benjamin Sharpington by his wife Elizabeth Wilsted, by whom he had an only child, Esther Wilkins, baptised 4th July 1724, married 14 June 1743, Michael Hay, and died 25 Aug. 1745, leaving one son Ann Hawkes Hay, of whom later.

Judge Wilkins m. 2d on May 2d, 1733, Johanna, daughter of Thomas and Johanna Roberts, and granddaughter of Philip Roberts of the Parish of Vere, by whom he had children: i. Martina, bap. 16 Feb. 1738; ii. Isaac; iii. Philip, bap. 6 Sept. 1744; iv.

THE FAMILY OF HAY

Thomas Lindsay, bap. 7 Jan. 1746. His will is dated 1750 and proved 1750, when he must have died.

The father of Judge Martin Wilkins was Isaac Wilkins, deceased, ante 1700, and his godfather was Martyn Wilkins of the Parish of St. Andrews, who married Mary Wilkins (vide Wills: Liber 9, folio 119, Jamaica records).

Isaac Wilkins, clergyman, only surviving son of Judge Martin Wilkins, by his 2d wife Johanna Roberts, and half-brother of Esther, who married Michael Hay, was born at Withewood, Jamaica, W. I., Dec. 1742, and d. at Westchester, N. Y., 5th Feb. 1830.

Sent to New York by his father to be educated, he was graduated at Columbia University (then King's College) A. D. 1760.

His parents dying when he was a child, his care devolved upon his maternal aunt, Mary Macey, wife of Thomas Macey.

He was m. 7 Nov. 1762, to Isabella, daughter of the Hon. Lewis Morris, son of Lewis Morris by his wife Isabella, daughter of Sir John Graham. He resided at Morisania for a few years after marriage and then purchased an estate known as Castle Hill in Westchester County, N. Y., and was a member of the Colonial Legislature in 1772.

When trouble arose between England and her American colonies, he boldly and openly proclaimed his allegiance to England, and was forced to leave the country in 1775, seeking refuge in England, and was allowed by the British Government an annuity of 125 pounds. Returning to New York before the close of the War of Independence, he sold his property in Westchester, and resided in Long Island until the return of peace. In 1784, he removed to Nova Scotia and took an active part in political affairs. He went back to New York again in 1794, studied for the Episcopal ministry, was ordained Deacon of the Church in Westchester, A. D. 1798, and soon called to the Rectorship; was ordained Priest in the same church 14 January 1801, and received the degree of Doctor of Divinity from Columbia A. D. 1811.

Lewis Morris Wilkins, son of Isaac Wilkins, D. D., was a member of the House of Assembly of Nova Scotia, Speaker of that body, and Judge of the Supreme Court.

Lewis Morris Wilkins, Jr., son of the above, was b. 24th May

1801 at Halifax, Nova Scotia, and d. 14 March 1885, having been graduated at King's College in 1819, and studied law, becoming an eminent Canadian Jurist.

Among the descendants of this family in South Carolina were and are: Martin, Berkeley, Gouveneur, and Sarah Wilkins—the latter still living in Charleston, S. C., and children of Gouveneur, recently deceased, residing at Greenville, S. C. The first wife of Major Screven of South Carolina was a member of this family of Wilkins, his 2d wife being Miss Van Rensselaer of N. Y.

Will of Judge Martin Wilkins

"In the name of God Amen. I, Martin Wilkins, of the Parish of St. Dorothy, in the Island of Jamaica, Planter, being of sound mind and memory do make and ordain this my last Will and Testament in manner and form following. Imprimis I will that all my just debts and funeral charges be paid leaving my body to be buried according to the discretion of my dearly beloved Executrix hereinafter mentioned. To my much respected sister Ann Mister I give twenty-five pounds to buy her a suit of mourning being sensible that with her Estate she can want no more from mine. To my wife's sister Mary Macey, widow, I give a Ring of five pounds value for her remembrance of me. To my dear and only grandson Ann Hawkes Hay and to his heirs forever, not excluding any right my son may have after my said grandson's death, I give all the lands and Negro Slaves with their issue and increase mentioned in an Indenture Tripartite, copy herewith, signed by his grandmother Ann Wilkins, Adam McQuestin, and myself, the nineteenth day of January in the year of our Lord one thousand seven hundred and nineteen, without taking advantage of any other writing, and without charging him, my said grandson, with the several Bonds, lare Debts, and a Chancery Suit I have paid since that time from my own Estate to satisfye the debts due from his grandmother's, the above lands and negroe slaves, provided no trouble, charges, or disputes, of any kind whatsoever by his Guardians, Himself, or Anybody in his stead, be given or made to my wife or son in regard to anything done by me in my lifetime. To my dearly beloved wife Johanna Wilkins I give for ever my Chariot, all my plate, jewels, household furniture, and half of my ready Cash, with half of what money which shall any ways be due to me by mortgage, bonds, notes, or accounts; I also give to my said wife during her natural life and whilst she continues my widow, the one half of the rent of my estate both real and personal not meaning any part of the above remaining moiety of cash, mortgage, bonds, notes, or accounts, wheresoever it be in any part of the world in lieu of her thirds. All the rest of my Estate both real and personal I give and bequeath to my only and most dear son Isaac Wilkins and his heirs forever. But should he die before he arrives to the age of twenty-one years or before he has legitimate issue, then I give to my wife and her heirs for ever all the negro slaves and their issue which were her property before our marriage at that time then living.

Col. Frederick J. Hay, eighth son and youngest child of Col. Ann Hawkes Hay, born at Haverstraw on the Hudson River, New York. A colonel in the War of 1812. (Painted by Fitzsimmons of New York)

Susan Cynthia Brown, wife of Col. Frederick J. Hay
(Painted by Fitzsimmons of New York)

And if both my son and grandson should die before they arrive to the age of twenty-one years or before they have legitimate issue, so far as I have power to devise or bequeath, notwithstanding anything I may have said to the contrary in this Will, this is my Meaning—I then give to my dearly beloved wife and her heirs my whole Estate both real and personal forever.

Lastly I herewith nominate and appoint my dear and good wife Johanna Wilkins whole and sole Executrix of this my last Will and Testament. In witness hereof I the said Martin Wilkins have to this my last Will and Testament and to another of equal date Indenture and Signification in all respect set my hand and seal this nineteenth day of December in the year of our Lord one thousand seven hundred and forty-eight.

MARTIN WILKINS.

Witnesses:—Arundel Burton, Dan Baylie, John Barjean.
(Island Record Office, Spanish Town, Jamaica, W. I.; Wills: Lib. 28, f. 29.)"

The following is extracted from the Indenture Tripartite, or 99-year lease of Ann Sharpington's Estate, which was bequeathed by his grandfather, Martin Wilkins, to his and her grandson, Ann Hawkes Hay. As the lease expired not until 1819, and Colonel Hay died A. D. 1785, and as it is positively known to the present generation of Colonel Hay's descendants—some of his grandchildren still survive—that his heirs never came into this property, it is an interesting question to ask, What became of this property? May not the heirs now living have a just claim on the landed tracts described fully in the lease? Would such claim be barred by the Statute of Limitation under the English law? Would ignorance on the part of the heirs that they had such a claim prevent a defence being set up by the present possessors under the Statute of Limitation? Or were these lands confisciated by Great Britain? These questions are left by the descendant, the historian, to be answered by the descendants of the legal profession.

The document is far too lengthy to be given completely, but we extract from it the important parts:—

A Ninety-nine Year Lease

"Island Record Office, Spanish Town, Jamaica, W. I. Deeds, Lib. 61, f. 53.

"This Indenture Tripartite made the nineteenth day of January in the year of our Lord one thousand seven hundred and nineteen between Martin Wilkins and Ann, his wife, of the one part, Mathias Philip * * * * * of the second part, and Adam McQuisting * * * * * * of the third part; Whereas the said Martin Wilkins and Ann his wife in right of the said Ann is possessed of, entitled to, and interested in several tracts of land and Negro Slaves in the Parish of St. Dorothy in the said Island and elsewhere devised to the said Ann by the last Will and Testament of John Sharpington, her late husband.

Now this Indenture Witnesseth that the said Martin Wilkins and Ann his wife for the better settling and making over all the said Estate, which belongs to them, in right of the said Ann, for and in consideration of five shillings current money of this island to them in hand * * * * * * Have granted Bargained Sold aliened released and confirmed * * * * * * All that parcell of land containing two hundred and ten acres * * * * * lying in the Parish of St. Catherine now St. Dorothy, bounded * * * * * * And also One other parcell of Land containing sixty acres * * * * * * bounding * * * * * and also those two parcells of land the one containing by estimacion sixty acres scituate lying * * * * * * the other parcell containing one hundred and forty acres bounded * * * * * * And also one other parcell of land containing thirty-one acres lying * * * * * * bounding * * * * * * And also all that parcell of land containing by estimacion sixty acres bounding * * * * * *; and also those negro slaves hereinafter named, that is to say:— John, Sam, Pant, Hurry, Tom, Charles, Cesar, Quacoe, Jemmy, Quam, Robin, Dick, Whon, Pegg, Nanny, Venus, Jenny, Rose, Whanny, Dido, Molly, Betty, Mouria, Grace, Priscillas, Dinah, Yabbah, Phibbah, Peter, Quan, Phaenick, Cuffee, Plutarch, Mercury, Hector, Bennebah, Clarinda, Cubba, Venus, Candice, Jibbah, Catalina, Bess; their issue, offspring, and increase. And all the other Estate which they the said Martin and Ann his wife are interested in or entitled to in the said Island of Jamaica or elsewhere in right of the said Ann his wife * * * * * * to have and to hold for the full term of Ninety Nine Years from the day of the date of these presents to be compleat and ended Upon the Trusts Limitations and Agreements hereinafter mentioned and declared concerning the same term and estate.

* * * * * * for the time being of and in the premises expectant upon the determination of the said Term of Ninety Nine Years shall be the true intent and meaning of these presents belong or appertain, surrender and yield up the said Estate and term of Years unto such person or persons requiring the same.

In Witness Whereof the parties first above named have to these presents interchangeably sett their hands and seals the day and year first above written.

"MARTIN WILKINS,
"ANN WILKINS,
"ADAM McQUISTING."

Michael Hay, Esq., m. 14th June 1743, Esther, only daughter of Judge Martin Wilkins by his 1st wife, Ann Sharpington (née Pichell), by whom one son:—

i. Ann Hawkes Hay, whose history follows in Section XXII.

Twenty-second Generation

COLONEL ANN HAWKES HAY, OF KINGSTON, JAMAICA, WEST INDIES, was the only child of Michael Hay, Esq., of Edinburgh, Scotland (removed to Jamaica, W. I.), by his wife Esther Wilkins (m. 14 June 1743), daughter of Judge Martin Wilkins of Jamaica Island by his 1st wife Ann Sharpington (Née Pichell or Pitchell), relict of John Sharpington. Colonel Hay was b. 14th August 1745, baptised on the 29th of the same month and year (Kingston records), and died in New York on the 18th of April 1785, at the age of forty years.

He m. 5th October 1763, Martha Smith (daughter of Judge William Smith, b. 1697 in the Island of Ely, England, who removed to New York in 1715), b. in New York 18 June 1745, and d. in South Carolina 30 March 1821, and was buried at Stoney Creek, near McPhersonville, S. C.

Ann Hawkes Hay accompanied his half-uncle, Isaac Wilkins, but two years older, to New York for the purpose of being educated, and there married while still at college. Returning to Jamaica with his bride, the young couple, both infants in the eyes of the law, at first lived in Kingston, but losing their first three children, they then settled at Haverstraw on the banks of the Hudson.

Soon came war between America and England to disturb their happy and quiet life; refusing two commissions offered him in the English army, Hay united himself with the cause of the patriots, and throughout the seven years of struggle that ensued was zealous and active in support of the land of his adoption.

In the opening years of the Revolution, he commanded a regiment of volunteers, and was entrusted with the defence of the western shore of the Hudson River in the vicinity of Haverstraw, and we find in the American Archives, Fifth Series, many letters from and to him relating to his movements and those of the enemy. Some of these letters are from Generals Washington and Clinton, others from the Legislature and Council of Safety, and prove how earnestly his heart and hopes were embarked in the cause of freedom, how indefatigable he was in its promotion, and in what high esteem he was held by the leaders of the army.

After the disbanding of his volunteers, he was appointed by General Washington to act as Quartermaster, and freely sacrificed his own fortune in providing for the needs of the Continental army. It is a tradition in the family that thus was his property in New York spent, and that what claims he had on lands still in Jamaica were lost to him by confiscation when he cast in his lot with the Americans.

It may be seen by following the births of his younger children born during the War of Independence, he is sometimes stationed at different points on the Hudson, and at others in New Jersey.

He is most complimentarily mentioned (we are told) in Paulding's Life of Washington, and William Abbatt in "The Crisis of the American Revolution" pays a handsome tribute to Colonel Hay.

When the war ended in 1783, Colonel Hay's American property had been lost, except a share in the Dean's Patent, which will be considered presently, and his Jamaica possessions, it is stated, were confiscated by the English Government.

He had no time to recover from the state of desolation in which his fortunes were left by his sacrifices and losses in the war, for he died in 1785 in New York City, leaving a helpless widow, the daughter of wealth and affluence, and eight surviving children, the eldest but seventeen years of age and the youngest one month old.

Judge William Smith, the father of Mrs. Hay, had died in 1769; William Smith, her elder brother, had proclaimed himself a loyalist and was now Chief Justice of Canada; Joshua Hett Smith, another brother, was suspected (unjustly) of having been the accomplice of General Arnold, and had removed to England, where he married Miss Middleton; the home at Haverstraw had been burned during the war; the claims resulting from Colonel Hay's portion of the Dean's Patent (60,000 acres on Grand Island and the shores of Lake Champlain) were in the possession of "squatters" and in litigation. Thus it happened that this was a period of struggle with this family, and while one brother, the eldest, remained in New York, where his descendants are now to be found, the remaining brothers came South, to Alabama and South Carolina.

In South Carolina, one of these brothers practiced law in Beaufort, married, and sent on for his mother and youngest brother, who later made a home in Barnwell District, married and left many children. Descendants of these and of a third brother, who followed later to South Carolina, are now scattered over the State, having always been held in high esteem, and made useful and, in some cases, eminent citizens of this country.

The professions and avocations of these descendants of Colonel Hay are as varied as their homes. Some are found in the high calling of the ministry, others are practitioners at the bar, many are skillful physicians, some insurance men, some fill chairs of learning at the leading educational institutions of the land, some are authors and some artists, while others are planters, directing their efforts to making two blades grow in soil that was wont to produce but one.

Living in an era of commercialism, not emulating others in their mad rush for wealth gained too often by sharp practice and founded too frequently on another's happiness, they are content to live uprightly and modestly, holding their word sacred as their bond.

All of this family in South Carolina that spring from the Hays of Erroll and Lochloy, are lovers of the beautiful in music, poetry, and art. Interpreting into language the hidden harmonies of the forest and its denizens, or giving expression to the lofty emotions of the mind, and the softer feelings of the heart, they reveal the beauty of the souls of things in nature and set to music melodies that lie beneath mere physical sound, translating that life which shines behind the outer world acting as a veil to hide its innate beauty from sight of the profane.

On July 11, 1769, letters patent were issued by King George III. to A. Hawkes Hay, Samuel Smith, his brother-in-law, and others, for 13,500 acres of land in Dean's Patent, in the town of Chazy, in what is now Clinton County, State of New York, and 15,500 acres in what is now known as South Hero Island, in Lake

Champlain, which island belongs to Vermont. This island was formerly called Grand Island. Clinton was divided from Washington County in 1788, and Washington from Tryon County in 1784. In the year 1800, after the death of Colonel Hay, this grant was visited by his sons, Michael and Thomas. They found that portion of the lands located on Grand Isle (formerly Hero Island) occupied under grants from Vermont — this being a part of the disputed territory which had caused the colonial war between New York and New Hampshire, in which Ethan Allen first came into prominence.

Another section lying along Lake Champlain they found occupied by citizens of French descent claiming the land by right of possession, and likewise under the Treaty between Great Britain and France conveying the Canadas and other disputed territory to England, but stipulating that French citizens should remain in possession of lands acquired and enjoyed by them previous to the war.

Michael made terms with some of these "squatters" and settlers, taking possession of what had been unoccupied, and his descendants are still living in that part of New York. In making these terms the sons of Colonel Hay acted under the legal advice of Aaron Burr, who had studied law in the office of their uncle, Joshua Hett Smith, and who on one occasion had risked his own life to save that of young Samuel Hay, who had fallen down a well at Harverstraw, his father's home.

From the number of deeds relating to Ann Hawkes Hay in Jamaica, copied by Mrs. Graham from the records at Spanish Town, we here give abstracts of a few. It will be remembered that Walter Richmond married Isabella, the sister of Colonel Hay, and was made his guardian after the decease of John McLean, who, with Henry Livingston, was guardian under Michael's will.

We introduce a few of these abstracts of deeds registered in Jamaica:—

"Lib. 136, fol. 172, 24th Aug. 1749.—Michael Hay of St. Andrews, Gentleman, transfers to John Barjean et ux, et al. the house Elizabeth Villears bought of Edward Morris in Orange St., Kingston, lately occupied by Dr. Copeland. Mentions his (3d) wife Elizabeth Hay, née Webb, widow of Archibald Campbell."

THE FAMILY OF HAY

"28th Nov. 1749. Lib. 140, fol. 84.—Michael Hay of St. Dorothy, wife Elizabeth, and Ann Mister, widow, deed certain property to Adam McQuisting. Mentions Mary Campbell of Scotland."

"Lib. 155, fol. 89.—Michael Hay, planter of St. Dorothy, Jasper Hall, and John Grant deed 380 acres of land in St. David to Andrew Ronaldson. Witness: James Alves."

"19th Dec. 1748.—Martin Wilkins, Esq., of St. Dorothy, et ux. Johanna lease lands to William Good for 15 years. Refers to Indenture made 19th Jan. 1719, etc. Further sets forth that reversion or remainder of the said * * * * * * being in Ann Hawkes Hay, a minor of the age of three years, the son of Michael Hay who intermarried with his only child and daughter who is now deceased, of the said Martin and Ann his wife, and the grandson of the said Martin Wilkins."

"Lib. 142, fol. 124, 4th Apl. 1750.—Ann Mister, widow, of St. Andrews, deeds lands to John Tod, merchant of Kingston, to the use of Michael Hay of the parish of St. Dorothy, planter, during the term of his natural life. After Michael's decease, John Tod must convey lands unto Ann Hawkes Hay, son of said Michael Hay by Esther his late wife, niece to the said Ann Mister."

"Lib. 162, fol. 108. 1st Feb. 1756.—Ann Hawkes Hay, a minor, by his duly appointed guardian, Michael Hay, planter, leases for 11 years to John Bird, gentleman of St. Dorothy, Hawkes Hill, 81 acres in St. Dorothy, etc."

"Lib. 163, fol. 24. 1st March 1756.—Ann Hawkes Hay, a minor, of the age of ten years, or thereabouts, by Michael Hay, Gentleman of Kingston duly appointed Guardian of his person and Estate, leases 300 acres of land in St. Dorothy called Sharpington Mountain, etc., to John Bonner, for seven years."

"Lib. 223, fol. 21. 9th Feb. 1767.—Ann Hawkes Hay of Kingston, and Martha his wife, deed to John Allen, Gent. of Kingston, certain lands. Mentions will of Ann Mister dated 6th July 1752, devising her entire estate to Michael Hay in trust for Ann Hawkes Hay. Said lands are described as Hunt's Bay Pen, etc. Also Lots 445 and 446 in Kingston—Orange St."

"Lib. 175, fol. 68. 28th Jan. 1759.—Michael Hay, Esq., administrator of the Estate of the Hon. Martin Wilkins, and guardian of his son Isaac Wilkins, a minor, leases certain lands to Anna Spencer, widow, of St. Andrews, and mentions Indenture between John Laugher et ux. Sussannah, and Martin Wilkins, dated 1st July 1742."

"Lib. 193, fol. 21. 27th Nov. 1759.—Michael Hay, Esq., of Kingston, deeds to Thomas Wilson, merchant, his late (3d) wife, Elizabeth's interest in several dwelling houses in parish and town of Kingston, etc. Mentions Indenture made 25th Nov. 1742 by John & Priscilla Innes, Martha, widow of Hugh Williams, and Elizabeth Webb—later wife of Michael Hay (these three were sisters)."

"Lib. 181, fol. 110. 30th Apl. 1760.—Michael Hay, Esq., of Kingston, leases to William Stevenson, Esq., of St. James, for seven years from 1st May 1760, 200 acres of land with buildings, etc., at Hunt's Bay in Parish of St. Andrews, called Hunt's Bay Pen; also a tract of Scotch grass land; also land adjoining Port Royal grass lots in Parish of Port Royal; also the dwelling house now occupied by Michael Hay in Orange St., Kingston; also 136 slaves duly named and appraised.

"The annual rent to be 1333 pounds, to be paid to Michael Hay, his heirs or Assigns." (This rent in annual interest on $100,000 worth of property. Michael died A. D. 1762, and this property is devised to his son Ann Hawkes Hay. It would appear that later a suit is entered against the Estate of Michael Hay by Isaac Wilkins, and by decree of Court of Chancery, this property is ordered for sale, but Ann Hawkes is permitted to redeem it by sale of other property. This Decree was made 20th Feb. 1765, and we now find record of the following sales by Ann Hawkes Hay, presumably to pay off the claim against the above Estate.)

"19th July 1765. Lib. 215, fol. 34.—Ann Hawkes Hay, Gentleman of Kingston, Jamaica, an infant (in law) by Walter Richmond his Guardian, deeds three negro slaves, Prince, Orenoque, and Blackwell, etc."

"Lib. 214, fol. 145. 1st Mch. 1765.—Ann Hawkes Hay, Esq., of Kingston, an infant by Walter Richmond his guardian, and Martha Hay his wife, also an infant, and Walter Richmond in right of Isabella his wife, and sister of Ann Hawkes Hay, beneficiaries under the will of Michael Hay, deed to Robert Law, 3 slaves, etc."

"Lib. 122, fol. 137. 1766. Deed of Gift.—'Know all men by these presents that I, Hawky Hay, Planter of St. Andrew, deed 1½ acres of land to, etc."

"Lib. 222, fol. 169. 9th Jan. 1768.—Ann Hawkes Hay, Esq., of Kingston, and Martha his wife, deed negro slaves to, etc."

"Lib. 218, fol. 116. 19th July 1765.—Ann Hawkes Hay through guardian deeds to William Murray, Esq., of Kingston, Lot No. 1172 for 110 pounds."

"Lib. 217, fol. 23. 1st Mch. 1765.—Ann Hawkes Hay through guardian deeds slave Nannie to Margaret Smith, spinster, for 50 pounds."

"Lib. 217, fol. 24. 1st Mch. 1765.—Ann Hawkes Hay through guardian deeds to John Allen the following negro slaves:— Venus, Teresia, Cuba and her two little children, Charlotte and Charles, for 200 pounds."

"Lib. 215, fol. 41. 19th July 1765.—Ann Hawkes Hay through guardian deeds negro slave Henrietta to, etc., for 37 pounds."

"Lib. 216, fol. 45. 10 July 1765.—Ann Hawkes Hay through guardian deeds two slaves to Alexander Forbes, Gentleman of Kingston, for 151 pounds."

"19th July 1765.—Ann Hawkes Hay, etc., deeds two slaves to Thomas Ingles for 102 pounds."

"Ann Hawkes Hay through guardian Walter Richmond, deeds property to Mr. Nunes and Mr. Silva, for 40 pounds. Mentions death of his guardian John McLean."

"Lib. 225, fol. 163. 22nd Dec. 1767.—Ann Hawkes Hay and wife Martha deed Hunt's Bay Pen to Philip Livingstone Esq. of Kingston."

"Lib. 244, fol. 3. 12th Nov. 1771.—Ann Hawkes Hay, Esq., of Kingston, and Martha his wife, deed to Wm. Patrick Browne 108 acres of land and 50 acres of mountain land. Mentions Capt. Thomas Fuller's Pen."

This is the last mention of Ann Hawkes Hay in records of Jamaica.

THE FAMILY OF HAY

Under marriages in Jamaica we select the following sent us by Mrs. Graham, and relating to Colonel Hay's family:—

"Alexander Grant of Westmoreland to Martha Mister, A. D. 1730."
"Martin Wilkins to Johanna Roberts, 2d May 1733."
"Benj. Sharpington to Elizabeth Wilsted 14th July 1693."
"Martin Wilkins to Ann Sharpington, widow, 16 Apl. 1719."
"John Sharpington to Ann Pitchell, 19 Nov. 1718."
"Michael Hay to Esther Wilkins, 14 June 1743."
"Walter Richmond to Isabella Hay, 15th May 1763."
"Martin Wilkins (god-father of Judge Martin Wilkins) to Mary Wilkins, 20 Jan. 1691."

Under Births and Baptisms

"Martina, dau. of Martin and Johanna Wilkins, 16 Feb. 1738."
"Philip, son to same, 6th Sept. 1744."
"Thomas Lindsay, son to same, 7th Jan. 1746."
"Esther, dau. of Martin & Ann Wilkins, 4 July 1724."
"Ann Hawkes Hay, son of Michael and Esther Hay, 14 June 1745."
"Ann Mister Hay, dau. of Ann Hawkes and Martha Hay, 14 July 1765."
"Mary Hay, dau. of the same, b. 6 Nov. 1766."

From the Record of Interments

"Esther, spouse of Michael Hay, was bu. in the Church, 25th Aug. 1745."
"Elizabeth, 2d spouse of Michael Hay, bu. in churchyard, 11 Sept. 1755."
"Michael Hay, Esq., was bu. in the Church, 13th Feb. 1762."
"Martha, spouse of Alexander Grant, ob. 17th Nov. 1733."
"Isabella, spouse of Walter Richmond, bu. in the Church, 26th Feb. 1772."

Whatever property Ann Hawkes Hay possessed in Jamaica when the Revolutionary War began, seems to have been forfeited as the result of his adherence to the cause of the American colonists; fortune was the price paid by this young Scotchman for devotion to the principles of liberty. At the close of the war he was a poor man. The following extracts are taken from the New York State Archives:—

"Proceedings of the Provincial Congress, Committee of Safety, and Convention of New York, Relating to Military Matters:—
(Pages 61 and 62 of New York in The Revolution by Bertholdt Fernow)
A. M. Feb. 16th, 1776.

"A letter from Andrew Onderdonck, Chairman of the Committee of the Haverstraw Precinct dated 30th January 1776 was read and filed, containing the following list of names of officers nominated for the Regiment of * * * * * *

Militia of the Precinct

Ann Hawkes Hay, Colonel.
Isaac Sherwood, Lieut.-Colonel.
John Smith, 1st Major.
William Ryder, Adjutant.
Garrett Onderdonck, Quartermaster.

* * * * * *

"Ordered that commissions be made out for the Field and other Officers of the Militia in the Precinct of Haverstraw. * * * * * *

"Ordered that Colonel Brasher, Mr. Scott, Mr. Wickham, Colonel Hay, Colonel Drake, Colonel P. Ten Broeck, Mr. Rhea, Colonel Nicoll, Mr. Moore, Mr. Vanderbilt, and Doctor Williams be a committee to settle the quota or number of men and officers under the rank of Field Officers to be raised in the different counties in this colony to constitute the Four Regiments ordered to be raised for the Continental Service, and defence of this colony, and that said committee report with all convenient speed."

"Die Solis 10th Ho. A. M. Feb. 18th, 1776.

"Colonel Hay from the Committee appointed to apportion the different quotas of men and officers under the rank of Field Officers to be raised in the different counties of this Colony to form four regiments ordered to be raised in this Colony, delivered in their report, which was read, and the same being read a second time and filed, is in the words following, to wit:—

" 'Your Committee appointed to levy the Quotas of Men to be raised in the different counties of this colony for the service of the United Colonies, report that it is their opinion that the number of men that can be raised in each county is as follows:—

" 'New York, 8 companies; Albany, 5 companies; Charlotte, 1 company; Dutchess, 4 companies; Westchester, 2 companies; Suffolk, 3 companies; Queen, 1 company; Kings and Richmond, 1 company; Orange, 2 companies; Ulster, 2 companies—in all 32 companies.—Is humbly submitted by your committee.

" '(Signed) Ann Hawkes Hay, Chairman.'

"The Congress agreed with the Committee in their said report."

"From New York in the Revolution as Colony and State by James A. Roberts, Comptroller, 2nd Edition, Albany, 1898, p. 157.

"Orange County Militia—2d Regiment:—

"Colonel, Ann Hawkes Hay; Lieut.-Col., Gilbert Cooper; Major John Smith; Major, John L. Smith; Adjutant, James D. Clark; Quartermaster, Joseph Johnson; Surgeon, John Ferrand," and goes on to name 12 Captains, 16 Lieutenants, 4 Ensigns, and about 1,000 privates among which appear the names of:—

"Gardner, William Sickles, Matthias Conklin, Jacob Sickles, John Coe, William Conklin, Dowah and James and John Vanderbilt, Adolph and Peter Wanamaker, John Backman, Samuel Bird, about 30 bearing the name Blauvelt, four of the name Garrison, James Horton, Richard Howard, about thirty of the name Conckling and Conklin, about 15 of the name Cooper, six of the name Demarest, Peter Depew, Cornelius and John Depue, six of the name Campbell, 12 of the name Coe, John Hutson, eight of the name Jones, ten of the name Mabie, Joel Mead, Charles and Jacob and Salenas and Mordica Mott, about fifteen of the name Onderdonck, six of the name Post, Joseph Roosevelt, ten of the name Secor, twenty of the name Smith, Charles Stewart, six of the name Springstein, four Snyder, six Tallman, and many others."

The above are some of the names constituting the 2d Regiment of Orange County Volunteers, commanded by Colonel Ann Hawkes Hay, and rendering important services on the Hudson River during the 1st year of the War of the American Revolution. The complete list may be seen in the publication appearing at the head of this extract. Many of these names have since been conspicuous in the history of the United States, in financial and political circles.

The following extracts from "Military Minutes of the Council of Appointment of the State of New York, 1783-1821," relate to three sons of Colonel Ann Hawkes Hay:—

"P. 148. Anno 1788. Orange County. In Lieut-Colonel John Robert's regiment, Michael Hay is mentioned as an Ensign."

P. 218. Anno 1792. In Lieut-Colonel David Burno's regiment, Thomas Hay is mentioned as Adjutant."

P. 258 A. D. 1793. In Brig-Gen. Hathorne's brigade, in Lieut-Colonel Commandant Seth Marvin's regiment, is mention of Michael Hay as Lieutenant."

"P. 332. Anno 1796. Orange County. Michael Hay is mentioned as Justice of the Peace."

"P. 617. Anno 1802. Orange County. Mention of a new troop of Horse in Gen. Wueisneis' Brigade, Samuel Smith, Captain, and Thomas Hay 1st Lieutenant."

"P. 731. Anno 1804. Washington County. In David Gray's regiment, mention is made of William Hay as Ensign;" and on "page 875, it is stated that said William Hay is promoted to Lieutenant."

It has been stated at the beginning of this section that Colonel Ann Hawkes Hay married Martha Smith in New York, both eighteen years of age. Her lineage will be found in the following sketches, published in the records of The Historical Society of New York:—

Famous New York Families — The Smiths

"Five generations of college men, whereof each has supplied distinguished lawyers to the community, is the simple but magnificent record of the Smith Family of New York.

"It has enjoyed the advantages of wealth, is connected with the old Knickerbocker blood, and through legal, medical, and literary services stamped itself upon the chronicles of the State.

1. William (1) the soldier, was b. in the Isle of Ely, Cambridgeshire, England, but removed thence, and settled at Newport Pagnell, Buckinghamshire, where he d. about 1682.

    He m. Elizabeth Hartley of Lancashire, by whom he had five sons and one daughter:—i. William; ii. James; iii. John; iv. Samuel; v. Thomas; from whom descend the New York branch; vi. Christiana. Of these sons, the eldest, William, removed to Jamaica, West Indies, and settled at Port Royal; he m. Frances Peartree, daughter of Colonel Wm. Peartree, mayor of New York in 1703; and from him descend the "Peartree Smiths," who played an important part in the Empire State during the Eighteenth Century—one of these Catherine, m. the Hon. Elisha Boudinot of New Jersey.

2. Thomas Smith, 5th and youngest son of William the Soldier, was b. 1675, at Newport Pagnell. He married Susannah Odell, and came to America with his three sons A. D. 1715, and immediately set about building the first Presbyterian Church in New York. He d. 1745 a man of large means. By his wife Susannah, he had the following children:—i. William, ii. Thomas, who owned a large tract of land in Orange County at Smith's Cove, now Turner's Station, on the Erie Railroad; iii. the Rev. John Smith, b. 5 May 1702, Minister at White Plains, where he d. 1771—one of his daughters married the Reverend Benjamin Talmadge of Brookhaven, L. I., and was the mother of Colonel Benjamin Talmadge of Revolutionary fame; iv. Odell, who d. young; v. Elizabeth, who m. Thomas Herbert of England; vi. Martha Smith, who married Edward Roberts.

3. Judge William Smith, eldest son of Thomas, was b. A. D. 1697, at Newport Pagnell, Buckinghamshire, England.

    He accompanied his father to America in 1715, settling at New York City, and became known as one of the great men of the period. Eighteen years of age when he arrived in America, he immediately entered Yale College, from which he was graduated in 1719, and took the degree of Master of Arts at that institution A. D. 1722. Acting as Professor at Yale for several years while studying law, he declined the Presidency of the institution and opened a law office in New York City A. D. 1724, and from this point on, until his death A. D. 1769, was a leading figure in colonial life, appearing in nearly every litigation of importance, and being a leader in each political issue, in politics a Whig—an advocate of the people against the Crown.

    With James Alexander, he defended John Peter Zenger, editor of the New York Weekly Journal, when Zenger was acquitted, 1735, and the liberties of the press preserved. For the bold stand he took

THE FAMILY OF HAY

in this trial, he was disbarred for two years by a tyrannical judge.

In 1736, he was Recorder; in 1748, one of the Incorporators of Princeton College, drawing up its first charter and the draft of the second, remaining to the end of life one of the most influential and honored members of the board.

The cause of higher education in New York being neglected in those days, the first steps toward a better condition were taken by Judge Smith, William Alexander, and three members of the Morris family. In the year 1754, with a number of distinguished friends, he arranged plans for a public library, obtained the charter, and started what is now the New York State Library.

The year 1751 saw him appointed Attorney-General; two years later he was a member of the Council, the following year was chosen one of the four representatives from New York to the General Congress at Albany. In 1760, the office of Chief Justice was offered him, but declined.

Three years later he accepted the position of Judge of the Supreme Court of the Province, which office he held until his death.

His educational ideas were applied to the training of his children, and all were good French and German scholars, all thoroughly versed in English literature, the sons versed in Greek and Latin and possessed of a fair knowledge of Hebrew.

He married Mary, daughter of Renè and Blanche Het, Huguenot emigres. From Baird's "History of the Huguenots," Vol. 2d, p. 28, we extract the following:—About the same time there arrived in the City of New York an interesting family from Marennes, in France. Jacques Dubois had held an important office under the Government of France when compelled at the Revocation to flee from the country. He left Marennes with his young wife Blanche Sauzeau, and their infant daughter, and an orphan boy named Daniel Mesnard, who had been committed to his care. The fugitives made their way first to Amsterdam, thence to Martinique Island in the West Indies, and finally to New York, where Dubois soon after died. His widow survived him only a few months. Their daughter Blanche grew up and became the wife of Rene Het; the orphan Daniel Mesnard, when arrived at man's estate, married the daughter of Francois Vincent, and founded a family still extant. * * * * * Renè Het emigrated also to New York from La Rochelle, France, A. D. 1681. He was a son of Joshua and Sarah Het of La Rochelle, was a merchant of New York, and agent in that city, with Andre Fresneau, of the Royal West Indies Company of France (vide Historical Magazine of New York, New Series, Vol. IV, p. 266).

Judge William Smith, by his wife Mary, had the following children:—

    i.   William Smith, b. 18 June 1728; d. in Quebec 3d Dec.

1793. He m. Janet, daughter of James Livingstone of New York and sister of Robert R. Livingstone of Clermont, by whom he had ten children. Believing rebellion to be a crime, he declared himself a loyalist in the war of 1776, but refused to take up arms against his countrymen. Residing on Long Island during the war, he was the friend and adviser of Clinton, and was sent as a commissioner to try and save the life of the noble and unfortunate Major Andrè.

After the War for Independence had ended, he was made Chief Justice of Canada, to which province he removed, where he died. He wrote "Smith's History of New York," edited by his son.

ii. Susannah Smith, b. 24th Dec. 1729. She married Robert James Livingstone of New York, eldest son of James and Maria Livingstone, and had among other children:—Mary Livingstone, who married Captain Gabriel Maturin of the British Army; Colonel Williams S. Livingstone, a brave and gallant officer of the Revolution, known from his reckless daring as "Fighting Bill," who married Catherine Lott; Susannah Livingstone, born 30th July 1758, and married the Rev. James Francis Armstrong, who was paster for thirty years of the 1st Presbyterian Church in Trenton, N. J.; Robert James Livingstone, Jr., who joined the American Army at the age of sixteen, and was severely wounded at the Battle of Trenton; the Hon. Peter R. Livingstone, b. 1766, d. at his residence, "Grassmere," near Rhinebeck, A. D. 1847, was member of the State Senate from Dutchess County, and of the Constitutional Convention A. D. 1821, and married Joanna, daughter of Judge Robert R. Livingstone (one of whose daughters married General William Montgomery, killed at Quebec); Judge Maturin Livingstone, who was graduated at Princeton, was a very distinguished man, and married Margaret, only daughter of Morgan Lewis (a famous general in the War of the Revolution and Governor of New York), by Gertrude, daughter of Judge Robert R. and Margaret Beekman-Livingstone—they had among other children:—Julia, b. 1801 and m. Major Joseph Delafield; Gertrude Livingstone, who m. Major Rawlins Lowndes, Susan Livingstone, m. William T. Lowndes, Margaret A. Livingstone, m. Alexander A. Hamilton, son of James A. Hamilton, and Blanche Livingstone, who married Lydig M. Hoyt.

iii. Mary Smith, b. 26th March 1732, married John Smith

and left one daughter, Mary Smith, who married Richard Bancker.

iv. Sara Smith, b. 3d Aug. 1733, married the Rev. Abraham Keteltas of Jamaica, Long Island, and died 12th Oct. 1815.

v. Thomas Smith the Patriot, b. 11 Mch. 1734 and died 1795. He was a member of the Committee of Safety and of the Provincial Congress of New York. He married Elizabeth Lynsen, by whom he had a large family.

One of his daughters married John C. Spencer, Secretary of War, and their son was hanged at sea by a brutal captain for an alleged conspiracy of mutiny. It is said that the unfortunate young man only planned a practical joke to frighten a tyrant who was a cruel martinet in his discipline of the crew. The sudden announcement of his death is said to have cost the life of his lovely mother, and the reason of a first cousin Sarah, daughter of Joshua Hett Smith, who died in South Carolina and was buried at the Boiling Springs, ten miles south of Barnwell, C. H.

Another daughter married William Denning of New York.

A son Thomas Smith, married Mary, daughter of John Taylor, died at his home in Haverstraw, N. Y., A. D. 1815, and among other children, left a son John Taylor Smith, one of the most prominent lawyers of Rockland County, who left a son:—Charles Bainbridge Smith, a prominent lawyer in New York, and the present representative of the family in that city.

vi. Elizabeth Blanche Smith, who m. John Torrans of South Carolina, and is buried there in the Circular Churchyard.

vii. Dr. James Smith, b. 1738; graduated at Princeton and received the best medical education in Europe.

He was active in establishing the Chair of Materia Medica and Chemistry at Columbia College, New York, which college (then King's) was founded largely by his father Judge William Smith. He married a wealthy widow, Mrs. Alexander of Jamaica, and left children.

viii. Anne Smith, who married Mr. Bostwick of New York.
ix. John Smith, b. 1741, a lawyer of New York.
x. Catherine Smith, m. John Gordon of South Carolina.
xi. Martha Smith, b. 18 June 1744, m. Colonel Ann Hawkes Hay. Their children are given presently.
xii. Samuel Smith, b. A. D. 1745. He died unmarried.
xiii. Margaret Smith, married Alexander Rose of Charleston, S. C., and was grandmother of Dr. Arthur Rose of that city,

whose children are still living there.

Alexander Rose was a lineal descendant of the family of Rose, barons of Kilravock, Nairnshire, Scotland, and of Lilias Hay, of the same stock as Colonel Ann Hawkes Hay, who married Martha Smith above, the sister of Margaret Smith.

It seems a strange chance that two young Scotchman whose families had several times intermarried in their native country, whose ancestral castles—Inshoch and Kilravock—were but a few miles apart, probably without knowledge of the many ties that bound them in kinship, should marry sisters in a foreign land. The posterity of both Ann Hawkes Hay and Alexander Rose now live in South Carolina.

xiv. Joshua Hett Smith, b| 27th May 1749, was admitted to the bar.

Aaron Burr studied law for a time in his office. Acting under his orders, at a time when no one suspected Arnold's good faith, Smith, who was living at Haverstraw in the house of his brother Thomas the Patriot, went out into the Hudson with two oarsmen to meet the Vulture, received Major Andre into his boat, and escorted him to the shore for the memorable interview with the traitor of the Revolution.

When the Vulture was fired on by Colonel Livingstone—a cousin of Smith— and dropped farther down the river, it was but common courtesy to invite Andrè to his house.

The following day he was requested by Arnold, the commanding officer of that district whom all trusted, to conduct his guest back to the British lines. Ignorant of the nature of Andrè's mission, he obeyed Arnold's order, rode with André for a short distance up the Hudson, then crossed the stream and escorted him down on the eastern side, leaving him when he deemed it safe, and returning to his brother-in-law, Colonel Hay's headquarters, quietly prepared to pass the night in company with his wife who was staying with her siser-in-law, Martha Hay.

It was due to the foresight of Colonel Talmadge—also a cousin of Smith—that Andrè, when captured, was not delivered a prisoner to General Arnold. Smith was rudely arrested in the presence of his wife at the house of Colonel Hay, charged with treason, and she never recovered from the shock, but died in consequence.

Tried and acquitted before a military court of all complicity in Arnold's treachery, Smith yet found it necessary to leave the country and go to England, where he wrote his book, and married his second wife, Miss Middleton. His later life was embittered by the consciousness that many believed in his guilt—we are, alas! too prone to believe evil

Dr. Joel Wyman, founder of the Wyman Family in South Carolina. He married Catherine Clementine Hay, daughter of Lewis Scott Hay and Harriet Yonge Johnson of S.C. (Courtesy of Mrs. John Frampton, Charleston, S.C.)

Dr. William D. Ellis and his wife, Susan Emily Hay, fifth child of Lewis Scott Hay and Harriet Yonge Johnson. (Courtesy of Frampton E. Ellis of Atlanta, Ga.)

of others—and many even now hold him to have been a traitor and Arnold's accomplice.

He was the innocent victim of Arnold and circumstantial evidence; unjustly is his memory clouded by the suspicion of disloyalty and treason.

He had one child, Sarah Smith, who married her cousin Thomas, a son of Colonel Hay, and with two of her daughters she passed the last days of her life at the "Boiling Springs," in Barnwell County, S. C., her mind clouded by the sad death of her cousin, young Spencer, and her grave may be seen from the window of the cottage in which we are writing this sketch of her father.

His descendants are honored citizens of South Carolina.

Colonel Ann Hawkes Hay, by his wife Martha Smith, had the following children—the record is copied from the Family Bible of one of his grandchildren, and is as follows:—

i. William Richmond, their first son, born on Monday morning about half past nine o'clock, July 30th, 1764, in the City of New York, and baptised in the house on the same day, by the Rev. Joseph Treat, minister of the Presbyterian Church of the City of New York. He died 27th Sept., 1766, and was buried in the churchyard in Kingston, Jamaica, West Indies, at the age of two years.

ii. Ann Mister Hay, their 1st daughter, was born on Thursday morning, at 5 o'clock, 11 July, 1765, in Kingston, Jamaica, and was baptised in the house on Sunday, the 14th of the same month, by the Rev. Mr. Atkins, rector of the Church of England, in Kingston. Her god-father was Walter Richmond, and her god-mothers were Isabella Richmond and Louisa Pelton.

She died 27th Oct., 1766, and was buried in the same grave with her brother.

iii. Mary Hay, their 2d daughter, was born on Thursday, noon at 1 o'clock, 6th Nov., 1766, in Kingston, Jamaica, and was baptised at the house by the Rev. Mr. Hudson, curate of the Church of England in Kingston.

Her god-father was Mr. Nathaniel Grant, and her god-mothers were Mary Fitch and Mrs. Grant.

She died 27th November, 1767, and was buried in the grave with her brother and sister.

iv. Michael Hay, their second son, was born on Saturday night, at 10 minutes before 12 o'clock, 30th July, 1768, in the City of New York and was baptised the next day by the Rev. Joseph Treat, minister of the Presbyterian Church of New York.

(His posterity are now living in New York, near Chazy, Clinton County.)

v. William Smith Hay, their 3d son, was born on Monday evening, at 15 mintues after 6 o'clock, 18th December, 1769, at Cornwall, Orange County, and was baptised in the house on Sunday, the 24th of the same month, by the Rev. Maffat Schonemack in the Province of New York.

He died on the 24th October, 1778, and was buried under a large chestnut tree at Haverstraw on the Hudson, in the County of Orange.

vi. Samuel Hay, their 4th son, was born on Sunday evening near 9 o'clock, on the 8th of September, 1771, and was baptised in the house by the Rev. John Rodger, D.D., assistant to Mr. Treat of the Presbyterian Church of New York.

He d. 5th May, 1804, and bu. at Grimball Hill, near Coosawhatchie, S. C.

He m. 22 June, 1797, Elizabeth Mary, dau. of Colonel John Kenney.

vii. Thomas Hay, their 5th son, was born on Monday evening, 15 minutes before 6 o'clock, the 25th of October, 1773, at Haverstraw, in the County of Orange, and was baptised in the house on Sunday, the 28th of November, by the Rev. Joseph Treat, minister of the Presbyterian Church, in the City of New York.

viii. Janet Scott Hay, their 3d daughter, was born on Friday, 15 minutes after 1 o'clock, 3d of November, 1775, at Haverstraw, in Orange County, and was baptised in the house by the Rev. Joseph Treat on Thursday, the 28th of November.

(She married Mr.———— Campbell and removed to Louisiana.)

ix. Martha Hay, their 4th daughter, was born on Sunday at 1 o'clock p.m. on the 22nd of November, 1777, at Ringwood Iron Works, in the State of New Jersey, and was baptised by the Rev. Mr. Hoyet, at Haverstraw on May the 30th, 1778.

x. Lewis Scott Hay, their sixth son, was born on Thursday, about 3 o'clock p.m. on the 2nd May, 1780, at Fishkill, N. Y., and was baptised by the Rev. Mr. Evans, chaplain of General Perre's (?) brigade on the 20th of June following, at the house of Colonel Dirick Brunkerhuff.

xi. William Hay, their 7th son, was born on Monday, between 2 and 3 o'clock p.m., on the 26th of August, 1782, at Haverstraw, N. Y., and was baptised by the Rev. Mr. Evans, chaplain of the New Hampshire Line, on Saturday, the 16th Nov., following.

xii. Frederick Jay Hay, their 8th son, was born on Saturday, the 5th of March, 1785, at Haverstraw, and was baptised by the Rev. Mr. Kew (or Kerr) of New York.

(His amplified history follows in Section XXV.)

Twenty-third Generation

SAMUEL HAY, OF BEAUFORT DISTRICT, SOUTH CAROLINA, was the sixth child of Colonel Ann Hawkes Hay by his wife Martha Smith. He was born on the 8th of September, 1771, possibly in Kingston, Jamaica (as we find his parents deeding 108 acres of land in the Island on the 12th November, 1771), and baptised by the Rev. John Rodger, D. D., Assistant to Mr. Treat, Minister of the Presbyterian Church of New York City. He died on the 5th of May, 1804, at his home, Grimball Hill, near Coosawhatchie, Beaufort District, S. C., and was buried there by the side of his youthful wife, whom it is said, he so tenderly loved that grief for her death caused his own not long after.

It has been already related that Samuel's life was once saved by Aaron Burr, who (then studying law at the office of his uncle, Joshua Hett Smith) clambered down and brought him safely out from a well into which he had fallen. On another occasion General Washington was a guest of Colonel Hay at Haverstraw; and riding a fiery steed on the lawn was almost thrown from his horse startled by a salute to the General fired from a toy cannon by young Samuel Hay. General Washington thanked the youthful patriot for the compliment, then wrote him an order on the ordnance department for one pound of powder.

But fourteen years old when his father died, two years after the close of the Revolutionary War, Samuel received a good education, studied law, and removed from New York to Beaufort, S. C., and practiced law at the Beaufort bar, where the records show he was Ordinary (Probate Judge) for Beaufort District.

Having met success in Beaufort, he sent back to the North for his widowed mother and her youngest son, Frederick. She lived for many years and died on the 30th of March, 1821, and was buried at Stoney Creek, near McPhersonville, S. C.—the history of Frederick is given later. Samuel Hay married at her home, Grimball Hill, on the 22d of June, 1797, Elizabeth Mary, b. 26th Aug., 1776, the eldest daughter of Mr. John Kenney by his wife Miss Mulholland, to whom he was married on the 15th of February, 1773. Elizabeth Mary Hay died on the 29th of August, 1803. Three daughters were born to Mr. Kenney and his wife, Miss Mulholland:—

    i. Elizabeth Mary, b. 26 Aug. 1776, and m. 22d June 1797, Samuel Hay.

    ii. Eleanor, b. 31 Aug. 1779, and m. 20th Feb. 1800, Dr. John Bellinger, grandson to the Landgrave Edmund Bellinger of South Carolina.

    iii. Susan Emily, b. 20th Nov. 1781, and m. 23d Apl. 1804, Charles J. Jenkins, by whom a son:—Charles J. Jenkins, the noble War Governor of the State of Georgia, whose memory is revered by all who knew him.

After the death of his 1st wife, Mr. Kenney married on the 12th Dec. 1798, Rachel (née Porcher) relict of William Ross; she married after the death of Mr. Kenney, on the 23d of July 1811, Colonel James Postell, and reared her step-grandchildren, William and Mary Hay.

Samuel Hay, by his wife Elizabeth Mary, left two infant children:—

    i. William Henry Hay, b. 10th Sept. 1801. History follows in Section XXIV.

    ii. Eliza Mary Hay, b. 9th Aug. 1803. Her history is given in Section XXIV, under that of her brother.

THOMAS HAY, seventh child of Colonel Ann Hawkes Hay by his wife Martha Smith, was born 25th October, 1773, at Haverstraw, N. Y., and baptised by the Rev. Joseph Treat of New York. He married his first cousin Sarah, only child of Joshua Hett Smith, and died in New York, she d. "The Boiling Springs," S. C., 8 Dec., 1849, aged 75 years and 4 months, and they left the following children:—

    i. William Hay, who died unmarried at Haverstraw, N. Y.

    ii. Matilda Hay, who owned a home at the "Boiling Springs," Barnwell District, S. C., and died unmarried, and is buried there.

    iii. Charlotte Hay, b. in New York, A. D. 1807, d. at the "Boiling Springs," S. C., 11 Aug. 1856. She was unmarried.

    iv. Frederick Hay, died unmarried in Alabama.

THE FAMILY OF HAY

v. Augustus Hay, died unmarried at the "Boiling Springs," S. C.
vi. Martha Hay, Married Dr. Thomas Hutson, Sr., of South Carolina, and has many descendants now living—some in McPhersonville, some in Charleston, and others elsewhere in South Carolina.
   Dr. Thomas Hutson, Sr., was the 1st cousin of his wife Martha; he was the son of Martha, a daughter of Colonel Ann Hawkes Hay.

JANET SCOTT HAY, eighth child of Ann Hawkes Hay by his wife Martha Smith, married a Mr. Campbell, and removed to Louisiana.

MARTHA HAY, ninth child of Colonel Ann Hawkes Hay by his wife Martha Smith, was born 22d Nov., 1777, at Ringwood Iron Works in the State of New Jersey, and baptised by the Rev. Mr. Hoyet.

She married William Main Hutson of South Carolina, descended from the Rev. William Hutson and his wife Mary Woodward-Chardon, by whom she had children:—

i. Dr. Thomas Hutson, Sr., who married 1st his cousin Martha, daughter of Thomas Hay and wife Sarah Smith (dau. of Joshua Hett Smith), and by her left children, among whom may be mentioned Dr. Thomas Hutson, Jr., of McPhersonville, S. C., (who had daughters:—Augusta; Charlotte Matilda, m. Ben Martin; Emeline Colcock, m. her cousin Mac Hutson; Florie, m. Robert Heyward; and a son Ogier, m. Miss Owens, and is a surgeon in the U. S. Army), and Matilda. By a second marriage, Dr. Hutson, Sr., had children:—Willie, John, Jane DeSaussure, Mellicent, Sally, and Annie.
ii. Isaac Hutson, a distinguished lawyer of Barnwell, S. C., b. 3 Sept. 1819, d. 1887, who married Sarah, the sister of the celebrated Presbyterian divine, Dr. Ben Palmer of South Carolina and New Orleans, by whom are surviving children:—Sophie, and the Rev. Edward Palmer Hutson.
iii. Jane Hutson, m. Dr. Louis DeSaussure and left children:—Charles DeSaussure of Memphis, Tenn.; and Thomas DeSaussure of Millegeville, Georgia.
iv. William Maine Hutson, a prominent lawyer of Orangeburgh, S. C., who married Mary Mackay, and left children.
v. Maria Hutson, m. Dr. William Townsend, Sr., and had a son:— William Townsend, of whose descendants later.
vi. Esther Main Hutson, died unmarried.
vii. Mary Hutson, died unmarried.
viii. Ann Barnwell Hutson, died unmarried.

THE FAMILY OF HAY

LEWIS SCOTT HAY, tenth child of Colonel Ann Hawkes Hay by his wife Martha Smith, was born at Fishkill, on the Hudson River, New York. He followed his brother Samuel to the State of South Carolina, and married, A. D. 1807, Harriet Yonge Johnson, who died 1865.

He died in Barnwell District, S. C., A. D. 1843, and by his wife left the following children:—

    i. Martha Hawkes Hay, married and left descendants.
    ii. Harriet Yonge Hay married and left descendants.
    iii. Clementine C. Hay, married and left descendants.
    iv. Doctor Lewis Scott Hay, married and left descendants.
    v. Susan E. Hay, married and left descendants.
    vi. Frederick J. Hay, married and left descendants.
    vii. Rosa Isabel Hay, married and left descendants.
    viii. Louisa Hay, died unmarried.
    ix. Adeline D. Hay, married and left descendants.
    x. Eugene Gordon Hay, married and left descendants.

Many descendants of these, too numerous to mention, are successful planters, prominent lawyers, and eminent physicians; and one has been recently elevated to the bench in Georgia, having previously won distinction at the Atlanta bar.

Twenty-third Generation

(Continued)

COLONEL FREDERICK JAY HAY OF THE BOILING SPRINGS, BARNWELL DISTRICT, SOUTH CAROLINA, was the twelfth and youngest child of Colonel Ann Hawkes Hay by his wife Martha Smith, and was born at Haverstraw, on the Hudson River, New York, 5 March 1785, one month before his father's death, and died at "The Boiling Springs," S. C., 10 Aug., 1849.

While yet a lad, his mother, Martha Smith Hay, and himself were sent for by his brother Samuel to rejoin him at Beaufort, S. C., where he had established a law practice at the Beaufort bar.

Frederick m. on the 15th Feb., 1810, Susan Cynthia, only daughter of Mr. Brown by his wife Miss Murdoch, of Virginia parentage. She was the only child of two only children, and a wealthy heiress, gentle, fair, and beautiful in character. She was b. 8th of August, 1792, and d. in Barnwell, 27th Nov., 1868, and bu. at the "Boiling Springs" (ten miles south of Barnwell), where her husband had built a beautiful home at this most healthful spot in the State, surrounded by scenery of a natural beauty rarely equaled. The house was burned in 1864 by Sherman's soldiers. Some of their posterity now live at "The Boiling Springs," forming a hamlet of related families, cherishing the old Scotch traditions and at peace with all the world.

Frederick was a colonel in the War of 1812. With his large means, he assisted liberally many of his young relatives, having the sympathy and co-operation of his wife, who was greatly beloved for her many virtues and admired for her graces.

Their lives were founded upon the principle, "It is more blessed to give than to receive."

Frederick J. Hay, by his wife Susan, had the following children:—

i. Mary Louisa Hay, b. 8 Aug., 1812, d. 24 March, 1894.
ii. Charles Colcock Hay, b. 12 April, 1814.
iii. Dr. Frederick Jay Hay, b. 21 Jan., 1816, d. 1891.
iv. The Rev. Samuel Hutson Hay, b. 14 March, 1818, d. 24 Feb., 1886.
vi. William Augustus Hay, b. Dec., 1819, d. 28 July, 1846.
vi. Lewis Scott Hay, b. 30 Jan., 1822, died unmarried.
vii. Dr. Thomas Theodore Hay, b. 11 March, 1824, is still living.
viii. Oscar Payne Hay, b. 17 Jan., 1828, d. Sept., 1905.
ix. Alfred Octavius Hay, b. 13 Feb., 1830, died in infancy.
x. Susan Cynthia Hay, b. 27 June, 1831, d. 12th July, 1907.
xi. Martha Hutson Hay, b. 26 Aug., 1834, is still living.

We now give a brief sketch of each of these, excepting the 6th and 9th children, who died unmarried; and the 10th and 11th, who married their first cousins, Samuel and Richard Hay, whose histories are presented in Section XXIV.

MARY LOUISA HAY, the 1st child of Colonel Frederick Hay by his wife Susan, was born at McPhersonville, Beaufort District, S. C., 8 Aug., 1812, and baptised by the Rev. Mr. Brown.

She married at "The Boiling Springs," Barnwell District, A. D. 1831, Richard A. Gantt, b. 1796, d. 1874, and bu. at "The Boiling Springs," where he made his home, son of Judge Richard Gantt, eminent jurist of South Carolina, one of three associate justices of the Court of Appeals, by his wife Sarah, dau. of Sherwood Allen, of the State of Virginia. (Judge Richard Gantt was the son of Dr. Thomas Gantt of Maryland by his wife Susannah Mackall, also of Maryland.)

Mrs. Gantt died at "The Boiling Springs," S. C., 24 March, 1894, and is bu. there, having by her husband the following children:—

i. Colonel Frederick Hay Gantt, b. 10 Oct., 1833, died unmarried 10 Nov., 1885.
During the Civil War of 1861-65, he was a Colonel in the C. S. A., commanding the 11th regiment of S. C. Infantry, in General Hagood's Brigade. After the war ended, he studied law and for ten years before his death was the Solicitor of the 2d Circuit of his native state.
ii. Captain Richard Plantagenet Gantt, b. at "The Springs" on the 10th Dec., 1834, and is still living at his home there. He was an officer

THE FAMILY OF HAY

of the 11th Infantry, commanded by his brother, and was with him in many battles in Virginia. He is now a planter of Barnwell County, living at "The Boiling Springs."

He m. 1 Aug., 1866, Ella Elliott, daughter of George C. Mackay by his wife Abbie Jenkins, both of Beaufort District. She was b. 16 Sept., 1845, and d. 14 Dec., 1904, and was bu. at "The Springs," having had by her husband the following surviving children:— i. Anna Maud; ii. Frederick Hay; iii. Elizabeth Mackay; iv. Edith Plantagenet; v. Mary Louisa; vi. Richard; vii. Alma Devereux; viii. Waldo Douglas; ix. Charles Drayton.

iii. Santa Anna Gantt, b. 4 May, 1837, died unmarried 24 March, 1898.
iv. Eldred Lucas Gantt, b. 23 Feb., 1839, was killed at Petersburg, Va., while acting Adjutant of the 11th S. C. Infantry, having been mortally wounded 24 June, 1864, dying two days later.

The Rev. Hugh Perroneau Dawes Hay, in his beautiful poem, "The Phantom Host" (which by many is incorrectly attributed to "Father Ryan"), refers to his cousin in the lines:—

"Then strode the brave Malony,
Kind, genial Adjutant,
And next him walked the truthful
The Lion-hearted Gantt."

vi. A baby, died unnamed.
vi. Gussie Gantt, died an infant.
vii. Lewis Gantt, died an infant.
viii. Mary Louisa Gantt, married her cousin, the Rev. Samuel Hay, of whom later.
ix. Susan Cynthia Gantt, died at the age of four years.
x. John Mackall Gantt, living at "The Boiling Springs," S. C., married his cousin, Ellen Reynolds, dau. of the Rev. Samuel Hay, Sr., by whom 2 children:—Sam and Fred.
xi. Sarah Eliza Gantt, living at "The Boiling Springs," S. C.
xii. Longstreet Gantt, married Lavinia Skinner, is now living at Winnsboro, S. C., and has children:—Evelyn, Louise, Joseph, Annie, and Julia.

CHARLES COLCOCK HAY, 2d child of Colonel Frederick Hay by his wife Susan, was born at his father's plantation home, "Green Oak Forest," Barnwell District, six miles south of Barnwell Court House, on the 12th of April, 1814, and died many years ago.

He entered the South Carolina University, which he attended for several years, displaying great brilliancy of scholarship, and standing first in his class. On account of delicate health, he left college before graduating. He married Sarah Peyton, a descendant of the family of Peytons of Virginia, by whom he had the following surviving children:—

    i.   Charles Colcock Hay, died young.
    ii.   William Hay, m. Sallie Odum and has children:—Ross and William.
   iii. Helen Hay, m. her cousin Lewis, son of Dr. Thomas Hay, and have children:—Arthur, m. Miss Gardner; and Erroll, who married Dr. Lowrie.
   iv. Peyton Hay, m. Minnie Stroman, and has children:—Clarence, Sarah, and Emma.
    v.   Arthur Erroll Hay, died young.

Charles C. Hay and his daughter Helen are among those members of the family who have written poetry greatly admired and which at some future day we hope to see published in a volume. We give one poem of the father and one of the daughter:

The Rose

"Most beauteous flower, the loveliest
Of all the glittering train,
That Flora leads at vernal morn
Upon the dewy plain;
The modest violet hides its head,
The lily's cheek grows pale,
When on the heath thy charms appear,
Thy breath upon the gale!

"Bright harbinger of sunny days,
Emblem of youth and love,
Nature hails thee as Noah did
The olive and the dove;
At thy approach, fond zephyr comes
In all a wooer's pride,
On gladsome wing to whisper love,
And claim his beauteous bride.

"Fair and bright, thy nuptial bower
'Neath skies of azure hue;
Joyous the hymneal song
That nature swells for you;
From sunny hill and verdant plain
Congratulations rise,
Birds blithely sing, and laughing brooks
Send back their glad replies.

"But ah, how fleeting are thy charms!
How brief thy vernal day!
Like youth and love, alas, too soon
Thou art doom'd to fade away;
The breeze that warmly kiss'd thy cheek
Now coldly passes by.
And leaves thy tender form to droop,
To wither and to die.

"So thus too oft confiding hearts
In purest love imbued,
Feel first the chilling slight from those
Who flatter'd and who sued,
And, like the blighted rose that was
So fair but yesterday,
Sink with their beauties to the tomb,
Unmourned to pass away.
—Charles Colcock Hay.

A daughter of the above thus daintily describes the dawning of the day:

Aurora

"Sweet Morn, decked in her gleams of light,
Steals o'er the eastern sea,
Waking the slumbering earth from dreams,
And bidding its darkness flee,
Her gentle touch uplifts the wings
Of sable-plumaged night,
As down the slope of western hills
He slowly takes his flight;
Soft zephyr breathes a sad farewell,
Mid showers of pearly tears—
Sparkling dew-drops—gifts more rare
Than all the gems she wears,
Her veil of floating mist removed,
She lingers there the while,
And blushing views within the deep
Her mirrored, dawning smile—
Then gathering up her fleecy robes,
Clouds of silver sheen,
She folds them round her mystic form,
And hastens o'er the scene.
Her gilded sandal's radiant track
Tips each purple wave,
That onward dancing, glittering goes
To some far, coral cave;

And then she steps from ocean's tide
Upon the verdant lea,
To touch with roseate finger tips
Each shrub and flower and tree.
She stoops to kiss the lily's cheek,
To sip the dew distilled,
From the perfumed, snowy cups
Sweet fairy hands had filled,
Next thro' the deep green forest glade
Her silver arrows fly,
To bear upon their diamond points,
The light caught from her eye;
While flashing there in every hue
The spangled hammocks swung,
Among the trees, by silken threads
The busy spiders hung.—
Then o'er the mountain cliffs she climbs,
To tinge, with pink and gold,
The mantling mist-clouds resting there,
Their towering peaks enfold.
Far, o'er the crags and rippling rills,
She lightly speeds away,
To meet her king with glory crowned,
And herald there the day,
From out a flood of crimson light,
He comes to claim his bride,
To seat her on his gorgeous throne,
In all her regal pride,—
'Tis thus Aurora, pure and bright,
In splendor weds the day,
Then lays aside her diadem
To sink beneath his sway.

—Helen Hay.

DR. FREDERICK JAY HAY, 3d child of Colonel Frederick Hay by his wife Susan, was born at "Green Oak Forest," Barnwell District, S. C., 21st January, 1816, and baptised by the Rev. Mr. Brown. He died at "The Boiling Springs," A. D. 1891, and was buried there.

He was graduated in medicine at the Charleston Medical College, about 1838, and married on the 7th of March, 1839, in Charleston, S. C., Caroline Hasell, daughter of Matilda Perry by her husband Christopher Gadsden, son of Thomas Hasell by his wife Mary Somers of Georgetown, S. C.

THE FAMILY OF HAY

For many years after his marriage Dr. Frederick Hay practiced medicine in Charleston, spending the summers in turn at Barnwell, at "The Boiling Springs," and his beautiful plantation home, "Errolton." In the year 1859 he removed to a plantation known as "Tranquil Hill," near Summerville, S. C., and practiced medicine until the year 1871, in Summerville and the vicinity, and then returned to his home at "The Boiling Springs," where he followed his profession until his death in the year 1891.

Dr. Hay was known as a physician of skill and ability; he was especially fortunate in his treatment of typhoid fever, having never lost a case in his entire practice. He was, moreover, of a scientific turn of mind, well versed in the knowledge of the fauna and flora of his native State and country. Some of his contributions to science and discoveries in natural history were preserved in a work undertaken by Dr. Holbrook, the well-known Professor of Anatomy, at the Medical College of Charleston, who was Dr. Hay's intimate friend.

The friend to all who knew him, and venerated by them in return, he died at "The Boiling Springs" in his seventy-sixth year, and by his wife, Caroline Hasell, who d. ———, left children:—

i. The Rev. Hugh Peronneau Dawes Hay, b. 17 January, 1840, an Episcopal clergyman, now in charge of churches at Bluffton, Hardeeville, and Shirley, S. C.

   A soldier in the war of 1861-65, he rendered his country faithful service, and is admired as a writer of prose and poetry. One of his poems—"The Phantom Host"—has been recited at several Confederate reunions, and been published in Dr. Wharton's collection of Southern Poetry, who accredits it incorrectly to "Father Ryan."

   He married Mary Pinckney, of Charleston, S. C., daughter of Robert Pinckney by his wife Martha Salina Gaillard, and by her, now deceased, has sons:—i. Percy Douglas Hay, m. May Mitchell and has children: May, Percy, and Gladys; ii. Alfred Pinckney Hay, m. his cousin, Mary Louisa, daughter of Captain Richard P. Gaunt, and has children: Edith and Henry; iii. Harry Hasell Hay; iv. Eldred Gaunt Hay.

   The Rev. Mr. Hay has daughters:—i. Mary Pinckney Hay; ii. Ruth Hay, m. James, son of Mr. Haskell Rhett of Beaufort by his wife Rosa Means, and has children:—Ruth, James, Haskell, Mary; iii. Lena Pinckney Hay, m. her cousin, Henry Cumming,

THE FAMILY OF HAY

son of Judge Samuel and Susan Hay, and has a little daughter:—Lena St. Clair Hay.

ii. Hasell Hay, living at her home at "The Boiling Springs."
iii. Dr. Christopher Gadsden Hay, b. A. D. 1847, and now residing at Beaufort, S. C., where he is U. S. Health Officer for one of the harbors leading into Beaufort.

He was a gallant young Confederate soldier for the last two years of the Civil War, and married his cousin, Mary, daughter of Mr. Oscar Payne Hay, by whom children:—Alvan, Jean, and Hugh.

iv. Morritt Hay, died in infancy.

We give the following poem by the Rev. Hugh Peronneau Dawes Hay, hoping that its publication here may serve to prevent its being published elsewhere as one of "Father Ryan's" pieces. The Alfred Pinckney of these verses was a brother-in-law of Mr. Hay, and Gantt was his young cousin who fell at Petersburgh, Va., while Pat Maloney was a young hero from Barnwell, none of whom would have come under the observation of Father Ryan —and yet it is very reluctantly that admirers of the Alabama poet will cede the claim of the South Carolina author. He has written others of greater beauty:

The Phantom Host

My form was wrapped in slumber,
That steals from the heart its cares,
For my very life was weary
With its barren waste of years;
But my soul with rapid pinions
Fled swift to the light that beams
From a phantom sun and planets,
For the dreamer and his dreams.

I stood in a wondrous woodland,
Where the sunlight nestled sweet,
In cups of snowy lilies,
Which grew about my feet;
And while the forest arches
Stirred gently with the air,
The lilies underneath them
Swung their censors pale in prayer.

I stood amazed and wondering,
And a grand, Memnonian strain

THE FAMILY OF HAY

Came sweeping thro' the forest
And died, then rose again;
It swelled in solemn measure,
Till my soul with comfort blest,
Sank down among the lilies,
With folded wings to rest.

Then to that mystic music,
Thro' the forest's twilight aisle,
Passed a host with muffled footstep,
In martial rank and file;
And I knew those grey-clad figures,
So slowly passing by,
Were the souls of Southern soldiers
Who for freedom dared to die.

In front rode Sidney Johnston,
His brow no longer wrung,
By the vile and senseless slander
Of a prurient, rabble tongue;
And near him, mighty Jackson
With placid front, as one
Whose warfare was accomplished,
And crown of glory won.

There Hill, too, pure and noble,
Passed in that spirit train,
He had joined the martyred army
From the South's last battle plain;
Then next in order followed
The warrior priest, great Polk,
With joy to meet the Master,
For he'd nobly borne his yoke.

Then Stuart, the bold, the daring,
With matchless Pelham rode,
With earnest, chastened faces,
They were looking up to God;
And Jenkins, glorious Jenkins,
With his patient, fearless eyes,
And the brave, devoted Garnett,
Journeyed on to paradise.

Before a shadowy squadron,
Rode Morgan, keen and strong,

THE FAMILY OF HAY

And I knew by his tranquil forehead,
He'd forgotten every wrong;
There peerless Pegram marching,
With a dauntless, martial tread,
And I breathed a sigh for the hero,
The young, the early dead.

'Mid spectral, black horse troopers,
Passed Ashby's stalwart form,
With that proud, defiant bearing
Which spurned the battle's storm;
But his glance was mild and tender,
For in that phantom host,
It dwelt with lingering fondness
On the brother he had lost.

Then strode the brave Malony,
Kind, genial adjutant,
And next him walked the truthful,
The lion-hearted Gantt.

There to that solemn music,
Passed a triad of the brave,
Hayne, Taylor, Alfred Pinckney,
All had found a soldier's grave;
They were young and gentle spirits,
But they quaffed the bitter cup,
For their country's flag was falling,
And they fell to lift it up.

Aye, there passed in countless thousands,
In that mighty phantom host,
True hearts and noble patriots,
Whose names on earth are lost;
There "the missing" found their places,
Those who vanished from our gaze,
Like brilliant meteors flashing,
Then lost in glory's blaze.

Yes, they passed—that noble army—
They passed to meet their Lord,
And a voice within me whispered,
"They but march to their reward."

—Hugh Peronneau Dawes Hay.

Written in compliance with his wife Mary Pinckney's request that he write a poem in memory of her brother Alfred Pinckney, who was killed in Virginia in the war of 1861-65.

THE REV. SAMUEL HUTSON HAY, 4th child of Colonel Frederick Hay by his wife Susan, was b. 14th of March, 1818, at "Green Oak Forest," and was baptised by the Rev. Mr. Brown. He died 24th Feb., 1886.

He was exceptionally studious as a child, displaying marked intellectual ability of a high order, reading Virgil at the age of ten years in the regular course of his education. Like his brothers, Charles Colcock and Oscar Payne Hay, who stood among the very first in large classes, he entered the South Carolina University and won by his scholarship distinguished honor. Under the influence of its President, Bishop Elliott, he felt he was divinely called to the sacred ministry, and took a course of Theology at the Presbyterian Seminary in Columbia, S. C.

While at college he met the lady who became his wife, Miss Mary Peck, a granddaughter of Professor Park. He was first called to the church at Beech Island; in 1843, he took charge of the church at Winnsboro, and after two years returned to live with his father at "The Boiling Springs," whose failing health required his son's assistance in managing his plantation. Called to the Camden Church in 1853, he remained there until 1880, and then removed to McClellville, S. C.

With a longing for the scenes of his youth, he removed in 1883 to Allendale as the Evangelist of the Charleston Presbytery, and in 1885 returned to his early home, "The Boiling Springs," where he died and was buried, 1886.

With intense patriotism, on the eve of the Civil War, he preached a celebrated sermon from the text, "In the name of our God, we shall set up our banners," and during the progress of subsequent hostilities was often forced to face ruthless raiding parties of Sherman's army at his own door.

A finished scholar and devoted parent, he educated all his children himself; a devout Christian, it was said of him, "He deserves no credit for being good, he cannot be otherwise," and his life illustrated the two commandments—Love for God and Love for Man.

He died finally, widely revered and without one enemy in the world, and yet was a man of strongly marked character. He left at his death a widow whom he loved most tenderly in life, and many children, whose proudest heritage might well be that they are sons and daughters of the just.

By his wife Mary he had the following children:—

i. Frances Snowden, m. Colonel Del Kemper of the C. S. A., at one time a professor at the citadel, Charleston, S. C., and later U. S. Consul to China.
   They left children:—May; Zaida; Erroll; and Del Kemper.
ii. James Thornwell Hay, who was admitted to the bar, and practiced law in Camden, S. C.; he was a distinguished State Senator from Kershaw County, and has recently died, leaving a widow and several children—one of whom, named for his father, is a promising young physician.
iii. Frederick Jay Hay, who is now in charge of the Mechanical and Industrial department at "Farm School," near Asheville, N. C. By his wife Miss Richards, he has children:—Sophie; Sam; Louise; John; Fred; Mary Peck; Lisle; and Nellie Hay.
iv. The Rev. Samuel Hutson Hay, Jr., a Presbyterian minister, now of Camden, S. C.
   He married his first cousin, Mary Louisa Gantt, daughter of Richard Gantt by his wife Louisa Hay, and by her has children:—Harold Hawkes; ii. Samuel Hay.
v. The Rev. Thomas Park Hay, a Presbyterian minister, now living at Gainesville, Fla.
   He married 1st Susan Venning, by whom a daughter Olive; he married 2d Miss Jennie Mikell, and has a son:—Thomas.
vi. Mary Susan Hay, married her cousin, Dr. Walter Scott Hay, son of Dr. Lewis Scott Hay, by his wife Ann Fraser of Charleston, S. C., and by her husband, who is deceased and b. at "The Boiling Springs," has children:—Erroldine, Malcolm, Lewis Scott, Nelleen, and Walter Smith Hay.
vii. Burwell Boykin Hay, on the publishing staff of a newspaper in Atlanta, Ga., married Annie Wynne, and by his wife has a daughter:—Minnie Lee Hay.
viii. Ellen Reynolds Hay, youngest dau., married her first cousin, John Mackall Gantt, son of Mr. Richard Gantt by his wife Louisa Hay, and lives at "The Boiling Springs," S. C.
   By her husband she has two sons: Sam and Fred.
ix. Dr. William Smith Hay, graduated at medicine, and is a practicing physician at Allendale, S. C. He married Burney Clarke and by her has one son:—Samuel Burney Hay.

THE FAMILY OF HAY 157

WILLIAM AUGUSTUS HAY, the 5th child of Colonel Frederick Hay and his wife Susan, was born at "Green Oak Forest," Barnwell District, S. C., on the 25th of December, 1819, and died near Barnwell, 28 July, 1846; he was buried at "The Boiling Springs."

He was graduated at the South Carolina University, and having been admitted to the bar, entered upon the practice of law at Barnwell C. H., establishing the reputation of being a young lawyer of unusual ability and brilliancy. Like his cousin, William Henry Hay, he died suddenly in the very flower of life.

He married at her home in Barnwell, S. C., Susan O'Bannon, the sister of Dr. James O'Bannon, who having survived her husband by many years, died in Barnwell, A. D. 1901, and is buried at "The Boiling Springs." They had children:—

    i.   Frances Jane Hay, died in infancy.
    ii.   Harriet Ford Hay, married William Hutson Townsend, son of Dr. William Townsend, Sr., by his wife Maria, the 5th child of Martha (daughter of Colonel Ann Hawkes Hay) by her husband William Maine Hutson (vide Section XXIII—A).

        Her husband dying many years ago, Mrs. Townsend is now living with her two children in Columbia, S. C.

        By her husband, she has children:—i. William Hay Townsend, studied law in the office of Colonel William Elliott of Beaufort, S. C., and having practiced law for several years in Barnwell, as a partner in the firm of Bellinger and Townsend, removed to Columbia, where at one time he was the Assistant Attorney-General of South Carolina.

        Resigning from this office, he has set up an office for himself in Columbia, where he is a successful practitioner at the bar, skilled especially in the civil law.

        ii. Edith Townsend, living in Columbia with her mother and brother.

DOCTOR THOMAS THEODORE HAY, 7th child of Colonel Frederick Hay by his wife Susan, was born at "The Boiling Springs," S. C., on the 11th of March, 1824, and was baptised by the Rev. Mr .Brown.

He studied medicine and was graduated at the Medical College of Charleston. He was especially gifted in the power of diagnosis, and excelled in the treatment of children's diseases. It is said he never lost a case of diphtheria in all his practice, saving by his skill many patients suffering from this disease so fatal in days preceding the discovery of anti-toxine.

Having retired from active life, and one of two living grandchildren of Colonel Ann Hawkes Hay of the American Revolution, this venerable and beloved representative of the family of Hay of Erroll and Lochloy is now living at Raleigh, N. C., where he settled to be with his children, his life full of years and honor.

He married on the 10th April, 1845, Rhoda Furse, who died at Kings Mountain, N. C., leaving children:—

    i. Lewis Gordon Hay, married his first cousin, Helen, daughter of Charles Colcock Hay. He is now deceased and left children, Erroll, who m. Dr. Lowrie of York County, S. C., living in Luxora, Ark.; and Arthur, who married Miss Gardner and lives in Indian Territory.

    ii. Mary Ella Hay, lives with her father in Raleigh, N. C.

    iii. Rosalie Hay, lives with her father in Raleigh, N. C.

    iv. Thomas Theodore Hay, went from "The Boiling Springs," S. C., to Raleign, N. C., to begin a business career as clerk in an Insurance Company. He soon developed such marked ability that he became the manager and general agent for a leading life and several fire insurance companies, and by energy and integrity has risen to a very high point of success. He now resides in Raleigh, N. C., and in addition to the business of insurance, is president of "The Raleigh Press Brick Company." He married Isabel Cameron, daughter of Major Seaton Gales of Raleigh, by his wife Mary A. Cameron, and by her has children:—i. Mary Seaton Hay, m. William Branch Jones, a prominent lawyer of Raleigh, by whom a little girl, Isabella Cameron Jones; ii. Belle Cameron Hay, m. Frank Morton Stronach, a successful business man and manufacturer of Raleigh, Vice-President and Secretary of the Raleigh Press Brick Company, by whom a son, Thomas Hay.

    v. Walter Douglas Hay, who was junior partner of the firm of T. T. Hay and Bro.

    He married Nannie Burwell of Raleigh, now deceased, by whom an only daughter living:—Nannie, attending school in Raleigh.

    vi. Leila Hay, m. Benjamin, son of Dr. Peeples, by whom one child.

    vii. Gilbert Hay, engaged in the Marine and Fire Insurance business, living at Waco, Texas. His name came down from Gilbert Hay, Lord of Erroll, grandson of Gilbert, 3d Earl of Strathearn. (See Section or Chapter III.)

    He m. Alice Henrietta Marshall of Texas, by whom a son:—Marshall Downes Hay.

    viii. Albert Hay, twin to Gilbert, died a young man full of promise, whose

THE FAMILY OF HAY   159

death was greatly deplored by all who knew him.
ix.   Oscar Payne Hay, unmarried, living in Raleigh, N. C., where he is an agent of real estate.

There were also the following children who died young:—Robert, Charles Colcock, Florence and Louise (twins).

OSCAR PAYNE HAY, the 8th child of Colonel Frederick Hay by his wife Susan, was born at "The Boiling Springs," S. C., and baptised by the Rev. Mr. Moderwel of Augusta, Ga. He d. in Beaufort, S. C., and was bu. at the place of his birth, in September, 1905.

He was graduated at the South Carolina University with distinction in a large class, and among his classmates were his lifelong friends, Major Theodore Barker, Judge Simonton, the Rev. Mr. Campbell, and Dr. William E. Huger of Charleston, and Colonel McMaster of Columbia, S. C.

Mr. Oscar Hay was widely known over the State, and was generally beloved and honored by his many friends, for his courage, gentleness and integrity. He married his first cousin, Sarah Porcher Hay, daughter of William Henry Hay by his wife Mary Caroline Gantt, and by his wife, who died A. D. 1904, had children:—

i.   Mary Hay, married her cousin Christopher Gadsden Hay, M. D., an account of whom has been already given.
ii. Caroline Petigru Hay, married Richard M. Bostick, and died at "The Boiling Springs," S. C., 5th Oct. 1887; her death was followed four months later by that of her only daughter, 4 months old, named for her mother.

Twenty-fourth Generation

WILLIAM HENRY HAY OF "THE OAKS," BARNWELL, SOUTH CAROLINA, was the only son of Samuel Hay (6th child of Colonel Ann Hawkes Hay) by his wife Elizabeth Mary Kenney.

He was born at Grimball Hill, near Coosawhatchie, Beaufort District, S. C., and but two years old when his father died, with his baby sister Eliza Mary,—the mother having died one year before the father—was carefully and affectionately reared by the step-grandmother, Mrs. Rachel Postell, née Rachel Porcher, at "Grimball Hill."

He was b. on the 10th of September, 1801, and died at the early age of twenty-nine years, of peritonitis, in the village of Barnwell, on the 27th of November, 1830, while attending court.

He was a strikingly handsome man, and, as in the case of his father, his career as a brilliant lawyer was cut short at a period when life opened full of promise.

He m. on the 27th of November, 1821, Mary Anna Caroline (born at her father's home, "Mount Vintage," Edgefield Disrict, S. C.), daughter of Judge Richard Gantt of Maryland, by his wife Sarah Allen of Virginia. The lineage of Mary Ann Caroline will be found in the following sketch of:—

The Family of Gaunt

1. Thomas Gaunt (or Gantt), the 1st, came to the Province of Maryland, A. D. 1660, and received in a grant from Lord Baltimore, the lands of "Myrtle Range," at White's Landing, Calvert County.

    It is stated he was descended from the Rev. John Gaunt of Highfield House, co. Stafford, England, rector of Dudley, and brought with him to Maryland a young son, Edward, by his wife Miss Graham, who died in England.

    According to the Gaunt Family Bible, this Edward had a son who was Thomas the 2nd.

    Dr. Christopher Johnston, State Historian of Maryland, in cor-

THE FAMILY OF HAY

respondence with the writer, takes issue with this, and says he finds by the evidence of wills that Thomas, the 2d, was the son of Thomas Gaunt, 1st, who d. 1692, by his wife Anne Greenfield, who d. 1726, and was the daughter of Thomas Greenfield (b. 1649 and resided in the Province of Maryland till 1715, when he died in Prince George's County, having been a Burgess for Calvert and Prince George's Counties, and Member of the Colonial Council, at one time Acting Governor), by his wife Martha, daughter of James Trueman (b. 1622, d. 1672, having been a Justice for Calvert County from 1669 to 1670), by his wife Anne Storer who d. 1714. Thomas Gaunt the 1st was His Majesty's Justice of the Peace 1689 and Justice of Calvert County.

2. Thomas Gaunt the 2d, son of Thomas the 1st, d. in Prince George's County, Md., in 1765, having held the position of Gentleman's Justice of the Quorum from 1725 to 1728; Commissioned Justice, 1732; Burgess for Prince George's County from 1722 to 1728; Justice of Prince George's County, 1726-33; of the Quorum from 1728; and Presiding Justice from 1732.

   He married 1709, Priscilla Brooke, daughter of Anne and Colonel Thomas Brooke (b. about 1659, d. 7 Jan. 1730, was Justice for Calvert Co.; Commissioner for laying out Towns; Member of Council 1692 to 1707 and 1715-1724; Justice of Court 1695; Com.-Gen. of the Province; President of the Council and Acting Governor of Maryland), the son of Eleanor Hatton by her husband Major Thomas Brooke (b. at Battle, England, 23 June 1632; and d. in Maryland 1676; was Captain of Militia for Calvert 1658; was Major in 1660; Sheriff of Calvert Co. 1660-67; Presiding Justice of County Court 1667), the son of Mary Baker and her husband Robert Brooke (b. in London, England, 3 June 1602; d. at Brooke Place Manor, Md., 1655; was Commander of Charter Company 1650; Member of Council 1650; Head of the Provincial Council 1652).

3. Thomas Gaunt the 3d, M. D., son of Thomas the 2d, was b. in Maryland 1710; and d. 1785 in Prince George's County, Md.

   He was Justice of Prince George's Co., 1738-41; 1748-52; and Justice of Quorum in 1740.

   He m. Rachel Smith, daughter of Sarah (d. 1757 and dau. of George Young), by her husband Colonel John Smith of Calvert County, b. 1676, d. 1737, and Justice of the Provincial Court of Md. 1729 to 1737; and of the Quorum from 1730.

4. Thomas Gaunt the 4th, M. D., son of Dr. Thomas Gaunt the 3d, was b. in Prince George's County, Md., about 1736; he was Justice of Prince George's County 1773-75; and Member of the Maryland Convention of 1775; was a Member of the Provincial Council; a Signer of the Declaration of Rights by the Freemen of America, which hangs in the State House at Annapolis; was Superintendent of

THE FAMILY OF HAY

Fortifications 1775; was a Member of the Committee of Correspondence in 1775; and in 1777 was a Member of the Council of Safety. He m. Susannah Mackall, who d. 1757, and was daughter of Mary Hance by her husband James John Mackall (who held colonial offices), son of Susannah Parrott by her husband Colonel John Mackall of Calvert Co., d. 1739 (his son James John, was b. 1717 and d. 1772), son of Mary d. 1718, by her hubsand James Mackall, Esq., of Calvert County, Md.

Mary Hance, wife of James John Mackall, was the daughter of Mary Hutchins, by her husband Benjamin Hance of Calvert Co., b. 1692 and d. 1773, the son of Mary Sewell by her husband John Hance of Calvert County (m. 1687), d. 1709 and held colonial office.

Mary Hutchins was the daughter of Elizabeth Burrage, by her husband Francis Hutchins, who resided in the Province of Maryland to 1698, when he d. in Calvert County. He was a Burgess for Calvert 1682-84 and 1694-97, and Justice 1679-96.

James John Mackall was b. in Calvert Co., Md., 29 Nov. 1717, and d. 3d January 1772; and was a Burgess for Calvert Co., 1745-65.

5. Judge Richard Gaunt, son of Dr. Thomas the 4th, was b. in Calvert County, Md. in 1767; he studied law under the Hon. William Pinckney, and removed to the State of South Carolina, where he rose to the high office of Circuit Judge, and one of the three Justices of the Court of Appeals, at the same time as his friend Judge Charles J. Colcock.

He m. Sarah Allen, who is said to have been selected to dance by LaFayette, as being the most beautiful and graceful lady of the ballroom, in Augusta, Ga.

They had children:—Thomas Gaunt; Edward Gaunt; William Gaunt; Sarah Gaunt, m. Mr. Stone of Greenville, S. C.; Eliza Gaunt, m. William Thompson of Greenville, S. C.; Richard Gaunt, m. Louisa, eldest child of Colonel Frederick Hay (of her we have given an account in Section XXIII—B); and finally, Mary Ann Caroline Gaunt.

6. Mary Ann Caroline Gaunt, daughter of Judge Richard Gaunt, was born at Mount Vintage, Edgefield District, S. C., on the 11th of June, 1803, and died———.

She married on the 27th of November, 1821, at her father's home, William Henry Hay, son of Samuel and Elizabeth Mary Hay. (Vide the 1st part of Section XXIII—A.)

William Henry Hay, by his wife Mary Caroline Guant, had the following children:—

i. Mary Caroline Hay, born 3d October 1822, at Columbia, S. C., lived with her sister Sarah, died about 1901, and was buried at "The Boiling Springs," S. C., where she died, unmarried.

THE FAMILY OF HAY

Sarah Porcher Hay, born at Columbia, S. C., 20th April 1824, and died in Beaufort, S. C., 1903, and was buried at "The Boiling Springs," S. C.

She married her first cousin, Oscar Payne, son of Colonel Frederick Hay, and for his sketch vide Section XXIII—B.

Judge Samuel Jenkins Hay was born at his father's home, "The Oaks," near Barnwell, S. C., history follows.

Richard Gaunt Hay was born 20th October 1827, at "The Boiling Springs," S. C.

During the war of 1861-65 he was a gallant officer in the C. S. A., being major of the 11th Regiment of Infantry, Hagood's Brigade. After the war ended he was elected a member of the Legislature, just preceding the rule by "Carpet Baggers," "Scalawags," and negroes. He was well known in insurance circles, was universally beloved and admired, and was a strikingly handsome man of courtly manners.

He married his first cousin, Martha Hutson Hay, the youngest child of Colonel Frederick Hay, one of two surviving grandchildren of Colonel Ann Hawkes Hay of the American Revolutionary War.

They had children:—i. Mary Caroline, died at the age of three years; ii. Martha Hutson, died an infant; iii. Sarah Henrietta, died in infancy; and iv. Marion Haywood Hay, m. her cousin Frederick Hay Gaunt, son of Captain Richard P. Gaunt, (an account of whom has been given in Section XXIII—B), and by him has children:— Richard, Marshall, Frederick, and Elizabeth Marion Gaunt, now living at "The Boiling Springs."

William Henry Hay, called Marion Hay, studied law in Mr. Patigrin's offices in Charleston, S. C., d. s. p.

Twenty-fifth Generation

JUDGE SAMUEL JENKINS HAY OF INGLESIDE, BARNWELL, SOUTH CAROLINA, was the eldest son and 3d child of William Henry and Mary Caroline Hay. He was b. at his father's home, "The Oaks," just without the limits of Barnwell, on the 23d of November, 1825, and died at his home, "Ingleside," Barnwell, S. C., on the 14th day of June, 1881, and buried at "The Boiling Springs," S. C.

He was adopted at an early age by his distinguished kinsman, Governor Charles J. Jenkins of Georgia, and was graduated at Erskine College, S. C., the valedictorian of his class, having established a record of brilliant scholarship. He studied law in the office of Governor Jenkins, and was junior partner in the law firm of Jenkins, Walton, and Hay, of Augusta, Ga.

After his marriage he returned to his native State, and settled at Barnwell, where he practiced law until his death.

He was elected District Judge by the Legislature of 1865, and a little later resigned the office under a radical administration. He refused to hold the office of Probate Judge offered him at the period of radical control of the government of South Carolina, but accepted the office later under democratic rule.

Many stories are related that show his chivalrous nature, and readiness to aid the weak imposed upon by those stronger than themselves.

On one occasion he denounced the dishonesty of a desperado whom he saw playing unfairly at cards and winning money from one of his friends. The man, enraged, called for pistols, that he might have satisfaction for his wounded honor. Only one could be found and young Hay proposed they cast lots for it and the first shot. It was won by the gambler and as Hay stood quietly before him with folded arms and without change of expression or tremor in voice, looked down the barrel of the weapon and bade his antagonist "Fire!" the latter, aiming for a few moments, threw down his weapon, exclaiming he could not kill so brave a man—the slightest indication of fear would have meant instantaneous death for the young champion of fair play, but his dauntless mien won the generous admiration even of one accustomed to scenes of bloodshed and crime.

This incident happened in early life, and later on amid all the stormy scenes of "Military Despotism" and "Radical Misrule," which characterized the lawless period of Reconstruction, Judge Hay fearlessly performed his duty, at times issuing warrants for the arrest of United States marshals, who were illegally seizing the citizens of Barnwell and dragging them off for trial at the point of their pistols. He has been known, alone, to quell the tumult of a "radical mob," brandishing their weapons and clamoring for the blood of Barnwell's citizens. When a boy he won the reputation of being "a John C. Calhoun" among his companions, was their referee for all disputes, which were settled as he decided; later in life, confidence in him was so great that he arbitrated many "affaires d'honneur," which he adjusted, when possible, by peaceful methods.

Once when a negro had been hung up by Federal troops for refusing to disclose the spot in which his master's family had secreted their articles of value and was at the point of death, Samuel Hay rode to the scene and cut him down when no one else dared do so, the Federals threatening to shoot down whoever interfered with the execution.

In strong contrast to his fearless temperament and on occasion tiger-like energy in support of justice arrayed against injustice, and defense of the weak oppressed by the strong, was his unobtrusive modesty of mien and deportment in the ordinary avocations of life, and his shrinking from all notoriety.

The following extracts are taken from sketches of Judge Hay written just after his death, which will show the veneration in which he was held by the community in which he lived:—

"Never prince bore in his breast a knightlier soul than that of Samuel Hay, now smiling down from its 'high place' of repose upon the scenes of his pilgrimage and the friends of his true heart * * * * * * * He displayed at all times and in a thousand crises the courage of a lion where innocence was to be defended or wrong set right. No man in his presence dared lightly take the name of woman on irreverent lips, and on one occasion, at least, like the chevalier of a vanished time, he offered his own brave heart as the shield of a maligned lady's honor, and at no period of his life would he have hesitated to repeat the challenge and maintain it with his life.

"In patriotism he was no less bold and brave. During that 'Reign of Terror' in South Carolina, when few were willing to lift a lance for Freedom, Mr. Hay's pen was the very *first* to advocate 'Straight-out Democracy,' by which policy the State was eventually redeemed. This fact is immortalized among the files of our staunch old paper, 'The Barnwell Sentinel,' whose columns were frequently enriched by this gifted and graceful mind, that like the modest violet sought ever to hide in the shade while passing zephyrs bore its ineffable perfume to the outer world.

"The tenderest of all the Muses had kissed his fancy in its dreams, and charming verse flowed as freely as noble prose from his facile pen. Had he been half so ambitious as he was daring in thought and trained in scholarship, the world of letters would mourn his loss today, as much as the sphere within whose orbit he was content to move.* * * * * * And when He comes in glory to gather His own, they, who, like our friend, have gone about the quiet byways silently doing their life-work, will be called to the rewards of His inflexible justice. * * * * * *"

From another sketch is extracted the following:—

"His loss will be felt not alone by his family but by the community at large. He was a 'Chevalier Bayard sans peur et sans reproche,' a gentleman of the old school (which, alas! is passing away with the present generation), with high sentiments of honor grounded upon sound principles worthy the emulation of all. * * * * * * * His administration of justice was characterized by ability, integrity and strict impartiality. With him duty was ever paramount to interest and he did not weigh one against the other * * * * * * * It was especially in the walks of private life that the beauty of his character shone forth and those who knew him best loved him most. * * * * * * *

Judge Samuel J. Hay married at her home, "The Boiling Springs," Barnwell District, S.C., his cousin, Susan Cynthia Hay.

She was the daughter of Colonel Frederick J. Hay, by his wife Susan, and was born 27th June 1831, at "The Boiling Spjrings," and died on the 12th July 1907, in Charleston, S. C., and buried at "The Boiling Springs." Lovely in form and feature, her disposition was one of great gentleness and tender affection, and her character pure and elevated above the things of earth. Brave and courageous under trials and affliction, she was a fit helpmate to her husband, whom she outlived by twenty-six years.

We think the following lines, written by Judge Hay, most fittingly descriptive of the resting place of his wife who has recently crossed the river to rejoin him, so long awaiting the reunion:—

> Tread lightly here, for Jesus keeps
> Watch where his heavy laden sleeps
> With weary eye and dim!
> He guardeth well the promised rest
> And takes the sleeper to his breast
> Who fell asleep in Him.
>
> Tread lightly! for the mortal clay
> That mingles with the dust today,
> In cold corruption sown—
> With immortality put on.
> Will join upon the judgment morn,
> The throng about the throne.
>
> Tread lightly here! beneath thy feet
> A saint, in slumber soft and sweet,
> Awaits the trumpet's call;
> To rise when graves give up their dead,
> With crown of glory on her head,
> And meet the Lord of all.
>
> Tread lightly here! beneath the sod,
> Reposing in the peace of God,
> Let his beloved sleep!
> In mercy He hath closed those eyes,
> Too loving for this world of sighs,
> And destined here to weep.
>
> Safely the gentle law of love,
> By which she walked, hath led above
> To virtue's bright reward:
> Too pure in heart on earth to stay,
> Her tears have all been wiped away,
> In mansions of the Lord!

The children of Judge Samuel J. Hay by his wife Susan are as follows:

i. Charles Jenkins Hay, living in Barnwell, S. C., where he was admitted to the bar, having studied law in Mr. Hutson's office. At one time Trial Justice of Barnwell, he is now Secretary and Treasurer of the Town Council, and is Past Master of the Barnwell Masonic Lodge.
ii: Susan Emily Hay, living in Charleston, S. C.

iii. Richard Marion Hay, an insurance man and planter; he lives at "The Boiling Springs," S. C.

   He married Miss Sallie Glover of Charleston, S. C., daughter of Sanders Lestarjette Glover by his wife Julia Mathews, Charleston, and has children:—Samuel Marion Hay; Lestarjette Glover Hay; Emily Kathleen Hay.

iv. William Henry Hay, bookkeeper of the People's National Bank of Charleston, S. C.

v. Patti Lee Hay, married her cousin Charles J. Colcock, son of Colonel Charles J. Colcock, C. S. A., by his wife Lucy Frances Horton, and has a surviving daughter:—Erroll Hay Colcock, vide Section XXIV—B.

vi. Mary Erskine Hay, lives in Charleston, S. C.

vii. Henry Cumming Hay, planter, insurance, and real estate agent, living at "The Boiling Springs," S. C.

   He married his cousin, Lena Pinckney, daughter of the Rev. Hugh Peronneau Dawes Hay by his wife Mary Pinckney, for whose sketch vide Section XXIII—B.

   They have a daughter:—Lena St. Clair Hay.

viii. Gertrude Agnes Hay, living in Charleston, S. C.

ix. Samuel Montgomery Hay, died young.

We conclude this section (or chapter) with another poem by **Judge Samuel J. Hay**, and one by the Rev. Dawes Hay, reserving others of equal beauty for which we have no space here for publication.

The River of Death

There's a mystical stream called the River of Death,
And I've stood on its haunted shore,
While a crowd swept along from the world's sunny heath—
Some with shout as of triumph, with garland and wreath,
Some weeping and wailing and gnashing their teeth,
Others come with no thought of the cold waves beneath,
As they step from the brink to the River of Death,
Its waters unknown to explore.

It is fearful to gaze on the wonderful throng
Who visit that perilous stream;
There the great with whose glories the wide world hath rung,
And the brave into strength of proud manhood just sprung,
And the lovely and fair such as poets have sung,
And the gay o'er whose lives scarce a cloudlet hath hung,
And the rich and the poor, and the old and the young,
Flit by like the forms in a dream.

THE FAMILY OF HAY

Thro' the valley of shadow this river doth sweep,
With a wild and mystical sound,
Now 'tis fearfully loud, now 'tis wondrously deep,
Now soft as the strains that lull'd childhood to sleep,
Plaintive now—anon wailing—then heard but to weep,
Such the varying tones that its wild waters keep,
And that echo flings back from each shadowy steep
Of the ghoul-haunted region around.

Full many, I ween, gayly enter that vale,
To the sound of the timbrel and lute;
And they speed on their way light as flakes of white sail,
As the blue waters sparkle and dance to the gale,
When this world seems too fair for its fashions to fail,
Where gay song and sweet laughter and gladness prevail,
Tho' the river's deep voice may be heard in the dale,
If the revellers a moment are mute.

They will not believe that their broad summer way,
Windeth down to the waters space;
While the birds sing so sweetly, the woods are so gay,
And charm'd odors are floating wherever they stray—
Oh! they heed not the preacher, nor mark with dismay
How the shadows steal forth in a noiseless array,
Till in blackness of darkness, they feel the cold spray
Of the River of Death in their face.

Yet thro' all these gay windings, one path doth extend
Which always may safely be trod.
Tho' the storm's mark be on it, fear not to descend,
For a light with its course thro' the valley doth blend,
Which shines more and more as the gloom doth impend,
Where it spans the dark river, and thence doth ascend
To its Source in the day-spring of days without end,
All ablaze with the glory of God.

—Samuel Jenkins Hay.

The Flag of Manassas

Baptiz'd in blood where Jackson fell,
Flag of the South, wave on!
Oft sinking 'neath the rising knell
For those we cannot love too well,
The victor's shout may scarcely swell,
Fields may be lost and won:
But while on earth man strikes for right,
And God above is just,
Thro' stormy day and starless night
Thy stars shall be our guiding light,
Tho' torn and tatter'd in the fight,
Thou shalt not trail the dust!

Thy bars upon the breeze are spread
To break a tyrant's chain;
The cause for which our fathers bled,
In which the first of mortals led,
And fought 'til vict'ry corwn'd His head,
Our God will still sustain:
Tho' we have sinn'd against His grace,
Ungrateful for the past,
He will not always hide His face,
When humbl'd we our steps retrace,
He'll lead us like His chosen race
Thro' wars 'Red Sea" at last.

Then wave, thou Flag of Liberty,
Already laurel crown'd!
The voice of blood pour'd out for thee,
Rich blood to make a nation free,
Is rising from the ground:
Its pleading tones, our Maker hears,
And will not hear in vain,
He'll wipe away the widow's tears,
And guard the orphan's tender years,
And break our foeman's guilty spears,
And truth and right maintain.

—Samuel J. Hay.

Judge William D. Ellis as a young soldier in his Confederate uniform. (Courtesy of Frampton E. Ellis of Atlanta, Ga.)

Phoebe Caroline Prioleau, wife of Judge William D. Ellis. (Courtesy of Frampton E. Ellis of Atlanta, Ga.)

Eugene Gordon Hay, youngest child of Lewis Scott Hay and Harriet Yonge Johnson (Hay) and grandchild of Col. Ann Hawkes Hay. (Courtesy of Mr. Frank Hay of

Mrs. Eugene Gordon Hay, neé Julia Caroline Oakman. (Courtesy of Mr. Frank Hay of Charleston, S. C.)

Deus Misereatur

'Tis the sound of a nation's agonized wail,
'Tis the voice of a people borne high on each gale,
'Tis the blood of the murder'd which cries from the vale,
    Pitying Savior, attend us!
'Tis the groan of the weak in their strife with the strong,
'Tis the moan of the desolate patient of wrong,
While the pathway to peace looks rugged and long,
    Pitying Savior, defend us!

'Tis the deep smother'd sob in the hush of the night,
For the lov'd and the lost who have vanish'd from sight,
For the friend or the brother struck down in the fight,
    Pitying Savior, behold us!
Will a day never dawn—a day of release,
Oh, hasten the time when these troubles shall cease,
And soon in the light of Thy love, Prince of Peace,
    Pitying Savior, enfold us!

Oh, comfort the hearts now broken with woe,
Oh, lift up the heads in sorrow bow'd low,
And spread o'er this storm Thy celestial bow,
    Pitying Savior, O hear us!
And when thro' the aisles of Thy church there shall sweep,
A mighty "Te Deum," while the thunders that sleep
In the organ, now wake with a grand, joyous leap,
    Pitying Savior, be near us!

                —Hugh Peronneau Dawes Hay.

Twenty-fourth Generation — B

ELIZA MARY HAY OF McPHERSONVILLE, BEAUFORT DISTRICT, SOUTH CAROLINA, was the 2d child and only daughter of Samuel and Elizabeth Mary Hay of Grimball Hill, and a granddaughter of Colonel Ann Hawkes Hay and his wife Martha Smith.

She was born at "Grimball Hill," Beaufort District, S. C., on the 9th day of August, 1803, and died at McPhersonville, S. C., and was buried at Stoney Creek, ten miles south of that village. Her mother died in the 27th year of her age, twenty days after this daughter's birth, and her father one year later in the 33d year of his age. Her brother William Henry, and herself thus left orphans when babies, were reared by their step-grandmother, Mrs. Rachel Postell, née Porcher. A peculiarly tender affection lasting to the end of life existed between the orphans; and their uncle, Colonel Frederick Hay (who had been sent for with Martha Smith Hay his mother by Samuel Hay the father of these children to come to him in South Carolina from Haverstraw, N. Y.), was always devoted to them. She married at McPhersonville, S. C., on the 15th July 1819, Thomas Hutson Colcock, eldest son of Judge Charles J. Colcock.

Eliza Mary Hay by her husband Thomas H. Colcock (born 10 August 1807, died 6 May 1851, bu. at Stoney Creek, near McPhersonville, S. C., a member of the "Nullification Convention," and although he had been admitted to the bar, was a Southern Planter of the olden time), had the following children:—

    i. Colonel Charles Jones Colcock, whose history follows in Section XXV—B.
    ii. William Hutson Colcock, b. 2 Nov. 1821, m. 15 Apl. 1840, Mary Ellen, dau. of Colonel William Lynn Lewis, descendant of Colonel John Lewis, the pioneer settler of Augusta Co., Va., by whom children:—i. William Lewis, b. 1840, d. 1842; ii. Elizabeth Hay

THE FAMILY OF HAY

Colcock, b. 19 July 1842, m. John Bailey and had issue, Lewis, Minnie, m. Richard Reed of Kentucky; John, d., Thomas, Errol, m. Langdon Cheves Mobley of Florida; Elizabeth, d., Lily, Peyton, and Lawton; iii. Thomas Hutson Colcock, b. 27 Oct. 1845, m. Sallie, dau. Mr. Joseph Lawton, both d.s.p.; iv. Anna Stuart Colcock, b. 26 Nov. 1847, m. 27 Sept. 1860, Abram Marshall Martin of Beaufort Co. (later Hampton Co.), S. C., removed to Ocala, Fla., of which town he was at one time mayor; he is now deceased, leaving by his wife, still living in Ocala, the following children, Elizabeth Mary, b. 1873, m. Edward Hoffman (3 sons, Abram Sandiman, Henry Sinclair, and Edward Herman); Annie Lewis, b. 1877, m. David S. Woodrow (one child, Annie Blair); Lavolotte Holmes, b. 1880.

iii. Captain Richard Hutson Colcock, b. 18 Aug. 1823, d. 15 Sept. 1901, and b. at Stoney Creek. He commanded the Charleston Light Dragoons in the war of 1861-65, and before the war resided in Charleston, S. C., and was junior partner in the firm of John Colcock & Co.

He m. his cousin Eliza Mary, dau. of Mr. John Colcock of the above cotton firm, and by her (still living in McPhersonville, S. C.) had children:—Mary Mellicent, Esther Hutson, John, d.; Eliza Mary, and Martha Anna.

iv. Samuel Hay Colcock, d.s.p.
v. Esther Hutson Colcock, b. Jan. 1831, d. July 1893; married William Douglas Gregorie of McPhersonville, S. C., now deceased, and left one surviving child:—Mary Woodward Colcock Gregorie, m. her cousin Marion Woodward, son of the Hon. William Ferguson Colcock, by whom several children.
vi. Thomas Hutson Colcock, b. in March, 1835, m. in Nov., 1874, Mary Fuller, dau. of Governor A. G. Magrath. She d. 1881, and he d. 29 June 1900, and both are bu. at Magnolia Cemetery, where they had previously interred their only children.

After the death of his first wife, Eliza Mary Hay, Thomas Hutson Colcock married a 2d time and left children, who have married and left descendants living in Washington, D. C., Yorkville and Spartanburg, S. C.

Twenty-fifth Generation — B

COLONEL CHARLES JONES COLCOCK OF CHARLESTON, SOUTH CAROLINA, was the eldest son of Eliza Mary Hay (vide XXIV—B) by her husband Thomas Hutson Colcock of McPhersonville, S. C.

He was born on the 30th of April, 1820, at "Green Oak Forest," three miles north of the "Boiling Springs," Barnwell District, S. C., where his mother, whose home was in Beaufort District, was on a visit to her uncle, Colonel Frederick Hay of the War of 1812, youngest son of Colonel Ann Hawkes Hay, of the War of 1775-83.

He first attended an excellent boarding school, "The Boiling Springs Academy," and at an early age was taken to Charleston, S. C., by his grandfather, Judge Charles J. Colcock, with whom he subsequently lived until grown, and was educated at the best schools in that city. Later he established the house of "Fackler and Colcock," succeeded by that of "Colcock, McCauley and Molloy," conducting an extensive cotton-factorage business, throughout the States of Alabama, Tennessee, and South Carolina, with headquarters in Charleston. In connection with this business, he owned a plantation adjoining "Foot-Point," managed by an overseer, and planted Sea-island Cotton.

Of strong magnetic personality, he wielded great influence in commercial and political circles, exerted frequently for the benefit of others and in promoting enterprises of a public nature.

He was a director of the Bank of the State; a director of the Memphis, Chattanooga and Charleston Railroad; established a line of steamers to run between Charleston and Savannah, touching at plantation wharves in the tide water region; and organized a company for constructing the Charleston and Savannah Railroad, of which he was an influential director. He was, also, the originator

THE FAMILY OF HAY

of the "The Foot-Point Land Company," which was chartered and began operations for building a railroad terminating at "Foot-Point,"—the natural and expansive deep-sea port of Broad River, where a great city was to be founded—but all these operations were arrested by the Civil War.

On the breaking out of this war, he was Captain of the **Ashley Dragoons** of Charleston, but soon raised the 3d South Carolina Cavalry Regiment, which he commanded throughout the ensuing struggle, and succeeding General "Live Oak Walker," as "acting general," having charge during the last eighteen months of the war, of the 3d Military District of the Confederate States Government, extending from the Ashepoo to the Savannah River, and along the coast. In November, 1864, he posted the troops and commanded at the "Battle of Honey Hill," near Grahamville, S. C., where, after a fierce contest of ten hours, 6000 Federals were driven back, with the loss of 1000 killed and wounded, by 1400 Confederates, who lost but 40 men. A detailed account of this battle is published in the "Charleston Sunday News," of date 10th Dec. 1899, and fills about 12 columns. He likewise commanded and led a brilliant cavalry fight at Florence, S. C., where credit for victory has been given to a general who had crossed the river and was many miles away, having left Colonel Colcock in command of the rear of the retreating Confederate Army.

After the War between the States had ended, it was Colonel Colcock who first suggested that the large store of provisions accumulated by the Federal Government on the Southern coast, should be advanced to the planters, and thus many Southern planters, whose resources had been exhausted by the protracted struggle, were enabled to reclaim their lands and resume their occupation. The Government later, with great generosity, canceled this obligation by a people, the results of whose industrial operations had been swept away by the cotton caterpillar for several consecutive years.

Encouraged by high prices of sea island cotton, Colonel Colcock made the mistake of not resuming the "Factorage Business" subsequent to the war, but operated several large plantations, and although the crops were always promising, they were destroyed by the "worm"; losing heavily, he finally removed to a short-staple-cotton plantation in Hampton County, where he died of pneumonia, A. D. 1891, on the 22d of October, and was buried at "Stoney Creek" cemetery, near McPhersonville. A tablet to his honor has been placed in the Hampton Court House by the survivors of his regiment, and a Confederate camp named for him. In a memorial tribute to Colonel Colcock, in brochure, Captain William A. Courtenay writes:—"It may be said of him as of another knightly leader of men—

> "Wher'er he fought,
> Put so much of his heart into his act,
> That his example had a magnet's force,
> And all were swift to follow whom all loved."

It has been seen he was the eldest son of Eliza Mary Hay by her husband Thomas Hutson Colcock, whose lineage will be found in the following sketch.

The Family of Colcock

Thomas Hutson Colcock (for record of whose children see Eliza Mary Hay, Section XXIV—B), b. 10 Aug. 1797, was admitted to the bar 1818, m. 1st, 15 July 1819, Eliza Mary Hay. He was a member of the Nullification Convention 1832-33. Following the avocation of a planter in Beaufort District, S. C., he d. 6 May 1851, and was bu. at Stoney Creek Church. He was eldest son of Judge Charles Jones Colcock, b. in Charleston, S. C., 11 Aug. 1771, baptised at St. Michael's Church, on the 30th October following, by the Rev. Robert Cooper, whose sponsors were his great-aunt, Mrs. Rebecca Motte of the arrow incident of the Revolution, Jacob Motte, and Robert William Powell.

Graduated at Princeton College, N. J., A. D. 1788, Judge Colcock studied law in the office of the Hon. Henry William DeSaussure and was admitted to practice at the Charleston bar in 1792. Not long after, he was elected Solicitor of the Southern Circuit, returned twice to the South Carolina House of Representatives, 1804 and 1808, was elected by the Legislature Circuit Judge, Associate Judge, and one of the three Judges of the Court of Appeals, over which he at times presided. He was next elected President of the Bank of the State, holding this responsible position until his death. He commanded a fine cavalry company at Ninety-Six, S. C.,

THE FAMILY OF HAY

was a patron of the Charleston Library, being one of the "Brick Members," one of the founders of St. Peter's Church, burned in the fire of 1861, was President of the Board of Trustees of the Charleston Medical College, a member of the South Carolina Society, and installed Grand Master of the Grand Lodge of South Carolina Ancient York Masons. A. D. 1816.

He d. in the sixty-eighth year of his age, 26 January 1839, at Charleston, and was buried in St. Peter's churchyard.

He married at her father's home, near McPhersonville, S. C., A. D. 1795, Mary Woodward, b. 23 Nov. 1774, daughter of Major Thomas Hutson, an officer in Marion's Volunteers of the Revolution (pay warrants to him for services as Captain and Major are on file in the archives at Columbia), by his wife Esther, daughter of William Maine by his wife Judith, daughter of Henry Gignilliat by his wife Esther (aunt of Gen. Francis Marion), daughter of Judith Baluet by her husband Benjamin Marion, son of Perinne Boutignon by her husband Jean Marion, son of Gabriel Marion of Rochelle, France.

Henry Gignilliat was the son of Jean Francois Gignilliat, born at Venay, in Switzerland (son of Abraham Gignilliat by his wife Marie de Ville) by his wife Suzanne Le Serrurier, French Huguenot refugees, settling in South Carolina on the Santee River, just after the revocation of the Edict of Nantes, A. D. 1685; Suzanne was the dau. of Jacques Le Serrurier (one of this name was a marshall of France).

Jacques Le Serrurier by his wife Elizabeth Le Ger, had four daughters:—i. Catherine, who m. the Hon. Henry Le Noble and were progenitors of many of the Marions, DeVeaux, DuBoses, Hamptons, Mazycks, Ravenels, and Dwights; ii. Marianne Le Serrurier, married Isaac Mazyck; iii. Madame Pierre of St. Julian, from whom descend the families of Jervey and others; iv. Suzanne Le Serrurier, m. Jean Francois De Gignilliat, from whom derive the family of Colcock, and a branch of Hutson, etc.

The children of the Rev. William Hutson by his wife, Mrs. Chardon, née Mary Woodward, were:—Mary Hutson, m. Arthur Peronneau; Elizabeth, m. Isaac Hayne, the martyr; Richard Hutson, the Chancellor, an exile to St. Augustine and first Intendant of Charleston; Major Thomas Hutson, m. Esther Maine, as mentioned above; Esther Hutson, m. William Hazzard Wigg; and Anne Hutson, m. Gen. John Barnwell.

(From Jacques Le Surrurier and the Rev. William Hutson and his wives descend many families of the seaboard of South Carolina.)

Major Thomas Hutson, whose daughter married Judge Colcock, was a son of the Rev. William Hutson (who came out from England, and was minister of the First Circular Church of Charleston; he m. 2d the widow of Hugh Bryan and is buried with both wives in the churchyard of the Circular Church on Meeting Street, Charleston, S. C.), by his first wife Mrs. Chardon, née Mary Woodward (relict of Isaac Chardon, whose 1st wife was Marie, dau. of Isaac Mazyck and Marianne Le Surrurier), daughter of Colonel Richard Woodward (son of Dr. Henry Woodward, first permanent English settler in South Carolina, 1666, who was left in the Sanford expedition among the Indians at Port Royal, and taking formal possession of the country for England, learned the language of the Indians, and ever after remained their steadfast friend; he was later a member of the South Carolina Colonial Council, and m. Mary, dau. of Colonel John Godfrey, member of Council, and Acting Governor of the Colony), by his wife Sarah, b. 20 Nov. 1690, dau. of James Stanyarne, b. 1661, d. 1703, member of the South Carolina House of Commons under the Proprietary Government, by his wife Rachel (said to have been a daughter of Jonathan Fitch, member of the Colonial House of Commons).

Judge Colcock had the following children by his wife Mary Woodward Hutson:—

i. Thomas Hutson Colcock, b. 10 August 1797, was admitted to the bar 1818, m. 15 July 1819, Eliza Mary Hay, b. 9 Aug. 1803, and had children, whose records have been given in Section or Chapter XXIV—B, in the course of their mother's history.

By a second marriage he had children:—Eliza Hay, b. 1846, m. 1865, Adolphus Moore of Yorkville, S. C., d. 1886, leaving several children; Joseph W. Colcock, b. 1847, drowned at Galveston, Texas; William Hutson Colcock, b. 1849, d. 1890, m. 1872, Miss Twitty of Spartanburg, and had children, Ethel and a 2d dau.; and James Dunwody Colcock, b. 1851, m. 1883, Mary Elizabeth Park, by whom children, Edward Rowland and Thomas Hutson Colcock.

THE FAMILY OF HAY

ii. John Colcock, b. 6 Mch. 1799, d. 24 June 1872, leaving surviving issue:—Mellicent, b. 1828; Eliza Mary, b. 10 June 1830; and Martha Anna, b. 30 Jan. 1833; all living and the last two married and have issue. Mr. John Colcock was a cotton factor in Charleston of the firm of "Colcock & Co.," doing an extensive business before the war of 1861-66.

iii. William Ferguson Colcock, b. 5 Nov. 1804, d. 1889, was graduated with first honors at the South Carolina College 1821; was admitted to the bar 1825, and entered upon the practice of law at Coosawhatchie, Beaufort District; was elected to the House of Representatives from Prince Williams Parish 1838-40-42-44-46, and was Speaker from 1840 to 1848; was elected to Congress from the 7th Congressional District of S. C. 1848 and re-elected 1850, and 1853 was appointed Collector of the Port of Charleston by President Pierce, holding that office until 1865. He was likewise a Regent of the Smithsonian Institute at Washington, D. C.

He m. 1st 1829, Sarah Huguenin, who dying six months later, he m. 2d Emmeline Lucia, sister to his first wife and by her had children:—i. Edgar Huguenin, b. 1840, d. 1858; ii. Emmeline Sarah, b. 1841, d. 1861; iii. William Ferguson, b. 1843, m. Henrietta Toomer and has a surviving daughter, Annie Toomer, authoress and artist; iv. Cornelius Julius, b. 1845, admitted to the bar, elected to the S. C. Legislature 1898, 1900, and 1902, m. 1890, Pauline Ladson Mew, and has children, Pauline Ladson, Clarence Huguenin, and May Clementine; v. Mary Anna, b. 1847, m. 1869, Dr. Joseph Dewees, and d. 1889, leaving children, Emmeline, m. Joseph W. Lyman of Louisiana, Amelia Lequeux, and Henrietta; vi. Theodora Octavia, b. 1849, m. 1868, Charles Jones Colcock Hutson (deceased) and has living children, Richard, married and Clerk of the U. S. Court of South Carolina; William Colcock, married and has issue, Mary Anna, James Gregorie, Theodora Colcock, Louise d'Aubrey; vii. Henry Hay, b. 1851; viii. Franklin Pierce, b. 1853, m. 1899. Isabel Fraser Cunningham, and has a daughter, Laurie Isabel; ix. Marion Woodward, b. 1856, m. 1st 1884, Sarah Hutson, dau. Dr. Thomas W. Hutson, Sr., see XXIII—A, sketch of Thomas Hay; m. 2d 1900, Mary Woodward Colcock Gregorie, dau. of Esther Colcock by her husband William D. Gregorie, by the 1st marriage, Marion, Dessie, Franklin, Henrietta, and by the 2d marriage, children, William, Harry and Esther; x. Adelaide Huguenin Colcock, b. 3 Sept. 1858.

iv. Richard Woodward Colcock, b. 6 June 1806, entered West Point 1822, from which he was graduated 1826, in the class with Albert Sidney Johnston. He resigned a Lieutenancy in the army to study law and was admitted to the bar at Columbia, S. C., in 1842. In view of his high character and military training, he was appointed

Superintendent of the Citadel Academy, in 1844, into which he introduced the military feature; later he was appointed to a position in the Custom House of Charleston, and d. 14 Aug. 1856, and bu. in St. Michael's churchyard.

Having m. 1843, his cousin Millicent Jane Bacot, by her he left at his death surviving children:—i. Charles J. Colcock, b. 4 Apl. 1844, recently deceased, who m. 1870, Margaret Seabrook Smith (and had children, Margaret Hamilton, m. 1900 George Carroll of Jacksonville, Fla.; Daniel DeSaussure, b. 1879; Mai North, b. 1882, m. John Alfred Calhoun of Charleston and has two children; Millicent Woodward Colcock, b. 1886); ii. Daniel DeSaussure Colcock, b. 22 Jan. 1846, m. 1st Augusta, dau. of the eminent Presbyterian Divine, Dr. Ben Palmer of S. C. and New Orleans, she d. 1875, and he m. 2d 1880, Mattie Rugeley, dau. of A. J. Rugeley by his wife Ellen Blair (and has the following children:—1st marriage, Augusta Palmer, b. 1874, and by the last marriage, Richard Woodward, b. 1880, Mary Rugeley, b. 1882; Daniel De Saussure, b. 1884, and William Ferguson, b. 1898; iii. Richard Hutson Colcock, b. 5 May 1850, m. in New Orleans, La., 1873, Agnes Hannah Stockman (by whom children:—Isabel, b. 1874, m. 1900; Walter Wingate Carré of New Orleans; John, b. 1875; Richard Hutson, Jr., b. 1877; Agnes, b. 1880; James Stockman, b. 1896).

v. Charles Jones Colcock, died young.

The parents of Judge Charles Jones Colcock were John Colcock, Jr., and his wife Millicent, daughter of Joseph Jones (and sister of Major John Jones, who fell in the war of 1776-83, at the siege of Savannah) by his wife Mary (daughter of Robert, eldest son of Colonel Miles Brewton), sister of Miles Brewton, Jr., who m. Mary Izard and built the famous colonial mansion known as No. 25 King Street, Charleston, S. C., in which he entertained Josiah Quincy, Jr., in 1773, and his brother-in-law, Lord William Campbell, in 1775, used as Colonel Balfour's headquarters in the Revolution and as General Howard's headquarters in the war of 1861-65. Mary Brewton, grandmother of Judge Colcock, had the following half-sisters:—Frances Brewton, b. 1733, m. 1753, her first cousin Charles Pinckney, and was mother of the celebrated Charles Pinckney; Rebecca Brewton, b. 15 June 1737, m. 1758, Jacob Motte, and is noted for the arrow incident of the Revolutionary War. (An interesting and correct account of this story, which rests upon the authority of a letter from her grandson Charles Coteswoth Pinck-

THE FAMILY OF HAY 181

ney, to the Columbia Carolinian, is published in the second volume of "The South Carolina Historical and Genealogical Magazine," page 149, in a sketch written by its editor, Mr. A. S. Salley, Jr., now State Historian.)

John Colcock, Jr., was b. at Charleston, S. C., 6 June 1744, and d. 21 August 1782. He was admitted to the practice of law at Charleston in the Court of Common Pleas, 1767; was Secretary and Correspondent of the Charleston Library Society (now the Charleston Library) in 1769; was Justice of the Peace for Berkeley Co. in 1769; in 1772, was Deputy Clerk C. & P. for the Southern Circuit (Districts of Ninety-Six, Orangeburg, Charleston, and Beaufort); in 1775-76 was Assistant to the Commissary-General (Thomas Farr, Jr.) of S. C.; was a member of the First Provincial Congress of S. C. 1775; and was Secretary of the Privy Council in the opening year of the Revolutionary War. His defence of Isaac Hayne, the martyr, may be read in Ramsay's History of the Revolution, and in Gibbes' Documentary History of South Carolina. (For a sketch of John Colcock, see Vol. iii. p. 218, South Carolina Historical Magazine, by A. S. Salley, Jr.) He was m. in St. Michael's Church, 30 Oct. 1768, to Millicent Jones of whom above; and was the fourth child of Captain John Colcock, merchant of Charleston, and Justice of the Peace, by his wife Deborah Milner, to whom he was m. in Charles Town, 13 July 1732.

Captain John Colcock came out from England in command of a sailing vessel and was the son of parents of that kingdom, but abandoned the sea after marriage, and settled down in Charles Town as a merchant, being appointed Justice of the Peace by Lieutenant-Governor Lyttleton. He is the ancestor of all of the name in South Carolina, and d. at the close of 1756. (Vide Vol. III, p. 217, of "The South Carolina Historical and Genealogical Magazine.")

Colonel Charles J. Colcock, eldest son of Eliza Mary Hay by her husband Thomas H. Colcock,—whose maternal lineage is contained in the consecutive chapters of this volume, and whose paternal lineage is presented in the foregoing sketch—was three times married:—

He married 1st, in Charleston, S. C., A. D. 1838 or 1839, Mary Caroline Heyward, granddaughter of Thomas Heyward, Jr., a Signer of The Declaration of Independence, by whom the first two children mentioned below.

He married 2d at her home near Huntsville, Ala., on the 8th of January, 1851, Lucy Frances Horton, daughter of the Hon. Rhodah Horton by his wife Lucy Otey, first cousin of Bishop James Hervey Otey of Tennessee, the originator and first Chancellor of "The University of the South," at Sewanee, by whom the third, fourth, and fifth child mentioned below (she d. in Charleston, Apl. 1862, and bu. at Magnolia Cemetery).

He married 3d near Robertville, S. C., Dec. 1864, Agnes, youngest child of Mr. Benjamin Bostick, who is still living, and by her had the last five children mentioned below.

Colonel Colcock by his three marriages had the following children:—

   i.   John Colcock, b. 7 Aug. 1843, was a member of the 3d. S. C. Cavalry during the Civil War, and d.s. 6 Mch. 1877.
   ii.   Caroline Ann Colcock, b. 4 Nov. 1840, d. 18 Sept. 1855.
   iii. Charles Jones Colcock, b. in Beaufort District, S. C., 17 Jan. 1852, attended the College of Charleston for two years, and was graduated at Union University, Schenectady, N. Y., where he taught mathematics for three years, and is now Head Master of the Porter Military Academy, Charleston, S. C., where he was prepared for college. He married his cousin, Patti Lee Hay, daughter of Judge Samuel Hay (vide Section XXV—A) by his wife, Susan, daughter of Colonel Frederick Hay, youngest son of Colonel Ann Hawkes Hay (Section XXII) and by her had children:—(He is the writer of this book.)

        i. Samuel Hay Colcock, died in Charleston at the age of six months, and was buried at Magnolia Cemetery.
        ii. Errol Hay Colcock, (a daughter) now a school girl.

   iv. Francis Horton Colcock, b. at Bellevue near Huntsville, Ala. Prepared for college at "The Holy Communion Institute," now changed to "The Porter Military Academy" in honor of its great and good founder; he was graduated at Union College A. D. 1877. He studied law in the office of General James Connor of Charleston, S. C., where he was admitted to the bar, and practiced law for a few years. He is now Professor of Mathematics at the South Carolina University, Columbia, S. C.

He m. Mary Robert, daughter of Mr. Seaborn Jones by his wife Jennie Bostick, of Screven County, Georgia, by whom children:—
i. Francis Horton, deceased; ii. Anna Eustace, m. Alva DePass, attorney-at-law in Columbia, and has a little daughter, Anna; iii. Charles

THE FAMILY OF HAY 183

Jones; iv. Frances Horton; v. Seaborn Jones Colcock.
- v. Errol Hay Colcok, b. at "Bellevue," Ala., 1 July 1859, d. in Hampton County of a congestive chill, 6 Oct. 1882, and bu. at Stoney Creek, Beaufort County.
- vi. Catherine Colcock, b. 9 Sept. 1865, now living in New Orleans with her husband, Robert Godin Guerard of Savannah, Ga.
- vii. Helen McIver Colcock, b. 3 Jan. 1867, now living in Grahamville, S. C.; she married Charles Colcock Gregorie, son of Dr. Thomas Gregorie of Grahamville, S. C., by whom the following children:— Agnes; Thomas; Charles, Louisa; Joseph Gregorie.
- viii. Woodward Hutson Colcock, b. 11 Sept. 1869, d. 23 Sept. 1885, is buried at "Stoney Creek."
- ix. William Bostick Colcock, b. 7 July 1872, living in Florida.
- x. Agnes J. Colcock, b. 22 July 1877, d. 19 Oct. 1884, at the early age of seven years.

THE FAMILY OF HAY

A reader of our manuscript having directed attention to the omission of the lines of descent of Colonel Hay from the Scandinavian Count Rognvald through the family of Bruce, and from the Emperor Charlemagne, and the Saxon King, Alfred the Great, we add the following tables, making them as concise as is consistent with historical clearness.

Conclusion

TABLE I.

Descent of Colonel Hay from the early Norse Kings:—

1. Rognvald, Count of Moeri and Earl of Orkney, was the son of Eistein, son of Thebotan Duke of Sleswick by his wife Ascrida, daughter of Rognvald, son of Olaus (Olaf) King of Norway.
2. Torf Eynor, his son, was also Earl of Orkney. For an account of his exploits, refer to the Saga of Harald Haarfager, introduced into the earlier part of this work.
3. Thorfinn, his son, Earl of Orkney, married Goriola, daughter of Duncan, Earl of Caithness.
4. Hlodver, their son, Earl of Orkney, married 2d Gudna, daughter of Kiarval, King of Ireland.
5. Sigurt Lodvison, their son, Earl of Orkney, married 1st Olith (Alice), daughter of King Malcolm II., and had a son the great Earl Thorfinn, m. 2d Thora, only child of King Hacon the Good, son of King Harald Haarfager by his wife Thora, and by her had sons, Somerled, Brusée, and Eynor.
6. Brusée, son, was Earl of a part of Orkney, and died A. D. 1033.
7. Rognvald Brucesson (son of Brusée) married Ostrida, daughter of Rognvald Wolfsen, and was Earl of Gothland.

He accompanied his cousin Ingigred, daughter of King Olaf, to Russia on her way to wed Jarislief, King of Russia (by whom she had sons, Valdimar and Visiwald).

Rognvald was granted the Earldom of Ladoga by the Queen. He had an adventurous career, going to the Holy Land to fight the Saracens, and residing for a time at Constantinople.

He was murdered A. D. 1046, by Aldred, son of Uchtred, Earl of Northumberland, and left two sons:—Eyliff and Ulf. It is said that these sons settled in Normandy, then in possession of their kinsman, Robert, Duke of Normandy, likewise descended from Count Rognvald; were baptised Christians, taking the names Regenvald and Robert, from whom descend the family of Bruce in England and Scotland.

We shall consider the posterity of Robert.

THE FAMILY OF HAY 185

8. Robert de Brusée, youngest son of Rognvald Brucesson, built in Normandy the castle of Brussée or Brux near Valognes, married Emma, daughter of Allan, Lord of Brittany, and had sons:—Alan, Lord Brix and Adelme (or Adam).

9. Adelme, or Adam Brus, 2d son of Robert, came to England with Queen Emma A. D. 1050, and upon her death retired to the north. Sixteen years later, on the invasion of England by Duke William, he was one of the Conqueror's generals, and, commissioned by him to subdue the north, was rewarded by a gift of 94 manors in Yorkshire, of which Skelton in Cleveland was the chief. He was likewise given lands in Scotland by Edgar, whom he had assisted in dethroning his uncle, Donald Bane.

   He married Emma, dau. of Sir William Ramsay, by whom he had sons:—Robert; William, Prior of Gisborough; Duncan; and a dau., Rossilina, who married Walter de Moreville, Great Constable of Scotland.

10. Sir Robert de Brus, Lord of Cleveland, son, married Agnes, daughter of Fulke of Paganell (his marriage a second time to an Agnes of Annand is said to be an invention—Annandale was a possession of his father Adelme) by whom sons:—Adam; and Robert le Meschin, to whom he gave Annandale and other Scotch estates.

    He was present at the Battle of the Standard and d. 1141.

11. Robert de Brus, 2d son, was the 1st Lord of Annandale. He was captured by his father at the Battle of the Standard, having espoused the cause of David I. Delivered by his father a prisoner to King Stephen, he was given by the latter to his own mother in ward, and held for a time at Skelton. His father now added to his Scotch possessions by the grant of Herts and Hertnesse in Durham. By his wife, Euphemia, he had sons:—Robert, who m. Isabel dau. of William the Lion, but died s.p.; and William.

12. William de Brus, 2d son, succeeded his brother, sat in the Parliament of King John, married Christina, d. 1215, and was buried at Gisborough Abbey. Issue:—Robert; William; John.

13. Robert le Noble, succeeded his father William de Brus. He married Isobel, 2d dau. of David, Earl of Huntingdon, by his wife Maude, daughter of Hugh, Earl of Chester (son of Ralph de Gernous, 4th earl, son of Ralph, or Randle de Meschnes, Viscounte de Bayeux, by Maud, sister of Hugh Lupus, 1st earl, nephew to King William I., being his half-sister's son and d. 1101).

    David Earl of Huntingdon, was the 3d son of Henry, Prince of Scotland (son of King David I. by Maud, dau. of Waltheof) by his wife, The Lady Adeline de Warren, dau. of William, Earl of Warren and Surrey, by his wife Gunnora, youngest daughter of William the Conqueror, by his wife Matilda of Flanders, whose descent from the Emperor Charlemagne will be given presently.

David of Huntingdon and his wife Adeline de Warren, had children:—John le Scot, m. Helena, dau. of Llewellen, Prince of Wales, poisoned by his wife; ii. Margaret, m. 1207, Alan, Lord of Galloway; iii. Isobel, m. Robert de Brus; iv. Maude, d.s.; v. Ada, m. Henry of Hastings—from these sisters descended the competitors for the crown in 1290. He was styled Lord of Annandale and, d. 1245, his wife, b. 1226, d. 1251, and both were buried at Saltre Abbey, near Stilton, beside David of Huntingdon. They left sons:—Robert and Richard.

14. Robert Brus, the Competitor, eldest son, was b. 1210, and d. at Lochmaben, 1295. He was Sheriff of Cumberland and Governor of Carlisle Castle, and had the delivery of his mother's estates as one of the co-heirs of John le Scot, Earl of Chester and Huntingdon, as well as many other estates in Scotland and England.

He was nominated a regent of Scotland and guardian of Alexander II., and his child-queen, Margaret, dau. of Henry III. He was signed with the Cross, and accompanied Edward to the Holy Land. Upon the death of "The Maid of Norway," he summoned his friends to his Castle, Turnberry, and advanced his claims to the Scottish throne, awarded by Edward I. to John Balliol.

He m. 1242-44, Isabel de Clare, daughter of Gilbert, 3d Earl of Gloucester, by whom 5 children.

15. Robert Brus, "viel counte of Carrick," eldest son, was born circa 1245, appointed Governor of Carlisle, he accompanied Prince Edward to the Holy Land. On his return, he met Marjorie, only daughter of Niel, Earl of Carrick, while hawking, and as she was a beautiful girl and rich heiress, he immediately lost his heart to her, and they were married A. D. 1271 when she was but 15 years of age. She had been left an infant daughter of Margaret (daughter of Walter the High Steward) by her husband Niel, 2d Earl of Carrick, one of the Guardians of Scotland in 1255, son of Duncan, 1st Earl of Carrick, who founded the Cross Raguel, son of Gilbert, d. A. D. 1186, son of Fergus, Lord of Galloway by his wife Elizabeth, dau.-nat. of King Henry I. The Earl of Gloucester was likewise descended from King Henry I.

Robert Brus, "viel counte of Carrick," had 5 sons and 7 daughters:—Robert le jeune Counte, later King; Edward fell at the Battle of Dundalk, 1318; Thomas and Alexander, beheaded at Carlisle; Sir Nigel or Niel, beheaded at Berwick.

Of the daughters, Lady Isabel Bruce m. Sir Thomas Randolph of Strathdon (vide Earls of Moray, Dunbar, and March in an earlier part of this work); Lady Mary Bruce m. Sir Alexander

Rev. Samuel Hutson Hay, Presbyterian Minister, son of Col. Frederick J. Hay. (From the original portrait painted by Fitzsimmons of New York City)

Mary Peck of Virginia, wife of Rev. Samuel Hutson Hay. (Courtesy of Mrs. Fred Gantt of Columbia, S.C. From the original portrait by Fitzsimmons of New York City)

THE FAMILY OF HAY

Fraser (vide Family of Fraser in this work); Lady Christian Bruce m. Gratney, 11th Earl of Mar (vide Families of Mar and of Sutherland in this work); Lady Matilda or Maud m. Hugh, Earl of Ross; Lady Margaret Bruce m. Sir William Carlyle; Lady Elizabeth Bruce m. Sir William Dishington; and an unknown daughter m. Sir David de Brechin.

King Robert I., son, b. at Turnberry Castle, 11 July 1274, when 17 years of age became Earl of Carrick. He was also Lord of Annandale, Lord of the Garioch, etc., in Scotland, and Lord of Herts and of Hertnesse in Durham, and of many other English possessions, for which he owed fealty to the English sovereign.

(For an account of his struggle for the Crown of Scotland, the reader is referred to the 1st part of this work.)

Marjorie Bruce, daughter, m. Walter the High Steward.

King Robert II., son, married 1st Elizabeth, daughter of Sir Adam Mure of Rowallan, in county of Ayr.

King Robert III., son, whose name at first was John, married Annabella, daughter of Sir John Drummond of Stobhall.

The Princess Mary, 3d child, married Sir George Douglas, Earl of Angus, brother of the hero of Otterburn. (Vide Family of Douglas in this work.)

The Lady Elizabeth Douglas, daughter, married, 1st Sir Alexander, 1st Lord Forbes, m. 2d Sir David Hay of Yester, from whom the Earls and Marquises of Tweeddale. (Vide Family of Douglas, this work.)

The Lady Forbes (a daughter) married Sir William Urquhart of Cromarty. (Vide Family of Urquhart in this work.)

Sir Alexander Urquhart of Cromarty, son, married Katherine, dau. of Sir James Ogilvie of Deskford. (Vide ibid.)

Katherine Urquhart of Cromarty, daughter, married William the Hay of Lochloy. Vide Part II. of this work; see also "The Bruces and the Cumyns," published at Edinburgh and London, in 1870, by William Blackwood and Sons, pages 618-19-20-21.) (A. D. 1511.)

John the Hay of Lochloy, son, married Isobel Dunbar, d. 1554. (Vide ibid.)

John the Hay,, Lord of Lochloy and Park, son. d. 1598, married Janet Sutherland, daughter of William Sutherland of Duffus, descended from the Earls of Sutherland and ancestor to the Lords Duffus of England. (Vide ibid; also Burke's Landed Gentry; also History of Nairnshire.)

George Hay, 2d son, died ante 1600. (Vide ibid; also "The History of Nairnshire," by George Bain.)

Sir Alexander Hay of Easter Kennet, Director in Chancery and

Clerk Register, and Lord of Sessions, son of George, charter 1582, married Mariot Farquhar. (Vide "The Bruces and the Cmyns," p. 619. An account of Sir Alexander is given in "The Dictionary of National Biography.")

29. Mr. John Hay, eldest son, married Mariot Drummond (vide ibid).
30. Mr. David Hay of Easter Kennet, Craigtown, Kennet Pans, and of Woodcockdale (sold Easter Kennet to Bruce, friar of Clackmannan for 16,000 merks, A. D. 1638, vide ibid) and married Jean Winrhame (vide copies of documents given in the 2d part of this work under the section devoted to David Hay of Easter Kennet).

    He was the 2d son of Mr. John Hay and his wife Mariot Drummond, and had two sons:—John Hay of Woodcockdale and James Hay of Carruber or Carriber.

31. James Hay of Carruber, 2d son, Clerk of Sessions, died A. D. 1702, married Madgdalen Robertson, of the family of Strowan, and had 4 sons and 2 daughters (vide Part II. of this work; also "The Bruces and the Cumyns").

32. Thomas Hay, son, Writer to the Signet, and Writer in Edinburgh, of Bridgehouse, sometimes referred to as "of Carriber," d. 1733, married Isabel Balfour, daughter of Michael Balfour, granddaughter of Sir David Balfour of Forret (vide the section of this work devoted to Thomas Hay of Bridgehouse, with copies of documents).

33. Michael Hay of Kingston, Island of Jamaica, d. 1762, married Esther, daughter of Judge Martin Wilkins of Jamaica, W. I. Eldest son of Thomas Hay by his wife Isabel Balfour (vide documents presented earlier in this work).

34. Colonel Ann Hawkes Hay, only son, b. 1745, removed to New York after his marriage to Martha, daughter of Judge William Smith of New York (vide the account of Colonel Hay presented earlier in this work).

    His descendants are now living in South Carolina, and in Raliegh, N. C.

TABLE II.

Descent of Colonel Hay from the Emperor Charlemagne and William I.:—
Referring to "The Family of Cumyn" in an earlier part of this book, it may be seen how Colonel Hay descends from the great emperor of the Franks through that line; two other lines of descent will now be given.

1. Pepin d'Heristal, d. A. D. 714. A ruler of the Franks, he became Major Domus of Australasia A. D. 676 by his victory at Testri over all the Franks, styling himself Dux et Princeps Francorum in 687.
2. Charles Martel, his son, was b. about 690, and d. 22 Oct. 741. He was Duke of Austria.

THE FAMILY OF HAY

3. Pepin the Short, his son, was King of the Franks. He aided the Pope in his wars, to whom he granted the exarchate of Ravenna, the Pentapolis, and territories of Bologna and Ferrara, thus laying the foundation of "The Papal States."
4. Charles the Great, or Charlemagne, was b. at Liege, Bavaria, 2 April A. D. 742. He was the great King of the Franks and Emperor of the Romans, and d. at Aachem, Germany, 28 Jan. 814.
5. Louis Le Pieux and Le Debonnaire, his son, was b. 778, and d. near Mainz, 840. He was Emperor of the Roman Empire.

    By his 1st marriage he had 3 sons, Lothair, Pepin, and Louis; when he married a second time and had a son, Charles, to whom he designated Alamannia with title of King, it caused a rebellion by the brothers in which the father was made prisoner, but later released and restored to his throne by Louis.
6. Charles the Bald, his son, was b. at Frankfort on the Maine 13 June 823, and d. near Mont Cenis, 6 Oct. 877. He was King of the Franks and Emperor of Rome. He invaded Italy and was crowned Emperor by Pope John V., A. D. 875.
7. Judith, his daughter, having married in turn, Aethelwulf and Aethelbald, married Baldwin I., Earl of Flanders, son of Ingelramn, son of Lideric, d. 836, son of Saluet, Prince of Dijon by his wife, Eringarde, dau. of Girard, Lord of Rousillon (Saluet was traditionally descended from King Priam of Troy, 1200 B. C.)
8. Baldwin II., son, Count of Flanders, builder of the walls of Bruges and Ypres, married Aelfryth, daughter of Aelfred the Great and d. 918.
9. Arnulph the Elder, their son, slew William Longsword, the Norman Duke, and m. Adela, dau. of the Count of Vermandois.
10. Baldwin III., his son, Count of Flanders, promoted the industrial interest of his country by establishing the first weavers of Ghent and laid the foundation of its liberty by appointing 12 vassals to constitute a Council. He d. A. D. 961.
11. Arnulph the Younger, his son, succeeded as Count of Flanders, and d. A. D. 989.
12. Baldwin IV. (Pulchra Barba), his son, succeeded, and fought successfully against the King of France and the Emperor Henry II., gaining from the latter the cession of Valenciennes, Walcheran, and the Island of Zealand. He d. A. D. 1036.
13. Baldwin V., his son, succeeded as Count of Flanders. He m. Adela, daughter of Robert of France.
14. Matilda of Flanders, his eldest daughter, married 1053, William, Duke of Normandy, and was crowned Queen of England at Westminster, A. D. 1067. She is noted for having embroidered the

Bayeux Tapestry. Her husband, William of Normandy, having conquered the kingdom A. D. 1066, became King William I. of England.

15. Gunnora, his youngest daughter, married William de Warren, created Earl of Surrey by William Rufus, his brother-in-law, and d. 1135.

16. The Lady Adeline de Warren, their daughter, m. Henry, Prince of Scotland, eldest son of King David I., who predeceased his father.

17. David, Earl of Huntington, their youngest son, married Maud, daughter of Hugh, 5th Earl of Chester, son of Randel or Ralph, 4th earl, son of Ralph de Meschines, Vicount de Bayeux of Normandy, 3d Earl, by Maud, sister of the 1st Earl, Hugh Lupus, nephew of King William I.

18. The Lady Isobel, daughter, m. Robert Bruce, le Noble, from whom the descent of King Robert Bruce (and of Colonel Hay) may be seen by referring to Table I., generations 13 to 34, inclusive.

TABLE III.

1. Charles III., King of France, was b. A. D. 879, and d. A. D. 929. He was the son of King Louis II., the son of Charles the Bald, the son of King Louis Le Debonnaire, son of Charlemagne.

   In the year 911 he ceded Normandy, with the hand of his daughter Gisela, to the Norse viking, Rollo, son of Earl Rognvald, from whom we have seen were descended King Robert I., and the earls of Strathearn.

2. Rollo, banished from Scandinavia by King Harald Haarfager, sailed around Scotland and Ireland, ascended the Seine and forcibly seized Rouen and the lands between the Seine and the Epte, extorting from Charles III. of France the cession of Normandy, and the hand of his daughter Gisela. He d. in the year 930.

3. William Longsword, their son, succeeded as Duke of Normandy, and ruled his dukedom from 927 to 943, when he was murdered by Arnulph, Count of Flanders, in an island of the Somne.

4. A daughter of William Longsword married Kenneth III., King of Scotland, and it will be found by referring to the first pages of this history that they were progenitors of Colonel Hay.

   Richard the Fearless, d. 996, succeeded his father as the 3d Duke of Normandy, and married a daughter of Count Hugh of Paris (styled Hugh the Great Count of Paris, who refused the Crown of France, conferring it on Rodolph, Duke of Burgundy, and married 1st a daughter of Edward the Elder, and married 2d Hedwig, sister of Otho the Great, Emperor of Germany and the Roman Empire, and dau. of Henry I., King of Germany, b. 876,

d. 936, surnamed The Fowler, who was one of the great rulers of Germany, and first of the Saxon line to reign over that country, he consolidated the monarchy and defeated the Huns A. D. 933, son of Otho, Prince of Saxony), the brother of Eudes, King of France, and son of Robert, Duke of France, son of Robert the Strong, styled Count of Paris, slain A. D. 866, by the Norman chief, Hastings.

5. Richard the Good succeeded his father and was the 4th Duke of Normandy from 996 to 1036.

6. Robert le Diable, 5th Duke, died at Nicea, 1035, returning from Palestine, sending to his son the message, "I am being borne to Paradise by four black devils," in allusion to the Moorish slaves who were bearers of his litter in which he was ill. Robert, the 6th Duke, succeeded. Under the law of the country, he was not allowed to marry a subject, but was faithful to Herleva, daughter of Fulbert, the tanner, by whom he had a son:—

7. William the Conqueror, 7th Duke of Normandy, married his cousin Matilda of Flanders, daughter of Count Baldwin.

It is related she at first refused to marry William; enraged, he pushed her down, and rolled her over the ground. This rough wooing seems to have won her heart, for marrying William, she made him a devoted wife, and the two were crowned A. D. 1067, King and Queen of England. From William I. and Queen Matilda, the descent of King Robert Bruce (and of Colonel Hay) has been already traced to Table II., 14-8; and then in Table I., 13-34.

(There are likewise two additional lines of descent through King Henry I., which have been already given.)

TABLE IV.

Descent of Colonel Hay from King Alfred the Great:—
Cedric, a Saxon Ealderman, founded a settlement in England on the Hampshire coast, A. D. 495, assumed the title of King of the West Saxons 519, and conquered the Isle of Wight, A. D. 530. From him descended:—

1. Eegberht, King of Wessex, b. 775, d. 837, reigned 802-837.
2. Ethelwulf, King of Wessex, his son, d. 858, married Osburgh, dau. of Oshac, his cupbearer.
3. Aelfred the Great, King of West Saxony, his son, b. at Wantage, Berkshire, A. D. 849, d. A. D. 901, reigned 871-901. He married Elswitha.
4. Edward the Elder, his son, succeeded to the throne 901, and died at Parndon, Northamptonshire, 925.

5. Eadmund the Magnificent, his son, was born circa 922, and was assassinated on the 26th May 946, by Leofa, a robber, at Pucklechurch, Gloucestershire. He was King of Mercia and Wessex, subdued Cumbria, which he bestowed on Malcolm II. of Scotland.
He married Aelgifu.

6. Edgar the Peaceful, his son, b. 944, d. 975, succeeded his brother Eadwig to the throne. He ceded Lothian to Kenneth; and married Elfrida.

7. Aelthelred the Unready, b| 968, d. 1016, his son, married 2d the Lady Emma, dau. of Richard, son of William, son of Rollo, and by her was father of Edward the Confessor.
By his 1st wife, Aelfaod, he had a son:—

8. Edmund Ironsides, b. circa 989, ruled over West Saxony, while Canute the Dane governed East England. He was a brave Prince and an able sovereign.

9. Aedward the Aetheling, his son, was sent, while a child, to Denmark by the the Danish King, Hardicanute. Was later recalled from Hungary, where he had married a Hungarian lady of rank, by his uncle Edward the Confessor, but was not recognized by the people as King, the Crown being usurped by Harold, son of Earl Godwan.
He had a son Edgar Aetheling, and two daughters, who were given refuge at the Court of Malcolm of Scotland.

10. The Princess Margaret, daughter of Aedward the Aetheling, styled St. Margaret for her saintliness, her charity to the poor, and her many other virtues.
She married Malcolm III., styled Malcolm Cawnmohr, over whose fierce and generous nature she exerted a softening influence. They had sons:—Edgar, Alexander, and David I., successively kings of Scotland.

11. David I, succeeded his brothers, who died without issue, as King of Scotland. He married Maud, daughter of Waltheof by his treacherous wife, Judith, niece of William the Conquerer.

12. Henry, Prince of Scotland, their son, predeceased his father. He married the Lady Adeline de Warren, daughter of William, Earl of Warren and Surrey. He was a noble young prince, greatly admired and beloved. His early death was deplored not alone in Scotland but at the English Court.

13. David, Earl of Huntingdon, their 3d son, married Maud, daughter of Hugh, Earl of Chester, descended from King Henry I. of England.

14. Isobel, their daughter, married Robert Bruce, Lord of Annandale, styled "Le Noble," first competitor for the crown.
(For descent of Colonel Hay from this pair, refer to Table I, from 13 to 34.)

All are familiar with the life of Alfred the Great—warrior, statesman, poet, musician, and scholar of his day and generation. He was the founder of Oxford University and of English prose. The following version of The Lord's Prayer is one of his translations and will serve as a sample of the English of the ninth century:

"Faeder ure thu the earth on heafenum, si thin mama gehalgod, to be cume thin rice, Gewurthe hin willa on earthn swa swa on heafenum, urne ge daegwanlican hlaf syle us to daeg; and forgyf us ure gyltas, swa swa we firgivath urum gyltendum, and ne geladde thu us or consenung ac alyse us of yfle."

Recommending to them for an inspiration the virtues of their great progenitor, and hoping they may model their lives upon His whose servant he was, we bid our reader farewell.

Appendix

DEDICATED
TO THE REMEMBRANCE OF
ANN HAWKES HAY.
CITIZEN OF HAVERSTRAW PRINCINCT,
YOUNG MAN EXTRAORDINARY OF THE
AMERICAN REVOLUTION,
COLONEL OF THE THIRD REGIMENT OF
THE ORANGE COUNTY MILITIA,
SPIRITED COMPEER OF THE YOAST-MABIE MEETINGS
THAT DRAFTED THE ORANGETOWN RESOLUTIONS,
DELEGATE TO THE NEW YORK CITY
ELECTORAL CONVENTION,
MEMBER OF THE SECOND PROVINCIAL CONGRESS,
SELF-SACRIFICING QUARTERMASTER,
LOYAL FRIEND OF WASHINGTON,
A LOCAL MAN WHOSE LIFE SHED
A BRILLIANT LUSTER ON THE FOUNDERS' PLEDGE OF
"OUR LIVES, OUR FORTUNES AND OUR
SACRED HONOR."

From the plaque reproduced in the Haverstraw High School Annual

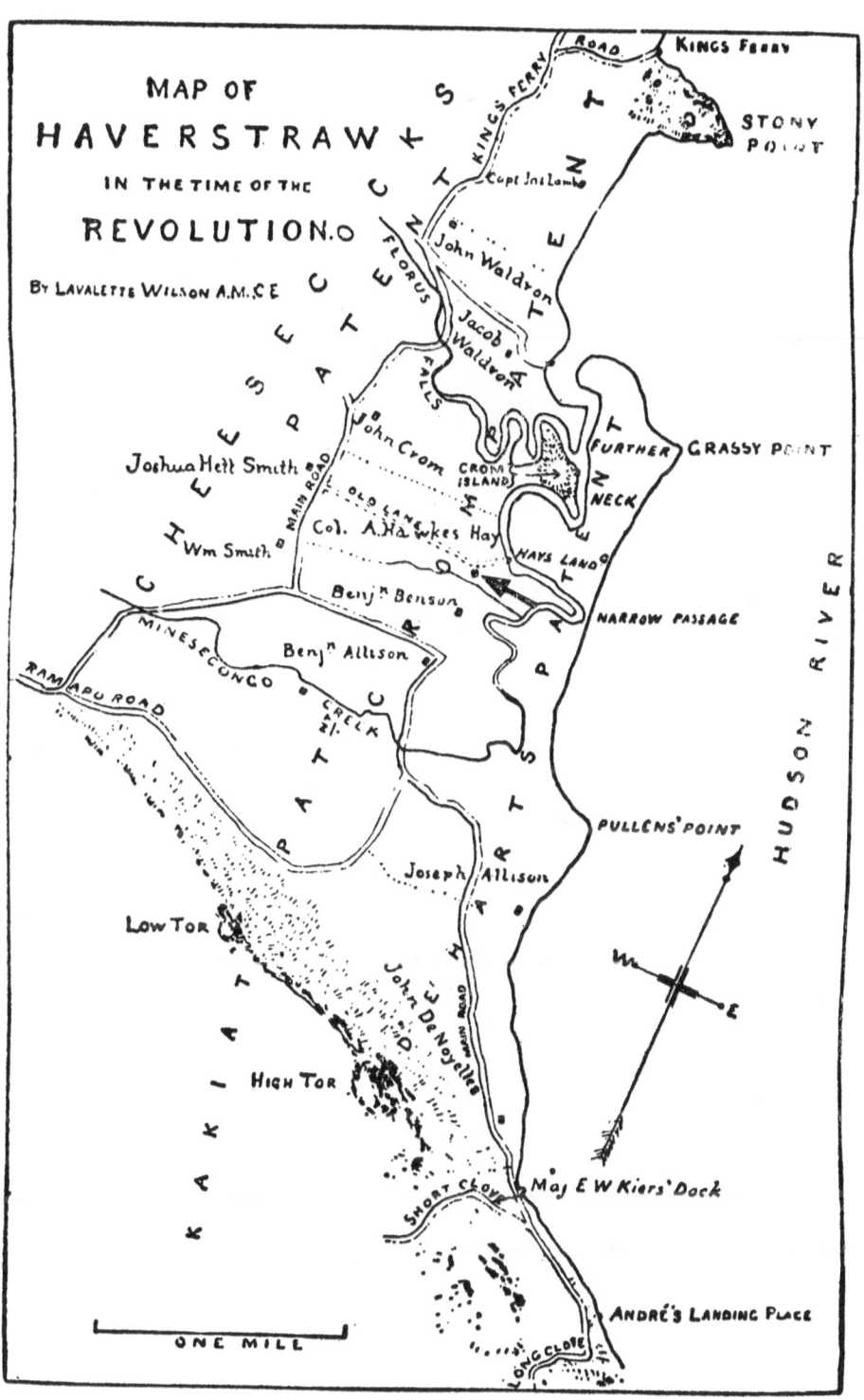

Small arrow points to Col. Hay's home

LATER LINES

Since "The Family of Hay" was published in 1908, several generations have been added to the clan and this appendix is an attempt to bring the lines down to include the last additions to the family.

Some of the descendants could not be reached. Therefore several blank pages are left at the back of the book so that those desiring to do so, may bring down their lines in writing as our grandparents did in the old "Family Bible."

COLONEL ANN HAWKES HAY
YOUNG MAN EXTRA-ORDINARY

From The RECENSIO, the annual of the Haverstraw, N. Y. High School. Written by Mr. Harry Hale Smith, historian of Haverstraw. Col. Ann Hawkes Hay is featured in the 1957-58 issue.

> (The Banners are dancing;)
> The red shields advancing,
> The Hay, the Hay, the Hay!
> Mac Garadh is coming;
> Give way, give way!
> The Hay, the Hay, the Hay!
> Cry Hollen Mac Garadh!
> Give way!

When the great families of the British North Country assembled for their periodic "gatherings", it was customary to show prowess by military exercises and by athletic games, but there were always, it may be assumed, contests in poetry as well, for the gathering itself must be celebrated in verse. At the head of this column is a fragment of verse adapted from "A GATHERING" written by Captain James Hay in 1715. It gives their battle cry and celebrates their warlike tradition. Captain James Hay himself borrowed from an earlier poem of the clan in Gaelic.

Of such a military tradition were the Hays of Erroll and Lochloy, and of such a tradition came the man who was the eyes and ears of General Washington in the Haverstraw precinct—then consisting of what is now Stony Point, Ramapo, the present Haverstraw township and Clarkstown. (The other Precinct in "Orange County South of the Mountains" was Orangetown. The Haverstraw precinct was set up by the province in June, 1719.) This scion of the Hays of Erroll and Lochloy was the center of military intelligence and communication, the bureau of purchase and a forwarding agency, as well, for the Continental forces in this district. He was the center of recruitment, the active commander of a company of volunteers, as well as the commander of the Third Regiment of Orange County Milita, having the defense of the West Shore of the Hudson from Stony Point to Ft. Lee as his assignment. He was our delegate to the New York City Convention that elected our representatives to the Second Continental Congress, and he was the statesman who headed the Provincial Congress Committee which apportioned among the several counties, the number of recruits to be furnished to the Continental Forces.

General John Morin Scott called him, in a letter to Washington, "a gentlemen uncommonly spirited in the publick cause", and General Washington himself wrote of him as a "faithful and indefatigable officer".

This man with a back-breaking assignment of duties, this man who received and merited the high praise of his superiors—this Haverstraw man was—Colonel Ann Hawkes Hay. He was a young man at the time of all these enumerated duties—and a young man whom the enemy appreciated and respected, for twice he was offered a Commission in the Royal Army by the British authorities in this county, and not improbably through the efforts of some of his Tory-in-laws. Colonel Hay declined the commissions with emphasis. He was the son of Michael Hay, a wealthy Jamaica planter, born in Edinburgh, Scotland. His mother, Esther, was the daughter of Kingston's Judge Martin Wilkins by his first wife, Ann Sharpington.

All the records indicate that the Hays were people of wealth and substance. The Hay who was to lead a New York township into and through a great war was born in August 14, 1745. He was, therefore, thirty-one years old in 1776. Like many another islander the man who was to become Colonel Hay came to New York City to be educated. He came with his half uncle, but two years older; moreover, like many another college boy, he married when eighteen, while yet in school. His choice of wife was Martha Smith, daughter of Judge William Smith, Sr. of the Provincial Courts, who was born in the Isle of Ely, England and came to New York in 1715. As an attorney he had, until disbarred, defended the accused in the famous Peter Zenger case, and laid the ground work for Andrew Hamilton of Philadelphia who succeeded Smith as Zenger's attorney. Martha Smith was the sister of Tom, Hett, John and William Smith of Haverstraw. This family fact accounts probably, for Hay and his wife coming to Haverstraw at all. He had lived in Jamaica at first, after his marriage, but

APPENDIX — THE FAMILY OF HAY

the Hays there lost their first three children. They came to the scattered community on the Hudson for reasons of health and to be near his wife's relatives.

When Colonel Hay came to Haverstraw, he was a man of means, but being general Quartermaster did not add to, but drained his fortune. In order to purchase supplies, at all, so distrustful were the Whig farmers of the Continental Congress that it was necessary for Colonel Hay to guarantee payment. This necessity together with furnishing transport depleted his funds.

After the treason of Arnold, the British instituted the policy of burning the homes of the Militia officers, and one day a landing, in force, was made, when the family was away and help was not near, Colonel Hay's house was burned. The family had anticipated this as a possibility, and had buried their silver and other valuables and family records, and other papers in the garden; but an intimidated slave belonging to the Hays revealed the hiding place, and all these buried articles were carried off by the British. Colonel Hay's no inconsiderable property in Jamaica was then confiscated by the Crown. Carried away by the British were, it appears, the family genealogical records, which it was left for later generations of Hays to reconstruct from the archives in Scotland. Through about thirty-four generations, the family traces its lineage to Cedric, the Saxon, who flourished in 495 A. D., and this lineage would also include, of course, Alfred, the Great, of England.

Through seven years of war, Colonel Ann Hawkes Hay continued zealous in behalf of the land of his adoption, and left an example, applauded by such thoughtful writers as Paulding in his LIFE OF WASHINGTON, and Abbott in his CRISIS OF THE AMERICAN REVOLUTION.

Colonel Hay died suddenly in New York in the year 1786 leaving a large family (twelve children), which shortly divided. (The first 3 had died in infancy.) Some moved to the South and some to Northern New York State.* The descendants of this substantial Revolutionary stock still flourish in the Carolinas and in Clinton County in up-state New York.

How pleasant in the ears of Americans should be the oath of association which at that time of greatest danger, this man signed:

---

* At the time of his death, Colonel Hay was not altogether without property, though we should probably say now that he was "land poor." He had acquired in 1769 a tract of land in two parcels—one of 13,500 acres and one of 15,500 acres—on South Hero Island, Lake Champlain, and in the Township of Chazy in what is now Clinton County, but the title was clouded by conflicts of state claims and by the claims of actual squatters. Ultimately this inheritance was visited by two of Colonel Hay's sons—Michael and Thomas, and eventually part of this inheritance was recovered through the advice of their attorney, Aaron Burr. Descendants of Colonel Hay still live in Clinton County,

"Do in the most solemn manner, resolve never to become slaves; and do associate under all the ties of religion, honor and love of our country."

The more impressive thing is that he kept the oath.

A LETTER FROM A NEW YORK MEMBER OF THE CLAN TO HIS SOUTHERN COUSIN—KATE ERROLL HAY OF ALLENDALE, SOUTH CAROLINA

West Chazy, New York,
Oct. 23, 1899

My dear cousin:

I was pleased to receive your kind letter and to be made aware that I have a kinswoman in whom I am quite sure I recognize a kindred spirit. I feel highly honored in the discovery of such a cousin and in being the recipient of such a letter.

I assure you I appreciate your patriotism and pride of family and I shall look forward with the highest anticipation to the time—be it near or far distant—when I shall have the pleasure of meeting you personally.

I've never known much of our great grandmother's family, the Smiths, except as they were mentioned historically in connection with the Revolution.

You spoke of having a portrait of Judge William Smith, our honored ancestor. In case you have one to spare I shall be delighted to receive your kind offer, also any photographs of the Hay family at the South, especially one of your own which I would highly prize.

I was twelve years old when my grandfather Hay died and remember many of the ancedotes and stories he used to relate in regard to his own immediate family.

I may state here that I have one grandson. He is six years old and his name is Erroll Hay Nicklin. His mother is the youngest of my two daughters and resides in Englewood, N. J. She is a widow and in certain contingency, the son's last name will be dropped and he will be known by the name of Erroll Hay.

Enclosed I send you two papers, one written by my mother and the other clipped from an English paper which shows that the old man and his two sons of the battle of Loncarty fame were not the head of the Hay family but that it dates far back of that.

Coming down to the present, in Irving's Life of Washington mention is made of Colonel Ann Hawkes Hay of Haverstraw on the Hudson, at whose

Susan Cynthia Hay, daughter of Col. Frederick J. Hay, married her cousin, Judge Samuel J. Hay. (From the original portrait painted by Fitzsimmons of New York City)

Martha Hutson Hay, daughter of Col. Frederick J. Hay, married her first cousin, Capt. Richard Gannt Hay. (From the original portrait painted by Fitzsimmons of New York City)

APPENDIX — THE FAMILY OF HAY

residence Washington and some of his officers made their headquarters when in that vicinity.

Colonel Hay married a daughter of Judge William Smith of New York and a sister of Joshua Hett Smith who was a near neighbor of their's in Haverstraw.

Not many days ago as I was taking down and brushing an old picture of the Smith house as it appeared in the time of the Revolution, numerous incidents connected with these families were recalled to mind some of which may be interesting in view of the fact that Michael Hay, son of Col. Ann Hawkes Hay, was one of the early settlers of Chazy in this county and that his son, Frederick Jay Hay now resides in the old homestead.

During the Revolution families often differed in the question of loyalty and a number of wealthy land owners remained neutral. But Col. Hay was a rank rebel from the start, so much so that he incurred the displeasure and hatred of Gov. Tryon. Col. Hay was an officer on whom Washington could always depend, and to him was assigned the duty of guarding the West Bank of the Hudson between Haverstraw and Fort Lee.

Here was the theatre of the capture of Major Andre when Benedict Arnold entered into a conspiracy for the betrayal of West Point and the dependent Post and furnished the unfortunate Andre with plans and explanatory papers. Late at night Arnold and Andre met at a short distance from the Smith house and held their conference. Andre remained over night sleeping at the home of Joshua Hett Smith. He was disguised and called himself Anderson.

In the morning Smith who had been requested by Arnold to do so, carried him some miles on his Journey: Andre had not proceeded for many miles after Smith left him before he was detected and captured and the papers and plans found on his person.

Joshua Hett Smith was arrested and held on charge of participating with Arnold and Andre, but was acquitted as being innocent of all knowledge of the plot.

It was not long after the execution of Andre that the British Governor Tryon sent a band of armed men to burn Col. Hay's house which they accomplished after robbing the premises of silverplate and other valuables.

The wife of Col. Hay was alone with her children and servants, her husband being on duty a number of miles distant.

With her family she fled to the house of her brother, Joshua Hett Smith, where she remained until the war closed.

Michael Hay, the eldest son of Col. Hay, was a lad of ten or eleven years at the time of these stirring events and when he became an old man he would relate with a great deal of enthusiasm the little incidents which then came under his observation.

He delighted in talking of Washington and telling what his boyhood thoughts were about him and the different officers who came with him to visit his father where they would sometimes remain two or three days. This was when the army was crossing the river and the Hudson was the theatre of war at that time. He liked General Knox, he was so pleasant and funny. He thought General Green a fine looking man. Colonel Hamilton was a small man. He was disappointed when he saw Lafayette. He had no beard and looked like a young slender boy instead of a General in the Continental Army.

I will relate one little incident in his own words which I have heard the old gentleman repeat a great many times.

"One day Washington and some of his officers had dined at my father's house. He was getting ready to leave. Most of the officers had already gone. The boys of the neighborhood had collected near the house and we made it up between ourselves that as soon as Washington should mount his horse to leave we would fire off thirteen leaden cannon that we had in our possession—to represent the thirteen states and pay Washington a compliment at the same time.

The General rose and walked to the door, my father accompanying him. Washington's servant stood holding his horse at a short distance from the house. The General, after making some remarks to my father, walked to his horse but had not become fairly seated in the saddle when crack! crack! crack! went the thirteen cannon! Washington's horse took fright, gave a plunge, then stood on his hind feet almost upright. Then gave another plunge continuing in that way for a little while. My father commenced to scold us for being so thoughtless. Washington spoke up very quickly, saying, 'Never mind, Col. Hay. The boys are good boys. Have one of them get on a horse and overtake General Knox with the artillery. He has charge of the ammunition. Tell him to give you some powder.' He then spoke a few brief but pleasant words to us. He said he hoped and thought we would all grow up to be good men and true to our country. He then made a low bow to us and bade us adieu. We were all very happy to have our good intentions understood and appreciated and were highly elated over the prospect of having plenty of powder for our cannon!"

In 1811 Michael Hay left the beautiful town of Haverstraw and with his family moved to Chazy in this county on lands from his uncle Samuel Smith, where we now reside.

He found few inhabitants then. The roads were mostly paths cut through the woods and traveling was usually on foot and on saddle horses. The country, for the most part was covered with a thick growth of forest trees, infested with bears, wolves and panthers, and through it all, the red man roved at will.

Michael Hay died about nineteen years ago. He was very charitable and so did not accumulate a large property but managed to leave each of his sons an inheritance.

Your affectionate cousin.
Lafayette Hay

COLONEL ANN HAWKES HAY

Ann Hawkes Hay was born on the 14th day of August, 1745, at Kingston, Island of Jamaica, West Indies, being the only child of his father, Michael Hay of Scotland, by his wife Esther Wilkins, daughter of Judge Martin Wilkins. He came to New York about the year 1760 to be educated at King's College, now Columbia University.

Michael Hay—the father—along with other brave Highland Lairds were "out for the Stuart in the rising," and after the defeat of the Highlanders at Culloden, took refuge in the British Indies; his cousins, the Earls of Carlyle and Kinnoul having been governors of the island.

Along with Michael went his cousin Thomas, Lord Erskine.

In Hone's Year Book of 1832, I find:

In May 1732 died John Erskine the eleventh earl of Mar. He was knight of the thistle, twice secretary of state, a promoter of the Union, and had been repeatedly returned as one of the sixteen peers to represent Scotland in Parliament.

The earl of Mar was twice married. His first lady was Margaret, daughter of Thomas Hay, earl of Kinnoul, by whom he had issue John, who died an infant, and Thomas, Lord Erskine. His second countess was Frances, daughter of Evelyn Pierrepont, duke of Kingston.

While still at College in New York, Ann Hawkes Hay married Martha Smith, daughter of William Smith, Judge of the court of the King's Bench, New York. After College the couple spent a few years in his home at Kingston, Jamaica, but losing their first three children on the Island, they moved to Haverstraw, New York, where her family, the Smiths lived. The site of the Hay home and Hay's Landing on the River may still be seen.

When war between America and England threatened Ann Hawkes enthusiastically sided with the country of his adoption, and though twice offered a commission by the British Army, it was emphatically refused and he became a Colonel in the Continental Army.

This year there has been issued a very attractive booklet from New York entitled "Historic Rockland County and the 350th Hudson-Champlain Anniversary Celebration—1609-1959." Quoting from Mr. Harry Hale Smith, Historian, who writes of Colonel Hay in the Booklet: "The distinguished Colonel Ann Hawkes Hay was made Revolutionary Defender of that part of Rockland County lying along the Hudson River from Stony Point to New Jersey. In addition to his combat duties, he was General Quartermaster and purchasing Agent for the Continental Army. When the Continental Congress did not get the funds, this man guaranteed to the Orange County farmers payment on a private basis. Colonel Hay died a poor man because of the financial support given the Revolutionary forces. Colonel Hay won high praise from his fellow officers, particularly from General Washington, whose eyes and ears and strong right arm he was in the District."

"In the American Archives, Fifth Series, there are many letters to and from him, relating to his movements and those of the enemy. Several of these letters are from Generals Washington and Clinton, others from the Legislature and Council of Safety. They prove how earnestly his heart and hopes were in the cause of freedom, how indefatigable he was in its promotion and in what high esteem he was held by the leaders of the army. Later General Washington appointed him Quartermaster and Colonel Hay freely sacrificed his own fortune in providing for the Continental Army. It may be seen by the births of his younger children born during the war, that he was sometimes stationed at different points on the Hudson and at others, in New Jersey. He is most complimentarily mentioned in histories of that period, and William Abbott in the "Crises of the Revolution" pays a handsome tribute to Colonel Hay."

When the war ended in 1783, having sacrificed his fortune, he had no time to recover from his losses when he died in New York City, leaving a helpless widow, daughter of wealth and affluence, and eight surviving children, the oldest but 17 and the youngest only one month old."

History mentions an incident in connection with Aaron Burr and one of his sons when a little chap. Young Samuel fell down the well at his father's home at Haverstraw. Aaron Burr, who was visiting there at the time, risked his own life by jumping down the well and pulling the little boy out.

Because of Colonel Hay's siding with the Colonists, the British Government confiscated his large plantations on the Island of Jamaica, the English Army

APPENDIX — THE FAMILY OF HAY

burned his home at Haverstraw overlooking the Hudson River—a Negro slave betraying the place where the family silver was buried, they even took that too. His private fortunes he had sacrificed to equip his regiment in the Continental Army, so that this young Scotsman lost everything through espousing the cause of American independence.

On October 5, 1763, while at college, Ann Hawkes Hay married **Martha Smith**, the daughter of Judge William Smith of New York and his wife, Mary Hett Smith. Both were just 18 years of age. They had the following children: 1, 2, 3—the first three died as infants.

4. Michael Hay, second son born in Haverstraw July 30, 1768, married and his descendants moved to Clinton County, New York.
5. William Smith Hay, third son born at Cornwall, Orange County, December 18, 1769, died young.
6. Samuel Hay, fourth son, was born September 8, 1771 at Haverstraw and later moved to South Carolina where he practiced law in Beaufort. He married Elizabeth Mary Kenney, daughter of Colonel John Kenney.
7. Thomas Hay, fifth son, born at Haverstraw on October 25, 1773, married his first cousin, Sarah, daughter of Joshua Hett Smith. He died in New York.
8. Janet Scott Hay born November 3, 1775 at Haverstraw married Mr. Campbell and moved to Louisiana.
9. Martha Hay born in New Jersey November 22, 1777 came to South Carolina and married William Main Hutson and left children.
10. Lewis Scott Hay born at Fishkill, New York on May 2, 1780 moved to South Carolina and married Harriet Yonge Johnson.
11. William Hay born at Haverstraw August 26, 1782.
12. Frederick Jay Hay born at Haverstraw March 5, 1785—one month before his father's death. Samuel Hay had established a law practice in South Carolina and sent for his widowed mother and baby, Frederick Jay Hay— so they moved to South Carolina and Frederick married there, Susan Cynthia Brown. The other children followed to the South, Michael remaining in New York State.

(Detailed Lines Follow)

APPENDIX — THE FAMILY OF HAY

SAMUEL HAY

Samuel Hay, sixth child of Colonel Ann Hawkes Hay and his wife, Martha Smith, was born at Haverstraw, N. Y., Sept. 8, 1771. After receiving his education he moved to Beaufort, South Carolina—the first of the family to come South. He married Elizabeth Mary Kenney, daughter of Colonel John Kenney and his wife Miss Mulholland.

Colonel Kenney and his wife had three daughters:

1. Elizabeth Mary, married June 1797, Samuel Hay and had two children:
   (a) William Hay
   (b) Eliza Mary Hay
2. Eleanor married Dr. John Bellinger, grandson of the Landgrave Edmund Bellinger of South Carolina.
3. Susan Emily married April 1804, Charles J. Jenkins, Governor of Georgia during the War Between the States.

After the death of his first wife, Mr. Kenney married Dec. 1798 Rachel (neé Porcher). After the death of Samuel Hay and his wife Elizabeth Mary, Mrs. Kenney reared her step grandchildren: William Hay and Eliza Mary Hay, who were still infants.

Samuel Hay and his wife Elizabeth Mary Kenney (Hay) left the following descendants:

I. William Henry Hay born on 10th of September 1801, and died when only twenty-nine years of age. He married at her father's home in Edgefield County, South Carolina, on the 27th of November, 1821, Mary Caroline Gantt, daughter of Judge Richard Gantt, formerly of Maryland and his wife, Sarah Allen of Virginia who, it is said, was selected by Lafayette to dance with him as being the most beautiful and graceful lady of the ballroom in Augusta, Georgia. William Henry Hay by his wife, Mary Caroline Gantt (Hay) had the following children:

A. Mary Caroline Hay born October 3, 1822, died unmarried.
B. Sarah Porcher Hay born in Columbia, South Carolina, April 20, 1824, married her first cousin, Oscar Payne Hay, son of Colonel Frederick Hay and his wife Susan Cynthia Hay. They had two children, Mary Hay and Caroline Hay. (Line given under Oscar Payne Hay.)
C. Judge Samuel Jenkins Hay born at his father's home, "The Oaks," near Barnwell, South Carolina, the 23rd of November, 1825. He was adopted early in life by his distinguished kinsman, Governor Charles J. Jenkins of

APPENDIX — THE FAMILY OF HAY

Georgia—in whose office he later studied law. He married at her home, the Boiling Springs, South Carolina, his cousin, Susan Cynthia Hay, daughter of Colonel Frederick J. Hay and his wife Susan Cynthia Brown (Hay). She was born June 27, 1831 and was lovely both in looks and character. A copy of her portrait with the curls is given in this book. (Children follow later.)

D. Major Richard Gantt Hay, fourth child of William Henry Hay and Mary Caroline Gantt (Hay) was born on the 20th of October, 1827. He became a gallant officer in the War of 1861-65 being a Major of the 11th Regiment of Infantry, Hagood's Brigade. He married his first cousin, Martha Hutson Hay, youngest child of Colonel Frederick J. Hay, son of Colonel Ann Hawkes Hay of the Revolutionary War. A copy of her lovely portrait in hoop skirt is in this book. They had four children, three of whom died in childhood. The fourth, Marion Heyward Hay, married her cousin Frederick Hay Gaunt, son of Captain Richard Gaunt and had four children. (Account of childen given under the Gaunt line.)

II. Eliza Mary Hay, only daughter of Samuel Hay by his wife, Elizabeth Mary Kenney (Hay) married at McPhersonville, South Carolina, 15th July 1819, Thomas Hutson Colcock—a southern planter of the olden time. Children:

A. Colonel Charles Jones Colcock. (His detailed line follows under "The Colcock Family").

B. William Hutson Colcock who married Mary Ellen Lewis, descendant of Colonel John Lewis, the pioneer settler of Augusta County, Virginia.

C. Captain Richard Hutson Colcock who married his cousin, Eliza Mary Colcock.

D. Samuel Hay Colcock. d.s.p.

E. Esther Hutson Colcock married William Douglas Gregorie of McPhersonville, South Carolina, and left one surviving child, Mary Colcock Gregorie who married her cousin Marion Woodward Colcock and had several children.

F. Thomas Hutson Colcock married Mary Fuller McGrath, daughter of Governor A. G. McGrath.

After the death of his first wife, Eliza Mary Hay, Thomas Colcock married a second time and left descedants now living in Washington, D. C., and Spartanburg and Yorkville, South Carolina.

THE COLCOCK FAMILY

This distinguished family has already been written up in the Hay book, but mention will be briefly made of the line of Charles J. Colcock, author of "The Family of Hay"—to whom all descendants of the Hays of Erroll and Lochloy owe the invaluable facts he collected and had printed for the family.

Thomas Hutson Colcock married on 15th July 1819, Eliza Mary Hay, only daughter of Samuel Hay and Elizabeth Mary Kenney of Grimball Hill Plantation, and a granddaughter of Colonel Ann Hawkes Hay and his wife, Martha Smith (Hay).

Colonel Charles Jones Colcock was the eldest son of Eliza Mary Hay and Thomas Hutson Colcock of McPhersonville, South Carolina, and the grandson of Judge Charles J. Colcock of Charleston, South Carolina with whom he lived until grown.

Colonel Colcock was married three times; *first*, to Mary Caroline Heyward in 1838. She was a granddaughter of Thomas Heyward, Jr., a signer of the Declaration of Independence.

He married *second* in 1851 Lucy Frances Horton at her home near Huntsville, Alabama.

He married the *third* time in 1864, Agnes Bostick, youngest child of Benjamin Bostick. They lived near Robertville, South Carolina.

Colonel Colcock by the three marriages had the following children:

A. John Colcock, officer in the 3rd South Carolina Regiment during the War Between The States.
B. Caroline Colcock died in girlhood.
C. Charles Jones Colcock who was for years Head Master of the Porter Military Academy, Charleston, South Carolina, married his cousin Patti Lee Hay, daughter of Judge Samuel Hay and his wife Susan Hay who was a daughter of Colonel Frederick Hay who was the youngest child of Colonel Ann Hawkes Hay. Their daughter, Erroll Hay Colcock, is living in Charleston, South Carolina.
D. Francis Horton Colcock, Professor of Mathematics for years at the South Carolina University in Columbia, married Mary Robert Jones of Screven County, Georgia—by whom the following children:
 1. Francis Horton Colcock, Jr. (deceased.)
 2. Anna Eustace Colcock married Alva DePass, Attorney in Columbia, South Carolina. They had a daughter Anna DePass.
 3. Charles Jones Colcock.

APPENDIX — THE FAMILY OF HAY

    4. Frances Horton Colcock.
    5. Seaborn Jones Colcock.
E. Erroll Hay Colcock died young.
F. Catherine Colcock married Robert Guerrard of Savannah, Georgia, and lived in New Orleans, Louisiana.
G. Helen McIver Colcock married Charles Colcock Gregorie, son of Dr. Thomas Gregorie of Grahamville, South Carolina. Their children were: Agnes, Thomas, Charles, Louisa and Joseph Gregorie.
H. Woodward Hutson Colcock died young.
I. William Bostick Colcock lived in Florida.
J. Agnes Colcock died in childhood.

THOMAS HAY

Thomas Hay, seventh child of Colonel Ann Hawkes Hay, was married to his first cousin Sarah, only child of Joshua Hett Smith, and died in New York. He left children:
1. William Hay died unmarried at Haverstraw, New York.
2. Matilda Hay died unmarried at Boiling Springs, South Carolina.
3. Charlotte Hay died unmarried at Boiling Springs, South Carolina.
4. Frederick Hay died unmarried.
5. Augustus Hay did not marry; died at Boiling Springs, South Carolina.
6. Martha Hay married her cousin, Dr. Thomas Hutson, Sr., of South Carolina.

JANET SCOTT HAY

Janet Scott Hay, eighth child of Colonel Ann Hawkes Hay and Martha Smith (Hay), was born at Haverstraw, New York, November 3, 1775. She married a Mr. Campbell and lived in Louisiana.

MARTHA HAY

Martha Hay, ninth child of Colonel Ann Hawkes Hay and Martha Smith (Hay), was born in New Jersey November 22, 1775, came to South Carolina and married William Main Hutson, and their son, Dr. Thomas Hutson, Sr., married his first cousin, Martha, daughter of Thomas Hay and his wife, Sarah

Smith, daughter of Joshua Hett Smith. They left children among whom may be mentioned Dr. Thomas Hutson, Jr., of McPhersonville, South Carolina, who had daughters Augusta, Charlotte, Matilda married Ben Martin; Emeline Colcock married her cousin, Mac Hutson; Florrie married Robert Heyward, and a son Ogier married Miss Owens and became a surgeon in the U. S. Army; and Matilda. By a second marriage, Dr. Hutson, Sr., had children—Willie, John, Jane DeSaussure, Millicent, Sally and Annie Hutson.

Jane Hutson married Dr. Louis DeSaussure and left children, among whom are Charles DeSaussure of Memphis, Tennessee, and Thomas DeSaussure of Millegeville, Georgia, and others scattered over the States.

HAY-DeSAUSSURE-CLARKE

A descendant of the Hays of Scotland and the DeSaussures, Thomas Hal Clarke is now living in Atlanta, Georgia and practicing law there. He married Mary Louise Hastings of Lovejoy, Georgia on July 12, 1951. They have three children:

1. Thomas Hal Clarke, Jr.
2. Mary Catherine Clarke.
3. Rebecca DeSaussure Clarke.

The parents of Thomas Hal Clarke were James Caleb Clarke and Mary Cox DeSaussure (Clarke). His paternal grandparents were Thomas Henry Clarke and Sally Boykin (Clarke).

His maternal grandparents were Charles Alfred DeSaussure and Ellen Chestnut Reynolds (DeSaussure).

LEWIS SCOTT HAY LINE

Lewis Scott Hay, sixth son of Colonel Ann Hawkes Hay and his wife, Martha Smith, was born at Fishkill on the Hudson River, New York State, 2nd May, 1780.

He followed his older brother, Samuel, to South Carolina and became a low country planter.

APPENDIX — THE FAMILY OF HAY

Lewis Scott Hay married Harriet Yonge Johnson, September 7, 1808. Harriet Yonge Johnson was born on Wadmallow Island April 12, 1792 and died in Greenville, South Carolina to which place the family had refugeed just ahead of Sherman's Army.

Her father was William Johnson, II, planter on Wadmallow Island, St. John's Parish, Colleton County and his wife was Catherine Rhoades.

Harriet Johnson's aunt, Susannah Johnson, married Colonel Francis Yonge.

Her father, William, II, and her uncle Richard Johnson who married Sarah Beckett, purchased in 1802 a large tract of land forming a portion of what was known as Wright's Barony on the Savannah River, in old Barnwell District. Johnson's Landing near present day Allendale, South Carolina, was named for them.

Since so many of the Hays are descended from Harriet Yonge Johnson, quotations from "The Sketch of the Johnson Family", owned by Mr. Frampton Ellis of Atlanta, Georgia, will be given here:

Johnson

"The first of this family of whom we find any record was William Johnson, planter of St. Paul's Parish, who married Hannah Beake. They both died in July, 1771. This William Johnson must have been of high social standing because his daughter, Susannah Johnson, married Colonel Francis Yonge, who was a member of the Governor's Council of the Province of South Carolina, and who administered on their estates.

Their only child, Harriet Peckham Yonge, married Gideon Hagood.

Besides his daughter, Susannah, William Johnson left two sons, William and Richard Johnson, who lived first on Wadmallow Island, South Carolina and later in Prince Williams Parish.

William Johnson II was born 1761 and died 1808 in Barnwell District (Charleston Courier, March 2, 1808). He married Catherine Rhoades. His will dated February 9, 1808 is recorded in Will Book, Barnwell County records.

Besides his brother, Richard Johnson, and his nephew, William Johnson, it mentions his wife, Catherine, and his children who were to be educated in Charleston, as follows:

1. Elijah Johnson.
2. Harriet Yonge Johnson who married Lewis Scott Hay.
3. Hannah Beake Johnson.
4. Catherine Rhoades Johnson.

5. Sarah Rhoades Johnson.
6. Susannah Johnson.
7. Eveline Rebecca Johnson.

These married and left descendants.

Richard Johnson (son of William and Hannah, his wife) was born 1760 and died in Barnwell District February 1825. He married Mrs. Sarah Stanyarne, formerly Beckett. They had the following children:

1. James B. Johnson.
2. Dr. William Stanyarne Johnson (1798-1859), married Sarah, daughter of Needham Green and left sons, including Alexander, Wickleff, Benjamin and James Johnson, and his daughters Mary who married James Ingram; Sarah Mitchell married first Joe Dill Lee, son of the Reverend William States Lee—eminent Presbyterian minister of Edisto Island, South Carolina. She married second, Samuel Joseph Walker. The last daughter, Catherine Johnson, married Samuel Dunbar and had a daughter, Sarah Dunbar, who married George Morrall and was the mother of Mrs. Peter Ervin of Atlanta, Georgia.
3. Richard Johnson, Jr. was born April 29, 1797 on Edisto Island and married Elizabeth Hewlett. Their children included William and Richard Johnson who lived in Savannah, Georgia, and Thomas Johnson who married Margaret Morrall.
4. Frances Johnson married and left descendants.
5. Sarah Johnson married Dr. John Fowke.
6. Mary Elizabeth Johnson married William Hewlett.
7. Catherine Johnson married first, Edwin Cater by whom one child, Thomas Johnson Cater, who left descendants in Perry and Macon, Georgia. She married second, Thomas Anderson by whom the following children: Richard, Samuel, Sarah Mary, Margaret Elizabeth and William Francis Anderson.

A descendant of Richard Johnson, Sr., uncle of Harriet Johnson Hay, is now living in Allendale, South Carolina, where he practices law; Thomas Oregon Lawton, Jr. born November 10, 1924 and married April 12, 1952 Bess White Macauley, daughter of Angus Hamilton Macauley and Margaret White Macauley of Chester, South Carolina. One child, Thomas Oregon Lawton, III, born October 19, 1957. The mother of Thomas Lawton, Jr. was Xania Easterling and her mother was Ella Johnson who married Alexander Salley Easterling 1853. Ella Johnson (Easterling) was the daughter of Adeline Powers Hays and Dr. Alexander Johnson (November 19, 1827-January 27, 1880) who was one of the sons of

APPENDIX — THE FAMILY OF HAY

Dr. William Stanyarne Johnson given above.

The father of Harriet Johnson Hay, William II, and her uncle Richard, and aunt Susannah Johnson were the children of William Johnson and Hannah Beake Johnson who died at St. Paul's Stono in 1771.

Lewis Scott Hay, sixth son of Colonel Ann Hawkes Hay by his wife Martha Smith (Hay) moved from Haverstraw, New York to South Carolina and married Harriet Yonge Johnson. They had the following children:

1. Martha Hawkes Hay married Bushrod Washington Davis.
2. Clementine Catherine Hay married Joel Wyman.
3. Dr. Lewis Scott Hay married Ann Fraser.
4. Harriet Yonge Hay married John E. Frampton.
5. Susan Emily Hay married Dr. William DeLoach Ellis.
6. Frederick Jay Hay married Adeline Wyman, sister of Joel Wyman.
7. Rose Isabel Hay married Mr. Elliott.
8. Louisa Hay died unmarried.
9. Adeline Hay married W. Oakman.
10. Eugene Gordon Hay married Julia Caroline Oakman.

Details given in lines following.

Hay-Davis

Martha Ann Hawkes Hay, daughter of Lewis Scott Hay and Harriet Yonge Johnson, married Bushrod Washington Davis. Children:

A. Bushrod Washington Davis, Jr. married his cousin, Loula Hay, daughter of Dr. Lewis Scott Hay and his wife, Ann Fraser (Hay). They had one son, Lewis Hay Davis (deceased).
B. Charles Frank Davis married Anne Louisa Green; children:
   1. Benjamin Wyman Davis married Miss Ruth; children. Gertrude, Clifton, Clara, Rosa and William Davis.
   2. Marian Davis married Gasque first and second, James La Roche. No children.
   3. Helen Davis married Jenkins; children: Davis, Harold and Josephine Jenkins—all of New York.
   4. Daisy Davis married Gasque. No children.
   5. Charles Frank Davis, Jr. (1877) married Pattie Miley; children:
      (a) Frank Marion Davis, Wadmallow Island, South Carolina.

    (b) Ralph Davis, John's Island, South Carolina.
    (c) Florence Martha Davis (Rogers), Huger, South Carolina.
    (d) Lease Davis (Meyer), Georgetown, South Carolina.
    (e) Bushrod Washington Davis, Wadmallaw Island, South Carolina.
    (f) Pattie Miley Davis (Smathers), Charleston, South Carolina.
    (g) Charles Frank Davis, III, Charleston, South Carolina.
6. Bushrod Washington Davis, III, son of Charles Frank Davis, Sr. and Anne Louisa Green; married Isabel Karcoff of New York; children:
    (a) Charles Harold Marion Davis (New York).
    (b) Isabel Davis (Marcinkas) (New York).
    (c) Howard Davis (New York).

C. Helen Davis (Smith), daughter of Bushrod Washington Davis and Martha Hay (Davis)

D. Mattie Davis Wyman, daughter of Bushrod Washington Davis and Martha Hay (Davis).

THE WYMAN FAMILY
(HAY - WYMAN)

Several years ago there appeared in the Columbia State Magazine an interesting article, entitled: "After Joel . . . came twenty-six other Physicians", nearly all of them graduated from the South Carolina Medical College at Charleston.

The record probably cannot be equalled in all this country.

Joel Wyman, the first of the family to come South, was born in Worchester, Massachusetts, December 6, 1800. He graduated at Amherst College with honors and received his M. A. Degree from there in 1828.

After graduation, he accepted a position as tutor at the Boiling Springs Academy, Barnwell County, South Carolina.

In a letter to his brother in Massachusetts he wrote: "As for myself, I am very pleasantly situated. I board with a genteel family by the name of Hay. He is very wealthy and has a family of fine children. He, as well as his lady, is very friendly to me providing every comfort. He originated from New York

APPENDIX — THE FAMILY OF HAY

and lives very much after the Northern style. I would exchange my position for none other in the country."

This is to be understood when we know how infatuated he became with one of the loveliest members of the Hay family, Catherine Clementine Hay, whom he later married.

Joel Wyman graduated in medicine in what was believed to be the first class to finish at the South Carolina Medical College 1831 and won the highest honors. The South Carolina Medical Society presented him with a handsome hand-made silver urn for the best Latin Thesis.

About a year after graduating, he married Catherine Clementine Hay, daughter of Lewis Scott Hay and Harriet Yonge Johnson (Hay). Six sons and three daughters were born to them.

I. William Hutson Wyman, the first physician son of Dr. Joel Wyman, Sr., graduated from the South Carolina Medical College in 1858. He was a surgeon in the Confederate Army and married Sarah Edwards. They had one physician son, Dr. Joel Wyman who graduated in 1881. Father and son died at a relatively young age in the practice of medicine.

II. Lallah Wyman, the oldest daughter of the first Joel, married Walter D. Smith, attorney. He died while serving as cavalry lieutenant in the Southern Army. Through the marriage of their daughter, Helen Smith, to Dr. C. P. Vincent, a graduate of the Medical College in 1885, there was born Dr. C. P. Vincent, Jr., who had a son, Dr. C. P. Vincent, III. The last is a great, great grandson of the original Joel Wyman and practices in Camden, South Carolina. From the first Dr. Vincent, there is another great, great grandson, Dr. Hugh Vincent.

III. Dr. Benjamin Wyman, medical graduate in 1869. Also served in the War as Captain in the 11th South Carolina Regiment, Hagood's Brigade. He married Mary Edwards and they had a daughter, Florence Wyman, who married Dan Crossland, and had a daughter, Mary, who married W. D. McNair, Sr. From this last marriage came Dr. W. D. McNair, Jr., practicing physician of Aiken, South Carolina, a great, great grandson of the first Joel.

IV. Holbrook Wyman, son of the original Joel Wyman, was not a physician himself, but had three sons and six grandsons who followed the profession. He married Clara Vincent and they had a number of children among whom the three physicians:

A. Holbrook Wyman, Jr., married first Pauline Lawton and second, Annie

Weatherbee. He graduated as physician in 1890 and had two sons follow him:
  1. Dr. Hugh Wyman of the class of 1925.
  2. Dr. Joel Wyman, class of 1943.
      These were great grandsons of the first Dr. Joel Wyman.
  B. Joel Wyman, another son of Dr. Holbrook Wyman, Sr., graduated in medicine in 1892. He married Ann Lucas Maybank and they lived in Denmark, South Carolina. Their descendants are given on the Maybank line.
  C. Delacy Wyman graduated in 1900. He married Allene Lawton and practiced medicine in Lena, South Carolina. There were several children, among whom a physician, Dr. Edward Holbrook Wyman graduated in 1931.
  D. Catharine Wyman, daughter of Holbrook Wyman, Sr., married the Reverend Dudley Jones, D. D. They had two sons to become physicians. There were also other children. Dr. Dudley Jones, Jr. graduated in 1934, and Dr. Parker Jones in 1943. These were great grandsons of the first Dr. Joel Wyman.
V. Marion Hay Wyman and
VI. Hastings Wyman were twin sons of Dr. Joel Wyman and his wife Clementine Hay. They were attending a military Academy and ran away to join their older brothers in the army of Virginia in 1861. They were not quite sixteen years old. Hay Wyman was mortally wounded in one of the engagements around Petersburg in 1863. The surviving twin, Hastings Wyman, served with the Confederate army until the end of the war. Afterwards he graduated at the South Carolina Medical College in 1875. He married first, A. Edwards; second, Martha Davis and third, Marian Aldrich. There were children and three physicians among them:
  A. Dr. Harry Wyman graduated in medicine in 1897. He has practiced in Aiken, South Carolina.
  B. Dr. Benjamin Wyman, Jr. finished in 1915. He is a practicing physician of Columbia, South Carolina and is now head of the State Board of Health. His son, Dr. Benjamin Wyman, III, followed him in his profession, graduating in 1950—a great grandson of Dr. Joel Wyman.
  C. Dr. Marion Hay Wyman (second Hay boy) is a Specialist in Columbia, South Carolina. Graduated from the medical college in 1910.
VII. Gertrude Wyman, daughter of the first Dr. Joel Wyman, married Howard Vincent and had children—one a pharmacist son—Howard Vincent, Jr.

APPENDIX — THE FAMILY OF HAY

VIII. Harriet Huldah Wyman, daughter of Joel and Clementine, married Lewis Hay Frampton and had children—one of whom a physician.
  A. Dr. James Frampton graduated at South Carolina Medical College in 1894 and has practiced for years at Mt. Pleasant, South Carolina.
  B. Mary Frampton married M. Freeman and they had a son to study medicine:
    1. Dr. C. Courtenay Freeman who finished at South Carolina Medical College in 1951.
  C. Other children of Harriet Wyman and Lewis Frampton are: Joel, John, Harry Hastings and Gertrude. The marriages and children are given on the Frampton line.

IX. Dr. Frampton Wyman, youngest child of Joel Wyman and Clementine Hay (Wyman), graduated from South Carolina Medical College in 1881. He married Rosamond Gordon Hack of South Carolina. They had children, one of whom was:
  A. Dr. Harry Hastings Wyman, Jr. who graduated in medicine and practiced in Aiken, South Carolina. He had a son:
    1. Dr. Dibble Wyman finished at the South Carolina Medical College in 1951—a great-grandson of the first Dr. Joel Wyman.
  B. Virginia Gordon Wyman, daughter of Dr. Frampton Wyman, married her first cousin, Vincent Wyman. They had four children. One a physician:
    1. Dr. Frampton Wyman who graduated in 1927. He married Bonnie Atkinson of Chicago, Illinois and they have children.
    2. Hugh Vincent Wyman, Jr. married Miriam Prentiss.
    3. Edward Holbrook Wyman married Dorothy Pague of Portsmouth, Virginia.
    4. Virginia Wyman married Wesley Willingham Lawton of Lena, South Carolina and there are two children.

From the first Wyman physician in South Carolina, Dr. Joel Wyman, we see that there were four sons, nine grandsons, ten great grandsons and three great, great grandsons—in all twenty-six physicians, who followed him in his profession.

Since there are many descendants of his in the present generation, there is no doubt but that others will carry on the splendid medical heritage.

The original Dr. Joel Wyman also became a good Confederate soldier. Though born in Massachusetts, he felt that South Carolina was then his home. Also he had married a southern girl.

Of course his brothers and friends in Massachusetts had joined the Federal Army. Every night before a battle Joel prayed that he would not recognize or kill any of his brothers or friends should they be in the battle which would be fought the following day.

Besides fighting himself, Joel gave five of his sons to the cause and one, Marion Hay Wyman, gave his life for it.

"When the war was over, Joel and Clementine returned to their home in South Carolina only to find that Sherman's army had burned the beautiful house to the ground and they had to spend the night in the slaves quarters."

—H. V. Wyman—Aiken, South Carolina

To quote again, "Clementine Hay Wyman, while fleeing with her daughter, Mrs. Joel Wyman and family, before Sherman's advancing army, hoped to take the train at a station where they had been waiting for it. But when it stopped, the engineer said his train was already heavily laden with refugees and he would not allow them to get aboard.

Clementine cried out: 'I am the daughter of a Mason and the wife of a Mason. Is there no one here to help me?'

A man went up to the engineer with a pistol in his hand and ordered him to take the party aboard.

He did so."

—Dr. J. F. Wyman, Aiken, South Carolina

LEWIS SCOTT HAY, M. D.

Dr. Hay was the son of Lewis Scott Hay, sixth son of Colonel Ann Hawkes Hay of the Revolutionary War and his wife, Martha Smith (Hay).

He married Ann Hagood Fraser of Walterboro and Charleston, South Carolina. She was the daughter of Joseph Fraser and Matilda Hagood who was the daughter of Johnson Hagood Esq. and his wife, Ann O'Hear.

Johnson Hagood was known as Johnson Hagood the Elder, to distinguish him from his grandson, General Johnson Hagood, C. S. A. and also from General Johnson Hagood of World War I, who commanded the American troops in France. His daughter, Matilda, married Joseph Fraser whose daughter, Ann Fraser, married Dr. Lewis Scott Hay.

APPENDIX — THE FAMILY OF HAY

The Hays and Frasers had fought side by side in the Wars of Scotland and had inter-married over there. Then later these two representatives of the Highland Clans were again united in matrimony in the low country of South Carolina.

Since the Hays in this country are descended from the Frasers of Scotland through marriage over there, it may be interesting to them to read the following:

The Fraser Clan.

The Frasers were of Norman descent as the name indicates. The early spellings vary greatly but they undoubtedly came from France to lower Scotland and then later settled in the Highlands around Inverness. A short distance from the city stands their ancestral home, Beaufort Castle, home of the Lovat Frasers since 1511 and is still inhabited by them. The present building is on the site of the old Beaufort Castle burned by the Hannoverian soldiers in 1746—which itself superseded earlier strong holds burned by the English.

The Clan became so large that it was eventually broken up into smaller clans but all held allegiance to the Chief Clan—the head of which was given a Barony and created Lord Lovat in 1400.

The Hays are descended from the Chief Clan—the Lovat Frasers. This Clan has served Scotland well in all the wars of the country. They were strong adherents of Wallace and Bruce. Alexander Fraser was an intimate friend of the Bruce—fought for him at Bannockburn and two years later, married his sister, the Lady Mary, widow of Sir Neil Campbell of Lochow.

They fought for their young Queen, Mary Stuart, and several hundred of the clansmen fell fighting for Prince Charlie in the fatal battle of Culloden Moor. A whole Regiment of the Fraser Highlanders fought valiantly against the French in North America and were, to a great extent, responsible for General Wolf's victory at Quebec in 1759.

The 71st Regiment Fraser Highlanders of over 2,300 men fought throughout the War of the Revolution.

They distinguished themselves in South Africa and have since fought in both World Wars. The present Chief—fifteenth Lord Lovat—is best known as leading the Commandos in France in World War 1939-1945 in which he won the D.S.O. and M. C. and was severely wounded. He is still living in his castle, is married and has four sons and two daughters.

Sir Bruce Fraser was the head of the British Admiralty during the War and signed the Peace Treaty for Great Britain with Japan on the S. S. Missouri anchored in Tokio Bay.

APPENDIX — THE FAMILY OF HAY

When America began to be settled, some of the Clan came over to try their fortunes in the New World. Among them John Fraser, who arrived in South Carolina in 1700 and settled near Coosawhatchie in the Indian lands. He often traded with the Yemassee Indians with whom his relations were most friendly. It was because of a warning from Sanute, a chieftain of the tribe, that he and his wife and child escaped the general massacre planned by the Spaniards and carried out by the Yemassees and Confederate tribes, which occurred on the 15th of April 1715 when the Indians destroyed the country south of Charles Town to within twenty miles of the city. The Frasers had time only to reach a canoe on the creek by their home—whence they made a perilous trip to Charles Town. (Taken from "The Charleston Sketch Book," by Charles Fraser, the artist).

Alexander Fraser, only child of John Fraser, settled on the plantation in Prince Williams Parish. He married and had several children, one of whom was the celebrated miniature painter, Charles Fraser, whose miniatures are all over the country. When the Marquis de Lafayette visited Charleston in 1825, he sat for Charles Fraser to paint his miniature for the city of Charleston.

Major William Fraser's son, Joseph Fraser, was the father of Ann Hagood Fraser, who married Dr. Lewis Scott Hay.

Another descendant of the O'Hears and Frasers of South Carolina now lives in Columbia, Mississippi, Anna MacNair Haney who married Dr. Seth Barron, practicing physician of Columbia, Mississippi. They have three girls:

1. Mary Lyn Barron
2. Bethany Barron
3. Lilla Gayle Barron

Anna MacNair Haney (Barron) was the daughter of John Jackson Haney whose mother was Sarah Ann Sanders and her father was Joseph Augustus Sanders of Walterboro, South Carolina who married Laura Witsell, also of Walterboro.

John Augustus Sanders' mother was *Eliza O'Hear* born November 14, 1793 in South Carolina. She died June 14, 1833 in South Carolina leaving descendants—among whom Anna MacNair Haney (Barron) of Mississippi.

Dr. Lewis Scott Hay and Ann Hagood Fraser of South Carolina had the following children:
A. Pattie Hay married Major Schmidt.
B. Sophie Hay married Cornelius Dickinson.
    (DICKINSON LINE WILL FOLLOW)
C. Lula Hay married her first cousin, Washington Davis. They had one son, Lewis Davis.

Frances Snowden Hay, daughter of the Rev. Samuel Hutson Hay and his wife, Mary Peck (Hay). She married Col. Del Kemper of Virginia, who became a general in the Confederate Army. Later, U.S. Consul to China.

A RARE FAMILY BADGE

This was worn by the members of the Hay Clan in battle during the early centuries. MAC GARADH is the Gaelic for HAY. MHOR means great.

APPENDIX — THE FAMILY OF HAY

D. Kate Erroll Hay did not marry.
E. Matilda Hay unmarried.
F. Minnie Hay married her cousin, John Frampton. They had no children but on the death of her sister, Sophie Hay Dickinson, she took her baby, Fraser Dickinson, and reared her in their home where she remained until her marriage to Roger Pinckney. (Children under Dickinson line).
G. Walter Scott Hay, M. D. married his cousin, Mary Susan Hay.

WALTER SCOTT HAY, M. D.

Dr. Walter Scott Hay of Allendale, South Carolina became the physician much loved by all of his section of the country—the "family doctor" of the old days.

He married his cousin, Mary Susan Hay—both great, grandchildren of Colonel Ann Hawkes Hay—Walter through his grandfather, Lewis Scott Hay, Sr.—6th son of Colonel Ann Hawkes Hay and Mary Susan through her grandfather Colonel Frederick Jay Hay—8th son of Colonel Ann Hawkes Hay—thus uniting these two lines in their children: Anne, Erroldine, Malcolm Fraser, Lewis Scott, Walter Scott, Nelleen and Walter Smith. Anne and Walter Scott died in infancy.

(A) Erroldine Hay married The Reverend Thomas Douglas Bateman from Derbyshire, England, a Presbyterian minister who became a naturalized citizen of this country; children:
  1. Margaret Hay Bateman died at eight months.
  2. Burney Hay Bateman died when one year old.
  3. Thomas Douglas Bateman, Jr., now the Associate Editor of the Commercial Dispatch of Columbus, Mississippi, married Chebie Ann Gaines, a native of Columbus. Her father is George Stark Gaines, formally of Mobile, Alabama and her mother, Anne Stephenson, from the Columbus section. Children:
     (a) Anne Hay Bateman
     (b) Margaret Gaines Bateman
     (c) Thomas Douglas Bateman III
(B) Malcolm Fraser Hay, Public Accountant, did not marry.
(C) Lewis Scott Hay, M. D. married Katharine Witsell of Charleston, South Carolina. They had no children but adopted her nephew and niece, Alec

Kroeg and Katharine Kroeg of Charleston, South Carolina.
- (D) Nelleen Hay married Dr. Ben J. Hammet of Blackville, South Carolina, now a practicing dentist of Allendale, South Carolina. They have one child:
  1. Ben Hay Hammet, a Journalist and Director of Public Relations and Alumni Affairs at Presbyterian College, Clinton, South Carolina. He married Jane Jenkins of Montgomery, Alabama and their children are:
     - (a) Ben Hay Hammet, Jr.
     - (b) Lewis Jenkins Hammet
     - (c) Erroll Scott Hammet
- (E) Walter Smith ("Chancellor") Hay, Senior Road Designer for the Georgia State Highway, Atlanta, Georgia, married Ruth Napier Lakenan of Virginia lineage. They have one child:
  1. Walter Smith ("Chancellor") Hay, Jr. who is with Goodbody and Company Investment Brokers, Atlanta, Georgia. He married Sara Banks Mills of Griffin, Georgia.

DICKINSON LINE

Sophie Fraser Hay, daughter of Dr. Lewis Scott Hay and Anne Hagood Fraser married Henry Cornelius Dickinson, children: Lillian Hay, Herbert, Percy Lee, Minnie Clare, Iona, Henry Gordon, Ruth, Fraser.

I. Lillian Hay Dickinson married Edward Smart; children: Walter, Miriam, Sophie Clare, Edward Henry, and Louerrol Smart.
  - (A) Walter Smart married first Annabelle Upchurch, and second, a widow, Lucy Bisbane—no children.
  - (B) Miriam Smart married George Baggott—no children.
  - (C) Sophie Clare Smart married Stacy Walters; children: Lillian Clare and Fay Catherine Walters.
    1. Lillian Clare Walters married Paul Herbert Hester, Jr. Children: Lillian Jenelle and Barbara Ann Hester.
    2. Fay Catherine Walters married Rodney Cudd, Jr. Children: Fay Catherine and Anna Clare Cudd.
  - (D) Edward Henry Smart married Rita Kidd; children: Edward Henry Smart, Jr. and Walter Samuel Smart.

APPENDIX — THE FAMILY OF HAY

   1. Edward Henry Smart, Jr. married Muriel Yancy Patrick and had two children, Sherry Olivia Smart and Edward Henry Smart, III.
   2. Walter Samuel Smart and his wife, Vivian Bland Smart had one son, Herbert Ivan Smart and a daughter, Susan Elaine Smart.
  (E) Louerrol Smart married Fred Wilkie; children: Frances Gray Wilkie and Fred Wilkie, Jr.
   1. Frances Gray Wilkie not married.
   2. Fred Wilkie, Jr. married Elva Glenn and they have two children: Charles O'Bryan and Gary Alexander Wilkie.
II. Herbert Dickinson, son of Sophie Fraser Hay and Henry Cornelius Dickinson, married a widow, Belle Cordray Strong; children: Herbert Donald, Henry Clyde, Edwarda, Annie Lou Dickinson.
  (A) Herbert Donald Dickinson did not marry.
  (B) Henry Clyde Dickinson married Vernie Adams and had one son, Fred Edward Dickinson.
  (C) Edwarda Dickinson married J. J. Ray and they have two daughters, Alice and Jane Ray.
   1. Alice Ray married Joseph Cabaniss. They have one son, Stephen Cabaniss.
   2. Jane Ray married Robert Kennedy. They have two children: Robert and James Kennedy.
  (D) Annie Lou Dickinson married John Eldon Kirkland; children:
   1. Evelyn Juanita Kirkland married Stanley Ross Roberts and they have two children: Karan and Susan Roberts.
   2. Helen Ray Kirkland married Ralph Warren Sibley; children: Stanley Warren and Mark Kirkland Sibley.
   3. Mell Elizabeth Kirkland married Maxwell Earle Rizer; children: Carey Franklin and Donald Earle Rizer.
   4. John Eldon Kirkland married Charlotte Perkins; children: Ann, John and Jeannie Rae Kirkland.
   5. The Rev. Harold Norman Kirkland married Sophie Dunbar; children: Stephen and Dana Kirkland.
III. Percy Lee Dickinson, son of Sophie Fraser Hay and Henry Cornelius Dickinson, married Mamie King; children:
  (A) Christopher King Dickinson, not married.
  (B) Henry Cornelius Dickinson died in infancy.
  (C) Percy Lee Dickinson, Jr. married Leila Armfield; children: Richard

Lee Dickinson, who married Elizabeth Davis and have two girls, Kevin and Kim Dickinson.

(D) Elizabeth Leila Dickinson married first J. Compton and they had two boys: Jimmie and Robert Compton. Elizabeth married second David Hilton; children: Thomas, William and Johnnie Hilton.

(E) Walter Edwin Dickinson married Jeannie Draze; children: Barry and Terrie Dickinson.

(F) William McLeod Dickinson married Martha Veno and had a daughter, Mattie Lou, who married Carl Le Grand and they have one son, J. Le Grand.

(G) Sophie Hay Dickinson married Ralph Davis; children: Ralph Cecil, Robert Dickinson, Olivia Margarette, Roy William and Ruth Alice Davis.

1. Ralph Cecil Davis, Jr. married Carmelita Cometo. They have one son, Ralph Davis, III.
2. Robert Dickinson Davis married Norma Roberts and have a son, Timothy Allen Davis.
3. Olivia Margarette Davis married Duane Evans. They have three sons: David Duane, Larry Michael and Eugene Lee Evans.
4. Roy William Davis married Roberta Phyllis Boardman. They have two daughters: Rhonda Phyllis and Susan Deborah Davis.
5. Ruth Alice Davis, unmarried.

(H) Mary King Dickinson married Ray Sprouse; children:
1. Mary Ellen Sprouse.
2. Ray Sprouse who married Loretta Kelley.
3. William King Sprouse married Becky Jackson and have a son, Christopher King Sprouse.
4. Barbara Ann Sprouse.

IV. Minnie Clare Dickinson died when a girl.

V. Iona Dickinson, daughter of Sophie Fraser Hay and Henry Cornelius Dickinson, married Willie Maher and they have one daughter, Minnie Maher, not married.

IV. Henry Gordon Dickinson died unmarried.

VII. Ruth Dickinson, daughter of Sophie Fraser Hay and Henry Cornelius Dickinson, married Leon Bamberg; children: George and Leone Bamberg.

(A) George Bamberg married Mattie Sue Hill; no children.
(B) Leone Bamberg married first George Davis; children:

APPENDIX — THE FAMILY OF HAY

   1. George Davis, Jr., who married Margaret McIntyre and they have one son, George Davis, III.
   2. Leone Ruth Davis married Charles Paris and they have one child, Pamela Diane Paris.
  (B) Leone Bamberg married second, James Wilkie Massey.
VIII. Fraser Dickinson (Frampton) married Roger Pinckney; children: Sophie Adele, Roger Pinckney, Jr., Gladys Hay, Robert Pinckney Leake, Theodore Guillard.
  (A) Sophie Pinckney married Roy Fyfe; children:
     1. Roy Fyfe, Jr. married Margaret Sams Fuller; children: Elizabeth Pinckney and Roy Fyfe, III.
     2. Margaret Ellen Fyfe married Philip Hill.
  (B) Roger Pinckney, Jr. married Chloe Martin; children: Roger Pinckney, III, Martin and Eve Pinckney.
  (C) Gladys Hay Pinckney—not married.
  (D) Robert Pinckney Leake married Helen Lindsay—no children.
  (E) Theodore Guillard Pinckney married Winnifred Caldwell; children: Theodore Guillard, Jr. and Patricia Gail Pinckney.

FRAMPTON LINE

Harriet Johnson Hay, daughter of Lewis Scott Hay and Harriet Yonge Johnson, was born in South Carolina April 2, 1817. She married John Edward Frampton, a Signer of the Ordinance of Secession of South Carolina. They had the following children: Theodora Pope, Lewis Hay, Mary Pope, John, James, Henry Wilkins, Eugene Hay, Joel Wyman, Edward, Herbert Granville, M. D., Charles Hay and Linwood.

   I. Theodora Pope Frampton married Pressley Smith; no children.
  II. Lewis Hay Frampton, born December 17, 1844; married Harriet Huldah Wyman; children: James, Joel Wyman, John, Harry Hastings, Mary Pope and Gertrude Wyman.
     A. James Frampton, M. D. married first, Elizabeth Buist Lucas and had one child, Bessie Lucas Frampton, who married Julian Huger LaBruce and had one child, Edith LaBruce, who married John Magill Mitchell,

Jr. and they had two children: Elizabeth LaBruce Mitchell and Edith Frampton Mitchell.

A. James Frampton, M. D. married second, Edith Ladson Gregorie; children: James Gregorie, Edmund Gregorie and Joel Wyman Frampton.
  1. James Gregorie Frampton married Margaret Elizabeth Darby and had five children: Margaret Elizabeth, James Gregorie, Edith Gregorie, Edmund Wyman and Camilla Darby Frampton.
     (a) Margaret Elizabeth Frampton married Justus Clyde Gilfillan, Jr. They had two children: Mary Margaret Gilfillan and Justus Clyde Gilfillan, III.
     (b) James Gregorie Frampton, Jr., married Peggy Jo Johnson.
     (c) Edith Gregorie Frampton married Robert Venning Royall, III; children: Eleanor Williams Royall and Margaret Frampton Royall.
     (d) Edmund Wyman Frampton.
     (e) Camilla Darby Frampton.
  2. Edmund Gregorie Frampton married Mary Geraldine MacNeal; children: Mary Geraldine Frampton and Edmund Gregorie Frampton, Jr.
  3. Joel Wyman Frampton married Frances Lesesne Robinson and had three children: Frances Robinson Frampton, Joel Wyman Frampton and John Grimball Frampton.
B. Joel Wyman Frampton married first, Leize Jenkins and had three children, each of whom died in infancy.
B. Joel Wyman Frampton married second, Lucille Cobia. There were eight children: Joel Wyman, Jr., Walter Cobia, Henry Wilkins, Charles Hay, Harriet Wyman, Lewis John, Jesse Sharpe and Gertrude Lucille Frampton.
  1. Joel Wyman Frampton, Jr. married Margaret Camille Zeigler; children:
     (a) Joel Wyman Frampton, III who married Sylvia Gayle Bobo.
     (b) Charles Hay Frampton.
  2. Walter Cobia Frampton married Amy Huchting; children: Walter Cobia, Jr. and Terre Frampton.
  3. Henry Wilkins Frampton married May Wylie Hutto and had three children: Rebecca Frampton, John Frampton and Kathleen Frampton.
  4. Charles Hay Frampton died young.

APPENDIX — THE FAMILY OF HAY

  5. Harriet Wyman Frampton married Bozydar Henry Orszula.
  6. Lewis John Frampton married Blanche Lenora Donnelly; children: Lynn Frampton, Lewis John Frampton, Jr. and Lisa Frampton.
  7. Jesse Sharpe Frampton married Virginia LaVergne Murray.
  8. Gertrude Lucille Frampton married Marion Alexander Todd, Jr.; children: Ann Todd, Marion Alexander Todd, III and Elizabeth Todd.

C. John Frampton married Virginia Aiken Taylor. They had one child, Virginia Taylor Frampton.

D. Harry Hastings Frampton married Vivian Griffis and had one child, Harry Hastings Frampton, Jr.
  1. Harry Hastings Frampton, Jr. married Barbara Lou Kalber; children: Harry Hastings, III, Carrie Lee and Vivian Griffis Frampton.

E. Mary Pope Frampton married James Oswald Freeman and had seven children: James Oswald, Jr., Lewis Frampton, John Frampton, James Frampton, Willington Edmonston, Campbell Courtenay and Harry Wyman Freeman.
  1. James Oswald Freeman, Jr., not married.
  2. Lewis Frampton Freeman married Helen Butler Pegues and had one child, Helen Butler Freeman.
  3. John Frampton Freeman married Mary Louise Coleman; children: Mary Louisa Freeman and Harriet Wyman Freeman.
  4. James Frampton Freeman married Sara Jo Gamble and had one child, Sara Ellen Freeman.
  5. Willington Edmondston Freeman married Mary Crawford Locke; children: Mary Locke, John Frampton, Robert Locke and Ellen Wyman Freeman.
  6. Campbell Courtenay Freeman married Dorothy Anne Dudley; children; Dorothy Anne and Campbell Courtenay Freeman, Jr.
  7. Harry Wyman Freeman married Margaret Ballantyne Smith; children: Harry Wyman Freeman, Jr. and Margaret Ballantyne Freeman.

F. Gertrude Wyman Frampton married Hall Thomas McGee, who for years has been General Manager of the Charleston News and Courier. They have two children:
  1. Hall Thomas McGee, Jr. married Margaret Anne Pringle; children: Anne Pringle McGee and Hall Thomas McGee, III.
  2. John Frampton McGee married Ann Beverly Canby and had two

children: Beverly Canby McGee and Catharine Frampton McGee.
III. Mary Pope Frampton daughter of John Edmond Frampton and Harriet Johnson Hay married David Maybank. (Their children are given in Maybank line).
IV. John Frampton married his cousin Minnie Oakman Hay; no children.
V. James Frampton married Annie McLeod and had eleven children: Lewis Hay, Harriet Hay, William McLeod, Minna McLeod, Henry Wilkins, Rena Lawton, Annie Mikell, Mary Pope, Tillie, Thomas Hutson and James.
   A. Lewis Hay Frampton; unmarried.
   B. Harriet Hay Frampton married George Gadsden Creighton; children: Annie Frampton, George Gadsden and William McLeod.
      1. Annie Frampton Creighton married Frederick Eugene Nigels; children:
         (a) Harriet Frampton Nigels married Thomas Grey Kevin, Jr., and had two children: Anne Nigels Kevin and Thomas Grey Kevin, III.
         (b) Frederick Eugene Nigels, Jr. married Betty Rose Coleman and had three children: Frederick Eugene Nigels, III, Leslie Creighton Nigels, and Scott McLeod Nigels.
         (c) McLeod Creighton Nigels married Anne Clary.
      2. George Gadsden Creighton, unmarried.
      3. William McLeod Creighton married Katherine Crawford.
   C. William McLeod Frampton married Isabel Aldrich Addison and had four children: George Creighton, Isabel Patterson, Julia Aldrich and William McLeod Frampton.
      1. George Creighton Frampton married Julia Salley and had one child, George Creighton Frampton, Jr.
      2. Isabel Patterson Frampton married James D. Whaley and had a child, Liza Whaley.
      3. Julia Aldrich Frampton married Greswold Gwynette; children: Greswold, Jr., Isabel Patterson and William McLeod Gwynette.
      4. William McLeod Frampton married Frances Moore; childen: Anne Aldrich, William McLeod, Jr. and Donald Moore Frampton.
   D. Minna McLeod Frampton married Washington Clark Seabrook and had one child, James Frampton Seabrook.
      1. James Frampton Seabrook married Alice Gadsden; children: James Gadsden, Baynard McLeod and Edwards Seabrook.

APPENDIX — THE FAMILY OF HAY

  (a) James Gadsden Seabrook married Barbara Minott; children: Elizabeth and Renee de Liesseline Seabrook.
  (b) Baynard McLeod Seabrook, unmarried.
  (c) Edwards Seabrook, unmarried.
E. Henry Wilkins Frampton married Nellie Woodberry and had three children: Alice Woodberry, Nellie and Henry Wilkins Frampton, Jr.
  1. Alice Woodberry Frampton married Charles Frank Davis, Jr. and had two children: Charles Frank, III and Henry Frampton Davis.
  2. Nellie Frampton married Harry Bogle Hills; children: Nellie Frampton and Harriette Bogle Hills.
    (a) Nellie Frampton Hills married Grover C. Criswell, Jr. and had one child, Grover C., III.
    (b) Harriette Bogel Hills, unmarried.
  3. Henry Wilkins Frampton, Jr. married Jeanna Jerdone.
F. Rena Lawton Frampton married Edward John Hanahan. They had one child, James Frampton.
  1. James Frampton Hanahan married Catherine Hammond Fair; children; Eve, Rena Frampton and Edward John Hanahan.
    (a) Eve Hanahan married Otis Lane Renfroe and had one child, James Lane Renfroe.
    (b) Rena Frampton Hanahan, unmarried.
    (c) Edward John Hanahan, unmarried.
G. Annie Mikell Frampton married William Porcher Gelzer and had three children: Anne McLeod, William Porcher, Jr., and Mary Pope Frampton Gelzer.
  1. Anne McLeod Gelzer married Arthur Carleton Lockwood; children: Nancy Mikell and John Carleton, Jr.
  2. William Porcher Gelzer, Jr., married Anne Baker; children: Kathleen Baker and Susan Neyle Gelzer.
  3. Mary Pope Frampton Gelzer married David Pollock Reese; children: David Pollock, Jr., Peggy Frampton and Anne McLeod Reese.
H. Mary Pope Frampton married Henry Hoyt Dowling; children: Mary Pope and Rena Frampton.
  1. Mary Pope Dowling married Edward Hall Pinckney, Jr. Children: Mary Dowling and Margaret Frampton Pinckney.
  2. Rena Frampton Dowling married Thomas Edgar Phillips; children: Thomas Edgar, Jr., and Henry Frampton Phillips.
I. Tillie Frampton, unmarried.

J. Thomas Hutson Frampton married first, Leila Harvey and had a daughter, Margie.
   1. Margie Frampton married James Morris.
J. Thomas Hutson Frampton married second, Louise Davis and had one child, Louise Hutson Frampton.
K. James Frampton, unmarried.
VI. Henry Wilkins Frampton married Lilly Lilienthal. No children.
VII. Eugene Hay Frampton; unmarried.
VIII. Joel Wyman Frampton; unmarried.
IX. Edward Frampton married his cousin Julia Caroline Hay. (Children have been given on Eugene Gordon Hay line).
X. Herbert Granville Frampton, M. D., married Marie Louise Horlbeck; children: Joseph Maybank Frampton, William Horlbeck Frampton, M. D., and Eliza Lucas Frampton.
   A. Joseph Mayband Frampton, unmarried.
   B. William Horlbeck Frampton, M. D., married Pauline Haltiwanger; one child, Wallace Frampton.
   C. Eliza Lucas Frampton married W. Lennox Kirkland and had one child, Marie Louise Kirkland.
XI. Charles Hay Frampton married Saidie Cuttino Mellichamp and had five children:
   A. William Mellichamp Frampton
   B. Lewis Hay Frampton married Sarah Catharine Tupper. Children:
      1. Lewis Hay Frampton, Jr.
      2. Charles Tupper Frampton
      3. John Edward Frampton
   C. Louise Elliott Frampton married Joseph Seabrook Oliver. Children:
      1. Margaret Frampton Oliver married Albert Edward Eads, Jr. and had a daughter Rosemarie Eads.
      2. Joseph Seabrook Oliver, Jr.
   D. Rosa Mellichamp Frampton married Osgood Darby Hamlin. Children:
      1. Harriet Frampton Hamlin
      2. Elizabeth Welch Hamlin
      3. Osgood Darby Hamlin, Jr.
   E. Harriet Johnson Frampton is the daughter of Charles Hay Frampton and Saidie Cuttino Mellichamp. She lives in Charleston, South Carolina, and is with the Charleston News and Courier.
XII. Linwood Frampton, unmarried.

Dr. Walter Scott Hay, great grandson of Col. Ann Hawkes Hay through his sixth son, Lewis Scott Hay.

Mary Susan Hay, wife of Dr. Walter Scott Hay, and great-grandchild of Col. Ann Hawkes Hay through his eighth son, Col. Frederick Jay Hay.

MAC GARADH MHOR

The Countess of Erroll, Chief of Clan Hay. (Courtesy of Newcastle Chronicle & Journal, Ltd.)

APPENDIX — THE FAMILY OF HAY

MAYBANK LINE

Harriet Johnson Hay, daughter of Lewis Scott Hay, Sr. and Harriet Yonge ınson (Hay), married John Edward Frampton.

Their daughter, Mary Pope Frampton, married in 1804, David Maybank; ldren: Joseph, John Frampton, Ann Lucas, Theodore DuPre, Mary Erroll and rriet Hay Maybank.

I. Joseph Maybank, M. D. (the beloved physician) of Charleston, South Carolina, married Harriet Lowndes Rhett; children: Burnett Rhett, Joseph, Harriet Rhett, John Frampton, Claudia Rhett, Theodore DuPre, and Aiken. Aiken died young.

- (A) Burnett Rhett Maybank, Governor of South Carolina and later U. S. Senator from the State, married Elizabeth de Rossett Myers, daughter of Judge Thomas Myers of Charleston, South Carolina. They had three children: Roberta Macon, Burnett, Jr. and Elizabeth de Rossett Maybank.
    1. Roberta Macon Maybank married George Paul and after his death, William Prioleau of Columbia, South Carolina, by whom she had a daughter and son.
    2. Burnett Rhett Maybank, Jr., now Lt. Governor of South Carolina, married Marian Mitchell, daughter of Julian Mitchell and Marian Roberta Mitchell of Charleston, South Carolina and they have two children: Marian Maybank and Burnett Rhett Maybank, III.
    3. Elizabeth de Rossett Maybank married Theodore Guerrard of Charleston, South Carolina and have one daughter—Elizabeth Guerrard.
- (A) Burnett Rhett Maybank, U. S. Senator, married second, Mary Pelzer Cecil of Charleston, South Carolina.
- (B) Joseph Maybank, son of Dr. Joseph Maybank and Harriet Rhett Maybank, married first, Jane Pelzer, daughter of Frank Pelzer and Mary Randolph Pelzer of Charleston, South Carolina. They had two sons: Joseph Maybank, Jr. and Francis Pelzer Maybank.
    1. Joseph Maybank, Jr.
    2. Francis Pelzer Maybank married Celestine Preston Frost, daughter of John Preston Frost and Laura Green Frost.
- (B) Joseph Maybank, Sr., married second, Josephine Creech. They have a little daughter, Mary Hay Maybank.

- (C) Harriet Rhett Maybank married Harold Bowen, M. D. of the U. S. Navy and had four children:
    1. Harold Bowen who married Duval Owens of Atlanta, Georgia.
    2. Harriet Bowen married Dr. Woodruff, M. D. of Anniston, Alabama.
    3. William Bowen not married.
    4. John Bowen still young.
- (D) John Frampton Maybank married Lavinia Huguenin of Charleston and Summerville, South Carolina. Children:
    1. Lavinia Maybank who married George Grimball, lawyer of Charleston, South Carolina.
    2. Harriet Maybank, not married.
    3. Triplets: David Maybank
        Thomas Maybank
        John Maybank
- (E) Claudia Rhett Maybank married John Christian of Anniston, Alabama and St. Louis, Missouri. They had two girls, Josephine and Caroline Christian.
- (F) Theodore DuPre Maybank married Mary Green of Charleston, South Carolina. No children.

II. John Frampton Maybank, Cotton Exporter, son of David Maybank and Mary P. Frampton Maybank, married Eleanor Sophia Johnson, daughter of William Johnson and Mary Mellichamp, both of Charleston, South Carolina. They had the following children:
- (A) Mary Sarazin Maybank, married Rees Ford Fraser of Georgetown and Charleston, South Carolina. No children.
- (B) William Johnson Maybank died young.
- (C) Eleanor Johnson Maybank married in 1929 Jefferson Withers Trotter of Camden, South Carolina and they had one son, Jefferson Withers Trotter, Jr., now living in Charleston, South Carolina.
- (D) David Maybank married Marian Tabor of Columbia, South Carolina. They had three children:
    1. David Maybank, Jr.
    2. Darrell Maybank who married Benjamin Hagood, son of James Hagood of Charleston, South Carolina and have two sons: James and Benjamin Hagood, Jr.
    3. John Frampton Maybank born in 1947 in Charleston, South Carolina.

APPENDIX — THE FAMILY OF HAY

- (E) Ann Lucas Maybank married William Lowndes Cain of Columbia, South Carolina and they have two children: Eleanor Johnson Cain and William Lowndes Cain, Jr.
- (F) Theodora Pope Maybank married in 1939 Joseph High Williams, son of T. T. Williams and Harriet High Williams of Atlanta, Georgia.
- (G) John Edward Frampton Maybank married Mary Deas Gadsden, daughter of Christopher Gadsden of Charleston, South Carolina and Miss Prioleau of the Beaufort South Carolina Section.

III. Ann Lucas Maybank, daughter of David Maybank and Mary Pope Frampton (Maybank) married Joel Wentworth Wyman, M. D. of Denmark, South Carolina. Children:
- (A) Clara Evelyn Wyman who married Bruce Creighton Baker and had two children:
    1. Joel Wyman Baker married Mary Florence Zeigler and
    2. Mary Floyd Baker who married John Witherspoon Bell, Jr.
- (B) Frank James Wyman married Selma Swain; children: Sallie Ann Wyman and Frank James Wyman, Jr.
    1. Sallie Ann Wyman married Harry Berry.
    2. Frank James Wyman, Jr. married Margaret Dick.
- (C) Joel Wentworth Wyman, Jr. married Camille Carden; children: Camille Rosalie Wyman and Jo-Ann Wyman.
- (D) Rosalie Wyman married Robert Fred Whitesides; children: Clara Ann Whitesides, Robert Fred Whitesides, Jr., Judy Whitesides and Joel Wyman Whitesides.

IV. Theodore DuPre Maybank, son of David Maybank and Mary Pope Frampton (Maybank) moved to Anniston, Alabama and married Nell Neil of Georgia. They left one daughter, Mary Pope Maybank, who married Oscar Kilby, son of Governor Thomas Kilby of Alabama and Anne Clark, his wife. They had one son, Thomas Kilby, officer in the U. S. Army, Paratrooper, who died in the Korean War.

V. Mary Erroll Maybank did not marry.

VI. Harriet Hay Maybank, daughter of David Maybank and Mary Pope Frampton (Maybank) married Edward Royall. They had four children:
- (A) Mary Maybank Royall married William Hazzard Barnwell, Jr. Their children are:
    1. Mary Pope Barnwell married a lawyer, William Hutchinson Vaughan.

APPENDIX — THE FAMILY OF HAY

      2. William Hazzard Barnwell, III is now a student at Sewanee University (1959).

(B) Robert V. Royall (an engineer) married Eleanor Williams and have two sons:
      1. Edward M. Royall, II, a lawyer, married to Helen Johnson.
      2. Robert V. Royall, Jr. married Edith Gregorie Frampton.

(C) Sallie DuPre Royall married John W. Ward, M. D. of Daylestown, Pennsylvania (now deceased). They had two children:
      2. Sallie DuPre Ward married Gerald Moore (an architect) and lives in West Springfield, Massachusetts.
      2. John W. Ward Jr.—a student at Valley Forge Military Academy (1959).

(D) Edward M. Royall married Noreen Harmon. They had five children:
      1. Harriet Maybank Royall (died in childhood).
      2. Edward M. Royall, III married Jacquelin Beeler.
      3. Mary Ellen Royall and
      4. Patricia Ann Royall—High School Students (1959).
      5. David Maybank Royall—lower school Porter Military Academy (1959).

ELLIS LINE

Susan Emily Hay, fifth child of Lewis Scott Hay and Harriet Yonge Johnson, was born in South Carolina in the year 1821 and died in Atlanta, Georgia in 1873. She married Dr. William DeLoach Ellis in 1843 at her plantation house in South Carolina—"Hay Villa". They left the following children: William D., Rose M., Harriet, Tallulah, Daniel W., and Frampton.

I. William D. Ellis, son of Susan Emily Hay and Dr. William D. Ellis and a prominent Judge of Atlanta, Georgia, married Phoebe Caroline Prioleau; children:
    A. William D. Ellis, Jr., married Blanche Lipscomb; children:
        (a) Frances Adgate Ellis, married Ewell Gay and had three children:

APPENDIX — THE FAMILY OF HAY

        1. Ewell Gay, Jr., married Mildred Ewing and had three children: Adgate, Ewell, III, and Merrill E. Gay.
        2. William Ellis Gay, married Mary McGaughey, had two children: William Ellis Gay, Jr. and Margaret Haverty Gay.
        3. Frank L. Gay, married Elizabeth B. Durshuck.
  (b) William D. Ellis, III, married Frances Tennent; children:
        1 Wingfield
        2. Lamar
        3. Douglas
  (c) Rutherford L. Ellis, married Martha Hodgson; children:
        1. Margaret Ellis, married John S. Langford and has two children: John S. Jr. and Martha.
        2. Rutherford Ellis, Jr., married Daisy Almond.
  (d) Lamar H. Ellis, married Sarah Hewlett and has two children:
        1. Lamar
        2. Blanche L.

B. Phoebe Prioleau Ellis, married Edward L. Bishop; no children.

C. Prioleau Ellis, married Annie Stuart; three children:
  (a) Annie Stuart, married E. Fay Pearce and had one child:
        1. E. Fay Pearce, Jr.
  (b) Prioleau, Jr. married Cathleen Gordon; two children:
        1. Prioleau, III, married Chloe Lain and has four children: Prioleau, IV, Gordon Lain, Phoebe and Edward.
        2. Cathleen, married G. Arthur Seaver and has two children: G. Arthur, Jr. and Cathleen.
  (c) Phoebe, married Stuart Gould and had two children:
        1. Stuart, Jr.
        2. Phoebe, married E. J. Forio and has one child: E. J. Forio, Jr.

D. Harry Hay Ellis, married Grace Gregorie; no children.

E. Frampton Erroll Ellis, lawyer of Atlanta, Georgia, married Eloise L. Oliver; children:
  (a) Frampton E. Ellis, Jr., married Florence Miller; children:
        1. Florence Rickwood Ellis
        2. Frampton E. Ellis, III

(b) Dr. John Oliver Ellis, married Gene Palfrey; children:
   1. John Oliver, Jr.
   2. Gene Gorgas
(c) Eloise O. Ellis, married Charles R. Simons; children:
   1. Charles Simons, Jr.
   2. Allan Simons
   3. Eloise E. Simons
(d) Edward Prioleau Ellis, married Harriet Louise Witham; one child:
   1. Harriet Calhoun Ellis

F. Harriet Frampton Ellis, married William Haskell Rhett; children:
  (a) Phoebe P. Rhett, married W. Neal Baird and has two children:
   1. Harriet Ellis Baird
   2. Phoebe Rhett Baird

II. Rose M. Ellis, daughter of Susan Emily Hay and Dr. William D. Ellis, died unmarried.

III. Harriet Ellis, daughter of Susan Emily Hay and Dr. William D. Ellis, married William Wallace McLeod, coastal Carolina planter on James Island, S. C., children:
  A. Susan R. McLeod, died unmarried.
  B. Wilhelmena McLeod, did not marry.
  C. Rose Lulah McLeod, married Dr. E. H. Barnwell and they live on Wadmalaw Island, S. C.
  D. William E. McLeod, Carolina planter, lives in the beautiful antebellum McLeod home on James Island, S. C.

IV. Tallulah Hay Ellis, daughter of Susan Emily Hay and Dr. William D. Ellis, married John Fort, lawyer and scientist; children:
  A. Susan Emily Fort, married Daniel Redfearn; no children.
  B. Kate Haynes Fort, married Arthur Codington; children:
   (a) Tallulah Ellis Codington, married Fred Reed and had two children:
     1. Tallulah Ellis Reed, married William Wallace Lyons.
     2. Elizabeth Weaver Reed.
   (b) Catherine Fort Codington, married Paul Luther Shafer; children:
     1. Barbara Shafer
     2. David Luther Shafer

APPENDIX — THE FAMILY OF HAY

       3. Catherine Fort Shafer, married E. O. Walnati and they had one daughter, Susan Lucinda Walnati.
    (c) Arthur Bonnell Codington, married Phoebe Ann Arledge.
    (d) John Fort Codington, married Celia Ungar; children:
       1. William Codington
       2. Ida Kate Codington
       3. Dorothy Eldridge Codington.
    (e) Mary Bonnell Codington, married William Joseph Robertson; children:
       1. John Mason Robertson and
       2. William Joseph Robertson, Jr.
    (f) Emily Hay Codington, married Mark Pennington and had two children:
       1. Mary Katherine Pennington
       2. Paula Ann Pennington
  C. Martha Fannin Fort, married Frank Hartley Anderson; children:
    (a) Martha Fort Anderson
    (b) Frances Hartley Anderson
  D. Tomlinson Fort, married Madeline Keen Scott; children:
    (a) Tomlinson Fort, Jr.
    (b) James Scott Fort
    (c) John Fort
  E. John Porter Fort, married Louise Keith Frazier; children:
    (a) John Porter Fort, Jr.
    (b) James Frazier Fort
    (c) Keith Fort
  F. William Ellis Fort, married Sylvia Lewis and had three children:
    (a) William G. S. Fort
    (b) Sylvia Lewis Fort
    (c) Martha Fannin Fort

V. Dr. Daniel Ellis, son of Susan Emily Hay and Dr. William D. Ellis and a physician on James Island, S. C., married first Rena McLeod and had one daughter; Rose Ellis. Dr. Ellis married second Mary Rivers and had three children:
  A. Dr. Daniel W. Ellis, Jr.
  B. Mary Seabrook Ellis
  C. Catherine Rivers Ellis

VI. Frampton Ellis, son of Susan Emily Hay and Dr. William D. Ellis, died unmarried.

HAY - WYMAN

Frederick Jay Hay, son of Lewis Scott Hay and Harriet Yonge Johnson, married May 25, 1844, Adeline Wyman of Westminster, Massachusetts, sister of Joel Wyman who married Frederick Hay's sister, Clementine Catherine Hay of South Carolina.

Their children:
1. Ella Rosa Hay born Barnwell County, South Carolina.
2. Eudora Hay born Westminster, Massachusetts.
3. Adelaide Hay born New Castle County, Delaware.
4. Susan Wyman Hay born New Castle County, Delaware.
5. Arthur Hay born New Castle County, Delaware. His wife was Nellie Saunders, Canton, Massachusetts; married August 24, 1892.
    (a) Helen Adelaide Hay born Chicago University, of Chicago, Ill.
    (b) Davis Saunders Hay born in Chicago, Illinois.
6. Lewis Scott Hay, born Westminster, Massachusetts.

DESCENDANTS OF EUGENE GORDON HAY

Eugene Gordon Hay, tenth child of Lewis Scott Hay and Harriet Yonge Johnson, married Julia Caroline Oakman; children: Rosa Elliott, Carroll, Eugene Gordon, Jr., Eliza Oakman, Julia Caroline, Estelle, Plantagenet Gantt, Wellington Oakman, Lewis Scott (Holding) Hay and Ann Josephine Hay.

I. Rosa Elliott Hay married Christopher Walter, M. D. No children.
II. Carroll Hay unmarried.
III. Eugene Gordon Hay, Jr. married Eliza Sarah Seabrook. Children:
    A. Rosa Elliott Hay unmarried.
    B. Washington Seabrook Hay died in youth.

APPENDIX — THE FAMILY OF HAY

C. Beatrice Hay married Martin Kessler Kneece and had three children:
   1. Eugene Hay Kneece who married Agnes Delores Spillers. They had three children: Eugene Hay Kneece, Joe Kess Kneece and Colleen Delores Kneece, all unmarried.
   2. Effie Alberta Kneece married Leonard Mobley, and had two children: Linda Mobley and Rose Ann Mobley.
   3. Bebe Helen Kneece married Norman Edward Woodward and had two children: Kessler Kneece Woodward and Guy Jason Woodward.
D. Lewis Holding Hay married Agnes Winnie Crook and had one daughter, Jane Louise Hay who married Edward John Brogan and had one daughter—Patricia Louise Brogan.
E. Daniel Ellis Hay married Lydia Lebby Clement; children:
   1. Daniel Ellis Hay, Jr. who married Rose Warren Wilson, had the following children: Rose Ellis Hay, Lydia Lebby Hay, Anne Clement Hay, Kathryn Villeneuve Hay and Daniel Ellis Hay, III.
   2. William Clement Hay married Gertrude Vincent Seabrook and had one son, William Clement Hay, Jr.
   3. Lydia Legare Hay married Thomas Eugene Pederson; children: Lydia Jean Pederson and Sallie Hay Pederson.
F. Eugene Gordon Hay, III, son of Eugene Gordon Hay, Jr. and Eliza Sarah Seabrook, married Motte Legare Clement; children:
   1. Motte Legare Hay, unmarried.
   2. Eugene Gorden Hay, IV, married Charlotte Miles Hanckel and had three children: Charleen Hanckel Hay, Motte Legare Hay and Polly Brock Hay.
   3. Mary Clement Hay, married Daniel La Roache Jenkins; children: Daniel Legare Jenkins, Gordon Hay Jenkins and Robert Clement Jenkins.
   4. Ann Wyatt Hay married Arthur Lee Thomas and they had two children: Marianne Thomas and Rhoda Arrington Thomas.
G. Solomon Legare Hay, son of Eugene Gordon Hay, Jr. and Eliza Sarah Seabrook, married Mary Woodward Hoffman and had one son, Solomon Legare Hay, Jr.
   1. Solomon Legare Hay, Jr. married Patricia Trezevant Jones and they had three children: Charlotte Elizabeth Hay, Solomon Legare Hay, III, and Cynthia Cranston Hay.

APPENDIX — THE FAMILY OF HAY

H. Annie Berwick Hay, daughter of Eugene Gordon Hay, Jr. and Eliza Sarah Seabrook, married Linwood Frampton, her first cousin. (Children given under the Julia Caroline Hay Frampton line.)

IV. Eliza Oakman Hay, fourth child of Eugene Gordon Hay and Julia Caroline Oakman, married Joseph Murdaugh Dopson; children: Julia Oakman, Annie Josephine, Nathaniel Edward and Eugene Gordon Dopson.

A. Julia Oakman Dopson married William Hamilton Murdaugh and had four children:
1. Annie Liza Oakman Murdaugh married James Lawrence Rawl and had two children: William Lloyd and Julia Ann Rawl.
2. Lillian Eunice Murdaugh married Boswell Risher Ulmer, Jr., and had three children:
    (a) Catherine Elaine Ulmer married George Alton Worth and they had two children: Randolph Boswell Worth and Eric Kaven Worth.
    (b) Boswell Risher Ulmer, III, married Rebecca Jane Gibson. No children.
    (c) Julia Ann Ulmer, unmarried.
3. Edith Virginia Murdaugh married Emory Lamount Banister and had one son: Edmond Linton Banister.
4. Edgar Glenn Murdaugh married Frances Beamguard. They had a daughter, Glenda Fay Murdaugh.

B. Annie Josephine Dopson, daughter of Eliza Oakman Hay and Joseph Murdaugh Dopson, married Henry Joseph Murdaugh; children:
1. Jane Evelyn Murdaugh married William Cecil Mitchell and had two children: William Cecil Mitchell, Jr. and David Carl Mitchell.
2. Joseph Henry Murdaugh married Helen Jones. They had two children: Bonnie Camiel Murdaugh and Brenda Murdaugh.
3. Vernell Murdaugh married Henry Rudolph Mills children: Henry Rudolph Mills, Jr., Randolph Wayne Mills and Roger Lamor Mills.
4. Eugene Hay Murdaugh married Evelyn Ponds. Children: Donnie Eugene Murdaugh, Henry Seal Murdaugh, Peggy Sue Murdaugh and Robert Marshall Murdaugh.
5. Clinton Decator Murdaugh married Barbara Bowers. No children.
6. Wade Howard Murdaugh married Mary Eugenia Bessinger and

APPENDIX — THE FAMILY OF HAY

had two children: Cynthia Kay Murdaugh and Linda Marie Murdaugh.
   7. Jackie Elmer Murdaugh married Laura Patricia Caldwell and had one child, Marion Frances Murdaugh.
C. Nathaniel Edward Dopson, son of Eliza Oakman Hay and Joseph Murdaugh Dopson, married Josephine Edna Murdaugh; children:
   1. Nathaniel Issam Dopson, married Rose Nell Pellum and had one child: Kuren LaWanna Dopson.
   2. Lewis Henry Dopson married Maggie Gertrude Cook and had one daughter: Connie Lewis Dopson.
   3. Joseph Harold Dopson married Fannie Bowers. Children: Joseph Harold Dopson, Jr., Deborah Annette Dopson, Jonathan Andrew Dopson and Sharon Denise Dopson.
   4. Herman Harden Dopson married Mary Evelyn Breland; children: Edward Harden Dopson, Michael Lynn Dopson, Craig Vernard Dopson and Mary Catherine Dopson.
   5. Betty Josephine Dopson married William Wyatte Wilson and had a daughter, Brenda Josephine Wilson.
D. Eugene Gordon Dopson, son of Eliza Oakman Hay and Joseph Murdaugh Dopson, married Vera Dell Murdaugh. Children:
   1. Mary Elizabeth Dopson married James Osban Casteen and had three children: James Osban Casteen, Jr., Hazel Elizabeth Casteen and Joseph Timothy Casteen.
   2. Vera Ruth Dopson married Frederick Lawrence Schanberger. Children: Barbara Gene Schanberger, Frederick Lawrence Schanberger, Jr., Cathi Ann Schanberger, Richard Dopson Schanberger and John Michael Schanberger.
   3. Annie Kathryn Dopson married Daniel Richard Thomas and had one child, Sandra Marie Thomas.
   4. Alice Eugenia Dopson—unmarried.
   5. Rosalyn Dopson—unmarried.
V. Julia Caroline Hay, daughter of Eugene Gordon Hay and Julia Caroline Oakman, married Edward Frampton. Children:
A. Herbert Granville Frampton died in youth.
B. Julia Oakman Frampton married William George Hiers. No children.
C. Harriet Hay Frampton married first, Jefferson Taylor Logan and had a son, Edward Taylor Logan, who married Esther Tuten, no children. She married second, Lee Jones and third, Robert Whitson.

    D. Mabel Estell Frampton died in childhood.
    E. Linwood Frampton married his cousin, Annie Berwick Hay. children:
       1. Lillie Seabrook Frampton married Everett Franklin Allred and had two children; David Allred who died in infancy and Everett Franklin Allred, Jr., unmarried.
       2. Charles Aimar Frampton unmarried.
       3. Linwood Frampton, Jr. died in infancy.
       4. Herbert Washington Frampton unmarried.
       5. Edward Frampton unmarried.
       6. Eugene Gordon Frampton unmarried.
    F. Eliza Oakman Hay Frampton married William Ellison Folk and had two children:
       1. Caroline Oteria Folk who married Alvin Eusebius Caldwell and had one son, Alvin Eusebius Caldwell, Jr. who died in infancy.
       2. William Ellison Folk, Jr. married Virginia Uldine Ham and had three children (all unmarried):
          (a) Janet Carol Folk
          (b) William Ellison Folk, III
          (c) Julia Virginia Folk
VI. Estelle Hay, daughter of Eugene Gordon Hay and Julia Caroline Oakman, unmarried.
VII. Plantagenet Gantt Hay, son of Eugene Gordon Hay and Julia Caroline Oakman, married first, Mary Elizabeth Risher, by whom the following children: Carroll Gordon, Clara Isabel, Annie Elizabeth and William Risher Hay.
    A. Carroll Gordon Hay married Dorothy Anne Adams and had twelve children:
       1. Carroll Gordon Hay, Jr. who married Sophia Karpinski. No children.
       2. Plantagenet Gantt Hay, Jr. unmarried.
       3. James William Hay married Jenetta Anne Moye and had two children: James Andrews Hay and William Lawrence Hay.
       4. Dorothy Anne Hay married George Frank Miley. Children: George Franklin Miley, Jr. and Juliana Miley.
       5. Mary Judy Hay married William Mauldin Williams. No children.
       6. Joan Duke Hay married Raymond Leon Murden. Children: Jean Marie Murden and Michael Raymond Murden.
       7. Martha Julia Hay married James Richard Overcash. No children.

APPENDIX — THE FAMILY OF HAY

    8. Clara Isabel Hay unmarried.
    9. Virginia Gail Hay, daughter of Carroll Gordon Hay and Dorothy Anne Adams, unmarried.
   10. Patricia Land Hay also unmarried.
   11. Helen Marie Hay unmarried.
   12. Linda Risher Hay not married.

B. Clara Isabel Hay married Robert Shelly Blount. Children:
    1. Robert Shelly Blount, Jr. who married Lorraine Miller and had three children: Robert Shelly Blount, III, Donald Franklin Blount and Stephen Miller Blount.
    2. Mary Elizabeth Blount married Relmum Emory Cotton and had one child: Relmum Durham Cotton.
    3. William Hay Blount married Hannah Winifred Ulmer and had one child: William Risher Blount.

C. Annie Elizabeth Hay, daughter of Plantagenet Gantt Hay and Mary Elizabeth Risher, married Joseph Oliverus Pinckney; children:
    1. Mary Elizabeth Pinckney, deceased.
    2. Frances Aloysia Pinckney married Paul Vincent Cahill and had one son, Paul Vincent Cahill, Jr.
    3. Marie Anita Pinckney married Paul Joseph Viens; children: Paul Joseph Viens, Jr. and Theodore Viens.
    4. Elizabeth Anne Pinckney married Peter John Nantista. Children: Phyllis Anne Nantista, Susan Elizabeth Nantista, Mary Frances Nantista, Lucian Nantista, Peter Nantista and Carl Nantista.
    5. Genevieve Hay Pinckney married Daniel Joseph O'Connor. Children: Christine O'Connor, Daniel Joseph O'Connor, Ellen O'Connor, Patrick O'Connor and Michael O'Connor.
    6. Clara Lois Pinckney married Henry John Rowland; children: Henry John Rowland, Jr., Ralph Joseph Rowland, Annie Germaine Rowland and Mary Monica Rowland.
    7. Joseph Oliverus Pinckney married Virginia Ann Schans and had one daughter, Virginia Ann Pinckney.
    8. James Linehan Pinckney unmarried.
    9. Patricia Carolyn Pinckney unmarried.
   10. Carroll Gordon Pinckney unmarried.

D. William Risher Hay, son of Plantagenet Gantt Hay and Mary Elizabeth Risher, married Ruth Sanders. No children.

E. Eugene Gordon Hay, son of Plantagenet Gantt Hay, and his second

wife, Marion Izlar, married Lillian Gladdin Owens. Children:
1. Eugene Izlar Hay
2. Otto Hay
3. Mary Elizabeth Hay

VIII. WELLINGTON OAKMAN HAY

Wellington Oakman Hay, eighth child of Eugene Gordon Hay and Julia Caroline Oakman, married first, Annie Stanley Risher and had five children: Julia Catherine, Mary Eliza, Carrie, Frederic Jerome and Estelle Hay.

A. Julia Catherine Hay married, *first*, James Frank Mears, by whom a son, James Frank Mears, Jr.
  1. James Frank Mears, Jr. married Jeanne Hoover and had two children: Patricia Mears and Helen Hoover Mears.
A. Julia Catherine Hay married *second*, William Henry Harrison and had two children:
  1. Catherine Harrison married W. H. Whetstone and had one child, Kathy Whetstone.
  2. Mary Harrison married T. W. Cone and had two children: Billie Cone and Carol Cone.
B. Mary Eliza Hay married Robert S. Even. They had one child: Honorene Even.
C. Carrie Hay, third child of Wellington Oakman Hay and Annie Stanley Risher, married Jasper Quintus Peeples, son of Edwin Wiley Peeples and his wife, Hattie Johns. His grandfather was Alexander McBride Peeples and his grandmother, Rebecca Folk. They have one son, Jasper Quintus Peeples, Jr.
  1. Jasper Quintus Peeples, Jr. married Anne Guilbert and had three children: Jasper Guilbert Peeples, III, Jan Peeples and James Hay Peeples.
D. Frederic Jerome Hay married Grace Burt and had a daughter: Billie Hay, who married Royce Boone and they have a son, Danny Boone.
E. Estelle Hay married Walter Crandel Varn. Children: Majorie Ann Varn and Jean Marie Varn.
  1. Majorie Ann Varn married Jessie Gibbs and they have two children: John Walter Gibbs and Ann McGuire Gibbs.

APPENDIX — THE FAMILY OF HAY

    2. Jean Marie Varn married F. W. Scheper, III and have one child: Julye Scheper.
- F. Winnefred Oakman Hay, daughter of Wellington Oakman Hay and his *second* wife, Idamae Lester, married Cleat L. Calvert and have a son: Kirk Calvert.

IX. LEWIS SCOTT (HOLDING) HAY

Lewis Scott (Holding) Hay, a low country planter, son of Eugene Gordon Hay and Julia Caroline Oakman, married Edith McClung Beckett. Children; Theodore Beckett, Julia Oakman, Henry Muhler, Lewis Holding, Frank Seabrook, Elizabeth McClung, Edith Beckett, Mary Moffatt and Inez Berwick Hay.

- A. The Rev. Theodore Beckett Hay, D. D., married Elizabeth Brown and had the following children:
    1. Theodore Beckett Hay, Jr. married Ella Perkins Bailey and have three children:
        - (a) Eleanor Bailey Hay—unmarried.
        - (b) Corinne Calhoun Hay—not married.
        - (c) Theodore Beckett Hay, III—unmarried.
    2. Lucy Boyd Hay married John D. Ross and they have two children—both unmarried:
        - (a) John Barkman Ross
        - (b) Elizabeth Ann Ross
    3. Elizabeth Brown Hay—unmarried.
    4. Edith McClung Hay—unmarried.
- B. Julia Oakman Hay married Kenneth Wilson Leland and had three children:
    1. Kenneth Wilson Leland, Jr. who married Charlotte Louise Coleman and they had three children (all unmarried): Kenneth Wilson Leland, III, Robert Whitney Leland, Victoria Denise Leland.
    2. Julia Hay Leland married Phillip Emmanuel Gervais and had three children (all unmarried): Julia Leland Gervais, Louise Wilson Gervais, and Phillip Emmanuel Gervais, Jr.
    3. Aaron Whitney Leland unmarried.
- C. Henry Muhler Hay married Pauline Grimball Parrott and they had four children:

APPENDIX — THE FAMILY OF HAY

1. Henry Muhler Hay, Jr. married Mary Ann Donaldson and had a son, Robert Marshall Hay—unmarried.
2. Edward La Roache Hay—unmarried.
3. Paula Evans Hay—unmarried.
4. Richard Oakman Hay—unmarried.

D. Lewis Holding Hay, Jr. married Mary Elizabeth Lofton. They had one son, Lewis Holding Hay, III (unmarried).

E. Frank Seabrook Hay, son of Lewis Scott (Holding) Hay and Edith McClung Beckett, married Jane Williams Chaplin. They had four children:
   1. Frank Seabrook Hay, Jr. married Ruth Love Lee and their children are: Michael Scott Hay, Teresa Hay, Alan Oakman Hay and Jonathan Lee Hay (all unmarried).
   2. The Rev. Lewis Scott Hay married Carol Eloise Jones and had two children (unmarried): Katharine Knight Hay and Carol Makemie Hay.
   3. Jane Chaplin Hay married Thomas Jacob Wessel and had two children: Thomas Jacob Wessel, Jr. (unmarried). And Jean Wessel—unmarried.
   4. Emmie Neyle Hay married Hooper Alexander, III. No children.

F. Elizabeth McClung Hay married Francis Marion Mitchell and had four children:
   1. Elizabeth Hay Mitchell, married on July 18, 1959 The Rev. Marshall Banks Neil III Presbyterian Minister, The Rev. Mr. Neil had just graduated from Columbia Seminary, Decatur, Georgia.
   2. Edith Beckett Mitchell who married John Gray Brawley, Jr. No children.
   3. Francis Marion Mitchell, Jr.—unmarried.
   4. Lewis Hay Mitchell—unmarried.

G. Edith Beckett Hay married Malcolm Holmes Morrison and had three children: Lillian Epps Morrison, Mary Hay Morrison and Edith Beckett Morrison (all unmarried).

H. Mary Moffatt Hay died in childhood.

I. Inez Berwick Hay married Walter Ennis James, Jr. They have three children: Charlotte James, Walter Ennis James, III and Nell Bull James—all unmarried.

APPENDIX — THE FAMILY OF HAY

X. ANN JOSEPHINE HAY

Ann Josephine Hay, daughter of Eugene Gordon Hay and Julia Caroline Oakman, married Horace Edward Walpole. Children: Anna Louise, Catherine Singletary, Horace Benjamin, Eugene Hay, Rosa Elliott, Carmen and Horace Edward Walpole.

A. Anna Louise Walpole married Daniel Francis Jenkins and had six children:
   1. Benjamin Roper Jenkins married Eleanor Welsh McElveen. Children: Benjamin Roper Jenkins, Jr., Eleanor Carol Jenkins, and Jane Louise Jenkins.
   2. Ann Hay Walpole Jenkins married Madison P. Tucker. No children.
   3. Frances Louise Jenkins married William Dupre Atkinson. Children: James Frierson Atkinson, William Dupre Atkinson, Jr. and Francis Jenkins Atkinson.
   4. Richardine Hart Jenkins married William Gourley and had two children: William Gales Gourley and Daniel Francis Gourley.
   5. Carmen Walpole Jenkins married Lester Earl Bentz and had two children: Lester Earl Bentz, Jr. and Carmen Theresa Bentz.
   6. Daniel Francis Jenkins—unmarried.

B. Catherine Singletary Walpole married James Porcher Pinckney. Children:
   1. James Porcher Pinckney, Jr. who married Dixie Fender; children Katherine Ann Pinckney, Lynn Fender Pinckney and Constance Porcher Pinckney.
   2. Katherine Walpole Pinckney married John Conley Howle and had two children: John Edward Howle and Katherine Walpole Howle.
   3. Ann Hay Pinckney married Joseph James Wildgen; children: Joseph James Wildgen, Jr., Paul Porcher Wildgen and Christopher Charles Wildgen.
   4. Benjamin Eugene Pinckney married Ann Hogg; children: Jo Ann Pinckney, Mary Lu Pinckney and Benjamin Eugene Pinckney, Jr.
   5. Webster Porcher Pinckney married Jean Shelley. No children.
   6. Gene Hay Pinckney married Carol Arthur Ripley and had one daughter: Katherine Hasell Pinckney.

APPENDIX — THE FAMILY OF HAY

  7. Sarah Pinckney married Lawrence Howard Davis; children: Sarah Katherine Davis, Lawrence Howard Davis Jr. and Carol Katherine Davis.
  8. Louis Walpole Pinckney married Helen Kasper and had one child: Louis Walpole Pinckney, Jr.
C. Horace Benjamin Walpole married Adelaide Dotterer Hill; children: Horace Benjamin Walpole, Jr., Laura Hill Walpole and Adelaide Dotterer Walpole.
D. Eugene Hay Walpole, fourth child of Ann Josephine Hay and Horace Edward Walpole, married Cornelia deHeer Porcher. Children:
  1. Cornelia deHeer Walpole married John Henderson Bentz; children: John Henderson Bentz, Robert Reynolds Bentz, Thomas Eugene Bentz and Charles Walpole Bentz.
  2. Eugene Hay Walpole, Jr. married Estelle Rhett Hanckel and had two children: Estelle Rhett Walpole and Eugene Hay Walpole, II.
  3. Philip Genfron Porcher Walpole married Margaret Glenn Murray and had two children: Margaret Murray Walpole and Philip Gendron Porcher Walpole, Jr.
  4. Mary Scott Walpole married Edward Francis Allston. Children: Edward Francis Allston, Jr., Mary Scott Allston, and Harriett Wilkinson Allston.
  5. Horace Edward Walpole married Elizabeth Barnes. No children.
  6. John Bassnet Legare Walpole married Theodora Janet Wilson and had one son: John William Eddings Walpole.
  7. Lucia Lockwood Walpole—unmarried.
E. Rosa Elliott Walpole married Charles W. Williams. Children:
  1. Mary Selby Williams married Dale Sorenson and had two children: Dale Selby Charles Sorenson (deceased) and Francis Walpole Sorenson.
  2. Rosa Elliott Williams married George Bishopp and had two children: Rosa Elliott Bishopp and George Benjamin Bishopp.
  3. Catherine Walpole Williams—un-married.
F. Carmen Walpole—unmarried.
G. Horace Edward Walpole married Elizabeth Cox Reedy. No children.

Below—Ben Hay Hammet, American member of Clan Hay of the faculty of Presbyterian College, Clinton, South Carolina, dressed in the Hay plaid while visiting the Highlands of Scotland.

Townsend Hay, the Chief's Lieutenant for the American Branch of Clan Hay.

March of Clan to Delgaty Castle.

House at Beaufort, South Carolina, home of Col. Ann Hawkes Hay's first son to come South. The houses of two other brothers were burned by Sherman's army on its march to the sea.

Below—"Belmont", Joshua Hett Smith's house at Haverstraw on the Hudson, New York, known as Smith's "White House."

APPENDIX — THE FAMILY OF HAY

COLONEL FREDERICK JAY HAY

Colonel Hay, the twelfth and youngest child of Colonel Ann Hawkes Hay and his wife, Martha Smith (Hay), was born at Haverstraw on the Hudson River, New York, March 5, 1785—one month before the death of his father.

While still a young boy, he and his mother were sent for by his older brother, Samuel, to join him in Beaufort, South Carolina, where he had already established a law practice.

Frederick Hay married on the 15th of February, 1810, Susan Cynthia Brown, a wealthy heiress and beautiful in person and character.

Colonel Hay and his wife lived in a lovely colonial home at Boiling Springs, South Carolina and their estate extended from "The Runs" to the Savannah River. This home was burned by Sherman's soldiers in 1864.

Frederick was a Colonel in the War of 1812 and served throughout the war.

According to a Southern custom, an artist from New York City spent over a year on the plantation painting all the family. The artist was Fitzsimmons. The pictures in this book of Colonel Hay and his wife, Susan Cynthia Brown (Hay), their son, Rev. Samuel Hutson Hay and his wife, Mary Peck Hay and the two daughters of Colonel Hay, Susan Cynthia Hay in white with the curls, and Martha Hutson Hay in pink, both in hoop shirts—are all from the original portraits Fitzsimmons painted.

Colonel Frederick Jay Hay and his wife, Susan Cynthia Brown (Hay), had the following eleven children: Mary Louise, Charles Colcock, Frederick Jay, Jr., Samuel Hutson, William Augustus, Lewis Scott, Thomas Theodore, Oscar Payne, Alfred, Susan Cynthia, and Martha Hutson.

    I. Mary Louisa Hay married Richard A. Gantt. Their children are given on the Gantt line.

CHARLES COLCOCK HAY

    II. Charles Colcock Hay, born at his father's plantation house, "Green Oak Forest," Barnwell District, married Sarah Peyton, descendant of the family of Peytons of Virginia. Their children are:
        A. Charles Colcock Hay, Jr. died while young.
        B. William Hay married Sally Odum; children, Rose and William Hay.
        C. Helen Hay married her cousin, Lewis Hay, son of Dr. Thomas Hay.

Their children are given under the Thomas Hay line.
- D. Peyton Hay married Minnie Stroman; children: Clarence, Sarah and Emma Hay.
- E. Arthur Erroll Hay died in youth.

FREDERICK JAY HAY, JR., M. D.

III. Frederick Jay Hay, Jr., M. D., third child of Colonel Frederick Jay Hay and his wife Susan, married on the 7th of March, 1839, Carolina Hasell. He practiced medicine in Charleston, South Carolina for many years after his marriage, spending the summers at his beautiful plantation house, "Errolton", at the Boiling Springs. Their children are:
- A. The Reverend Hugh Peronneau Dawes Hay, an Episcopal clergyman. A soldier in the war of 1861-65, he rendered his country faithful service. He married Mary Pinckney of Charleston, South Carolina, daughter of Robert Pinckney and Martha Guillard and had the following children:
    1. Percy Douglas Hay married May Mitchell and had three children: May, Percy and Gladys Hay.
    2. Alfred Pinckney Hay married his cousin Mary Louisa (Marie) Gantt. Their children are given under the Gantt line.
    3. Mary Pinckney Hay.
    4. Ruth Hay who married James Rhett of Beaufort, South Carolina. Their children are: Ruth, James, Haskell and Mary Rhett.
    5. Lena Pinckney Hay married her cousin, Henry Cumming Hay, son of Judge Samuel Hay and Susan Hay. They had a daughter Lena StClair Hay.
- B. Hasell Hay, daughter of Dr. Frederick Jay Hay and his wife Susan, did not marry.
- C. Christopher Gadsden Hay, M. D., a gallant Confederate soldier in the War Between the States, married his cousin, Mary Hay, daughter of Oscar Payne Hay and had three children.
    1. Alvin Hay.
    2. Jean Hay.
    3. Hugh Hay.

APPENDIX — THE FAMILY OF HAY

THE REVEREND SAMUEL HUTSON HAY

IV. Samuel Hutson Hay, fourth child of Colonel Frederick Jay Hay and his wife Susan Cynthia Brown (Hay), attended South Carolina University and won distinguished honor by his scholarship. Then feeling he was called to the ministry, he studied Theology at the Seminary in Columbia, South Carolina.

While at the University, he met Mary Peck of Virginia, niece of Dr. Thomas Peck, eminent teacher of Theology at Hampden Sidney, Virginia.

Mary Peck was then visiting her grandfather, Dr. Park, Professor in the South Carolina University, when she met Samuel Hutson Hay, a student there, and later they were married and had the following children:

1. Frances Snowden Hay married Colonel Del Kemper of Virginia who became a General in the War Between the States. He was in later years U. S. Consul to China. Children:
    A. May Kemper died when young.
    B. Zaida Kemper did not marry.
    C. Erroll Kemper, unmarried.
    D. Del Kemper, Jr., unmarried.
2. James Thornwell Hay practiced law in Camden, South Carolina and was for many years State Senator from Kershaw County. He married his cousin, Josephine Oakman, by whom the following children: W. Oakman, James Thornwell, Josephine and Adele Hay.
    A. W. Oakman Hay married Cornelia Williams and had two sons:
        1. James Thornwell Hay, Jr., married Florence Boykin of Camden, South Carolina and they had a child, James Thornwell Hay, III, who married Helen Taffel of Martinsville, Virginia and their two sons are:
            (a) James Dudley Hay
            (b) Samuel Boykin Hay
        2. Oakman Hay, Jr., son of W. Oakman Hay and Cornelia Williams (Hay), married Mary Adelaide Hughes of Tuxedo, New York. They live in New York City and have three children:
            (a) Mary Hughes Hay
            (b) Ann Hawkes Hay
            (c) Susan Hay
    B. James Thornwell Hay, Jr., son of James Thornwell Hay and Josephine Oakman (Hay), married Margaret Boykin of Camden, South Carolina. No children.

APPENDIX — THE FAMILY OF HAY

    C. Josephine Hay, unmarried.

    D. Adele Hay married Benham Brooks of Columbia, South Carolina, and had one child:

        1. Mary Josephine Brooks who married Archibald Tripp and they had a son, Archibald Tripp, Jr. of Columbia, South Carolina.

3. Frederick Jay Hay, III, son of Reverend Samuel Hutson Hay and wife Mary Susan Peck Hay; married Annie Richards, children: Sophie Edwards Hay, Samuel Hutson Hay, Annie Louise Hay, John Richards Hay, Frederick Jay Hay, Mary Peck Hay, Jeanie Lisle Hay, Nellie Hay.

    A. Sophie Edwards Hay, married Leland Blackwood Salters, M. D. Children:

        1. Frederick Hay Salters, M. D. married Lucy Davis Hall. **Children:**
            (a) Lucy Davis Salters, married Bennie F. Bray, have daughter Lucy Hall Bray.
            (b) Sophie Hay Salters

        2. Leland Blackwood Salters, not married.

        3. Jane McClary Salters, married Robert Ellis Chapman; have son Robert Ellis Chapman.

    B. The Reverend Samuel Hutson Hay, D. D., LL.D., married **Rachel Buchanan McMaster**; children:

        1. Rachel McMaster Hay, married the Reverend Hollis **Enes** Hayward; children:
            (a) John Hollis Hayward.
            (b) Samuel Francis Hayward
            (c) Rachel Enes Hayward

        2. Louisa Righton Hay, married Thomas Moffat Burriss; children:
            (a) John Hay Burriss
            (b) Thomas Moffat Burris.
            (c) Francis McMaster Burriss
            (d) Louisa Hay Burriss

        3. John Frederick Richards Hay, died a prisoner of war of the Japanese, a decorated hero of Bataan, Philippine Islands, in World War II.

    C. Annie Louise Hay, married Alvin Lewis McCaskill; children:

        1. John Calvin McCaskill, married Olga Hines; son, John Calvin McCaskill.

APPENDIX — THE FAMILY OF HAY

    2. Annie Righton McCaskill, married Robert Garnett Hodgkin; children:
       (a) Annie Righton McCaskill Hodgkin.
       (b) Robert Garnett Hodgkin.
       (c) Gordon Hay Hodgkin

D. The Reverend John Richards Hay, D. D., married Sara Craig; children:
    1. The Reverend Edward Craig Hay, married Mary Thomas Stockton; children:
       (a) Edward Craig Hay.
       (b) Robert Stockton Hay.
       (c) Thomas Douglas Hay
       (d) Mary Sara Hay
    2. Samuel Hutson Hay, married Dorothy Ann Churchill; children:
       (a) Samuel Hutson Hay.
       (b) Dorothy Churchill Hay.
       (c) Frederick Jay Hay
       (d) Herrick Richards Hay.
    3. John Richards Hay, married Elizabeth Ann Collett; son John Richards Hay.

E. The Reverend Frederick Jay Hay, D. D., married Mildred Johnston; they have no children.

F. Mary Peck Hay, married Stephen McQueen Huntley, Ph.D.; one son, Stephen McQueen Huntley, who is a student in the Presbyterian Theological Seminary, Decatur, Georgia.

G. Jeanie Lisle Hay, a librarian, unmarried.

H. Nellie Hay; died in early childhood, 1907.

The Reverend Samuel Hutson Hay, Jr. married his first cousin, Mary Louisa Gantt, daughter of Richard A. Gantt and Louisa Hay (Gantt) and had the following children:

A. Harold Hawkes Hay, never married.

B. Samuel Hutson Hay, III, married Mary Broun Ordway of Murfreesboro, Tennessee and had two children:
    1. Sarah Ordway Hay died early in life.
    2. Samuel Hutson Hay, M. D., who married Katheryn Sidney Chambers of Carthage, Tennessee. They have four children:

- (a) Samuel Hutson Hay, Jr.
- (b) Mary Corinne Hay.
- (c) Katheryn Chambers Hay
- (d) Sarah Louise Hay (all young).

5. The Reverend Thomas Park Hay, D. D., married *first*, Susan Venning, by whom a daughter, Olive Hay. (Her line is given under her husband's, Oscar Hay, son of Dr. Thomas Theodore Hay.)

    The Reverend Thomas Park Hay, D. D., married the *second* time, Jennie Mikell of Edisto Island, South Carolina, by whom a son: Thomas Park Hay, Jr. now living in New York.

    A. Thomas Park Hay, Jr. married Sue McWhirter. They have a daughter, Dorothy Sue Hay, now Mrs. James D. Thornton and their children are: James Thornton, Jr. and Sue Hay Thornton.

6. Mary Susan Hay married her cousin Walter Scott Hay, M. D., son of Lewis Scott Hay, M. D. and Anne Fraser (Hay). The children are on Dr. Walter Scott Hay's line.

7. Burwell Boykin Hay married Annie Wynne of Atlanta, Georgia. They had a daughter, Minnie Lee Hay.

    A. Minnie Lee Hay married Andrew Carrol Burkett. Children:
    1. Ann Wynne Burkett married Marvin Raimond Ausley, Jr. Children:
        - (a) Margaret Lee Ausley
        - (b) Marvin Raimond Ausley, III
    2. Andrew Carrol Burkett died in childhood.
    3. Louise Patterson Burkett married Ike Winbourn Pearce and had three children:
        - (a) Katherine Anne Pearce.
        - (b) Barbara Lynn Pearce.
        - (c) Ike Winbourn Pearce II

8. Ellen Reynolds Hay, daughter of the Reverend Samuel Hutson Hay and Mary Peck (Hay), married her first cousin, John Mackall Gantt. Their children are given on the Gantt line.

9. The Reverend William Smith Hay, M. D., youngest child of the Reverend Samuel Hutson Hay and Mary Peck Hay, married Burney Clarke of lower South Carolina and they had one son, Samuel Burney Hay.

    A. Samuel Burney Hay, D. D., now President of Stillman College, Tuscaloosa, Alabama, married Frances Dearing, daughter of Mr. and

APPENDIX — THE FAMILY OF HAY

Mrs. Marcellin Dearing of Covington, Georgia. They have three children:

1. Burney Hay married the Reverend Allen A. Gardner, Jr. of Gulfport, Mississippi. They now live in Thomasville, Georgia, where he is pastor of the First Presbyterian Church. They have four children:
    (a) Dearing Gardner
    (b) Burney Gardner
    (c) Allen A. Gardner, Jr.
    (d) Sam Hay Gardner
2. Martha Hay married F. Burton Vardeman, Jr. of Covington, Georgia and they live in Tuscaloosa, Alabama. Children:
    (a) Frances Hay Vardeman
    (b) Frank B. Vardeman, III
    (c) Cile Clarke Vardeman
3. Samuel B. Hay, Jr. married Louly Trippe Fowler on July 25, 1959, daughter of Mr. and Mrs. Robert Raphael Fowler, all of Covington. They are making their home at Hayfields Farm, Covington, Georgia.

V.   WILLIAM AUGUSTUS HAY

William Augustus Hay, fifth child of Colonel Frederick Hay and his wife, Susan, was a young lawyer with a promising future but died suddenly. He married Susan O'Bannon and had two children:
1. Frances Jane Hay (died in infancy) and
2. Harriet Ford Hay who married William Hutson Townsend, son of Dr. William Townsend, Sr. by his wife Martha, fifth child of Martha, (daughter of Colonel Ann Hawkes Hay) by her husband, William Marlon Townsend. They had two children:
    (a) William Hay Townsend, lawyer of Columbia, South Carolina, did not marry.
    (b) Edith Townsend — unmarried.

VI.   LEWIS SCOTT HAY

Lewis Scott Hay died unmarried.

VII.   THOMAS THEODORE HAY, M. D.

Dr. Hay was the seventh child of Colonel Frederick Jay Hay and his wife Susan Cynthia Brown (Hay). A practicing physician, he was especially gifted as a diagnostician and in the treatment of children's diseases.

He married on the tenth of April, 1845, Rhoda Furse and they had the following children:

1. Lewis Gordon Hay married his first cousin, Helen Hay, daughter of Charles Colcock Hay. They had two children: Erroll and Arthur Hay.
    A. Erroll Hay married Sidney Arthur Lowry, M. D. No children.
    B. Arthur Hay marrried Mary Louise Gardner and their children are:
        1. Helen Hay who is running her father's and grandfather's Insurance Agency in Kings Mountain, North Carolina.
        2. John Hay died July 31, 1918.
2. Mary Ella Hay never married.
3. Rosalie Hay unmarried.
4. Thomas Theodore Hay, successful business man of Raleigh, North Carolina, married Isabel Cameron Gales, daughter of Major Seaton Gales and his wife Mary Cameron Gales. Children: Mary Seaton Hay and Isabel Cameron Hay.
    A. Mary Seaton Hay married William Branch Jones, prominent attorney of Raleigh, North Carolina and had two children:
        1. Isabel Hay Jones who married first Clyde G. White, by whom a son, William Armistead White.
            (a) William Armistead White married Mary Elizabeth Cummings.
        1. Isabel Jones White married second, Harrison H. Fain and they had a son, Harrison. Isabel, twice a widow, is now married to William C. Etheredge, successful food broker of Raleigh. Her baby boy Harrison, was legally adopted by Mr. Etheredge and given the name of Harrison Etheredge.
            (b) Harrison Etheredge is now married to Ruth Southern of Raleigh.
    B. Isabel Cameron Hay, daughter of Thomas Theodore Hay and Isabel Cameron (Hay), married Frank Morton Stronach, manufacturer of Raleigh, and had a son, Thomas Hay Stronach, who lives in Raleigh engaged in the Insurance business. He married Ann Putnam of Bos-

APPENDIX — THE FAMILY OF HAY

ton, Mass. and they have two daughters: Aline Cameron Stronach and Isabel Jane Hay Stronach.

5. Walter Douglas Hay, partner in the firm of the Hay brothers in Raleigh, son of Dr. Thomas Theodore Hay and his wife Rhoda Furse, married Nannie Burwell and had a daughter—
   A. Nannie Hay, who married Samuel Hamilton Wiley, who was for years Consul General to several foreign countries. He is now retired.
      They have two sons:
      1. Walter William Wiley
      2. Patrick Hamilton Wiley.
      3. They also had a daughter, Marian Erroll Wiley who died in 1952.
6. Leila Hay married Benjamin Peoples, son of Dr. Peoples, by whom one child, now deceased.
7. Gilbert Hay engaged in the insurance business in Waco, Texas, married Alice Henrietta Marshall of Texas, by whom two sons:
   A. Marshall Downes Hay who lives in Blawenburg, New Jersey, and is engaged in the pharmaceutical manufacturing business. He married Katherine Braswell Bogue of Raleigh, North Carolina and they have a son, Marshall Downes Hay, Jr.
   B. Gilbert Hay, younger brother of Marshall Downes Hay, married Virginia Darden by whom a son, Gilbert Hay, Jr.
8. Albert Hay—twin brother to Gilbert Hay—a young man with a promising future, died early in life.
9. Oscar Payne Hay, a son of Dr. Thomas Theodore Hay and his wife Rhoda Furse, was also in the insurance business of Raleigh. He married his cousin, Susan Olivia Hay on December 11, 1912. She was the daughter of the Rev. Thomas Parke Hay, D. D., who married first Susan Venning and had a daughter, Olive Hay. Oscar Payne Hay and Susan Olive Hay had the following children: Nell Rhoda, Rosalie Venning, Thomas Theodore, Oscar Payne, Jr. and Mary Olive Hay.
   A. Nell Rhoda Hay, unmarried.
   B. Rosalie Venning Hay married a Presbyterian minister, Massey Mott Heltzel, D. D., on September 19, 1939. Children: Sallie Olive, Jeanie Hay and Margaret Wilson Heltzel.
   C. Thomas Theodore Hay married Bonnie Blalock. Children: Susan Blalock and Martha Scott Hay Blalock.

D. Oscar Payne Hay, Jr. married Ruth E. Enloe. Children: Ruth Ann and Thomas Enloe Hay.
E. Mary Olive Hay, unmarried.

VIII. OSCAR PAYNE HAY

Oscar Payne Hay eighth child of Col. Frederick Hay and his wife Susan Hay; married his first cousin, Sarah Porcher Hay, daughter of William Henry Hay and his wife, Mary Caroline Gantt. They had two children:
1. Mary Hay married her cousin, Christopher Gadsden Hay, M. D. (Children have been given).
2. Caroline Petigru Hay married Richard Bostick. They had only one daughter who died at four months.

IX. ALFRED HAY

Alfred Hay, ninth child of Colonel Frederick Hay and his wife Susan, died in infancy.

X. SUSAN CYNTHIA HAY

Susan Cynthia Hay, daughter of Colonel Frederick Jay Hay and his wife, Susan Hay, married her cousin Judge Samuel Hay and had the following children:
1. Charles Jenkins Hay, lawyer of Barnwell, South Carolina. Did not marry.
2. Susan Emily Hay, living in Charleston, South Carolina, unmarried.
3. Richard Marion Hay married Sally Glover of Charleston, and had the following children:
    (a) Samuel Marion Hay married first Mabel Southerland Mitchell in 1915 and had two children:
        (1) Elizabeth Southerland Hay who married December 30, 1941, George Montraville Davenport, Jr. of Cordover, Alabama. They had two children: Elizabeth Hay Davenport born in Florida, and Juilette Mitchell Davenport born in Columbia, S. C.

APPENDIX — THE FAMILY OF HAY

  (2) Margaret Mitchell Hay born in Charleston, South Carolina, married in 1941, Robert Lee Stallings, Jr. of Bridgeton, North Carolina and they have two children: Mary Mitchell Stallings born in California and Robert Lee Stallings, III born in Illinois.

 (a) Samuel Marion Hay married second in 1927, Mary Elizabeth Mitchell of Mount Pleasant, South Carolina, sister of his first wife.

 (b) Lester Glover Hay unmarried.

 (c) Emily Kathleen Hay unmarried.

4. William Henry Hay, son of Susan Cynthia Hay and Judge Samuel Hay, did not marry.

5. Patti Lee Hay married her cousin, Charles J. Colcock, son of Colonel Charles Colcock, C. S. A., by his wife, Lucy Frances Horton. They had one daughter—Erroll Hay Colcock, living in Charleston, S. C.

6. Mary Erskine Hay unmarried.

7. Henry Cumming Hay married his cousin, Lena Hay, daughter of Rev. Dawes Hay. They had one child, Lena St. Clair Hay.

8. Gertrude Agnes Hay did not marry.

9. Samuel Montgomery Hay died young.

XI.   MARTHA HUTSON HAY

Martha Hutson Hay, youngest child of Col. Frederick J. Hay and his wife, Susan Cynthia Brown (Hay) married her cousin, Major Richard Gantt Hay of the Confederacy, and their children were: Mary Caroline, Martha Hutson, Sarah Henrietta and Marion Heyward Hay. The first three died early. Marion Heyward Hay married her cousin, Frederick Hay Gaunt, and have surviving children: Richard, Marshall, Frederick and Elizabeth Marian Gaunt—their marriages and children are given on the Gaunt line.

GANTT or GAUNT LINE

Mary Louisa Hay, oldest child of Colonel Frederick J. Hay and his wife Susan Cynthia Brown (Hay) married Richard A. Gantt, son of Judge Richard Gantt, distinguished Jurist of South Carolina.

APPENDIX — THE FAMILY OF HAY

Judge Gantt was the son of Dr. Thomas Gantt and his wife, Susannah Mackall Gantt of Maryland.

Richard A. Gantt and Mary Louisa Hay (Gantt) had the following children:

I. Frederick Hay Gantt, Colonel in the C. S. A. He commanded the 11th South Carolina Regiment in General Hagood's Brigade. He died unmarried.

II. Richard Plantagenet Gantt, Captain in the 11th South Carolina Infantry commanded by his brother, married Ella Elliott Mackay, daughter of George Mackay by his wife, Abbie Jenkins, both of the Beaufort district. They had the following children: Anna Maud, Frederick Hay, Elizabeth Mackay, Edith Plantagenet, Mary Louisa, Richard Leon, Alma Devereux, Waldo Douglas and Charles Drayton Gantt.

   A. Anna Maud Gantt married Gordon Woodruff. No children.

   B. Frederick Hay Gaunt, married in 1897, his cousin, Marian Heyward Hay, who was the daughter of Major Richard Gaunt Hay of the Confederacy. He had married his first cousin, Martha Hutson Hay, youngest child of Colonel Frederick Jay Hay. Their children are: Richard, Marshall, Frederick, Elizabeth Marion (died in infancy), and Margaret Gaunt. These children are triple descendants of Colonel Ann Hawkes Hay. They are as follows:

   1. Richard Hay Gaunt married Mary Catherine Bond of Houston, Texas. Children:
      (a) Margaret Bond Gaunt married William John Jackson, and they have three children: Ann Catherine Jackson, Michael Gerard Jackson and Elizabeth Mary Jackson.
      (b) Marian Hay Gaunt, unmarried.

   2. Marshall Gaunt married Mary Josephine Toney of Pine Bluff, Arkansas. They have one child:
      (a) Mary Marsha Gaunt

   3. Frederick Hay Gaunt married Gean Campbell of Seminole, Florida. Children:
      (a) Frederick Hay Gaunt who died in infancy.
      (b) Elizabeth Hay Gaunt
      (c) William Hay Gaunt
      (d) John Campbell Gaunt

   4. Martha Margaret Hay Gaunt married Walter Young Lightsey. They adopted a boy in 1947, Donald Martin Lightsey.

APPENDIX — THE FAMILY OF HAY

C. Elizabeth Mackay Gantt, daughter of Richard A. Gantt and Mary Louisa Hay, never married.
D. Edith Plantagenet Gantt, unmarried.
E. Mary Louisa ("Marie") Gantt married her cousin, Alfred Pinckney Hay. Children: Alfred Pinckney Hay, Jr. (who died in infancy), Edith Louise, Henry Hasell and Charles Hugh Hay.
   1. Edith Louise Hay married George Flanders and had twin girls:
      (a) Edith Josephine Flanders who married Roger Rossiter and they had three children: Patricia, Suzanne and Mark Roger Rossiter.
      (b) Marilynn Louise Flanders married Joe Hagberg. They had two children: John Hagberg and Ruth Ann Hagberg.
   1. Edith Louise Hay married second, George Classen of Savannah, Georgia. They had one son, Harry Classen who married Joy Sutton Vann. No children.
      Edith married the third time Fred Hudelmaier.
   2. Henry Hasell Hay, son of Alfred Pinckney Hay and Marie Gantt (Hay) married Edna McDaniel of Beaufort, South Carolina, and had the following children: Preston Hay and Martha Hay.
   3. Charles Hugh Hay, son of Alfred Pinckney Hay and Marie Gantt (Hay) married Mildred Weideman and had two children: Charles Hugh Hay, Jr. and Louise Hay.
F. Richard Leon Gantt, son of Richard Plantagenet Gantt and Ella Mackay (Gantt) married Margaret Hope McGill of Kings Mountain, North Carolina, by whom the following children:
   1. Frances Alma Gantt married William Harley. No children.
   2. Thomas Drayton Gantt married Anita Camelier and their children are: Thomas, Lynette, Margaret, Douglas and Brenda Gantt.
   3. Kathryn Mabel Gantt married Edward Arbogast; children: Margaret, Roy and Wendell Arbogast.
   4. Richard Leon Gantt, Jr. married Elizabeth Harley and their children are: Ellen Gantt and Frances Gantt.
   5. Marie Gantt married Edward Fowke and have the following children: Walter Fowke, Linda Fowke and Gail Fowke.
   6. Fuller Alexander Gantt unmarried.
   7. Joe Douglas Gantt married Elizabeth Elkins. They have one child, Hope Gantt.

APPENDIX — THE FAMILY OF HAY

G. Alma Devereaux Gantt, daughter of Richard P. Gantt and Ella Mackay Gantt, married Dr. William Steinmeyer. Children:
  1. Ella Rachel Steinmeyer married Edwin Lawton Ellis. Children:
     (a) Marian Devereaux Ellis who married Creighton S. Inabinet. Their children are: Lynn Rebecca and Creighton Inabinet.
     (b) Rachel Elizabeth Ellis, not married.
  2. John Henry Steinmeyer, son of Alma Gantt (Steinmeyer) and Dr. William Steinmeyer, married Evelyn Ives. Children: John Henry, Jr., Harold Evelyn and Dorothy Elizabeth Steinmeyer.
     (a) John Henry Steinmeyer, Jr. married Joyce Goding. They have twin daughters, Donna and Diane; also William Harold, Evelyn Ives and Dorothy Elizabeth Steinmeyer.
  3. Maud Douglas Steinmeyer, daughter of Alma D. and Dr. William Steinmeyer, married Albert H. Cory and their children are Albert Henry Cory, Jr. and Caroline Cory.
  4. William Marion Steinmeyer married Lois Glenda Hedden. No children.
  5. Alma Gantt Steinmeyer married first, Daniel Harrell and had a son Daniel Harrell, Jr. who married Rena Bell and they have a daughter, Debora Harrell.
  5. Alma Gantt married second, Claude Coppelmann by whom the following children: Douglas Ashby, Claude, Jr., William Frederick, John Richards, Glenn Hutson and Christopher Devereaux Coppelmann.
  6. Marie Elizabeth Steinmeyer married Douglas Stuart MacArthur. Children: Margaret Elizabeth and Kathryn Stuart MacArthur.
H. Waldo Douglas Gantt, son of Richard P. and Ella Mackay Gantt, married Mabel Parler and their children are: Mabel Louise, Annie Elizabeth and Lillian Douglas Gantt.
I. Charles Drayton Gantt, son of Richard P. and Ella Mackay Gantt, married Jessie Evalyn Fowke in 1917. Children:
  1. Laurie Ella Gantt who married Colonel Moss Yater from Knoxville, Tennessee. Children: Moss Whittborn and Marthana Drayton Yater.
  2. Louis Plantagenet Gantt married Mildred Knight Derieux. Children: Evalyn Mackay Gantt and Aegina Derieux Gantt.
  3. John Drayton Gantt married Jean Audrey Youmans. Children: Charles Hammond Gantt and Edith Ann Gantt.

APPENDIX — THE FAMILY OF HAY

III. Anna Gantt, daughter of Richard Gantt and Mary Louise Hay Gantt, died unmarried.
IV. Eldred Lucas Gantt was killed at Petersburg while Adjutant of the 11th South Carolina Infantry. He died unmarried.
V. VI. VIIth Child died in infancy.
VIII. Mary Louisa Gantt, daughter of Richard Gantt and Mary Louisa Hay (Gantt), married her cousin, the Rev. Samuel Hay, Jr. Children found on Hay line.
IX. Susan Cynthia Gantt died in childhood.
X. John Mackall Gantt, son of Richard Gantt and Mary Louisa Hay Gantt, married his first cousin, Ellen Reynolds Hay, daughter of the Rev. Samuel Hay, Sr., by whom two children:
- A. Samuel Gantt—unmarried.
- B. Frederick Hay Gantt married Elizabeth Cheatham of Durham, North Carolina, daughter of Dr. Arch Cheatham and Ida Shaw Cheatham. Their children are:
    1. John Mackall Gantt married Henriette Smythe of Laurens, South Carolina, daughter of Robert Wade Smythe and Harriette Wilmer Hughes (Smythe). Children: John Mackall Gantt, Jr. and David Huff Gantt.
    2. Frederick Hay Gantt, married Henrietta Mason, daughter of Mr. and Mrs. Augustus Mason of Laurens, S. C.

XI. Sara Eliza Gantt, daughter of Richard Gantt and Mary Louisa Hay (Gantt), did not marry.
XII. Longstreet Gantt, son of Richard Gantt and Mary Louisa Hay (Gantt), married Lavinia Skinner. They lived in Winsboro, South Carolina. Children:
- A. Evelyn Harvey Gantt married Ernest Ferguson and they have three sons:
    1. Joseph Ferguson
    2. Ernest Ferguson, Jr.
    3. Richard Ferguson
- B. Louise Gantt married Morris Lyles and they have children.
- C. Annie Gantt died unmarried.
- D. Joseph Skinner Gantt was killed in France during World War I.
- E. Julia Gantt married Arthur La Bruce.

APPENDIX — THE FAMILY OF HAY

The following families are descendants of the Hays of Erroll and Lochloy in Scotland, but have a different emigrant ancestor from Colonel Ann Hawkes Hay.

ERROLL B. HAY, JR.

Mr. Hay's family originates from the Hays of Erroll in Scotland. His immigrant ancestor in this country was William Hay born November 10, 1748, the ninth child of James Hay and Helen Rankin (Hay) in Kilsyth, Scotland.

I. William Hay came to Virignia in 1768 and married Elizabeth Cary, daughter of Miles Cary and Elizabeth Taylor (Cary).

II. John Hay, their son, married Mary Stith Maury and lived in Virginia.

III. Isaac Hite Hay, fourth child of John Hay, married Ann Maury Baldwin and moved to Vicksburg, Mississippi, where he was admitted to the Bar in 1837. Their only child was:

IV. John Baldwin Hay who, after the death of his parents, was educated in Athens, Greece, living there with his missionary aunt, Mary Briscoe Baldwin. He joined the U. S. Consular Service and married Cornelia Holmes Badger in Philadelphia, Pennsylvania, December 19, 1843.

V. Erroll Baldwin Hay, their son, was born in Beirut, Syria. After his mother's death, he and his brothers and sisters were brought up by their grandmother, Cornelia Holmes Moorehead, in Philadelphia, Pennsylvania. He served in World War I and married Mary Goodall Bradley, daughter of Thomas Bradley and Hanna Goodall of Philadelphia. Their son:

VI. Erroll Baldwin Hay, Jr., born November 10, 1903 at Wayne, Delaware County, Pa., joined the Bethlehem Steel Company in 1925, was transferred to Atlanta, Georgia in 1933. He married Charlotte King in 1935, daughter of Charles Preston King and Augusta Louisa Wylie, all of Atlanta. They have three children:
   1. Erroll Baldwin Hay, III.
   2. Laura Augusta Hay.
   3. Mary Bradley Hay.

VIRGINIA RUTH HAY (PAGE)

In a cemetery out on their plantation from Sardis, Mississippi, there are two graves with markers bearing these inscriptions:

1. John G. Hay from Nairnshire, Scotland, died 1821.

APPENDIX — THE FAMILY OF HAY

2. **James** Hay, Auldearn, Scotland, 1823-1866. Married Mary B. Hay. Their children are:
   A. Sophie Jane Hay.
   B. Harry Hampton Hay married Martha Frances Williams and had four children:
      1. Harry Hampton Hay, Jr., married and had three girls: Addie Hay, Pattie Hay, Henrietta Hay.
      2. Clarence Christopher Hay, son of Harry Hampton Hay, Sr. and Martha Williams (Hay).
      3. Gerald Gordon Hay, another son of Harry Hampton Hay, Sr., married Mary D'Orr and had two girls:
         (a) Gladys Grace Hay married Arnold Bonner and had a son: Arnold Hay Bonner who married and has a child. Janet Grace Bonner (1952).
         (b) Virginia Ruth Hay, daughter of Gerald Gordon Hay and his wife Mary D'Orr, married Damon Page and live on their Mississippi plantation.
      4. William Williams Hay was the fourth son of Harry Hampton Hay, Sr. and Martha Frances Williams (Hay).
   C. Alex Hay—Captain in Confederate Army.

COMPTON - HAY

The Compton history in America began in the Province of *Maryland* with John Compton as immigrant. He came from Northhampton, England and the name of the English estate is Compton Wyngates. He settled is Maryland on an estate of eight hundred acres called Brathwood.

Records show a marriage to Mary Douglas, 1675, daughter of Robert Clark and widow of Robert Douglas. Their children were:

A. John Compton, Jr. born 1667.
B. Samuel Compton born 1669.
C. Matthew Compton born 1671; married Susannah Briscoe, daughter of Colonel Philip Briscoe and Susannah Swann.
D. Gerard Compton born 1673.
E. Eleanor Compton born 1677; married Henry Hardy.
F. James Compton born 1679.
G. Ralph Compton born 1681.

1. William Compton, son of John Compton, Jr. (1667) married **Mary Clarke** and their son, Wiliam Clarke Compton, married Elizabeth Elgin in Charles County, Maryland. In 1778 they moved to Flint Hill, Culpeper County, Virginia. Children:
   (a) James Compton never married.
   (b) Eleanor Compton did not marry.
   (c) John Compton married Dorcas Clarke.
   (d) Walter Sidney Compton married Elizabeth Ann Adams.
   (e) Anne Compton married Robert Graham.
   (f) William Compton married Nancy Hay (House of Erroll, Scotland, February 27, 1802—Reuben Finnell, minister—Culpepper County, Virginia. Will Book I page 204).
   (g) Thomas Compton married Eliza Jackson.
   (h) Alexander Compton married Lucinda Irelans.
   (i) Elizabeth Elgin Compton married Gerard Ricketts.
   Relatives of William Compton who married Nancy Hay (House of Erroll, Scotland) are now living in Tennessee.

CAMPBELL - HAY - ROANE

John Campbell and Grace Hay were the immigrant ancestors of Annie Elise Roane (Winter).

He was born in Londonderry, Ireland, and came to Pennsylvania in 1726 with his wife, Grizel (Grace) Hay (Campbell). They had children.

David Campbell had a daughter, Anne Campbell who married Archibald Gilbert Roane in July 24, 1788. Whose father was Andrew Roane, immigrant to Pennsylvania.

Judge Archibald Gilbert Roane was the first Supreme Court Judge and the second Governor of Tennessee. Roane County was named for him.

His son, Dr. Andrew Roane, married Sarah Jane Clarke, cousin of George Rogers Clarke of Kentucky. They had a son: Archibald Roane, Jr., Circuit Court Judge and Legislator, one of the Trustees of the University of Mississippi. He married Catherine Washington Winter. They were the parents of Anne Elise Roane who married her cousin, Dawson Winter and had a son, Archibald Roane Winter who married Dorothy May Ellison. There are two little boys by this marriage:
   1. Robert Roane Winter
   2. John Page Winter

APPENDIX — THE FAMILY OF HAY

THE CLAN HAY SOCIETY OF AMERICA

The Chief
The Right Honourable
Diana Denyse Hay,
Countess of Erroll,
Lady Hay and Slains,
Mac Garadh Mhor
31st Chief of Clan Hay
30th Great Constable of Scotland

Clan Hay Society of America:
Townsend Hay
Route 1
Black Mountain,
North Carolina

Many Americans by blood are eligible for membership in the American Branch of the Clan Hay Society.

The Clan Hay Society was formed at a Clan Council in Scotland in 1951 with the definite object of promoting a spirit of kin and fellowship among various branches of the Clan all over the world; of fostering an interest in Scotland and its history; in collecting and preserving its history and traditions; and when funds permit, acquiring former Hay lands with a view of settling members thereon.

The Chief appointed Captain John Hay of Hayfield as her Commissioner. Under his very competent leadership the Clan Hay Society, though recently organized, has grown until it is the fourth largest clan Society in Scotland with branches in England, Canada, South Africa, Australia and New Zealand.

Delgaty Castle, one of the old castles belonging to the chiefs of the Hay Clan, is now the headquarters of the Clan Hay Society. No other Clan Society has an old family castle as their headquarters. Members of the clan all over the world are invited to visit it when in Scotland.

The Clan Hay Society in Scotland issues very interesting news letters from time to time to members. Also they have sent out five illustrated Clan Hay

APPENDIX — THE FAMILY OF HAY

magazines filled with all sorts of interesting information to all who are related to the Family and Clan of Hay. The Shield of the Chief is argent three escutcheons gules.

The history of the Hays is the history of Scotland. King Robert Bruce made Gilbert Hay Hereditary Great Constable of Scotland for services at the Battle of Bannockburn in 1314. This title has been continuously in the family of the Chief. The present Chief, the Countess of Erroll, is the 30th Great Constable.

Years later at the Battle of Flodden Field in 1513 when the Scots under King James IV were in battle against the troops of King Henry III of England, the Clan Hay was practically destroyed. The Chief, his brother and ninety other chieftains and officers of the name of Hay and every man on the Hay lands between the ages of 16 and 60 were killed. Of the entire Hay Regiment there was not a single survivor.

The Clan has fought in all the wars of Scotland and after the fatal battle of Culloden when Prince Charles was defeated, many of them sought refuge in other lands—especially America. And so today many now living over here are eligible to the Clan Hay Society.

The Chief appointed as her Lieutenant, Townsend Hay of Black Mountain, North Carolina, to organize the Clan Hay Society of America, which is another branch of the Hay Clan Society of Scotland and acknowledges the Great Constable of Scotland as Chief in all Hay Clan matters. This Branch is the first to be formed outside the British Commonwealth. We are informed that ten thousand potential members are in the United States. Mr. Townsend is doing a splendid work. He has quite extensive material regarding the Clan Hay both in this country and Scotland, the result of fifty years of labor.

Mr. Townsend Hay belongs to the same branch of the Hay family as that of John Hay, former Secretary of State and afterwards Ambassador to the British Court. And now his grandson, John Hay Whitney, is Ambassador to the Court of Queen Elizabeth II in London.

Mr. Townsend Hay's branch, like many other branches of the Hay Clan, left Scotland as a result of being "out for the Stewart" with the Earl of Mar, in the Jacobite Uprising of 1715. After their defeat, his ancestors moved to the Palatine on the Rhine and then to America in the 1740's—then Virginia, Pennsylvania, Maryland, Western Pennsylvania and to Wisconsin, where he was born in 1889.

Townsend Hay is now the Chief's Lieutenant and lives with his wife in Black Mountain, North Carolina.

"NOBLESSE OBLIGE"

These French words meaning "Nobility Obligates," apply to all members of the Family of Hay.

Proper pride of ancestry is praise worthy and to be desired.

The lives of the men and women portrayed in this book should inspire all of their descendants to try to live up to their standards.

To be brave and honorable and chivalrous. Above all to follow in the faith *they* knew and handled down to their children — The "Faith Of Our Fathers".

> "To you from fallen hands
> They throw the torch —
> Be yours to hold it high."

FINIS

Index

INDEX TO THE FIRST EDITION

A

Auldearn, Battle of—52
Aurora, Poem by Helen Hay—149

B

Bacot, Jane—180
Bailey, Erroll—173
Bailey, John—173
Bailey, Lawton—173
Bailey, Lewis—173
Bailey, Lily—173
Bailey, Minnie—176
Bailey, Peyton—173
Bailey, Thomas—173
Bain, Mr. George—39, 47, 64
Balfour, Sir Andrew—111
Balfour, Anna—109
Balfour, Sir David—110
Balfour, Isabel—109, 112
Balfour, James—109
Balfour, Jean—109
Balfour, Michael—109
Barnwell, General John—178
Bellenger, Dr. John—142
Bethune, Coat of Arms—111
Bethune, Dr. George—107, 111, 117
Bethune, Jean—117
Blair, Andrew—110
Bonallo, Rev. James—79
Bostick, Jennie—182
Bostick, Richard M.—159
Boyes, Thomas—103
Brewton, Francis—180
Brewton, Mary—180
Brewton, Col. Miles—180
Brewton, Rebecca—180
Brewton, Robert—180
Brown, Susan Cynthia—145
Bruce, King Robert—13, 14, 15, 16, 17
Bruce, David—97
Bruce, Helen—97
Bruce, James—97
Bruce, Marjorie—44
Bruce, Mary Elizabeth—100
Bruce, Robert—99
Bruce, Robert, Descent from Norse Kings—187

C

Caithness, Family of—72
Calhoun, John Alfred—180
Cardross, Lord—119
Carlisle, Earl of—112
Carre, Walter Wingate—180
Carroll, George—180
Cawdor, Early Thanes of—58
Chisholm, Family of—83
Chisholm, Muriel—83
Clarke, Burney—156
Colcock, Family of—176
Colcock, Adelaide H.—179
Colcock, Agnes—182
Colcock, Agnes J.—183
Colcock, Anna Eustace—182
Colcock, Anna Stuart—173
Colcock, Annie Toomer—180
Colcock, Augusta Palmer—180
Colcock, Caroline Ann—182
Colcock, Catherine—183
Colcock, Charles J.—180
Colcock, Charles Jones—178, 180
Colcock, Clarence—179
Colcock, Cornelius Julius—179
Colcock, Daniel De Saussure—180
Colcock, Dessie—179
Colcock, Edgar—179
Colcock, Edward Rowland—178
Colcock, Elizabeth Hay—172
Colcock, Eliza Mary—178
Colcock, Emmeline Sarah—179
Colcock, Erroll Hay—182
Colcock, Esther—179
Colcock, Esther Hutson—179
Colcock, Frances Horton—182
Colcock, Francis Horton—183
Colcock, Franklin—179
Colcock, Franklin Pierce—179
Colcock, Helen McIver—183
Colcock, Henrietta—179
Colcock, Henry—179
Colcock, Henry Hay—179
Colcock, Isabel—179
Colcock, James Dunwody—178
Colcock, James Stockman—180
Colcock, Capt. John—181
Colcock, John—179
Colcock, John, Jr.—180
Colcock, Joseph—178
Colcock, Laurie Isabel—179
Colcock, Mai North—180
Colcock, Margaret Hamilton—180
Colcock, Marion—179
Colcock, Marion W.—179
Colcock, Mary Mellicent—179
Colcock, Martha Anna—179
Colcock, Mary Anna—179
Colcock, Mary Clementine—179
Colcock, Mary Rugeley—180
Colcock, Mellicent—180
Colcock, Mellicent Woodward—180
Colcock, Patti Lee Hay—54, 182
Colcock, Pauline Ladson—179
Colcock, Richard Hutson—173
Colcock, Richard Hutson, Jr.—180
Colcock, Richard W.—179
Colcock, Samuel Hay—173
Colcock, Seaborn Jones—183
Colcock, Theodora Octavia—179
Colcock, Thomas Hutson—178
Colcock, William—178
Colcock, William Bostick—183
Colcock, William Ferguson—179
Colcock, William Hutson—178
Colcock, William Lewis—172
Colcock, Woodward Hutson—183
Culloden Moor, Battle of—53
Cumming Family—40
Cumming, Mrs. Bruce—76
Cumming, Carles Lenox—100

D

D'Aubigny, Matilda—32
De Pass, Alva—182
De Pass, Anna—182
Deus Misereatur, Poem of—170, 171
Deeds in Isle of Jamaica—228, 129
Dewees, Amelia L.—179
Dewees, Emmeline—179
Dewees, Henrietta—179
Dewees, Dr. Joseph—179
Douglas, Family of—67
Drummond, Mariot—94
Dunbar, Family of—80
Dunbar, Sir Archibald—80, 81
Dunbar, Isabel—80
Dundas, Mary—100

E

Early Scotch History—1, 23
Eighth Generation—47
Eighteenth Generation—96
Eleventh Generation—62
Elgin, Earl of—100
Ennobling of the Hays—24
Erroll, Earl of—101
Erskine, Alice—44
Erskine, Catherine—119

INDEX — THE FAMILY OF HAY

Erskine, Sir John—44
Erskine, Rachel—119
Erskine, Thomas—119

F

Fifteenth Generation—88
Fifth Generation—37
Findlater, Earls of—46
First Generation—24
Flag of Manassas, Poem of the 169, 170
Forbes, Family of—66
Fourteenth Generation—85
Fourth Generation—35
Fraser, Family of—37
Fraser, Ann—156
Furse, Rhoda—158

G

Gales, Isabel Cameron—158
Gantt, Family of—160
Gantt, Alma Devereux—147
Gantt, Anna Maud—147
Gantt, Annie—147
Gantt, Charles Drayton—147
Gantt, Edith P.—147
Gantt, Eldred Lucas—147
Gantt, Elizabeth Mackay—147
Gantt, Evelyn—147
Gantt, Frederick—147
Gantt, Col. Frederick Hay—146
Gantt, John Mackall—147
Gantt, Joseph—147
Gantt, Julia—147
Gantt, Longstreet—147
Gantt, Louise—147
Gantt, Mary Ann Caroline—160
Gantt, Mary Louisa—147
Gantt, Richard—147
Gantt, Capt. Richard Plantagenet—146
Gantt, Samuel—147
Gantt, Sarah Elizabeth—147
Gantt, Santa Anna—147
Gantt, Susan Cynthia—147
Gantt, Waldo Douglas—147
Gaunt, Elizabeth Marion—163
Gaunt, Frederick Hay—163
Gaunt, Marshall—163
Gaunt, Richard—163
Gathering of the Hays—26, 27
Gibson, Anna—105
Gignilliat, Henry—177
Glen, Agnes—98
Glen, Andrew—98
Glen, Gov. of South Carolina—98
Glencairn, Countess of—111
Glover, Sallie—168
Glover, Sanders L.—168
Gordon, Helen—107
Gordon, Margaret—46
Graeme, William—Baron Kerdale—56
Graham, Sir John—121
Graham, Mrs. Laura—113
Grant Coat of Arms—120
Grant, Mrs. Alexander—120
Grant, John—120
Gregorie, Agnes—183

Gregorie, Charles—183
Gregorie, Charles Colcock—183
Gregorie, Joseph—183
Gregorie, Louisa—183
Gregorie, Mary W. C.—179
Gregorie, Thomas—183
Gregorie, Dr. Thomas—183
Gregorie, William Douglas—179
Guerard, Robert Godin—183

H

Harald, Haarfager—72, 76
Hasell, Caroline—150
Hawkes, Basilia—116
Hawkes, Edward—115
Hawkes, Richard—116
Hay Bible Records—139
Hay Coat of Arms—116
Hay of Easter Kennet—91
Hay of Fosterseat—89
Hay Family in Jamaica—112, 113, 114
Hay, Adeline D.—144
Hay, Agnes—111
Hay, Albert—158
Hay, Alexander—61, 62, 82, 83, 90, 91, 93, 94, 95, 96, 97.
Hay, Sir Alexander—94,97
Hay, Alfred Octavius—146
Hay, Alfred Pinckney—154
Hay, Alvan—152
Hay, Andrew—62, 97, 102, 107, 108, 109, 110
Hay, Ann—109
Hay, Ann Hawkes — 1, 110, 111, 114, 115, 116, 117, 120, 125, 126, 127, 133, 139, 184, 188
Hay, Ann Hawkes, descent from King Alfred—191
Hay, Ann Hawkes, descent from Charlemagne and William I—188
Hay, Ann Hawkes, descent from Early Norse Kings—184
Hay, Ann Mister—139
Hay, Arthur—158
Hay, Arthur Erroll—158
Hay, Augustus—143
Hay, Barbara—108
Hay, Belle Cameron—158
Hay, Burwell Boykin—156
Hay, Caroline Petigru—159
Hay, Charles Colcock — 147, 148
Hay, Charles Jenkins—167
Hay, Charlotte—142
Hay, Christian—102
Hay, Dr. Christopher Gadsden—152, 159
Hay, Clarence—148
Hay, Clementine—144
Hay, Daniel—93
Hay, David—80, 83, 87, 90, 94, 95, 96, 98, 99
Hay, Edith—151
Hay, Egidia—46
Hay, Eldred Gaunt—151
Hay, Eleanor—142
Hay, Elizabeth—128, 129
Hay, Elizabeth Mary—142
Hay, Ellen Reynolds—147, 156

Hay, Emily Kathleen—168
Hay, Emma—148
Hay, Erroll—148, 158
Hay, Erroldine—156
Hay, Esther—131
Hay, Eugene Gordon—144
Hay, Euphemia—46
Hay, Frances Jane—157
Hay, Frances Snowden—156
Hay, Frederick—144, 156
Hay, Frederick Jay—141, 144, 145, 146, 147, 150, 156, 159
Hay, George—83, 88, 90, 101, 103, 109
Hay, Gertrude Agnes—168
Hay, Gilbert—158
Hay, Sir Gilbert—46
Hay, Gladys—151
Hay, Grizel—102, 112
Hay, Harold Hawkes—156
Hay, Harriet Ford—157
Hay, Harriet Young—144
Hay, Harry Hasell—151
Hay, Hasell—151
Hay, Helen—46, 97, 109, 150, 158
Hay, Henry—151
Hay, Henry Cumming—151
Hay, Hugh—152
Hay, Rev. Hugh, P. D.—151
Hay, Isabella—118, 119
Hay, James—61, 90, 97, 98, 101, 110
Hay, Sir James—46
Hay, James Thornwell—156
Hay, Janet Scott—140, 143
Hay, Jean—107, 110, 119, 152
Hay, John—46, 80, 84, 86, 88, 95, 98, 99, 103, 104, 113, 159
Hay, Sir John—44
Hay, Leila—158
Hay, Lena Pinckney—151
Hay, Lena St. Clair—152
Hay, Lestargette Glover—168
Hay, Lewis—148
Hay, Lewis Gordon—158
Hay, Sir Lewis John Erroll—26, 62
Hay, Lewis Scott—140, 144, 148, 156
Hay, Lisle—156
Hay, Louisa—146, 156
Hay, Malcolm—156
Hay, Margaret—98
Hay, Marie—108
Hay, Marion Haywood—163
Hay, Marshall Downes—158
Hay, Martha—140, 143, 144
Hay, Martha Hawkes—144
Hay, Martha Hutson—146, 163
Hay, Mary—139, 156, 159
Hay, Mary Caroline—147
Hay, Mary Ella—158
Hay, Mary Erskine—168
Hay, Mary Louisa—146
Hay, Mary Pinckney—152
Hay, Mary Seton—158
Hay, Mary Susan—156
Hay, Matilda—142
Hay, May—151
Hay, Michael—97, 104, 107, 108, 112, 118, 120, 128, 133, 139
Hay, Michael—his will—116
Hay, Minnie Lee—156

INDEX — THE FAMILY OF HAY 275

Hay, Morritt—152
Hay, Nannie—158
Hay, Nelleen—156
Hay, Olive—156
Hay, Oscar—158
Hay, Patti Lee—168, 182
Hay, Patrick—83
Hay, Percy Douglas—151
Hay, Peter—108
Hay, Peyton—151
Hay, Richard Gaunt—163
Hay, Richard Marion—168
Hay, Rosa Isabel—144
Hay, Rosalie—158
Hay, Ross—148
Hay, Ruth—151
Hay, Samuel—128, 140, 141, 156
Hay, Samuel Burney—156
Hay, Rev. Samuel Hutson—146, 155
Hay, Samuel Jenkins—165, 166
Hay, Samuel Marion—168
Hay, Samuel Montgomery—168
Hay, Sarah—148
Hay, Sarah Porcher—159
Hay, Sophie—156
Hay, Susan Cynthia—146, 166
Hay, Susan Emily—144, 167
Hay, Thomas—104, 106, 108, 110, 128, 133, 140, 142, 143, 156
Hay, Rev. Thomas Park—156
Hay, Thomas Theodore—158
Hay, Dr. Thomas Theodore—157
Hay, Walter Smith—156
Hay, Walter Douglas—158
Hay, Walter Scott—156
Hay, William—47, 63, 64, 65, 134, 140, 142, 148
Hay, William Augustus—146, 157
Hay, William Henry—142, 160, 162, 168
Hay, William Richmond—139
Hay, William Smith—140, 156
Hayne, Isaac—177
Heather-Bell, Poem of the—54
Het, Mary—135
Heyward, Mary Caroline—181
Heyward, Ogier—143
Heyward, Robert—143
Hoffman, Abraham S.—173
Hoffman, Edward—173
Hoffman, Edward H.—173
Hoffman, Henry S.—173
Horton, Lucy Frances—182
Huguenin, Emmeline Lucia—179
Huguenin, Sarah—179
Huntingdon, David of—14
Hutson, Ann Barnwell—143
Hutson, Anne—178
Hutson, Annie—143
Hutson, Augusta—143
Hutson, Charles J. C.—179
Hutson, Charlotte Matilda—143
Hutson, Rev. Edward Palmer—143
Hutson, Elizabeth—177
Hutson, Emmeline Colcock—143
Hutson, Esther—178
Hutson, Esther Main—143

Hutson, Florrie—143
Hutson, Isaac—143
Hutson, James Gregorie—179
Hutson, Jane De S.—143
Hutson, John—143
Hutson, Louise D'Aubrey—179
Hutson, Mac.—143
Hutson, Maria—143
Hutson, Mary—143
Hutson, Mary Anna—179
Hutson, Mary Woodward—177
Hutson, Mellicent—143
Hutson, Richard—177
Hutson, Sally—143
Hutson, Sophie—143
Hutson, Theodora C.—179
Hutson, Dr. Thomas—143, 179
Hutson, Dr. Thomas, Jr.—143
Hutson, Major Thomas—178
Hutson, Rev. William—143, 177
Hutson, William C.—179
Hutson, William Main—143

I

Inshoch, Castle—50
Izard, Mary—180

J

Jenkins, Governor Charles J.—142
Johnson, Harriet Yonge—144
Johnston, Christopher—160
Jones, Major John—180
Jones, Joseph—180
Jones, Mary Robert—182
Jones, Mellicent—180
Jones, Seaborn—182
Jones, William Branch—158

K

Keith, Christian—39
Keith, Family of—39
Kemper, Colonel Del—156
Kenney, Elizabeth Mary—142, 145
Kenney, John—142
Keteltas, Rev. Abraham—137
Kilravock, Family of—85
Kinnoul, Earl of—110
Kydd, Dr. John—118
Kydd, Martha—118

L

La Hay, Sir David—32
La Hay, John—31, 57, 58
La Hay, Nicholas—31
La Hay, Sir John—37, 39, 43, 44, 60
La Hay, Peter—30
La Hay, Robert—30, 31
La Hay, Thomas—30
La Hay, William—24, 62, 63, 79
La Hay, Sir William—30, 31, 34, 35
Lauderdale, Earl of—100
Lawton, Sallie—173

Le Serrurier, Jacques—178
Lewis, Mary Ellen—172
Lewis, Colonel John—172
Lewis, William Lynn—172
Livingstone, Janet—136
Livingstone, Robert James—136
Lyman, Joseph W.—179

M

Macbeth, 51
Macey, Mary—121
Mackay, Ella Elliott—147
Mackay, Mary—147
Mackintosh, Clan of—55
Mackintosh, Janet—55, 57
Magrath, Mary Fuller—173
Main, Ann—117
Main, William—177
Mar, Family of—89
Marjoribanks, Andrew—103
Martin, Abram Marshall—173
Martin, Annie Lewis—173
Martin, Elizabeth Mary—173
Mikell, Jennie—156
Mister, Ann—114
Mobley, Langdon Cheves—173
Moir, Robert Leslie—52
Moore, Adolphus—178
Moray, Earl of—57, 104
Morris, Isabella—121
Morris, Lewis—121
Motte, Jacob—180

N

New York Militia—132
Nicholson, Margaret—110
Nicholson, Sir William—110
Nineteenth Generation—101
Ninth Generation—57

O

O'Bannon, Susan—157
Odell, Susannah—134
Odum, Sallie—148
Ogilvie, Family of—66
Oglivie, Sir Walter—46
Orange County Volunteers—133
Orkney and Caithness, Family 72
Otey, Bishop James H.—182

P

Palmer, Augusta—180
Palmer, Dr. Ben—180
Palmer, Sarah—143
Parish Records in Jamaica—131
Park, Mary Elizabeth—178
Patton, Mr. Henry—96, 101
Paul, Sir James Balfour—44
Peeples, Benjamin—158
Perroneau, Arthur—177
Petenalin, Eva de—31, 32
Peyton, Sarah—148
Phantom Host, Poem of the—152

INDEX — THE FAMILY OF HAY

Pichell, Ann—120
Pinckney, Alfred—152
Pinckney, Charles—180
Pinckney, Charles Cotesworth—180
Pinckney, Mary—151
Pinckney, Robert—151
Porcher, Rachel—141, 145

R

Reed, Richard—173
Rhett, Haskell—151
Rhett, James—151
Rhett, Mary—151
Rhett, Ruth—151
Richmond, Walter—115
River of Death, Poem of the—168
Robert II, King—44
Roberts, Johanna—121
Robertson, Magdalen—101
Rose, Alexander—138
Rose, Dr. Arthur—83
Rose, Margaret—87
Rose, Marie—80
Ross, Earl of—46
Rugeley, Mattie—180

S

Saga of Harald Haarfager—72, 76
Saussure, De, Charles—143
Saussure, De, Louis—143
Saussure, De, Thomas—143
Scoto-Irish Kings, Table of—1
Second Generation—31
Setons of Touch—46
Seventeenth Generation—94
Seventh Generation—44
Sinclair, Sir John—46
Sixteenth Generation—91
Sixth Generation—39
Sharpington, Ann—120
Skinner, Lavinia—147

Smith Family of New York—133
Smith, Anne—137
Smith, Catherine—137
Smith, Charles Bainbridge—137
Smith Elizabeth—137
Smith, Elizabeth Blanche—137
Smith, James—137
Smith, John—136, 137
Smith, Rev. John—134
Smith, Joshua Hett—126, 137, 138
Smith, Margaret—137
Smith, Margaret Seabrook—180
Smith, Martha—137
Smith, Mary—136, 137
Smith, Samuel—137
Smith, Sarah—137
Smith, Susannah—134
Smith, Thomas—134, 137
Smith, William—134, 137
Smith, Judge William—126, 134
Soulis, De, Julianne—24
Spicer, Elizabeth—100
Stewart, Family of—44
Stewart, Earls of Angus—70
Stewart, Margaret—45
Stewart, Walter—45
Stockman, Agnes Hannah—180
Strathearn, Gilbert, Earl of—32
Stroman, Minnie—148
Stronach, Frank Morton—158
Sutherland, Alexander—82
Sutherland, Duke of—85
Sutherland, Janet—87
Sutherland-Duffus, Family of—86

T

Tenth Generation—61
The Rose, Poem of—148
Third Generation—32
Thirteenth Generation—79
Thirty vs. Thirty, Fight of—55, 56

Torrans, John—137
Townsend, Edith—157
Townsend, Dr. William—157
Townsend, William Hay—157
Townsend, William Hutson—157
Twelfth Generation—63
Twentieth Generation—105
Twenty First Generation—112
Twenty Second Generation—125
Twenty Fifth Generation—164
Twenty Fifth Generation-B—174
Twenty Fourth Generation—160
Twenty Fourth Generation-B—172
Twenty Third Generation—141

U

Urquhart of Cromartie—64
Urquhart, Katherine—64, 65

V

Venning, Susan—156
Villers, Elizabeth—115

W

Webb, Elizabeth—115
Wigg, William Hazzard—177, 178
Wilkins, Family of—120
Wilkins, Ann—114
Wilkins, Esther—114
Wilkins, Issac—115
Wilkins, Johanna—115
Wilkins, Martin—112, 122
Wilkins, Sarah—115
Wynne, Annie—156
Winrahame, Jean—96
Woodrow, David S.—173
Woodrow, Lavolotte Holmes—173
Woodward, Family of—178

INDEX TO THE APPENDIX AND LATER LINES

APPENDIX

A

Adams, Elizabeth Ann—266
Adams, Vernie—223
Aldrich, Marian—216
Addison, Isabel Aldrich—228
Alexander, III, Hooper—246
Alfred the Great—199
Almond, Daisy—235
Allen, Sarah—206
Allred, David—242
Allred, Everett Franklin—242
Allred, Jr., Everett Franklin—242
Alston, Edward Francis—248
Allston, Jr., Edward Francis—248
Allston, Harriet Wilkinson—248
Allston, Mary Scott—248
Anderson, Frank Hartley—237
Anderson, Francis Hartley—237
Anderson, Martha Fort—237
Anderson, Richard—212
Anderson, Samuel—212
Anderson, Sarah Mary—212
Anderson, Thomas—212
Anderson, William Francis—212
Andre, Major—201
Arbogast, Edward—261
Arbogast, Margaret—261
Arbogast, Roy—261
Arbogast, Wendell—261
Arledge, Phoebe Ann—237
Armfield, Leila—223
Arnold, Benedict—201
Atkinson, Bonnie—217
Atkinson, Francis Jenkins—247
Atkinson, James Frierson—247
Atkinson, William Dupre—247
Atkinson, Jr., William Dupre—247
Ausley, Margaret Lee—254
Ausley, Jr., Marvin Raimond—254
Ausley, III, Marvin Raimond—254

B

Badger, Cornelia Holmes—264
Baggott, George—222
Bailey, Ella Perkins—245
Baird, Harriet Ellis—236
Baird, Phoebe Rhett—236
Baird, W. Neal—236
Baker, Anne—229
Baker, Bruce Creighton—233
Baker, Joel Wyman—233
Baldwin, Ann Nanny—164
Bamberg, George—224
Bamberg, Leon—224
Bamberg, Leone—224
Banister, Edmond Linton—240
Banister, Emory Lamount—240
Bannockburn, Battle of—268
Barnes, Elizabeth—248
Barnwell, Dr., E. H.—236
Barnwell, Mary Pope—233
Barnwell, Jr., William Hazzard—233
Barnwell, III, William Hazzard—234
Barron, Bethany—220
Barron, Lilla Gayle—220
Barron, Mary Lyn—220
Barron, Dr. Seth—220
Bateman, Anne Hay—221
Bateman, Burney Hay—221
Bateman, Margaret Gaines—221
Bateman, Margaret Hay—221
Bateman, Rev. Thomas Douglas—221
Bateman, Jr., Thomas D.—221
Bateman, III, Thomas Douglas—221
Beake, Hannah—211
Beamguard, Francis—240
Beckett, Edith McClung—245
Beckett, Sarah—211
Beeler, Jacquelin—234
Bell, Jr., Jno. Witherspoon—233
Bell, Rena—262
Bellinger, Dr. John—206
Bellinger, Landgave Edmund—206
Bentz, Carmen Theresa—247
Bentz, Charles Walpole—248
Bentz, John Henderson—248
Bentz, Jr., Lester Earl—247
Bentz, Lester Earl—247
Bentz, Robert Reynolds—248
Bentz, Thomas Eugene—248
Berry, Harry—233
Bessinger, Mary Eugenia—240
Bishop, Edward L.—235
Bishopp, George—248
Bishopp, George Benjamin—248
Bishopp, Rosa Elliott—248
Blalock, Bonnie—257
Bland, Vivian—223
Blount, Donald Franklin—243
Blount, Mary Elizabeth—243
Blount, Robert Shelly—243
Blount, Jr., Robert Shelly—243
Blount, III, Robert Shelly—243
Blount, Stephen Miller—243
Blount, William Hay—243
Blount, William Risher—243
Boardman, Roberta Phyllis—224
Bobo, Sylvia Gayle—226
Bogue, Katherine Braswell—257
Bond, Mary Catherine—260
Bonner, Arnold—265
Bonner, Arnold Hay—265
Bonner, Janet Grace—265
Boone, Danny—244
Boone, Rayce—244
Bostick, Agnes—208
Bostick, Benjamin—208
Bostick, Richard—258
Bowen, Harriet—232
Bowen, Dr. Harold—232
Bowen, Harold—232
Bowen, John—232
Bowen, William—232
Bowers, Barbara—240
Bowers, Fannie—241
Boykin, Florence—251
Boykin, Margaret—251
Boykin, Sally—210
Bradley, Mary Goodall—264
Bradley, Thomas—264
Brawley, Jr., John Gray—246
Bray, Bennie F.—252
Bray, Lucy Hall—252
Breland, Mary Evelyn—241
Briscoe, Col. Philip—265
Briscoe, Susannah—265
Brogan, Edward John—239
Brogan, Patricia Louise—239
Brooks, Benham—252
Brooks, Mary Josephine—252
Brown, Elizabeth—245
Brown, Susan Cynthia—205, 249
Burkett, Andrew Carroll—254
Burkett, Ann Wynne—254
Burkett, Louise Patterson—254
Burr, Aaron—199, 204
Burriss, Francis McMaster—252
Burriss, John Hay—252
Burriss, Louisa Hay—252
Burriss, Thomas Moffat—252
Burt, Grace—244
Burwell, Nannie—257

C

Cabaniss, Joseph—223
Cabaniss, Stephen—223
Cahill, Paul Vincent—243
Cahill, Jr., Paul Vincent—243
Cain, Eleanor Johnson—233
Cain, William Lowndes—233
Cain, Jr., William Lowndes—233
Caldwell, Alvin Eusebius—242

278 INDEX — THE FAMILY OF HAY

Caldwell, Laura Patricia—241
Caldwell, Winnifred—225
Callett, Elizabeth Ann—253
Calvert, Clint L.—245
Calvent, Kirk—245
Camelier, Anita—261
Cameron, Mary—256
Campbell-Hay-Roane Line—266
Campbell, Mr. (to Louisiana)—205
Campbell of Louisiana—209
Campbell, Anne—266
Campbell, David—266
Campbell, Gean—260
Campbell, John—266
Canby, Ann Beverly—227
Carden, Camille—233
Carlyle, Earl of—203
Casteen, Hazel Elizabeth—241
Casteen, James Osban—241
Casteen, Jr., James Osban—241
Casteen, Joseph Timothy—241
Cater, Edwin—212
Cater, Thomas Johnson—212
Cecil, Mary Pelzer—231
Cedric, the Saxon—199
Chambers, Katheryn Sidney—253
Chaplin, Jane Williams—246
Chapman, Robert Ellis—252
Cheatham, Dr. Arch—263
Cheatham, Elizabeth—263
Christian, Caroline—232
Christian, John—232
Christian, Josephine—232
Churchill, Dorothy Ann—253
Clan Hay Society—267
Clarke, Anne—233
Clarke, Burney—254
Clarke, Dorcas—266
Clarke, George Rogers—266
Clarke, James Calet—210
Clarke, Mary—266
Clarke, Mary Catherine—210
Clarke, Rebecca De Saussure—210
Clarke, Thomas Hal—210
Clarke, Jr., Thomas Hal—210
Clarke, Thomas Henry—210
Clary, Anne—2 28
Classen, Harry—261
Classen, George—261
Clement, Lydia Lebby—239
Clement, Motte Legare—239
Clinton, General—204
Clinton County, New York—199
Cobia, Lucille—226
Codington, Arthur—236
Codington, Arthur Bonnell—237
Codington, Catherine Fort—236
Codington, Dorothy Eldridge—237
Codington, Emily Hay—237
Codington, John Fort—237
Codington, Ida Kate—237
Codington, Mary Bonnell—237
Codington, Tallulah Ellis—236
Codington, William—237
Colcock, Agnes—209
Colcock, Anna Eustace—208
Colcock, Caroline—208
Colcock, Catherine—209

Colcock, Col. Charles James—207, 208, 209
Colcock, Charles J.—259
Colcock, Charles Jones—208
Colcock, Charley Jones (Grandson)—208
Colcock. Eliza Mary—207, 208
Colcock, Ewell Hay—208, 209
Colcock, Esther Hutson—207
Colcock Family—208
Colcock, Frances Horton—208, 209
Colcock, Francis Horton—208
Colcock, Francis Horton, Jr.—208
Colcock, Helen McIver—209
Colcock, John—208
Colcock, Marion Woodward—207
Colcock, Capt. Richard Hutson—207
Colcock, Samuel Hay—207
Colcock, Seaborn Jones—209
Colcock, Thomas Hutson—207, 208
Colcock, William Bostick—209
Colcock, William Hudson—207
Colcock, Woodward Hutson—209
Coleman, Betty Rose—228
Coleman, Mary Louise—227
Coleman, Charlotte Louise—245
Cometo, Carmelita—224
Compton, Alexander—266
Compton, Anne—266
Compton, Eleanor—265
Compton, Elizabeth Elgin—266
Compton, Gerard—265
Compton-Hay Line—265
Compton, James—224, 265
Compton, John—265, 266
Compton, J. John—265
Compton, Matthew—265
Compton, Ralph—265
Compton, Robert—224
Compton, Samuel—265
Compton, Thomas—266
Compton, Walter Sidney—266
Compton, William—266
Compton, William Clarke—266
Cook, Maggie Gertrude—241
Cone, Billie—244
Cone, Carol—244
Cone, T. W.—244
Cotton, Relmum Durham—243
Cotton, Relmum Emory—243
Coppelmann, Christopher Devereaux—262
Coppelmann, Claude—262
Coppelmann, Jr., Claude—272
Coppelmann, Douglas Ashby—262
Coppelmann, Glen Hutson—262
Coppelmann, John Richards—262
Coppelmann, William Frederick—262
Cory, Albert H.—262
Cory, Jr., Albert Henry—262
Cory, Caroline—262
Craig, Sara—253
Crawford, Katherine—228
Creech, Josephine—231

Creighton, Annie Frampton—228
Creighton, George Gadsden—228
Creighton, William McLeod—228
Crook, Agnes Winnie—239
Crossland Dan—215
Crossland, Mary—215
Cudd, Anna Clare—222
Cudd, Fay Catherine—222
Cudd, Jr., Rodney—222
Culloden, Battle of—268
Cummings, Mary Elizabeth—256

D

Darby, Margaret Elizabeth—226
Darden, Virginia—257
Davenport, Elizabeth Hay—258
Davenport, Jr., George Montraville—258
Davenport, Juilette Mitchell—258
Davis, Benjamin Wyman—213
Davis, Bushrod Washington—213, 214
Davis, Jr., Bushrod Washington—213
Davis, III, Bushrod Washington—214
Davis, Carol Katherine—248
Davis, Charles Frank—213
Davis, Jr., Charles Frank—213
Davis, III, Charles Frank—214
Davis, Charles Harold Marion—214
Davis, Clifton—213
Davis, Daisy—213
Davis, Elizabeth—224
Davis, Florence Martha—214
Davis, Frank Marion—213
Davis, George—224
Davis, Gertrude—213
Davis, Jr., George—225
Davis, III, George—225
Davis, Helen—213, 214
Davis, Howard—214
Davis, Isabel—214
Davis, Lawrence Howard—248
Davis, Jr., Lawrence Howard—248
Davis, Lease—214
Davis, Leone Ruth—225
Davis, Lewis—220
Davis, Louise—230
Davis, Marian—213
Davis, Martha—216
Davis, Olivia Margaretta—224
Davis, Pattie Miley—214
Davis, Ralph—214, 224
Davis, III, Ralph—224
Davis, Ralph Cecil—224
Davis, Jr., Ralph Cecil—224
Davis, Rhonda Phyllis—224
Davis, Robert Dickinson—224
Davis, Roy William—224
Davis, Ruth Alice—224
Davis, Sarah Katherine—248
Davis, Susan Deborah—224
Davis, Timothy Allen—224
Davis, Washington—220
Davis, William—213
Dearing, Frances—254

INDEX — THE FAMILY OF HAY 279

Dearing, Marcellin—255
Delgaty Castle—267
De Pass, Alva—208
De Pass, Anna—208
Derieux, Mildred Knight—262
De Saussure, Charles—210
De Saussure, Charles Alfred—210
De Saussure, Dr. Louis—210
De Saussure, Mary Cox—210
De Saussure, Thomas—210
Dick, Margaret—233
Dickinson, Annie Lou—223
Dickinson, Barry—224
Dickinson, Christopher King—223
Dickinson, Cornelius—220
Dickinson, Edwards—223
Dickinson, Elizabeth Leila—224
Dickinson, Fraser—221, 222, 225
Dickinson, Fred Edward—223
Dickinson, Henry Clyde—223
Dickinson, Henry Cornelius—222, 223
Dickinson, Henry Gordon—222, 224
Dickinson, Herbert—222, 223
Dickinson, Herbert Donald—223
Dickinson, Iona—224
Dickinson, Kevin—224
Dickinson, Kim—224
Dickinson, Lillian Hay—222
Dickinson Line—222
Dickinson, Mary King—224
Dickinson, Martha Lou—224
Dickinson, Minnie Clare—222, 224
Dickinson, Percy Lee—222, 223
Dickinson, Jr., Percy Lee—223
Dickinson, Richard Lee—224
Dickinson, Ruth—222, 224
Dickinson, Sophie Hay—221, 224
Dickinson, Terrie—224
Dickinson, Walter Edwin—224
Dickinson, William McLeod—224
Donaldson, Mary Ann—246
Donnelly, Blanche Lenora—227
Dopson, Alice Eugenia—241
Dopson, Annie Josephine—240
Dopson, Annie Kathryn—241
Dopson, Betty Josephine—241
Dopson, Connie Lewis—241
Dopson, Craig Vernard—241
Dopson, Deborah Annette—241
Dopson, Edward Harden—241
Dopson, Eugene Gordon—240, 241
Dopson, Herman Harden—241
Dopson, Jonathan Andrew—241
Dopson, Joseph Harold—241
Dopson, Jr., Joseph Harold—241
Dopson, Joseph Murdaugh—240
Dopson, Julia Oakman—240
Dopson, Kuren Le Wanna—241
Dopson, Lewis Henry—241
Dopson, Mary Catherine—241
Dopson, Mary Elizabeth—241

Dopson, Michael Lynn—241
Dopson, Nathaniel Edward—240, 241
Dopson, Nathaniel Issam—241
Dopson, Rosalyn—241
Dopson, Sharon Denise—241
Dopson, Vera Ruth—241
D'Orr, Mary—265
Douglas, Mary—265
Dowling, Henry Hoyt—229
Dowling, Mary Pope—229
Dowling, Rena Frampton—229
Draze, Jeannie—224
Dudley, Dorothy Anne—227
Dunbar, Samuel—212
Dunbar, Sarah—212
Dunbar, Sophie—223
Durshuck, Elizabeth B.—235

E

Eads, Jr., Albert Edward—230
Eads, Rosemarie—230
Easterling, Alexander Salley—212
Easterling, Xania—212
Edwards, A.—216
Edwards, Mary—215
Edwards, Sarah—215
Elgin, Elizabeth—266
Elliott—213
Ellis Line—234
Ellis, Annie Stuart—235
Ellis, Blanche L.—235
Ellis, Catherine Rivers—237
Ellis, Cathleen—235
Ellis, Dr. Daniel—237
Ellis, David W.—234
Ellis, Jr., Dr. Daniel W.—237
Ellis, Douglas—235
Ellis, Edward—235
Ellis, Edward Prioleau—236
Ellis, Edwin Lawton—262
Ellis, Eloise O.—236
Ellis, Florence Rickwood—235
Ellis, Frampton—211, 234, 238
Ellis, Frampton Erroll—235
Ellis, Jr., Frampton E.—235
Ellis, III, Frampton E.—235
Ellis, Francis Adgate—234
Ellis, Gene Gorgas—236
Ellis, Gordon Lain—235
Ellis, Harriet—234, 236
Ellis, Harriet Calhoun—236
Ellis, Harriet Frampton—236
Ellis, Harry Hay—235
Ellis, Jr., John Oliver—236
Ellis, Lamar—235
Ellis, Lamar H.—235
Ellis, Margaret—235
Ellis, Marian Devereaux—262
Ellis, Mary Seabrook—237
Ellis, Phoebe—238
Ellis, Phoebe Prioleau—235
Ellis, Prioleau—235
Ellis, Jr., Prioleau—235
Ellis, III, Prioleau—235
Ellis, IV, Prioleau—235
Ellis, Rachel Elizabeth—262
Ellis, Rose—237
Ellis, Rose M.—234, 236
Ellis, Jr. Rutherford—235
Ellis, Rutherford L.—235
Ellis, Tallulah—234
Ellis, Tallulah Hay—236
Ellis, William D.—234

Ellis, Jr., William D.—234
Ellis, III, William D.—235
Ellis, Dr. William De Loach—213, 234
Ellis, Wingfield—235
Elkins, Elizabeth—261
Enloe, Ruth E.—258
Erskine, Lord—203
Erskine, John, Earl of Mar—203
Erwin, Mrs. Peter—212
Etheredge, Harrison—256
Etheredge, William C.—256
Erroll, Countess of—268
Evans, David Duane—224
Evans, Duane—224
Evans, Eugene Lee—224
Evans, Larry Michael—224
Even, Honorene—244
Even, Robert S.—244
Ewing, Mildred—235

F

Fain, Harrison H.—256
Fair, Catherine Hammond—229
Ferguson, Ernest—263
Ferguson, Jr., Ernest—263
Ferguson, Joseph—263
Ferguson, Richard—263
Fender, Dixie—247
Flanders, Edith Louise—261
Flanders, George—261
Flanders, Marilynn Louise—261
Flodden Field, Battle of—268
Folk, Caroline Oteria—242
Folk, Janet Carol—242
Folk, Julia Virginia—242
Folk, Rebecca—244
Folk, William Ellison—242
Folk, Jr., William Ellison—242
Folk, III, William Ellison—242
Forio, E. J.—235
Forio, Jr., E. J.—235
Fort, James Scott—237
Fort, James Frazier—237
Fort, John—236, 237
Fort, John Porter—237
Fort, Jr., John Porter—237
Fort, Kate Haynes—236
Fort, Keith—237
Fort, Martha Fannin—237
Fort, Susan Emily—237
Fort, Sylvia Lewis—237
Fort, Tomlinson—237
Fort, Jr., Tomlinson—237
Fort, William Ellis—237
Fort, William G. S.—237
Fowke, Edward—261
Fowke, Gail—261
Fowke, Jessie Evalyn—262
Fowke, Dr. John—212
Fowke, Linda—261
Fowke, Walter—261
Frampton, Alice Woodberry—229
Frampton, Anne Aldrich—228
Frampton, Annie Mikell—228, 229
Frampton, Bessie Lucas—224
Frampton, Camella Darby—226
Frampton, Carrie Lee—227
Frampton, Charles Aimar—242

INDEX—THE FAMILY OF HAY

Frampton, Charles Hay—226, 230
Frampton, Charles Tupper—230
Frampton, Donald Moore—228
Frampton, Edith Gregorie—226, 234
Frampton, Edward—230, 241, 242
Frampton, Edmund Gregorie—226
Frampton, Jr., Edmund Gregorie—226
Frampton, Edmund Wyman—226
Frampton, Eliza Lucas—230
Frampton, Eliza Oakman Hay—242
Frampton, Eugene Gordon—242
Frampton, Eugene Hay—230
Frampton, Francis Robinson—226
Frampton, George Creighton—228
Frampton, Jr., George Creighton—228
Frampton, Gertrude Lucile—227
Frampton, Gertrude Wyman—227
Frampton, Harriet Hay—228, 241
Frampton, Harriet Johnson—230
Frampton, Harriet Wyman—227
Frampton, Harry Hastings—227
Frampton, Jr., Harry Hastings—227
Frampton, III, Harry Hastings—227
Frampton, Henry Wilkins—226, 228, 229, 230
Frampton, Jr., Henry Wilkins McLeod—229
Frampton, Dr. Herbert Granville—230, 241
Frampton, Herbert Washington—242
Frampton, Isabel Patterson—228
Frampton, James—230
Frampton, Dr. James—217, 225, 226
Frampton, James Gregorie—226
Frampton, Jr., James Gregorie—226
Frampton, Jesse Sharpe—227
Frampton, Joel Wyman—226, 230
Frampton, Jr., Joel Wyman—226
Frampton, III, Joel Wyman—226
Frampton, John—221, 226, 227, 228
Frampton, John E.—213
Frampton, John Edmond—225, 228, 230
Frampton, John Grimball—226
Frampton, Joseph Maybank—230
Frampton, Julia Aldrich—228

Frampton, Julia Oakman—241
Frampton, Kathleen—226
Frampton, Lewis Hay—217, 225, 228, 230
Frampton, Jr., Lewis Hay—230
Frampton, Lewis John—227
Frampton, Jr., Lewis John—227
Frampton, Lillie Seabrook—242
Frampton, Line—225
Frampton, Linwood—230, 240, 242
Frampton, Jr., Linwood—242
Frampton, Lisa—227
Frampton, Louise Elliott—230
Frampton, Louise Hutson—230
Frampton, Lynn—227
Frampton, Mabel Estell—242
Frampton, Margaret Elizabeth—226
Frampton, Margie—230
Frampton, Mary—217
Frampton, Mary Geraldine—226
Frampton, Mary Pope—227, 228, 229, 231
Frampton, Minna McLeod—228
Frampton, Nellie—229
Frampton, Rebecca—226
Frampton, Rena Lawton—228, 229
Frampton, Rosa Mellichamp—230
Frampton, Terre—226
Frampton, Theodore Pope—225
Frampton, Thomas Hutson—228, 230
Frampton, Tillie—228, 229
Frampton, Wallace—230
Frampton, Walter Bobia—226
Frampton, Jr., Walter Bobia—226
Frampton, Dr. William Horlbeck—230
Frampton, William McLeod—228
Frampton, Jr., William McLeod—228
Frampton, William Mellichamp—230
Frampton, Virginia Taylor—227
Frampton, Vivian Griffis—227
Fraser, Alexander—220
Fraser, Ann—213
Fraser, Ann Hagood—218
Fraser, Clair—219
Fraser, Sir Bruce—219
Fraser, Charles—220
Fraser, John—220
Fraser, Joseph—218, 220
Fraser, Lovat—219
Frazier, Louise Keith—237
Fraser, Lord Lovat—219
Fraser, Rees Ford—232
Freeman, Campbell Courtenay—227
Freeman, Jr., Campbell Courtenay—227
Freeman, Dorothy Anne—227
Freeman, Dr. E. Courtenay—217
Freeman, Ellen Wyman—227
Freeman, Harriet Wyman—227
Freeman, Harry Wyman—227

Freeman, Jr., Harry Wyman—227
Freeman, Helen Butler—227
Freeman, James Frampton—227
Freeman, James Oswald—227
Freeman, Jr., James Oswald—227
Freeman, John Frampton—227
Freeman, Lewis Frampton—227
Freeman, M.—217
Freeman, Margaret Ballantyne—227
Freeman, Mary Locke—227
Freeman, Mary Louisa—227
Freeman, Robert Locke—227
Freeman, Sara Ellen
Freeman, Willington Edmondston—227
Frost, Celestine Preston—231
Frost, John Preston—231
Frost, Laura Green—231
Fuller, Margaret Sams—225
Furse, Rhoda—256
Fyfe, Elizabeth Pinckney—225
Fyfe, Margaret Ellen—225
Fyfe, Roy—225
Fyfe, Jr., Roy—225
Fyfe, III, Roy—225

G

Gadsden, Alice—228
Gadsden, Christopher—233
Gadsden, Mary Deas—233
Gaines, Chebie Ann—221
Gaines, George Stark—221
Gales, Isabel Cameron—256
Gales, Major Seaton—256
Gamble, Sara Joe—227
Gantt Line—262
Gantt, Aegina Derieux—262
Gantt, Alma Deveriaux—262
Gantt, Anna—263
Gantt, Anna Maud—260
Gantt, Annie—263
Gantt, Annie Elizabeth—262
Gantt, Brenda—261
Gantt, Charles Drayton—262
Gantt, Charles Hammond—262
Gantt, David Huff—263
Gantt, Douglas—261
Gantt, Edith Ann—262
Gantt, Edith Plantagenet—261
Gantt, Eldred Lucas—263
Gantt, Elizabeth Mackay—260, 261
Gantt, Ellen—261
Gantt, Evelyn Mackay—262
Gantt, Evelyn Harvey—263
Gantt, Francis—261
Gantt, Frances Alma—261
Gantt, Frederick Hay—260, 263
Gantt, Fuller Alexander—261
Gantt, Hope—261
Gantt, Joe Douglas—261
Gantt, John Drayton—262
Gantt, John Mackall—254, 263
Gantt, Jr., John Mackall—263
Gantt, Joseph Skinner—263
Gantt, Julia—263
Gantt, Kathryn Mabel—261
Gantt, Laurie Ella—262

INDEX—THE FAMILY OF HAY

Gantt, Lillian Douglas—262
Gantt, Longstreet—263
Gantt, Louis Plantagenet—262
Gantt, Louise—263
Gantt, Lynette—261
Gantt, Mabel Louise—262
Gantt, Margaret—261
Gantt, Marie—261
Gantt, Mary Caroline—206, 207, 208
Gantt, Mary Louisa—250, 253, 261, 263
Gantt, Judge Richard—206, 259
Gantt, Richard A.—249, 259, 260, 261
Gantt, Richard Leon—261
Gantt, Jr., Richard Leon—261
Gantt, Richard Plantagenet—260
Gantt, Samuel—263
Gantt, Sara Eliza—263
Gantt, Thomas—261
Gantt, Dr. Thomas—260
Gantt, Thomas Drayton—261
Gantt, Waldo Douglas—262
Gardner, Jr., Rev. Allen A.—255
Gardner, Jr., Allen A.
Gardner, Burney—255
Gardner, Dearing—255
Gardner, Mary Louise—256
Gardner, Sam Hay—255
Gasque—213
Gaunt Line—260
Gaunt, Elizabeth Hay—260
Gaunt, Frederick Hay—207, 260
Gaunt, John Campbell—260
Gaunt, Margaret Bond—260
Gaunt, Marian Hay—260
Gaunt, Marshall—260
Gaunt, Martha Margaret Hay—260
Gaunt, Mary Marsha—260
Gaunt, Richard Hay—260
Gaunt, William Hay—260
Gay, Adgate—235
Gay, Ewell—234
Gay, Jr., Ewell—235
Gay, III, Ewell—235
Gay, Frank L.—235
Gay, Margaret Haverty—235
Gay, Merrill E.—235
Gay, William Ellis—235
Gay, Jr., William Ellis—235
Gelzer, Anne McLeod—229
Gelzer, Katherine Baker—229
Gelzer, Mary Pope Frampton—229
Gelzer, Susan Neyle—229
Gelzer, William Porcher—229
Gelzer, Jr., William Porcher—229
Gervais, Julia Leland—245
Gervais, Louise Wilson—245
Gervais, Philip Emmanuel—215
Gervais, Jr., Philip Emmanuel—245
Gibbs, Ann McGuire—244
Gibbs, Jessie—244
Gibbs, John Walter—244
Gibson, Rebecca Jane—240
Gilfillan, Justus Clyde—226

Gilfillan, III, Justus Clyde—226
Gilfillan, Mary Margaret—226
Glenn, Elva—223
Glover, Sally—258
Godring, Joyce—262
Goodall, Hanna—260
Gordon, Cathleen—235
Gould, Phoebe—235
Gould, Stuart—235
Gould, Jr., Stuart—235
Gourley, Daniel Francis—247
Gourley, William Gales—247
Graham, Robert—266
Green, General—202
Green, Anne Louisa—213
Green, Mary—232
Green, Needham—202
Green, Sarah—212
Gregorie, Agnes—209
Gregorie, Charles—209
Gregorie, Charles Colcock—209
Gregorie, Edith Todson—226
Gregorie, Grace—235
Gregorie, Joseph—209
Gregorie, Louisa—209
Gregorie, Mary Colcock—209
Gregorie, Dr. Thomas—209
Gregorie, William Douglas—209
Griffis, Vivian—227
Grimball, George—232
Guerrard, Elizabeth—231
Guerrard, Robert—209
Guerrard, Theodore—231
Guilbert, Anne—244
Guillard, Martha—250
Gwynette, Greswold—228
Gwynette, Jr., Greswold—228
Gwynette, Isabel Patterson—228
Gwynette, William McLeod—228

H

Hack, Rosamond Gordon—217
Hagberg, John—261
Hagberg, Joseph—261
Hagberg, Ruth Ann—261
Hagood, Benjamin—232
Hagood, Jr., Benjamin—232
Hagood, Gideon—211
Hagood, James—232
Hagood, Johnson—218
Hagood, Matilda—218
Hagood's Brigade—207
Hall, Lucy Davis—252
Haltiwanger, Pauline—230
Ham, Virginia Uldine—242
Hamilton, Alexander—202
Hamilton, Andrew—198
Hamlin, Elizabeth Welsh—230
Hamlin, Harriet Frampton—230
Hamlin, Osgood Darby—230
Hamlin, Jr., Osgood Darby—230
Hammet, Ben Hay—222
Hammet, Jr., Ben Hay—222
Hammet, Dr. Ben J.—222
Hammet, Erroll Scott—222
Hammet, Lewis Jenkins—222
Hanahan, Edward John—229
Hanahan, Eve—229

Hanahan, James Frampton—229
Hanahan, Rena Frampton—229
Hanckel, Charlotte Miles—239
Hanckel, Estelle Rhett—248
Haney, Anna MacNair—220
Haney, John Jackson—220
Hardy, Henry—265
Harley, Elizabeth—261
Harley, William—261
Harmon, Noreen—234
Harrell, Daniel—262
Harrell, Jr., Daniel—262
Harrell, Debora—262
Harrison, Catherine—244
Harrison, Mary—244
Harrison, William Henry—244
Harvey, Leila—230
Hasell, Carolina—250
Hastings, Mary Louise—210
Haverstraw, N. Y.—197, 199, 202, 203, 205
Hay, Family in Scotland—268
Hays of Erroll and Lochloy—264
Hay, Adelaide—238
Hay, Adele—252
Hay, Adeline—213
Hay, Alan Oakman—246
Hay, Albert—257
Hay, Alex—265
Hay, Alfred—258
Hay, Alfred Pinckney—250, 261
Hay, Alvin—250
Hay, Col. Ann Hawkes—197, 198, 199, 200, 201, 202, 203, 204, 205, 206, 207, 251
Hay, Ann Josephine—242, 247
Hay, Ann Wyatt—239
Hay, Anne Clement—239
Hay, Annie Berwick—240, 242
Hay, Annie Elizabeth—242, 243
Hay, Annie Louise—252
Hay, Arthur—256
Hay, Arthur Erroll—250
Hay, Beatrice—239
Hay, Billie—244
Hay, Burney—255
Hay, Burwell Boykin—254
Hay, Carol Makemie—246
Hay, Caroline Petigru—258
Hay, Carrie—244
Hay, Carroll—238
Hay, Carroll Gordon—242
Hay, Jr., Carroll Gordon—242
Hay, Catherine Clementine—215
Hay, Charles Colcock—249, 256
Hay, Jr., Charles Colcock—249
Hay, Charles Hugh—261
Hay, Jr., Charles Hugh—261
Hay, Charles Jenkins—258
Hay, Charlotte Elizabeth—239
Hanckel, Charlotte Miles—239
Hay, Dr. Christopher Gadsden—250, 258
Hay, Clara Isabel—242, 243
Hay, Clarence—250
Hay, Clarence Christopher—265
Hay, Clementine Catherine—213, 238

INDEX—THE FAMILY OF HAY

Hay, Corinne Calhoun—245
Hay, Cynthia Cranston—239
Hay, Daniel Ellis—239
Hay, Jr., Daniel Ellis—239
Hay, III, Daniel Ellis—239
Hay, Davis Saunders—238
Hay, Dorothy Anne—242
Hay, Dorothy Churchill—253
Hay, Dorothy Sue—254
Hay, Edith Beckett—245, 246
Hay, Edith Louise—261
Hay, Edith McClung—245
Hay, Edward Craig—253
Hay, Edward LaRoache—246
Hay, Rev. Edward Craig—253
Hay, Eleanor Bailey—245
Hay, Ella Rosa—238
Hay, Ellen Reynolds—254, 263
Hay, Eliza Mary—206, 207
Hay, Eliza Oakman—238, 240
Hay, Elizabeth Brown—245
Hay, Elizabeth Mary—206
Hay, Elizabeth McClung—245, 246
Hay, Elizabeth Southerland—258
Hay, Emily Kathleen—259
Hay, Emma—250
Hay, Emmie Neyle—246
Hay, Erroll—256
Hay, Erroll Baldwin—264
Hay, Jr., Erroll Baldwin—264
Hay, III, Erroll Baldwin—264
Hay, Erroldine—221
Hay, Estelle—238, 242, 244
Hay, Eudora—238
Hay, Eugene Gordon—213, 238, 243
Hay, Jr., Eugene Gordon—238
Hay, III, Eugene Gordon—239
Hay, IV, Eugene Gordon—239
Hay, Eugene Izlar—244
Hay, Frederick Jay—201, 205, 213, 238
Hay, Frances Jane—255
Hay, Frances Snowden—251
Hay, Frank Seabrook—245, 246
Hay, Jr., Frank Seabrook—246
Hay, Frederick Jerome—244
Hay, Frederick Jay—253
Hay, Col. Frederick Jay—207, 249
Hay, Jr., Dr. Frederick Jay—250
Hay, III, Frederick Jay—252
Hay, Rev. Frederick Jay—253
Hay, Gerald Gordon—265
Hay, Gertrude Agnes—259
Hay, Gilbert—257
Hay, Jr., Gilbert—257
Hay, Gladys—250
Hay, Gladys Grace—265
Hay, Grace—266
Hay, Harold Hawkes—253
Hay, Harriet Ford—255
Hay, Harriet Johnson—212, 213
Hay, Harriet Young Hay—213
Hay, Harry Hampton—265
Hay, Jr., Harry Hampton—265
Hay, Hasell—250
Hay, Helen—249, 256
Hay, Helen Adelaide—238
Hay, Helen Marie—243

Hay, Henry Cumming—250
Hay, Henry Hasell—261
Hay, Henry Muhler—245
Hay, Jr., Henry Muhler—246
Hay, Henrick Richards—253
Hay, Hugh—250
Hay, Rev. Hugh Peronneau Dawes—250
Hay, Inez Berwick—245, 246
Hay, Isaac Hite—264
Hay, Isabel Cameron—256
Hay, James—265
Hay, Capt. James—197
Hay, James Andrews—242
Hay, James Dudley—251
Hay, Jane Louise—239
Hay, James Thornwell—251
Hay, Jr., James Thornwell—231
Hay, III, James Thornwell—251
Hay, James William—242
Hay, Jane Chaplin—246
Hay, Janet Scott—205, 209
Hay, Jean—250
Hay, Jeanie Lisle—253
Hay, Joan Duke—242
Hay, John—250, 264
Hay, John Baldwin—264
Hay, John Frederick Richards—252
Hay, John G.—264
Hay, John Richards—253
Hay, Jr., John Richards—253
Hay, Rev. John Richards—253
Hay, Jonathan Lee—246
Hay, Josephine—252
Hay, Julia Caroline—230, 238, 241
Hay, Julia Catherine—244
Hay, Julia Oakman—245
Hay, Kate Erroll—200, 221
Hay, Katheryn Chambers—254
Hay, Katharine Knight—246
Hay, Kathryn Villeneuve—239
Hay, Lafayette—203
Hay, Laura Augusta—264
Hay, Lena Pinckney—250
Hay, Lena St. Clair—250
Hay, Leila—257
Hay, Lester Glover—259
Hay, Lewis—249
Hay, Lewis Gordon—256
Hay, Lewis Holding—239
Hay, Jr., Lewis Holding—245, 246
Hay, III, Lewis Holding—246
Hay, Lewis Scott—205, 210, 211, 213, 238, 242, 245, 255
Hay, Dr. Lewis Scott—213, 218, 221, 246
Hay, Linda Risher—243
Hay, Louisa Righton—252
Hay, Louise—261
Hay, Loula—213
Hay, Louisa—213
Hay, Lucy Boyd—245
Hay, Lula—220
Hay, Lydia Lebby—239
Hay, Lydia Legare—239
Hay, Malcolm Fraser—221
Hay, Margaret Mitchell—259
Hay, Marshall Downes—257
Hay, Jr., Marshall Downes—257

Hay, Martha—205, 209, **255**, 261
Hay, Martha Hawkes—213
Hay, Martha Hutson—207, 259
Hay, Martha Julia—242
Hay, Martha Scott Blalock—257
Hay, Marian Heyward—207, 260
Hay, Mary—250, 258
Hay, Mary B—265
Hay, Mary Bradley—264
Hay, Mary Caroline—206
Hay, Mary Clement—239
Hay, Mary Corinne—254
Hay, Mary Eliza—244
Hay, Mary Elizabeth—244
Hay, Mary Ella—256
Hay, Mary Erskine—259
Hay, Mary Hughes—251
Hay, Mary Judy—242
Hay, Mary Louisa—249, **259**, 260, 261
Hay, Mary Moffat—245, 246
Hay, Mary Olive—257, 258
Hay, Mary Peck—253
Hay, Mary Pinckney—250
Hay, Mary Sara—253
Hay, Mary Seaton—256
Hay, Mary Susan—221, 254
Hay, Matilda—221
Hay, May—250
Hay, Michael—199, 201, 202, 203, 205
Hay, Michael Scott—246
Hay, Minnie—221
Hay, Minnie Lee—254
Hay, Motte Legare—239
Hay, Nannie—257
Hay, Nancy—266
Hay, Nell Rhoda—257
Hay, Nelleen—222
Hay, Nellie—253
Hay, Jr., Oakman—251
Hay, Olive—254, 257
Hay, Oscar Payne—206, 250, 257, 258
Hay, Jr., Oscar Payne—257, 258
Hay, Otto—244
Hay, Patricia Land—243
Hay, Pattie—220
Hay, Pattie Lee—208, 259
Hay, Paula Evans—246
Hay, Percy—250
Hay, Percy Douglas—250
Hay, Peyton—250
Hay, Plantagenet Gantt—238, 242
Hay, Jr., Plantagenet Gantt—242
Hay, Polly Brock—239
Hay, Preston—261
Hay, Rachel McMaster—252
Hay, Major Richard Gantt—207
Hay, Richard Marion—258
Hay, Richard Oakman—246
Hay, Robert Marshall—246
Hay, Robert Stockton—253
Hay, Rosa Elliott—238
Hay, Rosalie—256
Hay, Rosalie Venning—257
Hay, Rose—249
Hay, Rose Ellis—239

INDEX—THE FAMILY OF HAY 283

Hay, Rose Isabel—213
Hay, Ruth—250
Hay, Ruth Ann—258
Hay Family, Samuel—206
Hay, Samuel—204, 205, 206, 207
Hay, Judge Samuel—250, 258
Hay, Samuel Boykin—251
Hay, Samuel Burney—254
Hay, Samuel Hutson—253
Hay, Jr., Samuel Hutson—254
Hay, III, Samuel Hutson—253
Hay, Dr. Samuel Hutson—253
Hay, Rev. Samuel Hutson—251, 252
Hay, Jr., Rev. Samuel Hutson—253
Hay, Judge Samuel Jenkins—206
Hay, Samuel Marion—258, 259
Hay, Sarah—205, 250
Hay, Sarah Louise—254
Hay, Sarah Ordway—253
Hay, Sarah Porcher—206, 258
Hay, Solomon Legare—239
Hay, Jr., Solomon Legare—239
Hay, III, Solomon Legare—239
Hay, Sophie—220
Hay, Sophie Fraser—222
Hay, Sophie Edwards—252
Hay, Susan—250, 251
Hay, Susan Blalock—257
Hay, Susan Cynthia—207, 258
Hay, Susan Cynthia Brown—207
Hay, Susan Emily—213, 234, 258
Hay, Susan Olivia—257
Hay, Susan Wyman—238
Hay, Teresa—246
Hay, Rev. Theodore Beckett—245
Hay, Jr., Theodore Beckett—245
Hay, III, Theodore Beckett—245
Hay, Thomas Family—209
Hay, Thomas—199, 205
Hay, Dr. Thomas—249
Hay, Thomas Douglas—253
Hay, Thomas Enloe—258
Hay, Jr., Thomas Park—254
Hay, Thomas Theodore—257
Hay, Jr., Thomas Theodore—256
Hay, Rev. Thomas Park—254
Hay, Townsend—268
Hay, Walter Douglas—257
Hay, Dr. Walter Scott—254
Hay, Washington Seabrook—238
Hay, Winnefred Oakman—245
Hay, Dr. Walter Scott—221
Hay, Walter Smith—222
Hay, Jr., Walter Smith—222
Hay, Wellington Oakman—238, 244, 245
Hay, W. Oakman—251
Hay, William—205, 206, 249
Hay, William Augustus—255
Hay, William Clement—239
Hay, Jr., William Clement—239
Hay, William Henry—206, 207, 258, 259

Hay, William Lawrence—242
Hay, William Risher—242, 243
Hay, William Smith—205
Hay, Rev. William Smith—254
Hay, William Williams—265
Hay-Wyman—238
Hay, Virginia Gail—243
Hay, Virginia Ruth—264, 265
Hayward, Rev. Hollis Enes—252
Hayward, John Hollis—252
Hayward, Rachel Enes—252
Hayward, Samuel Francis—252
Hedden, Lois Glenda—262
Heltzel, Jeanie Hay—257
Heltzel, Margaret Wilson—257
Heltzel, Massey Mott—257
Heltzel, Rev. Massey Mott—257
Heltzel, Sallie Olive—257
Hester, Barbara Ann—222
Hester, Lillian Jenelle—222
Hester, Jr., Paul Herbert—222
Hewlett, Elizabeth—212
Hewlett, Sarah—235
Hewlett, William—212
Heyward, Mary Caroline—208
Heyward, Ogier—210
Heyward, Robert—210
Heyward, J. Thomas—208
Hiers, William George—241
Hill, Mattie Sue—224
Hill, Philip—224
Hills, Adelaide Dotterer—248
Hills, Harriette Bogel—229
Hills, Harry Bogle—229
Hills, Nellie Frampton—229
Hilton, David—224
Hilton, Johnnie—224
Hilton, Thomas—224
Hilton, William—224
Hines, Olga—252
Hodgkin, Annie Righton McCaskill—253
Hodgkin, Gordon Hay—253
Hodgkin, Robert Garnett—253
Hodgson, Martha—235
Hoffman, Mary Woodward—239
Hogg, Ann—247
Horlbeck, Marie Louise—230
Hoover, Jeanne—244
Horton, Lucy Frances—208, 259
Howle, John Conley—247
Howle, John Edward—247
Howle, Katherine Walpole—247
Hudelmaier, Fred—261
Hughes, Harriette Wilmer—263
Hughes, Mary Adelaide—251
Huguenin, Lavinia—232
Huntley, Stephen McQueen—253
Huntley, Jr., Stephen McQueen—253
Hutching, Amy—226
Hutson, Anne—210
Hutson, Augusta—210
Hutson, Charlotte—210
Hutson, Emeline Colcock—210
Hutson, Florrie—210
Hutson, Jane—210
Hutson, John—210
Hutson, Mae—210

Hutson, Millicent—210
Hutson, Matilda—210
Hutson, Sally—210
Hutson, Dr. Thomas, Sr.—209, 210
Hutson, Dr. Thomas, Jr.—210
Hutson, William Main—205, 209
Hutson, Willie—210
Hutto, May Wylie—226

I

Inabinet, Creighton—262
Inabinet, Creighton S.—262
Inabinet, Lynn Rebecca—262
Ingram, James—212
Irelans, Lucinda—266
Ives, Evelyn—262
Izlar, Marion—244

J

Jackson, Ann Catherine—260
Jackson, Becky—224
Jackson, Eliza—266
Jackson, Elizabeth Mary—260
Jackson, Michael Gerard—260
Jackson, William John—260
James, Charlotte—246
James, Nell Bull—246
James, Jr., Walter Ennis—246
James, III, Walter Ennis—246
Jenkins, Abbie—260
Jenkins, Ann Hay Walpole—247
Jenkins, Benjamin Raper—247
Jenkins, Jr., Benjamin Raper—247
Jenkins, Carmen Walpole—247
Jenkins, Charles J.—206
Jenkins, Daniel Francis—247
Jenkins, Daniel La Roache—239
Jenkins, Daniel Lagare—239
Jenkins, Davis—213
Jenkins, Eleanor Carol—247
Jenkins, Frances Louise—247
Jenkins, Gordon Hay—239
Jenkins, Harold—213
Jenkins, Jane—222
Jenkins, Jane Louise—247
Jenkins, Leize—226
Jenkins, Richardine Hart—247
Jenkins, Robert Clement—239
Jenkins, Susan Emily (Hay)—206
Jerdone, Jeanna—229
Johns, Hattie—244
Johnson, Dr. Alexander—212
Johnson, Benjamin—212
Johnson, Catherine Rhoades—Johnson, Catherine—212
Johnson, Eleanor Sophia—232
Johnson, Elijah—211
Johnson, Ella—212
Johnson, Evalina Rebecca—212
Johnson, Frances—212
Johnson, Hannah Beake—213
Johnson, Harriet Yonge—205, 211, 213
Johnson, Helen—234
Johnson, James B.—212
Johnson, Mary—212

Johnson, Mary Elizabeth—212
Johnson, Mildred—253
Johnson, Peggy Jo—226
Johnson, Richard—211, 212
Johnson, Jr., Richard—212, 213
Johnson, Sarah—212
Johnson, Sarah Mitchell—212
Johnson, Susanna—211
Johnson, Susannah—212, 213
Johnson, Thomas—212
Johnson, Wickliff—212
Johnson, William — 211, 212, 213, 232
Johnson, II, William—211, 213
Johnson, Dr. William Stanyarne—212
Jones, Carol Eloise—246
Jones, Rev. Dudley, D. D.—216
Jones, Jr., Dr. Dudley—216
Jones, Helen—240
Jones, Isabel Hay—256
Jones, Lee—241
Jones, Mary Robert—208
Jones, Parker—216
Jones, Patricia Trezevant—239
Jones, William Branch—256

K

Kalber, Barbara Lou—227
Karcoff, Isabel—214
Karpinski, Sylvia—242
Kasper, Helen—248
Kelley, Loretta—224
Kemper, Col. Del—251
Kemper, Jr., Del—251
Kemper, Erroll—251
Kemper, May—251
Kemper, Zaida—251
Kennedy, James—223
Kennedy, Robert—223
Kennedy, Jr., Robert—223
Kenney, Elizabeth Mary—205, 206, 207, 208
Kenney, Col. John—205, 206
Kevin, Anne Nigels—228
Kevin, Jr., Thomas Grey—228
Kevin, III, Thomas Grey—228
Kidd, Rita—223
Kilby, Oscar—233
Kilby, Thomas—233
Kilby, Gov. Thomas—233
King, Charles Preston—264
King, Charlotte—264
King, Mamie—223
Kinnoul, Earl of—203
Kirkland, Ann—223
Kirkland, Dana—223
Kirkland, Evelyn Juanita—223
Kirkland, Rev. Harold Norman—223
Kirkland, Helen Ray—223
Kirkland, Jeannie Rae—223
Kirkland, John—223
Kirkland, John Eldon—223
Kirkland, Marie Louise—230
Kirkland, Mell Elizabeth—223
Kirkland, Stephen—223
Kirkland, W. Lennox—230
Kneece, Bebe Helen—239
Kneece, Colleen Delores—239
Kneece, Effie Alberta—239
Kneece, Eugene Hay—239

Kneece, Joe Kess—239
Kneece, Martin Kessler—239
Knox, General—202
Kroeg, Alec—222
Kroeg, Katharine—222

L

La Bruce, Arthur—263
La Bruce, Edith—225
La Bruce, Julian Huger—225
Lafayette—202, 206
Lain, Chloe—235
Lakenan, Ruth Napier—222
Langford, John S.—235
Langford, Jr., John S.—235
Langford, Martha—235
La Roache, James—213
Lawton, Allene—216
Lawton, Pauline—215
Lawton, Jr., Thomas Oregon—212
Lawton, III Thomas Oregon—212
Lawton, Wesley Willingham—217
Leake, Robert Pinckney—224
Lee, Joe Sill—212
Lee, Ruth Love—246
Lee, Rev. William States—212
Le Grand, Carl—224
Le Grand, J.—224
Leland, Aaron Whitney—245
Leland, Julia Hay—245
Leland, Kenneth Wilson—245
Leland, Jr., Kenneth Wilson—245
Leland, III, Kenneth Wilson—245
Leland, Robert Whitney—245
Leland, Victoria Denise—245
Lester, Idamae—245
Lewis, Col. John—207
Lewis, Mary Ellen—207
Lewis, Sylvia—237
Lightsey, Donald Martin—260
Lightsey, Walter Young—260
Lilienthal, Lilly—230
Lindsay, Helen—225
Lipscomb, Blanche—234
Locke, Mary Crawford—227
Lockwood, Arthur Carleton—229
Lockwood, Jr., John—229
Lockwood, Nancy Mikell—229
Lofton, Mary Elizabeth—246
Logan, Edward Taylor—241
Logan, Jefferson Taylor—241
Lowry, Dr. Sidney Arthur—256
Lucas, Elizabeth Buist—225
Lyles, Morris—263
Lyons, William Wallace—236

M

MacArthur, Douglas Stuart—262
MacArthur, Kathryn Stuart—262
MacArthur, Margaret Elizabeth—262
McCaskill, Alvin Lewis—252
McCaskill, Annie Righton—253
McCaskill, John Calvin—252
McCaskill, Jr., John Calvin—252

Macauley, Angus Hamilton—212
McCauley, Bess White—212
McDaniel, Edna—261
McElveen, Eleanor Welsh—247
McGaughey, Mary—235
McGee, Anne Pringle—227
McGee, Beverly Canby—228
McGee, Catherine Frampton—228
McGee, Hall Thomas—227
McGee, Jr., Hall Thomas—227
McGee, John Frampton—227
McGill, Margaret Hope—261
McGrath, Gov. A. G.—207
McGrath, Mary Fuller—207
McIntyre, Margaret—225
Mackay, Ella Elliott—260
Mackay, George—260
McLeod, Annie—228
McLeod, Rena—237
McLeod, Rose Lulah—236
McLeod, Susan R.—236
McLeod, Wilhelmena—236
McLeod, William E.—236
McLead, William Wallace—236
McMaster, Rachel Buchanan—252
McNair, Sr., W. D.—215
McNair, Jr., Dr. W. D.—215
MacNeal, Mary Geraldine—226
McWhirter, Sue—254
Maher, Minnie—224
Maher, Willie—224
Malnati, E. O.—237
Malnati, Susan Lucinda—284
Marshall, Alice Henrietta—257
Mitchell, Mary Elizabeth—259
Mackall, Susannah—260
Mar, Earl of—268
Martin, Ben—210
Martin, Chloe—225
Massey, James Wiklie—225
Maury, Mary Stith—264
Maybank Line—231
Maybank, Ann Lucas—216, 233
Maybank, Burnett Rhett—231
Maybank, Jr., Burnett Rhett—231
Maybank, III, Burnett Rhett—231
Maybank, Claudia Rhett—232
Maybank, Darrell—232
Maybank, David—228, 231, 232
Maybank, Jr., David—232
Maybank, Eleanor Johnson—232
Maybank, Elizabeth de Rossett—231
Maybank, Francis Pelger—231
Maybank, Harriet—232
Maybank, Harriet Hay—233
Maybank, Harriet Rhett—232
Maybank, John—232
Maybank, John Edward—233
Maybank, John Frampton—232
Maybank, Joseph—231
Maybank, Dr. Joseph—231
Maybank, Lavinia—232
Maybank, Marian—231
Maybank, Mary Erroll—233
Maybank, Mary Hay—231
Maybank, Mary Pope—233
Maybank, Mary Sarazin—232
Maybank, Roberta Mason—231

INDEX—THE FAMILY OF HAY 285

Maybank, Theodora Pope—233
Maybank, Theodore Du Pre—232, 233
Maybank, Thomas—232
Maybank, William Johnson—232
Mears, Helen Hoover—244
Mears, James Frank—244
Mears, Jr., James Frank—244
Mears, Patricia—244
Mellichamp, Mary—232
Mellichamp, Saidie Cuttino—230
Mikell, Jennie—254
Miley, George Frank—242
Miley, Jr., George Franklin—242
Miley, Juliana—242
Miley, Pattie—213
Miller, Florence—235
Miller, Lorraine—243
Mills, Henry Rudolph—240
Mills, Jr., Henry Rudolph—240
Mills, Randolph Wayne—240
Mills, Roger Lamar—240
Mills, Sara Banks—222
Minott, Barbara—229
Mitchell, David Carl—240
Mitchell, Edith Beckett—246
Mitchell, Edith Frampton—226
Mitchell, Elizabeth Hay—246
Mitchell, Elizabeth La Bruce—226
Mitchell, Francis Marion—246
Mitchell, Jr., Francis Marion—246
Mitchell, Jr., John Magill—225
Mitchell, Julian—231
Mitchell, Lewis Hay—246
Mitchell, Mabel Southerland—258
Mitchell, Marian—231
Mitchell, Marian Roberta—231
Mitchell, May—250
Mitchell, Jr., William Cecil—240
Mobley, Leonard—239
Mobley, Linda—239
Mobley, Rose Ann—239
Moore, Francis—228
Moore, Gerald—234
Moorehead, Cornelia Holmes—264
Morrall, George—212
Morrall, Margaret—212
Morris, James—230
Morrison, Edith Beckett—246
Morrison, Lillian Epps—246
Morrison, Malcolm Holmes—246
Morrison, Mary Hay—246
Moye, Jenetta Anne—242
Mulholland, Miss—206
Murdaugh, Annie Liza Oakman—240
Murdaugh, Bonnie Camiel—240
Murdaugh, Brenda—240
Murdaugh, Clinton Decator—240
Murdaugh, Cynthia Kay—241
Murdaugh, Donnie Eugene—240
Murdaugh, Edgar Glen—240
Murdaugh, Edith Virginia—240
Murdaugh, Eugene Hay—240

Murdaugh, Glenda Fay—240
Murdaugh, Henry Joseph—240
Murdaugh, Henry Seal—240
Murdaugh, Jackie Elmer—241
Murdaugh, Jane Evelyn—240
Murdaugh, Joseph Henry—240
Murdaugh, Josephine Edna—241
Murdaugh, Lillian Eunice—240
Murdaugh, Linda Marie—241
Murdaugh, Marion Frances—241
Murdaugh, Peggy Sue—240
Murdaugh, Robert Marshall—240
Murdaugh, Vera Dell—241
Murdaugh, Vernell—240
Murdaugh, Wade Howard—240
Murdaugh, William Hamilton—240
Murden, Jean Marie—242
Murden, Michael Raymond—242
Murden, Raymond Leon—242
Murray, Margaret Glenn—248
Murray, Virginia La Vergne—227
Myers, Elizabeth de Rossett—231
Myers, Judge Thomas—231

N

Nantista, Carl—243
Nantista, Lucian—243
Nantista, Mary Frances—243
Nantista, Peter—243
Nantista, Peter John—243
Nantista, Phyllis Anne—243
Nantista, Susan Elizabeth—243
Neil, III, Rev. Marshall Banks—246
Neil, Nell—233
Nicklin, Erroll Hay—200
Nigels, Frederick Eugene—228
Nigels, Jr., Frederick Eugene—228
Nigels, III, Frederick Eugene—228
Nigels, Harriet Frampton—228
Nigels, McLeod Creighton—228
Nigels, Leslie Creigton—228
Nigels, Scott McLeod—228
North, Eric Kaven—240

O

Oakman, Josephine—251
Oakman, Julia Caroline—213, 238
Oakman, W.—213
O'Bannon, Susan—255
O'Connor, Christine—243
O'Connor, Daniel Joseph—243
O'Connor, Jr., Daniel Joseph—243
O'Connor, Ellen—243
O'Connor, Michael—243
O'Connor, Patrick—243
Odum, Sally—249
O'Hear, Ann—218
O'Hear, Eliza—220
Oliver, Eloise L.—235
Oliver, Joseph Seabrook—230

Oliver, Jr., Joseph Seabrook—230
Oliver, Margaret Frampton—230
Orange County—204
Orange County Militia—198
Ordway, Mary Brown—253
Orszula, Bozydar Henry—227
Overcash, James Richard—242
Owens, Duval—232
Owens, Lillian Gladdin—244

P

Page, Damon—265
Palfrey, Gene—236
Paris, Charles—225
Paris, Pamela Diane—225
Paul, George—231
Parler, Mabel—262
Parrott, Pauline Grimball—245
Patrick, Muriel Yancy—223
Pearce, Barbara Lynn—254
Pearce, E. Fay—235
Pearce, Jr., E. Fay—235
Pearce, Ike Winbaum—254
Pearce, Ike W.—254
Pearce, Katherine Anne—254
Peck, Mary—251
Pederson, Lydia Jean—239
Pederson, Sallie Hay—239
Pederson, Thomas Eugene—239
Peeples, James Hay—244
Peoples, Alexander McBride—244
Peoples, Benjamin—257
Peoples, Edwin Wiley—244
Peoples, Ian—244
Peoples, Jasper Quintus—244
Peoples, Jr., Jasper Quintus—244
Peoples, III, Jasper Guilbert—244
Pegues, Helen Butler—227
Pellum, Rose Nell—241
Pelzer, Frank—231
Pelzer, Jane—231
Pelzer, Mary Randolph—231
Pennington, Mark—237
Pennington, Mary Katherine—237
Pennington, Paula Ann—237
Perkins, Charlotte—223
Peyton, Sarah—249
Phillips, Henry Frampton—229
Phillips, Henry Frampton—229
Phillips, Thomas Edgar—229
Phillips, Jr., Thomas Edgar—229
Pierrepont, Evelyn—203
Pinckney, Ann Hay—247
Pinckney, Benjamin Eugene—247
Pinckney, Jr., Benjamin Eugene—247
Pinckney, Carroll Gordon—243
Pinckney, Clara Lois—243
Pinckney, Constance Porcher—247
Pinckney, Jr., Edward Hall—229

INDEX—THE FAMILY OF HAY

Pinckney, Elizabeth Anne—243
Pinckney, Eve—225
Pinckney, Frances Aloysia—243
Pinckney, Gene Hay—247
Pinckney, Genevieve Hay—243
Pinckney, Gladys Hay—225
Pinckney, James Linehan—243
Pinckney, James Porcher—247
Pinckney, Jr., James Porcher 247
Pinckney, Jo Ann—247
Pinckney, Joseph Oliverus—
Pinckney Katherine Ann—247
Pinckney, Katherine Hasell—247
Pinckney, Katherine Walpole—247
Pinckney, Louis Walpole—248
Pinckney, Jr., Louis Walpole—248
Pinckney, Lynn Fender—247
Pinckney, Marie Anita—243
Pinckney, Martin—227
Pinckney, Margaret Frampton 229
Pinckney, Mary—250
Pinckney, Mary Dowling—229
Pinckney, Mary Elizabeth—243
Pinckney, Mary Lu—247
Pinckney, Patricia Carolyn—243
Pinckney, Patricia Gail—225
Pinckney, Robert—250
Pinckney, Roger—221, 225
Pinckney, Jr., Roger—225
Pinckney III, Roger—225
Pinckney, Sarah—248
Pinckney, Sophie Adele—225
Pinckney, Theodore Guillard—225
Pinckney, Jr., Theodore Guillard—225
Pinckney, Virginia Ann—243
Pinckney, Webster Porcher—247
Pogue, Dorothy—217
Ponds, Evelyn—240
Porcher, Cornelia de Heer—248
Porcher, Rachel—206
Prentiss, Miriam—217
Pringle, Margaret Anne—227
Prioleau, Phoebe Caroline—234
Prioleau, William—231
Putnam, Ann—256

R

Rawl, James Lawrence—240
Rawl, Julia Ann—240
Rawl, William Lloyd—240
Ray, Alice—223
Ray, J. J.—223
Ray, Jane—223
Recensio, The—197
Redfearn, Daniel—236
Reed, Elizabeth Weaver—236
Reed, Fred—236
Reed, Tallulah Ellis—236
Reedy, Elizabeth Cox—248
Reese, Anne McLeod—229
Reese, David Pollock—229
Reese, Jr., David Pollock—229
Reese, Peggy Frampton—229
Renfroe, James Lane—229

Renfroe, Otis Lane—229
Reynolds, Ellen Chesnut—210
Rhett, Harriet Lowndes—231
Rhett, Haskell—250
Rhett, James—250
Rhett, Mary—250
Rhett, Phoebe P.—236
Rhett, Ruth—250
Rhett, William Haskell—236
Rhoades, Catherine—211
Richards, Annie—252
Ricketh, Gerard—266
Ripley, Carol Arthur—247
Risher, Annie Stanley—244
Risher, Mary Elizabeth—242
Rivers, Mary—237
Rizer, Carey Franklin—223
Rizer, Donald Earle—223
Rizer, Maxwell Earle—223
Roane, Andrew—266
Roane, Dr. Andrew—266
Roane, Annie Elise—266
Roane, Judge Archibald Gilbert—266
Roberts, Karen—223
Roberts, Norma—224
Roberts, Stanley Ross—223
Roberts, Susan—223
Robertson, John Mason—237
Robertson, William Joseph—237
Robertson, Jr., William Joseph—237
Robinson, Frances Lesesne—226
Ross, Elizabeth Ann—245
Ross, John Barkman—245
Ross, John D.—245
Rossiter, Mark Roger—261
Rossiter, Patricia—261
Rossiter, Roger—261
Rossiter, Suzanne—261
Rowland, Annie Germaine—243
Rowland, Henry John—243
Rowland, Jr., Henry John—243
Rowland, Mary Monica—243
Rowland, Ralph Joseph—243
Royall, David Maybank—234
Royall, Edward—233
Royall, Edward M.—234
Royall, II, Edward M.—234
Royall, III, Edward M.—234
Royall, Eleanor Williams—226
Royall, Harriet Maybank—234
Royall, Margaret Frampton—226
Royall, Mary Ellen—234
Royall, Mary Maybank—233
Royall, Patricia Ann—234
Royall, Robert V.—234
Royall, Jr., Robert V.—234
Royall, Robert Venning—226
Royall, Sallie Du Pre—234
Ruth, Miss—213

S

Salley, Julia—228
Salters, Dr. Frederick Hay—252.
Salters, Jane McClary—252
Salters, Dr. Leland Blackwood—252
Salters, Lucy Davis—252

Salters, Sophie Hay—252
Sanders, Joseph Augustus—220
Sanders, Ruth—243
Sanders, Sarah Ann—220
Saunders, Nellie—238
Schanberger, Barbara Gene—241
Schanberger, Cathi Ann—241
Schanberger, Frederick Lawrence—241
Schanberger, Jr., Frederick L.—241
Schanberger, John Michael—241
Schanberger, Richard Dopson 241
Schans, Virginia Ann—243
Scheper, III, F. W.—245
Scheper, Judge—245
Schmidt, Major—220
Scott, General John Morin—198
Scott, Madeline Keen—237
Seabrook, Baynard McLeod—229
Seabrook, Edwards—229
Seabrook, Eliza Sarah—238
Seabrook, Elizabeth—229
Seabrook, Gertrude Vincent—239
Seabrook, James Frampton—228
Seabrook, James Gadsden—229
Seabrook, Renee de Liesseline 229
Seabrook, Washington Black—228
Seaver, Cathleen—235
Seaver, G. Arthur—235
Seaver, Jr. G. Arthur—235
Shafer, Barbara—236
Shafer, Catherine Fort—237
Shafer, David Luther—236
Shafer, Paul Luther—236
Shaw, Ida—263
Shelley, Jean—247
Sibley, Mark Kirkland—223
Sibley, Ralph Warren—223
Sibley, Stanley Warren—223
Simons, Allan—236
Simons, Charles R.—236
Simons, Jr., Charles R.—236
Simons, Eloise E.—236
Skinner, Lavinia—263
Smart, Edward—222
Smart, Edward Henry—222
Smart, Jr., Edward Henry—223
Smart, III, Edward Henry—223
Smart, Herbert Ivan—223
Smart, Louerrol—223
Smart, Miriam—222
Smart, Sherry Olivia—223
Smart, Sophie Clare—222
Smart, Susan Elaine—223
Smart, Walter—222
Smart, Walter Samuel—223
Smith, Harry Hale—197, 204
Smith, Helen—215
Smith, Joshua Hett—201
Smith, Margaret Ballantyne—227
Smith, Pressley—225

INDEX—THE FAMILY OF HAY

Smith, Martha—203, 205
Smith, Martha (wife of Col. Ann H. Hay)—198
Smith, Mary Hett—205
Smith, Samuel—202
Smith, Sarah—210
Smith, Walter D.—215
Smith, Judge William—198, 200, 201, 203, 205
Smythe, Henriette—263
Smythe, Robert Wade—263
Sorenson, Dale—248
Sorenson, Dale Selby Charles—248
Sorenson, Francis Walpole—248
Southern, Ruth—256
Spillers, Agnes Delores—239
Sprouse, Barbara Ann—224
Sprouse, Christopher King—224
Sprouse, Mary Ellen—224
Sprouse, Ray—224
Sprouse, Ray, Jr.—224
Sprouse, William King—224
Stallings, Mary Mitchell—259
Stallings, Jr., Robert Lee—259
Stalling, III, Robert Lee—259
Stanyarne, Sarah—212
Stephenson, Anne—221
Steinmeyer, Alma Gantt—262
Steinmeyer, Diane—262
Steinmeyer, Donna—262
Steinmeyer, Dorothy Elizabeth—262
Steinmeyer, Ella Rachel—262
Steinmeyer, Evelyn Ives—262
Steinmeyer, John Henry—262
Steinmeyer, Jr., John Henry—262
Steinmeyer, Marie Elizabeth—262
Steinmeyer, Maud Douglas—262
Steinmeyer, Dr. William—262
Steinmeyer, William Harold—262
Steinmeyer, William Marion—262
Stockton, Mary Thomas—253
Stroman, Minnie—250
Stronach, Aline Cameron—257
Stronach, Frank Morton—256
Stronach, Isabel Jane Hay—257
Stronach, Thomas Hay—256
Strong, Belle Cordray—223
Stuart, Annie—235
Swain, Selma—233
Swann, Susannah—265

T

Tabor, Marian—232
Taffel, Helen—251
Taylor, Virginia Aikin—227
Tennent, Frances—235
Thomas, Arthur Lee—239
Thomas, Daniel Richard—241
Thomas, Marianne—239
Thomas, Rhoda Arrington—239
Thomas, Sandra Marie—241
Thornton, Jr., James—254
Thornton, James D.—254
Thornton, Sue Hay—254
Tuten, Esther—241

Todd, Ann—227
Todd, Elizabeth—227
Todd, Jr., Marion Alexander—227
Todd, III, Marion Alexander—227
Toney, Mary Josephine—260
Townsend, Edith—255
Townsend, Dr. William—255
Townsend, William Hay—255
Townsend, Jr., William Hutson—255
Townsend, William Marlon—255
Tripp, Archibald—252
Tripp, Jr., Archibald—252
Trotter, Jefferson Withers—232
Trotter, Jr., Jefferson Withers—232
Tryon, Gov.—201
Tucker, Madison P.—247
Tupper, Sarah Catherine—230

U

Ulmer, Jr., Boswell Risher—240
Ulmer, III, Boswell Risher—240
Ulmer, Catherine Elaine—240
Ulmer, Hannah Winifred—243
Ulmer, Julia Ann—240
Ungar, Celia—237
Upchurch, Annabelle—222

V

Vann, Joy Sutton—261
Vardeman, Cile Clarke—255
Vardeman, Jr., F. Burton—255
Vardeman, Frances Hay—255
Vardeman, III, Frank B.—255
Varn, Jean Marie—244, 245
Varn, Marjorie Ann—244
Varn, Walter Crandel—244
Vaughan, William Hutchinson—233
Venning, Susan—254, 257
Veno, Martha—224
Viens, Paul Joseph—243
Viens, Jr., Paul Joseph—243
Viens, Theodore—243
Vincent, Dr. C. P.—215
Vincent, Jr., Dr. C. P.—215
Vincent, III, Dr. C. P.—215
Vincent, Clara—215
Vincent, Howard—216
Vincent, Jr., Howard—216
Vincent, Dr. Hugh—215

W

Walker, Samuel Joseph—212
Walpole, Adelaids Dotterer—248
Walpole, Anna Louisa—247
Walpole, Carmen—248
Walpole, Catherine Singletary—247

Walpole, Cornelia de Heer—248
Walpole, Estelle Rhett—248
Walpole, Eugene Hay—248
Walpole, Jr., Eugene Hay—248
Walpole, II, Eugene Hay—248
Walpole, Horace Benjamin—248
Walpole, Jr., Horace Benjamin—248
Walpole, Horace Edward—247, 248
Walpole, John Bassnet Legare—248
Walpole, John William Eddings—248
Walpole, Laura Hill—248
Walpole, Lucia Lockwood—248
Walpole, Mary Scott—248
Walpole, Philip Genfron Porcher—248
Walpole, Jr., Philip Genfron Porcher—248
Walpole, Rosa Elliott—248
Walter, Dr. Christopher—238
Walters, Stacy—222
Walters, Fay Catherine—222
Walters, Lillian Clare—222
Ward, Dr. John W.—234
Ward, Jr., John W.—234
Ward, Sallie Du Pre—234
Washington, Gen. George—196, 198, 199, 201, 202, 204
Weatherbee, Annie—216
Weideman, Mildred—261
Wessel, Jean—246
Wessel, Thomas Jacob—246
Wessel, Jr., Thomas Jacob—246
Whaley, James D.—228
Whaley, Liza—228
White, Margaret—212
Whitesides, Clara Ann—233
Whitesides, Joel Wyman—233
Whitesides, Judy—233
Whitesides, Robert Fred—233
Whitesides, Jr., Robert Fred—233
Whitson, Robert—241
Whetstone, Kathy—244
Whetstone, W. H.—244
White, Clyde G.—256
White, William Armistead—256
Whitney, John Hay—268
Wildgen, Christopher Charles—247
Wildgen, Joseph James—247
Wildgen, Jr., Joseph James—247
Wildgen, Paul Porcher—247
Wiley, Marion Erroll—257
Wiley, Patrick Hamilton—257
Wiley, Samuel Hamilton—257
Wiley, Walter William—257
Wilkie, Charles O'Bryan—223
Wilkie, Frances Gray—223
Wilkie, Fred—223
Wilkie, Jr., Fred—223
Wilkie, Gary Alexander—223
Wilkins, Esther—203
Wilkins, Judge Martin—203
Williams, Catherine Walpole—248

Williams, Charles W.—248
Williams, Cornelia—251
Williams, Eleanor—234
Williams, Harriet High—233
Williams, Joseph High—233
Williams, Martha Frances—265
Williams, Mary Selby—248
Williams, Rosa Elliott—248
Williams, T. T.—233
Williams, William Mauldin—242
Wilson, Brenda Josephine—241
Wilson, Rose Warren—239
Wilson, Theodora Janet—248
Wilson, William Wyatte—241
Winter, Catherine Washington—266
Winter, Dawson—266
Winter, John Page—266
Winter, Robert Roane—266
Witham, Harriet Louise—236
Witsell, Katharine—221
Witsell, Laura—220
Woodberry, Nellie—229
Woodruff, Dr.—232
Woodward, Guy Jason—239
Woodward, Kessler Kneece—239
Woodward, Norman Edward—239
Worth, George Alton—240
Worth, Randolph Boswell—240
Wylie, Augusta Louisa—264
Wyman Family—214
Wyman, Adeline—213, 238
Wyman, Dr. Benjamin—215
Wyman, Jr., Dr. Benjamin—216

Wyman, III, Dr. Benjamin—216
Wyman, Camille Rosalie—233
Wyman, Catharine—216
Wyman, Clara Evelyn—233
Wyman, Clementine Hay—218
Wyman, Delacy—216
Wyman, Dr. Dibble—217
Wyman, Edward Holbrook—217
Wyman, Dr. Edward Holbrook—216
Wyman, Florence—215
Wyman, Dr. Frampton—217
Wyman, II, Dr. Frampton—217
Wyman, Frank James—233
Wyman, Jr., Frank James—233
Wyman, Gertrude—216, 217
Wyman, H. V.—218
Wyman, Harriet Huldah—217, 225
Wyman, Dr. Harry—216
Wyman, Harry Hastings—217
Wyman, Jr., Dr. Harry Hastings—217
Wyman, Hastings—216
Wyman, Holbrook—215
Wyman, Jr., Holbrook—215
Wyman, Dr. Hugh—216
Wyman, Jr., Hugh Vincent—217
Wyman, Dr. J. F.—218
Wyman, Jo-Ann—233
Wyman, Joel—213, 216, 217, 238
Wyman, Dr. Joel—214, 215

Wyman, Mrs. Joel—218
Wyman, Dr. Joel (Grandson)—216
Wyman, Joel Wentworth—233
Wyman, Jr., Joel Wentworth—233
Wyman, John—217
Wyman, Lallah—215
Wyman, Marion Hay—218
Wyman, Dr. Marion Hay—216
Wyman, Mattie Davis—214
Wyman, Rosalie—233
Wyman, Sallie Ann—233
Wyman, Vincent—217
Wyman, Virginia—217
Wyman, Virginia Gordon—217
Wyman, Dr. William Hutson—215
Wynne, Annie—254

Y

Yater, Col. Moss—262
Yater, Marthana Drayton—262
Yater, Moss Whitborn—262
Yonge, Col. Francis—211
Yonge, Harriet Peckham—211
Youmans, Jean Audrey—262

Z

Zeigler, Margaret Camille—226
Zeigler, Mary Florence—233
Zenger, Peter—198

www.ingramcontent.com/pod-product-compliance
Lightning Source LLC
Chambersburg PA
CBHW030334240426
43661CB00052B/1625